Badge and Buckshot

Badge and Buckshot
LAWLESSNESS IN OLD CALIFORNIA

By John Boessenecker

UNIVERSITY OF OKLAHOMA PRESS : NORMAN AND LONDON

Library of Congress Cataloging-in-Publication Data

Boessenecker, John, 1953–
    Badge and buckshot.

    Bibliography: p. 313.
    Includes index.
    1. Outlaws—California—History—19th century.
    2. Peace officers—California—History—19th century.
    3. Law enforcement—California—History—19th century.
    4. California—History—1850–1950.   I. Title.
    F866.B64   1987   979.4'04   87–40209
    ISBN 0–8061–2097–5

The paper in this book meets the guidelines for permanence and durability
of the Committee on Production Guidelines for Book Longevity of the
Council on Library Resources, Inc.

To Marta

Contents

Illustrations

Maps

Preface

LAWLESSNESS in the Old West has been the subject of thousands of books and magazine articles. Countless volumes have been written about the peace officers who brought law and order to the Plains, Rocky Mountains, and the Southwest: the Texas Rangers, the deputy U.S. marshals of Indian Territory, the Pinkertons, the Arizona Rangers, and innumerable gunfighting marshals and sheriffs. Even more has been written about the frontier's notorious outlaws: Jesse James, the Youngers, the Daltons, Butch Cassidy, Sam Bass, and the like. Relatively little, however, has been said of the outlaws and peace officers of old California. There are few books on California bandits and just one biography of a pioneer California lawman. For some reason the subject has been largely neglected by writers and historians.

In his classic work on California banditry, *Bad Company*, Joseph Henry Jackson wrote that "it was the middle Seventies before the last of the outlaw gangs was dispersed, and the early Eighties when the last of the great lone bandits, Black Bart, was caught." He added that robberies of this period "were fairly humdrum affairs and the robbers a colorless lot" and that "Black Bart was the last of the great stage robbers and Vasquez and his followers constituted the last of the gangs."

Jackson, however, was mistaken. It is true that frontier conditions had largely disappeared in California by the turn of the century. The once roadless, isolated backcountry of the Sierra, the coastal ranges, and the great valley became extensively populated. Good highways, bridges, rail systems, and telegraph and telephone lines put an end to the days when horseback outlaws could easily escape pursuing posses. Nonetheless, many California desperadoes plagued lawmen and grabbed headlines long after their purported demise in "the early Eighties." A handful of them have been the subject of books: Chris Evans and John Sontag, whose careers of train robbery and murder lasted from 1889 to 1893, leaving ten men dead and twelve wounded and resulting in California's most famous manhunt; the notorious Dalton boys, who got their start as train robbers in Tulare County in 1891; and Jim McKinney, the murderous badman who terrorized the

San Joaquin Valley until he was slain by Bakersfield lawmen in 1903. Very little else has been written about the numerous outlaws of post-gold rush California. Even less has appeared in print about the state's great peace officers. Richard Dillon's *Wells Fargo Detective* is the only complete biography of a pioneer California lawman. The fascinating stories of California's finest peace officers (among them Steve Venard, Ben Thorn, Tom Cunningham, John Boggs, and Doc Standley) have been long lost in the dusty pages of history. It is about time their stories are resurrected and the record corrected.

In this volume I have compiled the sagas of ten of California's once-noted lawmen and outlaws, as well as two remarkable tales of frontier violence. By no means do these stories constitute a complete history of lawlessness in Old California. Most are told here for the first time, researched primarily from pioneer newspapers and court records, and are devoid of hoary legends and half-truths. They give a clearer view of nineteenth-century law enforcement and present a perspective on California social history rarely examined by modern scholars.

This book is not, however, a sociological study of frontier crime. It is merely an attempt to chronicle a dramatic chapter of little-known Californiana. And perhaps it will also afford due recognition of the services rendered California by those long-forgotten lawmen of great moral and physical courage, who, with badge and buckshot, established a framework for law and order in a turbulent era.

Foster City, California   JOHN BOESSENECKER

Acknowledgments

THIS book would not have been possible without the generous help of many persons. I would like to thank Irene Simpson Neasham, Elaine Gilleran, Merrilee Gwerder Dowty, Bob Chandler, and Grace Evans, past and present archivists of the Wells Fargo Bank History Room, San Francisco, for their kind assistance over the years. To the long-suffering staff of the Bancroft Library in the University of California, Berkeley, who always responded cheerfully to numerous (and seemingly interminable) requests for materials, many thanks. I am also grateful for the help of John Keller and the late Estle Beard, who aided greatly in rooting out the story of the Coates-Frost feud. Additional thanks to Helen Turner; R. Tod Ruse; Fred Kern; Dick Reynolds; Stan Wincote; Standley Hildreth; Clyde Arbuckle; Gladys Hansen; Marjorie Jensen; Sally Zanjani; Pat Jones; Bill Kelly; Joseph P. Samora, Laren Metzer, and Genevieve Troka, of the California State Archives; Lila Lee, of the Mendocino County Historical Society; Lorrayne Kennedy, of the Calaveras County Museum and Archives; Sibylle Zemitas, of the California State Library; Harold G. Schutt, of the Tulare County Historical Society; Jim Hickson, of the Auburn-Placer County Library; Gerald Wright, of the California Historical Society Library; Nancy Valby, of the San Jose Historical Museum; Ann Odgers, of the Modoc County Museum; and John G. Boeck, of Yuma Territorial Prison State Park. Thanks also to the staffs of the Colorado Historical Society; Western History Department, Denver Public Library; California Room, San Jose Public Library; Arizona Historical Society; Pacific Center for Western Studies, University of the Pacific, Stockton; Pioneer Museum and Haggin Galleries, Stockton; and the Silver City (New Mexico) Museum. And last, a special word of gratitude to my good friend Bill Secrest, Fresno writer, historian, and expert on the outlaws and peace officers of old California, who generously loaned countless items of data from his voluminous archives on frontier crime.

To these and any others I may have neglected to mention, my heartfelt thanks.

J.B.

Badge and Buckshot

Introduction

MISCONCEPTIONS about frontier law enforcement abound. In film, television, and western novels, the sheriff kills the badman in a fast-draw gunfight and then rides off into the sunset, leaving the outlaw's carcass to rot in the dusty street. Those desperadoes lucky enough to be captured alive are routinely lynched or imprisoned without the legal niceties of a trial. Revisionist historians, on the other hand, would have one believe that the Old West's prisons were filled with persecuted ethnic minorities, innocent of the offenses they were charged with; that in the event of a crime, the nearest available Chinese, black, or Hispanic was snatched up and tossed behind bars with barely a nod at due process.

Such scenarios did occur, but they were the exception and not the rule. A perusal of the chapters that follow should demonstrate that the judicial system was alive and well in California from the early 1850s onward and, by and large, functioned swiftly and effectively to punish malefactors. The system was far from perfect; judges, attorneys, and peace officers could be incompetent and sometimes corrupt. Its failings were greatest during the freewheeling, rough-and-tumble 1850s, when many California courts handed out extremely lenient sentences to lawbreakers. Perhaps as a result, lynchings were common during this decade, such vigilantism frequently resulting not from a lack of judges and courts but from frustration and impatience with the established legal process.

The criminal justice system of nineteenth-century California was not radically different in structure from that which exists today. From 1850 to 1879 the district and county courts handled all felony cases, a felony being any crime punishable by death or incarceration in the state prison (such as murder, robbery, and burglary). By 1869, California was divided into seventeen judicial districts. District courts tried all murder, manslaughter, and arson cases, and county courts heard all other felonies. In 1880 the county and district courts were consolidated, and from that date to the present, felony cases were tried in superior court. Minor crimes (misdemeanors) were heard either in justice court or police court. Police judges and justices of the peace frequently were not lawyers, and they dispensed a rather informal brand of justice. Appeals were heard by the California Supreme Court, there being no intermediate appellate courts before 1904.[1]

Each county elected a sheriff every two years until 1893 when the sheriff's term was increased to four years. He was assisted by an undersheriff and a force of deputies, the number varying in proportion to the county's size and population. Few sheriffs served more than two terms, but a small number, including Tom Cunningham and Ben Thorn, were extraordinary exceptions, holding office for many years and achieving fame as law officers. Counties were divided into townships, with each township having at least one justice of the peace. To every justice court was attached an elected constable, who served as a court officer and bailiff, serving process and attachments and having full police authority to apprehend criminals.

Law enforcement in cities and towns was directed by the chief of police (frequently called city marshal and occasionally, captain of police). This office was usually appointive, but in some towns the voters elected the marshal. The size of these police forces ranged from just one man in the smallest of towns to some five hundred in San Francisco during the 1890s.

United States marshals were charged with enforcing federal laws and serving as court officers to the federal courts. They were appointed by the president, and in California the office customarily went to former sheriffs. From 1850 to 1866 California had two U.S. marshals: one in Los Angeles, serving the Southern District Court, and one in San Francisco, for the Northern District Court. In 1866 the Southern District was abolished and merged with the Northern District; but in 1886 Congress re-created the Southern District, and its court and marshal were once again located in Los Angeles.

If a peace officer killed a man who resisted arrest, he was required to explain his actions to a coroner's jury; the coroner investigated all homicides and accidental deaths. Convicted felons were sent to the state prison, which from 1851 to 1854 was a brig anchored variously at San Francisco, Angel Island, and Point San Quentin. In 1854 a stone prison cellblock was completed at San Quentin, and in 1880 a second prison was opened at Folsom. Convicts came to call a trip to the dreaded "Stones" at San Quentin "crossing the bay." Those convicted of federal crimes were also sent to San Quentin, since there was then no U.S. penitentiary in California.[2]

Condemned men were executed by hanging. This was normally

done on an outdoor scaffold set up for the occasion in the yard of the county jail or courthouse, presided over by the sheriff, and frequently witnessed by large crowds. Later all executions were removed from the public eye to San Quentin and Folsom prisons; the last local hanging in California took place at Fresno in 1893.

With those introductory words out of the way, let us turn the page and take a glimpse at the real Wild West, California-style.

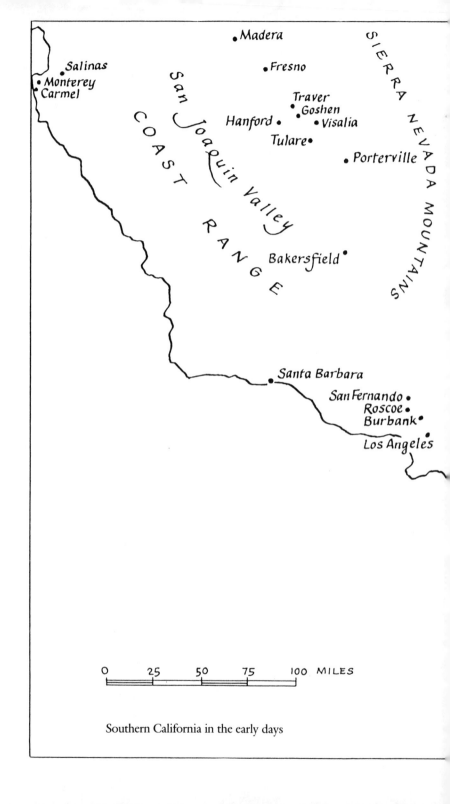

Southern California in the early days

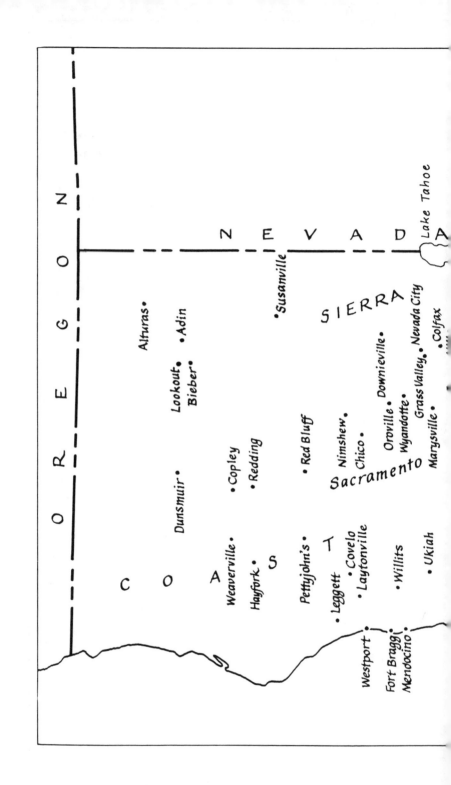

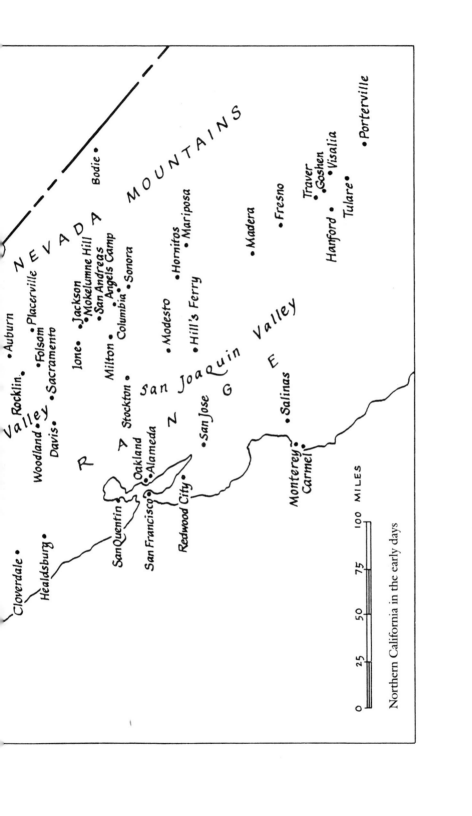

Northern California in the early days

PART ONE

With Badge and Buckshot: The Lawmen

"It is no use to go up against buckshot."
—BILL MINER

Outlaws' Nemesis: John C. Boggs

"IF J. Boggs is dead, I am satisfied." These few words, scrawled in pencil on a scrap of paper found clutched in the lifeless hand of Rattlesnake Dick, the notorious "Pirate of the Placers," speak volumes of the abject fear in which the road agents, mankillers, and sluice robbers of the mother lode held Placer County's once legendary constable and sheriff. From his shootout with Tom Bell's gang in 1856 to his capture of the men who perpetrated California's first train holdup in 1881, John Craig Boggs was the nemesis of some of the worst outlaws of the Old West. "Whole volumes might be written of the hairbreadth escapes and bloody fights in which Sheriff Boggs has figured," wrote one pioneer historian, adding, "Boggs seemed to bear a charmed life, for he fought these men wherever he found them, and always escaped without injury, although others were shot down beside him."[1]

Born in Greencastle, Pennsylvania, on October 18, 1825, he was the fourth of eight children of a prominent physician. Educated in the common schools of Greencastle, Boggs's brothers excelled in the classics and theology, and two of them became distinguished ministers of the Gospel. But young John was restless and adventuresome by nature, and school held little attraction for him. At age twenty he was appointed manager of an ironworks in Cumberland County, but when news of the California gold discovery reached the East Coast in December, 1848, Boggs saw his chance for the adventure of a lifetime. With a gift of $1,000 from his mother in his purse, he boarded the California-bound ship *Xylon* at Baltimore on February 3, 1849. The skipper of the *Xylon,* Captain Brown, proved to be rough and overbearing, treating the passengers inhumanely and putting them on short rations of water. Boggs and two others were elected as a committee to deal with Brown, and they succeeded in persuading him to dock at Rio de Janeiro to take on water. When the ship landed, most of the passengers complained to the U.S. consul of Brown's conduct, and he and his mate were sent home in disgrace.[2]

With a new captain, the long journey around the Horn resumed. One passenger, unable to stand the shipboard rigors of sickness and vile food, leaped overboard and was drowned. The *Xylon* finally reached San Francisco on September 14, 1849, where Boggs found a town of five thousand living in rudely constructed houses built on the sandhills, with the bay extending to the present site of Sansome Street. But John did not linger, setting off immediately upriver on a schooner for Sacramento. To his great surprise and pleasure, he stumbled upon his brother William, whom he had not seen in four years. The brothers secured pack mules and supplies and walked forty miles into the foothills to Wood's Dry Diggings, now Auburn. Boggs immediately began digging and washing for gold, little realizing that the Auburn area was to be his stomping grounds for the rest of his life and the scene of his most stirring encounters with desperadoes.

For three years John worked the mines in Placer, Nevada, and Yuba counties. Like most forty-niners, he seesawed between prosperity and poverty. Generous and good-natured, when he had money he spent it freely on his friends. Boggs never found the great wealth that attracted so many Argonauts to the placers, and in 1853 he took on steady employment as Auburn's first night watchman. For a year he patrolled the camp's streets and saved his wages and in October, 1854, took a trip home to visit his family in Pennsylvania. He returned to California in the spring and was appointed a deputy by Placer County Sheriff William T. Henson. The sheriff, his twenty-three-year-old undersheriff (B. F. Moore), and his nine deputies had their hands full with the unbridled lawlessness in the mining camps. Since Placer County lay on the main overland route to California, it was a natural stopping place for riffraff. Fugitives and desperadoes from the eastern states, disbanded volunteer soldiers, Sydney Ducks (former convicts from the Australian penal colony), and luckless miners who had never struck pay dirt were among the many rough characters who turned to crime in the mother lode.[3]

Highwaymen preyed upon lone travelers as well as the freighters which at that time carried more gold than stagecoaches did. The freighters brought gold dust to Sacramento, exchanged it for food and supplies, then returned to the mines. Holdups occurred frequently, as John Boggs recalled in later years: "I have known as many

John C. Boggs when he was
sheriff of Placer County.
Courtesy Bill Summers,
Placer County Sheriff's
Department.

as four different robberies on as many different roads in one day
within six miles of Auburn."[4]

Violent crime of all types was rampant, and the homicide rate was
particularly appalling. In 1855 the *San Francisco Alta* reported that 370
homicides had occurred in California during the first eight months
of that year. There were 36 lynchings and only 2 legal hangings. With
a statewide population of less than 300,000, this is an annual rate of
185 homicides per 100,000 people, more than sixteen times California's present homicide rate.[5]

Legions of cutthroats, freebooters, and ruffians infested the Placer
County foothills. Jim Webster, Ned Whitney, Buckskin Bill Riley,
Wabash Dan, Curley Bill, Spanish John, Cherokee Bob, Aaron Bracey,
Harrison Morgan, Dublin Jack, and One-Eyed Tom Williams are but
a sampling of those reckless renegades. But of them all, none was as

dangerous as Tom Bell, the most infamous outlaw to hit the gold-
fields since Joaquín Murrieta. Bell was six feet, two inches tall, slender and erect, with auburn hair worn long, a full beard, and a hide-
ously flattened nose. His true name was Thomas J. Hodges, and he
was an educated physician from Rome, Tennessee. After service as an
army doctor in the Mexican War he had joined the gold rush to California, where he pursued a career as a gambler, but quickly fell into
evil ways. On October 8, 1851, he landed in the state prison with a
five-year sentence for a grand larceny committed in Sacramento
County. He was only the twenty-fourth convict ever sent to the
prison, which at that time was a brig anchored in San Francisco
Bay. On May 12, 1855, Tom Bell, with Bill Gristy (alias Bill White),
and a half-dozen other convicts escaped from the recently constructed prison at San Quentin. By 1856, Bell was the leader of a well-
organized gang of thirty road agents. There were small groups in
each county between the Kings River and Marysville. His lieuten-
ants were Bill Gristy and Ned Conway, a red-bearded Irishman and
escaped convict whom Bell had met in San Quentin. Conway was
from a respectable New Orleans family.[6]

Tom Bell made his headquarters in the woods five hundred yards
behind the Mountaineer House, a hotel and tavern located eight
miles below Auburn on the Folsom road. The hotel was run by Jack
Phillips, a Sydney Duck. John Boggs and his fellow lawmen long suspected Phillips of harboring the outlaws and acting as a fence, but
they could get no evidence against him. The bandits used secret signs
and passwords to identify themselves to Phillips, and although Boggs
raided the Mountaineer House several times, Tom Bell and his men
were nowhere to be found. Sheriff Henson, Boggs, and the other
deputies hunted the desperadoes for months. Many false trails and
leads were followed up, but they never could capture the elusive Bell.
Undersheriff Moore later wrote, "Once we came so near to our game
that we found the droppings from their horses still smoking on the
ground."[7]

On August 12, 1856, Tom Bell and his band attempted to rob the
Camptonville stage, and in an exchange of gunfire a woman passenger was slain. A short time later a Jewish peddler named Rosen-
thal was robbed and murdered near the Mountaineer House by Bell
and several members of his gang. These brutal murders spurred
Boggs and the rest to even greater efforts. They rounded up a number of suspected gang members, including Charley Hamilton (a

black desperado), who admitted that he knew Tom Bell. Hamilton
made a deal with the officers: if they would promise him his freedom,
he would try to arrange the outlaw chief's capture. According to Undersheriff Moore, Hamilton "proved himself true and loyal ever after.
Charley was an athletic Negro, and brave as he was black." He joined
the gang, and although several distrusted him, and he had two close
brushes with death at their hands, he succeeded in ingratiating himself with Tom Bell.[8]

Meanwhile, Deputy Sheriff Bob Paul, of Calaveras County, posed
as an outlaw and collected evidence against Jack Phillips. On September 29, 1856, Paul placed the hotelkeeper under arrest for harboring Tom Bell. At ten o'clock the next night John Boggs received a
telegraph dispatch from Charley Hamilton in Folsom: "Tom Bell and
two others just crossed Folsom Bridge. Meet me at the corner of Jack
Phillips' fence."[9]

Within minutes Boggs, Moore, Sheriff Henson, and Deputies
George Martin, Sim Barrett, and Dana Perkins were in the saddle
and heading out of town at a fast lope. The road was muddy from
recent rain, and the night was starlit, but a dusky haze had settled
over the foothills, making it extremely dark. The lawmen were half a
mile from Phillips's Mountaineer House when they heard a pistol
shot in the distance, followed by the sound of riders approaching.
Sheriff Henson and his men dismounted and took cover in the brush.
A few minutes later two horsemen appeared. Boggs recognized them
instantly as Charley Hamilton and his friend Joe Burrows, also black.
Hamilton quickly told the posse that, after sending the wire, he and
Burrows had trailed Tom Bell, Ned Conway, and a third desperado,
Texas Jack, and had seen the outlaws make camp in a cluster of trees
at Rock Corral, not far from Folsom. The two black men had con-
tinued on to warn the sheriff, and Burrows had foolishly shot a
coyote that crossed their path.

The officers swiftly drew up plans to attack Tom Bell's camp. They
mounted up and continued on for another two miles, past the Mountaineer House to the Franklin House (a hotel and tavern). By now it
was 12:30 A.M., and the posse was spread out along the road, for they
planned to surround the outlaw camp in three separate groups.
Boggs, Hamilton, and Burrows were in the lead, with Moore and
Perkins a hundred yards behind, while Henson, Martin, and Barrett
brought up the rear. John Boggs, eager to trap the slippery Bell,
thundered past the Franklin House at a full gallop, with Hamilton

and Burrows directly behind him. To avoid the mud in the highway, the possemen rode their horses on the elevated bank on one side of the road. A few hundred yards beyond the Franklin House, Boggs suddenly spotted three riders, single file, in the middle of the road, heading toward them. It was so dark, and Boggs was riding so fast, that he had already passed them when Hamilton cried out that it was Bell's gang.

Reining up and wheeling his horse, Boggs yelled a warning to the officers behind.

"Boys, here they are!"

Moore and Perkins suddenly found themselves confronting three of the most dangerous outlaws ever to straddle a horse. Pulling his six-gun, Moore shouted, "We're officers! Surrender!"

The desperadoes' horses were jaded, and Bell and his men stopped immediately at the command.

"Hold on, boys," Ned Conway said to Moore, at the same time throwing his sarape back over his shoulders and yanking out a long-barreled Colt. In an instant the orange flames of six-guns lit up the darkness. Tom Bell and Texas Jack jumped behind their horses, using them for cover, and opened fire at the two lawmen. Moore snapped a shot at Conway, and the pistol ball glanced the side of his head, knocking the bandit from his horse. Conway leaped to his feet and ran for the woods. At that moment John Boggs and his two informants galloped up. Boggs, pistol in hand, took dead aim at Conway, forty feet distant, and squeezed the trigger. The bullet ripped into the badman's back at the left shoulder, shattered his heart, and lodged in his right breast. Conway fell headlong into the mud, instantly killed.

Tom Bell and Texas Jack leaped back into their saddles, and the possemen continued to blaze away at them. The officers' horses, all fresh mustangs, bucked and reared at the gunfire, making it almost impossible to get a clear shot. The desperadoes thundered up the road for about two hundred feet, with the posse in pursuit. Suddenly Bell and Texas Jack dismounted and again opened fire on the lawmen. But Boggs and his companions charged them, and the outlaws sprang back into their saddles and fled toward the Franklin House.

Sheriff Henson had raced forward when he heard the shooting, and as he neared the Franklin House, he heard Tom Bell and Texas Jack approaching at a dead run. Henson, Martin, and Barrett quickly dismounted and took cover at the corner of the Franklin House barn.

As Bell and Texas Jack rode by, the sheriff and his deputies opened fire with shotguns, but none of the shots were effective. The eight possemen chased the outlaws up the Auburn road, but their quarry had a hundred-yard lead. After a short pursuit they found that the outlaws had abandoned their horses and vanished into the chaparral. The lawmen made a brief hunt in the darkness, then decided to wait until daylight for a full search. Borrowing a lantern at the Franklin House, they returned to the scene of the shootout and retrieved Ned Conway's body.

Meanwhile, Tom Bell fled four miles to the Pine Grove House (a hotel and tavern), where he stole a horse and headed south to a hideout on a ranch on the San Joaquin River, near Firebaugh's Ferry. Four days later, on October 4, 1856, he was captured and lynched by a posse from Stockton, led by Judge George Belt. Jack Phillips, Bill Gristy, and several other gang members were sentenced to terms in San Quentin. Texas Jack's fate is unknown.[10]

One member of the Tom Bell gang who managed to evade capture was Richard A. Barter, better known as Rattlesnake Dick. Tall, gentlemanly, and strikingly handsome, he was the son of a British army officer and was born in Quebec, Canada. He arrived in California in 1850 at the age of seventeen and settled at Rattlesnake Bar, on the North Fork of the American River, a camp that gave him his nickname. According to the usual story, Dick turned to a life of crime after twice being falsely accused of theft. True or not, on December 20, 1854, he was lodged in San Quentin on a charge of grand larceny and was released a year later. Dick was suspected of planning the Trinity Mountain packtrain holdup of March 12, 1856, when several of Tom Bell's band, including George Skinner (alias George Walker), Adolph ("Big Dolph") Newton, and Nicanora Rodríguez stole $25,000 in gold that was being transported from the Yreka mines.[11]

Bill Gristy and Skinner's brother, Cyrus, had stolen thirteen head of mules on the Bear River, supposedly to help carry the stolen gold, but Cy was captured and jailed in Auburn. George Skinner determined to free his brother, and on the night of April 22, 1856, he met with Bill Gristy and Nicanora Rodríguez at a tent on the American River, a mile from Folsom. They planned to join up with several other gang members and attack the jail. John Boggs and Undersheriff Moore were the only officers on guard at the Auburn lockup that night. By a remarkable coincidence, Jack Barkley, former captain of police at Marysville, and two other officers surprised the outlaws at their camp near Folsom. In a furious gunfight George Skinner was killed and Nicanora was wounded. Said Moore, "Thanks to the Marysville boys, Boggs and myself were thus saved an interesting nocturnal picnic. . . . Cy told us afterwards all about their plan, but would not explain how he got wind of it several days beforehand."[12]

In 1858, Rattlesnake Dick was the chief of his own gang, among them George Taylor, Aleck Wright, and Jim Driscoll. They committed numerous burglaries and highway robberies in Nevada and Placer counties and proved to be as dangerous and elusive as Tom Bell's gang. Of all the officers who hunted Rattlesnake Dick and his band, John Boggs was the most relentless. Greatly feared by the outlaws, he came to be known as the "Nemesis of Rattlesnake Dick." The brigand chief hated Boggs and claimed that the lawman had once sworn falsely against him in court. But, as was noted by the early historian of Placer County, Myron Angel, "It is more than likely, however, that the deadly enmity which Dick bore towards Boggs was occasioned by the latter's persistent pursuit of the young robber, and his frequent frustrations of Dick's plans."[13]

On one occasion Rattlesnake Dick set up a nighttime ambush for Boggs outside his house in Auburn, but John was not at home. When he returned, he found a note from the outlaw tacked to his gatepost: "Have been in waiting for you nearly all night."[14]

Boggs, however, held no ill will toward Rattlesnake Dick. Although he considered the highwayman "a bad, desperate young lawbreaker," he admired Dick's courage and daring. Nonetheless, Boggs was untiring in his efforts to capture the outlaw. On April 28, 1858, while on a visit to Folsom, John received a message that Rattlesnake Dick and George Taylor had just boarded the Folsom-bound stage at Nevada City. Armed only with a warrant, a pair of handcuffs, and a single-barreled derringer, Boggs galloped toward Auburn, apparently hoping that he would arrive there before the stage and in time to get help from other officers in town. Instead he met the coach coming down the Widow Harmon grade, two miles below Auburn.

Boggs spotted Dick and Taylor riding atop the stage, chatting with A. W. Bee, a San Francisco newspaper reporter, and he ordered the driver to halt. Calling to the pair by name, Boggs commanded them to climb down from the coach, but they denied that they were the wanted men and began to parley with the officer. When Taylor demanded to see Boggs's warrant, he fumbled in his pockets for the paper, and both outlaws whipped out their six-shooters and opened fire. Boggs fired back with his single-shot, scaring the daylights out of Bee and sending the desperadoes scampering into the roadside chaparral.

A dejected John Boggs returned to Auburn with his wristless handcuffs, unserved warrant, and empty derringer. His friends got a great laugh out of his attempt to tackle such desperate highwaymen alone and with a single derringer. Boggs explained that George Taylor had thrown him off guard by demanding to see the warrant, and in later years he frankly admitted that his actions had been the most childish in all of his thirty years' experience in catching criminals, calling it "a stupid effort."[15]

John's next encounter with Dick proved more successful. He and Undersheriff George Johnston learned that the outlaw was near Nevada City and started in pursuit. They met Rattlesnake Dick in the woods, and in a running gunfight the bandit emptied his six-gun at the officers, then tripped and fell. In an instant Boggs and Johnston were on him, and soon Dick was in irons and on his way to the Nevada City calaboose. But few jails could hold the slippery brigand, and before long he was again at large.

Rattlesnake Dick finally met his end on the night of July 11, 1859. Just at dusk a citizen notified John Boggs that Dick had been seen riding toward Auburn from the south, accompanied by another desperado, believed to have been either Wabash Dan or Aleck Wright. Boggs and Sim Barrett immediately started south in search of the pair, while Undersheriff Johnston, Deputy W. M. Crutcher, and former deputy George Martin rode north on the road to Illinoistown. Johnston and his little posse met the outlaws on the road a mile from town. Rattlesnake Dick and his partner opened fire on the lawmen, killing Martin and shattering Johnston's left hand. Johnston fired back, and Dick reeled in the saddle but wheeled his horse and, with his companion, raced off into the shadows.

Large posses hunted the killers all night, and at dawn John Boggs and Sheriff L. L. Bullock found a corpse a mile from the scene of the gunfight, lying on a pile of brush on the roadside, partly covered with a saddle blanket. It was the body of Rattlesnake Dick. There were two bullet holes in his body and a third in his head. He was magnificently dressed in fine black trousers, light-colored vest, a light-drab Merino coat, and kid gloves. In one hand was a pistol, in such a position as to indicate that he had shot himself in the head. In the other was a slip of paper on which were scratched the words,

"Rattlesnake Dick dies, but never surrenders, as all true Britons do."
On the other side was written, "If J. Boggs is dead, I am satisfied." In
the darkness, Dick had mistaken Martin for Boggs, who haunted the
outlaw even at his death.[16]

Although Tom Bell and Rattlesnake Dick were the best known,
many other rough customers made life in Placer County dangerous
in the days of gold. One of these was Aaron Bracey, a black man who
settled on a small ranch a quarter mile from Auburn. On March 5,
1856, he killed a Chinese who he claimed had broken into his cabin.
On February 18, 1858, he quarreled with a neighbor, James Murphy,
over a strip of land and struck him over the head with a pick, punc-
turing his skull. Bracey went to the courthouse and gave himself up
to Sheriff Charles King, claiming that the pick had slipped from his
hands and accidentally hit Murphy. The officers put Bracey in a jail
cell, then rushed to his ranch and found Murphy dying, blood and
brain oozing out of a dollar-sized hole in the back of his head. Before
he died, Murphy revealed that he had argued with Bracey, and, upon
turning to leave, Bracey had struck him from behind with the pick.

Murphy, an Irish bricklayer with a wife and two children, was
highly respected in Auburn, and his fellow countrymen became in-
censed over the cowardly attack. Fearing mob violence, John Boggs,
Sheriff King, and a number of other officers remained on guard at the
jail that night. King arranged with fifty citizens to stay awake in their
homes and respond immediately to the jail upon hearing the ringing
of the courthouse bell. At two-thirty that morning, the ever-vigilant
Boggs was on watch in front of the courthouse. Suddenly he sprinted
inside and yelled to Sheriff King that a mob was headed for the jail.
The sheriff rushed downstairs, but as soon as he and Boggs stepped
outside, they were seized and pinioned by a crowd of seventy men
swarming onto the courthouse steps. One deputy managed to reach
the courthouse bell and sound the alarm, but he and the other officers on duty were quickly captured and disarmed. A number of citizens responded to the alarm, but none lifted a finger to help the
lawmen.

As members of the mob broke down the gate to the jailyard with
sledgehammers, Sheriff King managed to break loose and rushed
into the yard. The leader of the mob shoved a six-shooter into his
chest and ordered King to hand over the jail keys. Ignoring the command, the sheriff tried to wrestle the pistol from the lyncher, but he

was overpowered, carried out of the yard, and held under guard with Boggs and the other officers. In less than ten minutes the heavy blacksmith sledges had cracked the padlocks on the jail's two iron doors. Aaron Bracey's cell door was smashed open, and he was dragged outside. As the murderer was marched out of town, a priest, Father Quin, pleaded with the vigilantes to stop. Quin was rudely seized and thrown over a fence by the frenzied lynchers, who repeatedly beat Bracey over the head with pick handles and bludgeons.

"Well, Bracey, this is a dark night to go to heaven in!" taunted one of the mob.

Bracey was taken to a tall pine tree a mile and a half from town and hoisted up by a rope. But the knot slipped under his nose, and he gasped, "Gentlemen, I can't die so."

"Lower him down and put the knot under his ear," commanded one of his executioners.

"Choke him first!" yelled another. "And then run him up!"

The knot was adjusted, and once again he was yanked up, slowly strangling to death. A crowd of two hundred watched the disgraceful, bloodthirsty affair but took no active part in it. The lawmen were released by their captors, and the mob drifted away. The *Placer Herald* credited Sheriff King and John Boggs with doing their best to resist the mob and pointed out, "This is the first time that a prisoner has ever been forcibly taken from our officers." Added the editor, "While all admitted the justness of the fate of the criminal, many deprecated the manner of punishment."[17]

John Boggs had much better luck tracking down dangerous outlaws than warding off lynch mobs. One of the most desperate bandits in the placers was a murdering ruffian named Edward Eugene ("Ned") Whitney. He was a member of a loose-knit band of highwaymen, burglars, and sluice robbers that had its headquarters at Harrison Morgan's saloon in Forest Hill and at a cabin in Boston Ravine, near Grass Valley. These cutthroats particularly preyed upon Chinese, who were generally inoffensive and unlikely to resist. The robbers also knew that, if they were caught, there would be no one to testify against them, for at that time blacks and Chinese could not testify against whites in California courts.

On one occasion, two members of the gang, L. P. Stone and nineteen-year-old Ben Pascoe, were arrested for robbing Chinese and brought to Auburn for trial, but since there were no white witnesses, the freebooters were discharged. Two months later they were once again in the toils of the law. On October 3, 1858, Stone, Pascoe, and Henry ("Spanish John") Cavelho raided a camp of Chinese miners on the Bear River, near Dutch Flat. But these Chinese were far from docile and defended themselves with rocks, hatchets, and pistols. Stone was shot in the leg, and Pascoe received an ugly hatchet wound in the thigh. The brigands fled, but not before they had shot and killed two of the Chinese. The three robbers, with Ned Whitney, were captured at the cabin in Boston Ravine and lodged in the Nevada County jail on a charge of murder. Pascoe confessed, implicating Stone and Spanish John but exonerating Whitney, who was released. Whitney decided to move to more healthy climes and immediately departed for Columbia with two other members of the band, Richard Wallace and the saloonkeeper, Harrison Morgan, both ex-convicts.[18]

Whitney and his partners holed up in a cabin outside Columbia with several ruffians of the same stripe. Following a series of burglaries by these outlaws, Joel N. McDonald, a former Stockton police officer, went undercover and joined the gang in a burglary on the night of November 26. McDonald led six of the thieves, one of whom was believed to be Ned Whitney, to his cabin to divide the spoils. A posse of lawmen was lying in wait outside the place, but McDonald's cabinmate, who had carelessly been left ignorant of the plan, lit a candle inside. Spotting the light, the robbers immediately suspected a trap. One knocked McDonald down with a pistol, and another shot him in the head, causing instant death. The officers rushed out firing, but the killers escaped.

Three days later, Columbia City Marshal Bob Mullan and Constable John Leary, who had been trying to ferret out the murderers, saw Ned Whitney and a Dutchman named Miller, alias Walker, walking a drunk down Main Street, obviously intending to rob him. Constable Leary rushed around to Waldo Street to cut them off, unaware that Wallace and Morgan were concealed there, waiting for their partners. While Marshal Mullan closed in on the badmen from Main Street, Leary came up behind them on Waldo. In a brief gun duel, Ned Whitney shot and killed Constable Leary, and Marshal Mullan wounded Morgan. All four bandits escaped, but Mullan captured Morgan and Wallace later that night. On December 2, the enraged citizens of Columbia seized Morgan from his guard and lynched him from a flume on Gold Springs Road.[19]

Ned Whitney fled back to the Northern Mines and was soon again operating with impunity. On the night of March 20, 1859, Whitney, Buckskin Bill Riley, a ruffian named Lovering, and two other desperadoes entered Otto Thiele's store in Daneville, a small mining camp on the plains in the western part of Placer County. Forcing the owner to open the safe, they removed seventeen hundred dollars in coin and gold dust, then sat down and treated themselves to a grand feast, devouring sardines, oysters, home-baked bread, and wine. After exchanging their trail-worn clothes for new attire, they took off for the foothills.

In the morning Sheriff King received word of the outrage and immediately started for Daneville with John Boggs. They cut the robbers' trail and followed it to the Bear River, where they had swum across the stream. From here the trail led to the road to Nevada City, and the officers learned that the five brigands had boarded the Auburn–Nevada City stage, disembarking at Grass Valley.

Sheriff King soon returned to Auburn, but Boggs remained in Grass Valley and continued to hunt for the outlaws. Finally he heard that three ruffians matching their descriptions were camped in a cabin in French Ravine, two miles below town. At eight o'clock on the night of March 24, Boggs, with Nevada County Undersheriff J. B. Van Hagen, Deputy Sheriff Ed Burrell, and two citizens named Lockwood and Dennin, left town for the cabin. Burrell and Lockwood carried double-barreled shotguns, and the rest were armed with six-shooters.

The night was extremely dark, and the posse proceeded slowly and silently, not reaching the camp until midnight. A lamp burning inside showed that the cabin was occupied. While Van Hagen covered the rear, Boggs and the rest formed a rough skirmish line and crept cautiously toward the front of the cabin. When they were forty feet distant, Buckskin Bill Riley appeared in the doorway. Spotting the posse, he jumped back inside, yelling, "Look out, boys!"

Suddenly eight heavily armed desperadoes burst out of the cabin, flashes blazing from their gun muzzles. Boggs and his companions instantly responded with a barrage of fire, and a ball from Lockwood's shotgun perforated Buckskin Bill's left thigh. Boggs also fired at Bill, sending a bullet into his leg, and the outlaw dropped, his femur bone fractured. But a moment later Lockwood was out of the fight when a ball tore through his right arm, breaking the bone. Undersheriff Van Hagen started to run for the front of the cabin to help the possemen, but Boggs warned him back, crying, "There's a man shooting from the corner of the house!"

Van Hagen stayed put and did not fire a shot during the fight. Boggs, as usual, was still in the thick of the fray, firing as fast as he could at Ned Whitney, who crumpled to the ground, mortally wounded.

"I'm dying!" Whitney groaned. He had been struck by two balls from Boggs's six-shooter and a load of buckshot from Burrell's shotgun. Undaunted, the outlaws kept up a hot fire, driving the officers back. Boggs and the others quickly examined Lockwood, and seeing that he was in danger of bleeding to death, decided to retire from the battle. They took Lockwood to a doctor in Grass Valley, then, with reinforcements, returned to the camp. Arriving at daybreak, they found Buckskin Bill lying in front of the cabin, using the corpse of Ned Whitney as a pillow. Although the rest of the gang had fled, John Boggs had avenged the murder of Constable Leary. "This fight has made an inroad upon a precious pack of villains who have infested portions of Nevada and Placer counties for a long while," reported the obviously pleased editor of the *Placer Herald*.[20]

Jose Luis Cortes was yet another dangerous mining-camp ruffian. A Chileno whom the *Sacramento Union* called "one of the most desperate characters in the state," he had committed several murders in Calaveras County before fleeing to Forest Hill, northeast of Auburn. In January of 1859, John Boggs and Bob Paul, now undersheriff of Calaveras, made a daring arrest of Cortes and an accomplice at Forest Hill. Bundling their prisoners into a wagon, the officers headed for Auburn. Six miles from Todd's Valley, Cortes and his compadre slipped out of their handcuffs and leaped from the wagon. Paul tackled Cortes, but the other badman raced pell-mell for the timber. Boggs opened fire and winged him, but the outlaw kept running and escaped into the brush. The two lawmen, disappointed by the escape of one prisoner, returned Cortes to Mokelumne Hill for trial.[21]

In June, 1860, Brown's store at Mountain Springs (now Gold Run) was held up and robbed by a band of outlaws led by Billy Dickson, a former partner of Rattlesnake Dick. One "Curly" Smith was soon arrested as an accessory and lodged in jail in Auburn, where he was visited in his cell by two hard-looking women, Jenny Moore and Mrs. Murphy. Undersheriff George Johnston became suspicious of the pair and placed them under arrest. To his amazement, he discovered that "Mrs. Murphy" was really Billy Dickson in disguise. An amused local newspaperman was quick to dub the hapless badman "the gal that wore hoops."

From Curly Smith, Boggs and Johnston learned that the other members of the gang were three freebooters named Moody, Simpson, and Crozier. They traced Moody to Grass Valley. With Deputy Sheriff Ed Burrell, John Goad, and the Grass Valley night watch officer, Stephenson, they surrounded his cabin at midnight. The bandit sprang out the door, and at the order to "stand" he instead went for his six-shooter. Boggs did not have a clear field of fire, and he yelled at Stephenson to cut loose with his shotgun. Stephenson's double-barreled gun boomed, and Moody dropped with a scream, one leg completely shredded by buckshot. The badly wounded brigand was lodged in jail at Nevada City, and John Boggs set off on the trail of Simpson and Crozier. A month later the lawman bagged his prey in Stockton and returned them to Placer County to face punishment.[22]

When not fighting outlaws, John Boggs took an active role in Auburn's social and commercial life. In 1857 he married Lavisa C. Harrington, and to the couple were born two children, Isabella and John. That same year Boggs opened a saloon in Parkinson's Building in Auburn, and the next year he was elected constable of Auburn Township, a post he held for ten years. In 1861 he served as Auburn's first city marshal and took a leading role in the incorporation of the city. An ardent Republican, in 1863 he established the *Auburn Stars and Stripes,* the first Republican newspaper in Placer County, which he operated for two years.[23]

John Boggs was eager to be elected sheriff, but the office eluded him for years. Wrote historian Angel:

> It is strange . . . that Mr. Boggs was not elected sheriff of the county in those days, for he did his duty in every instance, and accomplished more for the county in ridding it of desperate characters than any sheriff that was elected, and he ran for the office often, but was invariably defeated. Politics, even at that early date in the history of this State, was pretty much the same as it is at the present time [1882], and partisan feeling overbalanced every consideration of efficiency for the office.[24]

Boggs was a candidate for sheriff in 1860 but was narrowly defeated by L. L. Bullock and ran again in 1862, losing once more by a close margin. He did achieve some success in politics in the 1860s, being reelected constable each election year. In 1867 he won the office of district assessor and two years later was chosen county assessor. In

1873 he again ran for sheriff and lost by only 48 votes. Retiring to his ranch in Newcastle, southwest of Auburn, he became one of the pioneer fruit growers in Placer County and one of the first to engage in the fruit shipping business.[25]

Thief catching, however, was in his blood, and he soon was appointed a special detective for the Central Pacific Railroad. But it was as a private citizen that John Boggs investigated the most volatile murder case in Placer County's history. On September 15, 1876, at the old Ryan ranch near Rocklin, a couple named Oder was found shot and hacked to death, and the ranch house had been ransacked and robbed. A half mile from the house, the owner, H. N. Sargent, was discovered horribly wounded, with five bullets in his body and one in his head. He died the following morning, but not before he described his assailants as three Chinese. The only one he could identify was Ah Sam, a well-known young man who had worked as a cook for several Auburn families.

The infuriated citizens arose en masse, formed vigilance committees, and drove out all the Chinese from Rocklin, Roseville, Penryn, and Loomis. The Chinese quarter of each town was demolished, the huts, shops, and joss houses leveled to the ground. Within a few days the only Chinese left in that part of the country was John Boggs's cook, whom the lawman would not allow to be driven off in such a high-handed manner. Boggs offered the cook his protection, and, in gratitude, the Chinese promised to help hunt the killers. The cook was true to his word. With information he supplied, Boggs arrested one suspect, Ah Fook, in Folsom and about the first of February, 1877, learned that Ah Sam was working at the Gold Strike Mine, in Plumas County. But when John arrived at the mine, he found that the bird had flown. He spent several days hunting for Ah Sam without success but cautioned all the miners in the area to be on the lookout for him. On February 16, a group of miners whom Boggs had warned spotted Ah Sam near Rich Bar and corralled him in a pile of rocks. Refusing to surrender, the murderer shot and killed himself.[26]

When C. C. Crosby was elected sheriff of Placer County that fall, he wasted no time appointing John Boggs his undersheriff. Boggs served two years and in 1879 ran for sheriff himself, finally winning the office that had long eluded him. He took over in March of 1880 and served for three years (his term was extended for one additional year because of the adoption of the new state constitution in 1879).[27]

George H. Shinn, one of the leaders of the gang that pulled California's first train holdup in 1881. Courtesy Wells Fargo Bank History Room.

Perhaps it was his fate, but John Boggs always seemed to be the right man in the right time and place. Six months after he took office, California's first train holdup took place in his bailiwick. The ringleaders of this peccant plot were Ed Steinegal, a reckless miner from Gold Run, and George H. Shinn, a thirty-two-year-old, distinguished-looking gambler who, according to wanted notices, "plays short cards and is also fond of the society of fast women." Early in August, 1881, Steinegal recruited three young friends into the band: John Mason, an Iowa Hill teamster, and Reuben Rogers and Henry Frazier, both miners and members of respected families at Gold Run. Said Mason of Steinegal's proposal, "He said that he had a job in view where we could make plenty of money."[28]

The gang's hideout was a cabin on Rogers's mining claim at Pickering Bar, on the North Fork of the American River, not far from Iowa Hill. A trail led from Pickering Bar up the canyon to the Central Pacific Railroad tracks. Their plan was simple: to remove a section from the track at Cape Horn Mills (about five miles above Colfax), derail the train, and rob the Wells Fargo car. On August 30, Steinegal, Shinn, and Mason met at Rogers's cabin. John Mason later described their actions:

> I came down to the cabin about two P.M. and when I got there met Steinegal. He had a gun on his shoulder and one in a sack. He told me that he and Shinn had tools hid in the bushes. We had provisions brought to the cabin, enough to last three or four days. The tools which we had were taken from the Aurora blacksmith shop, about a mile and a quarter from Iowa Hill. There were two picks, two shovels, axes, a wrench, hatchet, sledge, two pair of gum boots, and about seven or eight pounds of nails. We had also some giant powder and caps. I did not see Rogers until the night of the wreck. We took no picks or shovels up to the railroad, but took an axe, a sledge, a wrench, and some giant powder and caps. On the night of August 31st we started up for the railroad track. When we got up to where the spring near the cut is we sat down and waited, I think about five minutes, for Rogers to come. He soon came. There was an understanding that we should meet him there. He came about eight or nine o'clock. . . . He had a gun and a sack which he said contained giant powder and two bottles of whiskey, a lantern, and a six-shooter. I think he had twenty-four cartridges of giant powder. He said the powder was to blow up the express safe. He also had a monkey wrench. When we came to the spring we took a drink of water and whiskey. Rogers forgot his monkey wrench there. From there Rogers, Steinegal, Shinn, and myself— there were four of us—went down to the railroad. While going down the road we passed Frazier, sitting on the left hand side coming down, and he said "halloo!" and wanted to know if that was us. We said "Yes," and asked him if he had the bar made. It had been understood that he was to make a bar, and if he had not made it we were to postpone the attack. He said it was ready. We went into the bushes and loaded up two guns. We went down to the place . . . and took a rail up. We had considerable trouble in getting the rail up, and broke one prong of the bar in doing it. Myself and Shinn started to pull some spikes, and Steinegal went down and Rogers up the track to act as guards, to prevent any one coming to interfere. The right-hand rail going up was displaced, with the lower end pressed in. Then we went to a little island of sand near the telegraph poles and put on our masks. Then we took three or four drinks of whiskey and broke the bottles, and then waited for the train to come.[29]

It was a few minutes before midnight when eastbound Central Pacific Train No. 1, pulled by two engines, steamed up the steep grade. As it rounded a slight curve, the lead locomotive rumbled off the track, followed by the second engine, a fruit car, and the express and baggage coaches, which jounced heavily across the ties. The forward

A freight train rounds the sharp bend of Cape Horn in the 1870s. This was the scene of California's first train holdup. Courtesy California State Library.

engine plunged into the ditch and turned onto its side, and the whole train groaned to a halt. The jolt caused much excitement in the coaches, and Senator James G. Fair (the famed "Bonanza King"), who happened to be on board, went through the cars, trying to calm the passengers.

The Wells Fargo messenger, Chadwick, slid open his door and was met by John Mason, who yelled, "You son of a bitch, fall out of there!"

Chadwick slammed the door shut, blew out his lights, drew his six-gun, and prepared to resist the bandits. But no attack came. One of the gang spotted the fruit cars and cried, "This is a freight train, boys!"

John Mason glanced toward the mail car and saw Shinn and Frazier standing motionless.

"What are you doing?" Mason demanded. "If you are going to do anything, why don't you do it?"

Frazier yelled back that he saw soldiers getting off the passenger cars. At that, Steinegal ran toward them and exclaimed, "It is too big to take!"

"Well, if we are going, we had better go quick," responded Mason, and the skittish holdup men broke helter-skelter for the timber and brush, leaving behind some of their tools as well as a note that they had deliberately planted to mislead lawmen. Mason and Frazier, in their haste to escape the nonexistent soldiers, fell headlong into the undergrowth. They got up, and Frazier said breathlessly, "We have done enough now. We better go home!"

Mason noticed that Rogers was missing and yelled for him but got no answer. The four scampered up the hillside like scared rabbits, coming onto the tracks above Cape Horn. Said Mason later, "After we got up on the railroad track, we met Rogers. When we met, there was some dispute as to who got scared first and as to who ran and who didn't."[30]

Then the band split up, with Rogers returning to his home in Gold Run, and the rest going down to the cabin at Pickering Bar. Meanwhile a train crewman ran back to Colfax and telegraphed the alarm to Auburn and Sacramento. The affair, although comical and half-hearted, nonetheless created a public sensation, for it was the first attack on a railroad train on the Pacific Coast since Big Jack Davis's gang engineered the West's first train robbery just across the state line at Verdi, Nevada, in 1870. Reported the *San Francisco Alta*, "The news of the attempted train robbery caused the greatest excitement throughout this city and State." Rewards of $2,000 were offered for each of the culprits.[31]

At daybreak Sheriff Boggs and his deputies were on the scene, making a careful search. They found nine masks, 24 Hercules giant powder cartridges, fuse, axes, a sledgehammer, three lanterns, and a note which read:

Sacramento, May 20
Dick, will be at Stump's Ret's, Ne City, Monday. Everything O.K.
349.

Boggs knew that Stump's Restaurant in Nevada City was a hang-out for hard characters and that the job might have been "put up" there. By this time he had help from a half dozen of the best detectives in California: Jim Hume and John Thacker, of Wells Fargo; Fred T. Burke, Len Harris, and Bill Hickey, of the Central Pacific; and Captain A. W. Stone, of the San Francisco police. They began run-

ning down numerous clues, but as was usual in such cases, most of
them were false. A "hard-looking customer" who had boarded the
westbound train near Cape Horn was arrested at Roseville, but investigation proved that he was not one of the gang. Fred Burke, who
had been instrumental in the capture of the Verdi train robbers,
found wagon tracks near Cape Horn but upon following the trail
found that they belonged to an innocent rancher. A Chinese in Grass
Valley reported that a group of suspicious strangers had asked for di-
rections to Nevada City. This news, coupled with the note found by
the tracks, focused the investigation at Nevada City, but the detectives soon became satisfied that they were barking up the wrong
tree.[32]

John Boggs was certain that the train wreckers were local men,
probably miners, who knew how to use giant powder. He learned
that Ed Steinegal had recently purchased a quantity of powder and
fuse and was living in a cabin at Pickering Bar. On September 9,
Boggs and Jim Hume rode down to the river and found Steinegal
and Mason at the cabin. The pair told the lawmen that they were
miners, but Boggs became suspicious when he saw that they had no
tools to work their claim. The sheriff searched their cabin and found
pieces of material that had been cut from the masks found at the scene.
Sunk in the river nearby, Boggs found shovels and picks weighted
down with rocks, with the wood handles cut off. Steinegal refused to
talk, but it did not take Boggs long to convince Mason that, if he
wanted to save his neck, he had better cooperate. Mason "squealed"
and, upon being promised that he would not be prosecuted, gave up
the names of his partners.[33]

That very day Reuben Rogers had eloped with a fetching young
lady from Iowa Hill, Miss Mary Sullivan. They were wedded in Nevada City and spent their honeymoon night at the Union Hotel. The
following day Boggs and Hume picked up Henry Frazier and learned
that Rogers had eloped. They sent a wire to the Nevada City marshal, Erastus Baldridge, requesting him to place the newly married
miscreant under arrest. The marshal interrupted the lovebirds in
their honeymoon nest and clapped young Rogers into the county
jail. His bride, a local newsman dutifully reported, "hastened after
him and piteously pleaded with the sheriff to be admitted to his cell.
Of course her petition could not be granted, and with a broken heart
and a dazed mind, she hastened back to her room to be alone with
her sorrow."[34]

That evening John Boggs had four of the train wreckers safely behind bars in Auburn. He made a tireless search for George Shinn and once was so close to catching him that both were together in the same building, but Shinn escaped through a window without being seen by the sheriff. Finally, on October 27, the indefatigable Fred Burke captured Shinn on the Doolin ranch in Antelope Valley, eighteen miles west of Maxwell, in the coastal mountains of Colusa County.[35]

The trials of the holdup men were among the most controversial in Placer County's history, taking more than a year to complete and becoming a veritable cause célèbre. The accused men employed several of the best attorneys in California to defend them, including Jo Hamilton, former attorney general, and the Hon. Niles Searls. The district attorney, William D. Lardner, was assisted by two special prosecutors hired by Wells Fargo and the Central Pacific. This proved to be a most unwise development, for it convinced many in Placer County that these powerful corporations, in throwing their weight behind the prosecution, were intent on persecuting the defendants. This negative sentiment was fueled by a general feeling of resentment against the railroad, which for many years was extremely unpopular in California. The Central Pacific was particularly hated in Placer County, for it had refused to pay its taxes for several years and owed $90,000 to the county treasury.

Ed Steinegal's trial began on November 11, 1881, with John Mason, who had been granted immunity, testifying against him. After three weeks it ended with a hung jury. He was retried the following February and was convicted of attempted robbery and sentenced to thirteen years in San Quentin. This verdict caused much surprise, for it had been widely expected that he would be acquitted. Local newspapers had run editorials criticizing the railroad during the trial.

George Shinn was next placed on trial, his case beginning on June 26, 1882. It too caused much caustic comment in the press, which charged that these trials were too expensive and were being prosecuted solely for the railroad's benefit. Shinn was nevertheless convicted, and on July 18 was sentenced to twelve years and eight months in San Quentin.[36]

Rogers and Frazier were tried jointly, and their case commenced on September 11, 1882. While in San Quentin, both Steinegal and Shinn had confessed, confirming Mason's story and admitting that Rogers and Frazier had been in on the job. Steinegal had offered

Ed Steinegal, arrested by John Boggs for the Cape Horn Mills train holdup. Courtesy Wells Fargo Bank History Room.

to come up to Auburn and testify against them. On September 13, Sheriff Boggs picked up Steinegal at the prison and brought him to Auburn on the evening train. The cars were filled with passengers returning home from the state fair in Sacramento, and many disembarked when the train pulled into Auburn at ten o'clock. Boggs was met at the depot by his twenty-one-year-old son and deputy, John. They walked up the crowded street to the jail, with the handcuffed prisoner in front of them. As they neared the courthouse, Boggs motioned toward the jail-yard gate and ordered, "Turn across here."

Two young women were just ahead of Steinegal, and he suddenly darted in front of them and fled at top speed into a dark alley across from the courthouse. Boggs and his son whipped out their six-guns but held their fire for a moment until the two girls got out of the way, then sent a volley of shots after the fleeing desperado. They pursued him down the alley, but Steinegal had escaped. Boggs offered a five-hundred-dollar reward for the fugitive, but he was never recaptured.[37]

This escape was a great embarrassment to John Boggs, and he was also tremendously frustrated by the outcome of the final trial of the train wreckers. Although Mason testified against Rogers and Frazier, members of Rogers's family swore that he was in bed at Gold Run at the time of the Cape Horn job. The fact that Rogers had married shortly after the holdup convinced many that he was innocent, and the trial resulted in a hung jury on September 30. They were retried, and on December 23 a jury acquitted them both, despite the fact that Steinegal and Shinn had been convicted on exactly the same evidence. The jurors evidently believed that since the two ringleaders were convicted, justice had already been served.[38]

John Boggs, much perturbed at the public sympathy shown to the holdup men, had already decided not to run for reelection. At the expiration of his term in March, 1880, he left public office forever. He devoted his energies full time to fruit growing but remained a potent force in Placer County politics. He later purchased a half interest in the Never Sweat Mine, near Michigan Bluff, and also invested in the oil lands of Kern County. Boggs remained in Newcastle and enjoyed caring for his orchard and the beautiful gardens he planted around his home. In 1898 he was appointed postmaster of Newcastle, and that same year, after forty-one years of happy married life, his wife, Lavisa, passed away. Still active and virile at the age of seventy-three, Boggs soon married Alice S. Watson, twenty-five years his junior. He lived to the age of eighty-three, savoring to the fullest the peace and prosperity that he had so often risked his life to make possible. He was still serving as postmaster when his heart finally failed him on May 28, 1909. The old lawman was buried in the Newcastle cemetery. Said the editor of the *Placer Herald*:

> Of an ardent and enthusiastic nature, he defended the side of any cause he had chosen without fear or favor. A strong partisan in politics, he worked strenuously for his party's success and yet when the election was over no one spoke bitterly of him because the warmth of his heart, his many good qualities, and his readiness to help with his purse and influence were known to all. This was manifested at the time when his body was born to its last resting place and the burial rites were witnessed with emotion by many who had opposed him the most strongly in politics.[39]

Such tribute is purely ephemeral, its praises fleeting, for while the evil Tom Bell and Rattlesnake Dick are celebrated to this day in popular history and legend, the memory of John Boggs, who filled his life with good deeds, has long since gone glimmering.

CHAPTER 2

Manhunter: Steve Venard

LIKE most of the occupants of the National Hotel in Nevada City, Steve Venard was lost deep in midnight slumber in his second-floor room, when a sudden loud pounding on the door jarred him awake. Crawling out of bed, Venard swung the door open and was confronted by the burly figure of R. B. Gentry, sheriff of Nevada County. The North San Juan stage had just been robbed, the sheriff told him. Three men had blown up the ·Wells Fargo box and escaped with $7,900. Gentry asked Venard to join his posse.

Venard hurriedly dressed. Snatching up his sixteen-shot, lever-action Henry rifle, the newest and deadliest long arm on the frontier, he joined Sheriff Gentry and, within minutes, thundered out of town with the rest of the posse. He had no way of knowing that this was to be a memorable day in the life of this former schoolteacher and Argonaut.

Stephen Venard was born in 1824 on the Allen Kirby farm southwest of Lebanon, Ohio. He was educated at the nearby Waynesville Academy and, as a young man, moved west to Newport (now Fountain City), Indiana, where he secured a position as a teacher in the town school. A quiet man with strong moral principles and plenty of nerve, Steve became involved in the Underground Railroad, which was then very active in Newport. When Southern slave owners put a price on his head, he decided it was time to head west. His chance soon came.[1]

The year was 1849, and gold fever was sweeping the country. Sol Woody, a salesman from Cincinnati, began organizing a company of Wayne County men, with plans to leave for California in the spring. Late in the year Woody discussed the venture with Venard and a fellow teacher, Henry Puckett. Both agreed to go at the end of the school term.

On March 30, 1850, the group of twenty-five gold seekers rolled out of Newport in eight covered wagons. Each wagon was drawn by

four horses, with two more led behind. They moved west over the
National road to Saint Louis, Missouri, where they boarded the
riverboat *Ambassador* for Independence. The trip up the Missouri
River, through treacherous waters in freezing, exceptionally severe
April weather, was an omen of the hardships that lay ahead.

Venard and his companions crossed the northeast corner of Kansas
to the Platte River, which they followed into Wyoming. They saw
many newly dug graves and passed numerous companies camped on
the trail with their sick and injured. On June 16 one member of the
band suddenly came down with cholera and died. The next day the
dreaded disease claimed another of the group. The gold seekers buried their dead and pressed on through Wyoming. On July 2, near
what is now the town of Glen Rock, a third man died, also of cholera.
They crossed South Pass to Bear River, where yet another of Steve's
friends was claimed by cholera.

In southern Idaho six of the company separated from the group
and headed toward Oregon; Venard and the rest of the group followed the Raft River south into Nevada. By now they had abandoned most of their baggage and some of their horses. The slow trek
through the desert, along the Humboldt River, was the most difficult
part of the entire journey, with scorching temperatures, scarce food,
and alkaline water. Nonetheless, they kept doggedly on, finally crossing the Sierra and arriving in California on September 19, 1850, end-
ing an odyssey of almost six months.[2]

Venard's first efforts at mining met with moderate success, and in
November he and five others built a cabin at Illinoistown (now part
of Colfax). At the end of December he went to the North Fork of the
American River, where, after five months' labor, he managed to
scrape together four or five hundred dollars in gold. He then made a
prospecting tour two hundred miles north but had little luck, so he
went south to Downieville and finally landed in Nevada City, flat
broke. There he went to work on another miner's claim, earning six
to ten dollars a day. On October 13, 1851, he wrote to his sister in
Waynesville:

> Since I have been in the country I have had some experience in back
> life having lived for two months at a time entirely alone enjoying the
> solitude of a mountain life undisturbed by anything save that of the
> nightly prowling of coyotes, or the almost incessant growling and
> squealing of the mice as they helped themselves to the scanty morsel
> which was left at supper.

Write on receipt of this and let me know how you are getting along and also our relatives and friends and most particularly the ladies for they are so scarce in this country that I had almost forgotten that there was any such angelic creatures on earth any more. And if you hear any good young housekeeper enquiring for employment just send her to me and I will pay her better wages to superintend my little house . . . than she can get in the state of Ohio where she would have to perform five times the labor.[3]

Steve liked Nevada City and made it his permanent home. In 1853 he and a friend, Sam Connell, opened a grocery store on Broad Street, and later Steve engaged in the freighting business. A few years later Venard, Connell, and several others were partners in operating the Empire Mining Company, on Cement Hill, just outside town. None of these ventures brought Steve the financial success he was seeking, and in 1855 he secured a position as deputy under Nevada County Sheriff W. W. ("Boss") Wright. On November 3, 1856, Wright was shot to death, and in a special election William Butterfield was chosen as the new sheriff. Venard and Butterfield were not on good terms, and Steve resigned.

Nevada City, like most other mining camps of the gold rush era, was populated primarily by young men, far from the stabilizing influences of home, wife, and family. In addition, the town had a generous infusion of gamblers, saloonkeepers, prostitutes, hack politicians, and riffraff of every stripe. The result was an unstable community, rife with graft and political corruption. Nevada City politics in the mid-1850s were controlled by the gamblers and saloon men and the rough crowd who patronized their businesses. In 1856 a former baker named Henry Plummer was chosen city marshal. It was a rigged election in which drunken toughs frightened honest voters from the polls, and out-of-town miners were herded in to vote for Plummer. The new marshal was destined to become one of the West's most-celebrated outlaws and ended up the victim of a lynch mob in 1864, while serving as sheriff of Bannack, Montana. But in Nevada City, Henry Plummer appears to have been a capable lawman and made many arrests of thieves and robbers, although in later years he was suspected of having actually been in league with the criminal element.

The town's respectable crowd was embarrassed that a man of Plummer's stripe occupied the office of city marshal, and a few weeks before the city election of 1857, they turned toward Steve Venard as an alternative candidate. But Venard's reputation for courage and honesty could not compete with the tactics used by the Plummer camp to secure votes, and on election day, May 4, 1857, he was defeated, receiving 305 votes to Plummer's 417. Reported the *Nevada Journal,* "Many good citizens did not go to the polls, but, as usual, enough outsiders voted to make up the delinquency."[4]

Venard continued to work in the mines and was periodically employed as a Nevada City police officer. During the early 1860s much of the camp's rough element, including Henry Plummer, drifted away to new diggings, particularly Nevada's Comstock Lode, making it possible for an honest lawman to win at the polls. On May 2, 1864, Venard was elected to a one-year term as city marshal at a salary of seventy-five dollars a month, plus six dollars for each arrest he made that resulted in payment of a fine.

Venard's new duties included numerous mundane tasks that few people today would ever dream could be the lot of a frontier lawman. Reported the *Nevada City Gazette* on June 4, 1864:

> Under the efficient superintendence of Marshal Steve Venard, the road between this place and Selby Flat—at least so much of it as lies within the city limits—is being put in excellent condition. About a dozen men are employed, and Steve promises to "make a road that will not wash out with every little shower." A portion of the road is already well graveled, and he has removed two rickety old wooden bridges, supplying their places with substantial stone culverts. Mr. Venard has the reputation of being one of the best road-makers in the county, and he has a fine opportunity to "spread himself" on this road.

Road building was but one of many skills that could be required of the pioneer peace officer. Reported the *Gazette* a few months later, Venard, "with a posse comitatus, composed of a lot of boys who enjoyed the fun hugely, was busily engaged yesterday arresting the dogs who were so unfortunate as to be at large without a tag. He has some ten or fifteen cooped up which, unless claimed today by their owners, will be made to suffer martyrdom."[5]

Collecting taxes was yet another duty at which Venard was markedly adept. "Steve Venard has a mighty taking way with him," reported the *Gazette*'s editor. "Sometimes he takes 'gay cusses' to the city prison. When he politely taps a man on the shoulder and mildly suggests that he'll 'take five dollars if you please—road and corporation taxes,' it is almost impossible to refuse him."[6]

Nevada City was a turbulent town during the Civil War, and vio-

Steve Venard as he looked at
the time of his fight with
the Shanks gang in 1866.
Courtesy *Richmond* (In-
diana) *Palladium-Item*.

lence was frequent between Unionists and Copperheads. Steve po-
liced the camp with a firm but fair hand. Almost six feet tall, broad-
shouldered, with wavy black hair and a full beard, he was a crack
rifleshot and well known for his judgment and fearlessness. Mild-
mannered and temperate, Venard did not take part in the town's
rowdy night life but instead spent his free hours pouring over the
books of the newly organized Library Association.[7]

   While Steve was serving on the city marshal's force, a ruffian named
George Shanks drifted into town. Shanks had served a term in San
Quentin for stage robbery. He hailed from New York City and had
once worked as a pressman for the *New York Tribune*. He liked to brag
that "his mother had said he would die with his boots on, and that he
would make her out a liar if he had half a show." In 1863, Shanks had
worked as a cook for the Barton brothers in their Nevada City hotel.
When the brothers fired him, he returned at night and opened fire
through a window, wounding William Barton. Shanks escaped and
enlisted in the army, but he later deserted. In the fall of 1865 he shot

up the town of Colfax, wounding one resident, Lew Kopp, and forcing all the businessmen to close their shops. A few months later Shanks got drunk and raised a row in Unger's Saloon, in Grass Valley. Officer J. D. Meeks attempted to arrest him, and Shanks drew his six-shooter, covering Meeks.

"I'm Jack Williams, the great American chief!" he boasted drunkenly before fleeing the saloon.

Jack Williams was a notorious outlaw who had been hanged at San Andreas in 1856; "chief" was a popular term for a gunman. Shanks quickly became known as "Jack Williams's Ghost."[8]

Grass Valley lay four miles south of Nevada City, with a stage road connecting the two camps. Shanks began holding up late-night travelers along this highway on a regular basis. Local officers were unable to capture the elusive bandit, and he became increasingly bold. On one occasion he stopped a traveler named Smith and attempted to steal his poke. Smith broke into a run, and Shanks chased him into the center of Grass Valley, firing two shots at him before his fleet-footed victim escaped. After a dozen holdups had taken place, George Hilton, a local man with a reputation as a fighter, boasted that he was going to walk the lonely road between You Bet and Grass Valley at night, Jack Williams's Ghost or not. On the evening of April 21, 1866, Hilton set out with a pistol and sixty dollars in his pockets. Rounding a turn in the road, Hilton ran head on into the "ghostly" robber. He saw five men standing in a row next to the bandit and, thinking they were other robbers, quickly raised his hands and was relieved of his poke and pistol. When the highwayman vanished into the darkness, Hilton discovered that the other five men had also been robbed. Shanks had heard of the boast and had stopped each traveler on the road until he got his man.[9]

Shanks found his road-agent career so profitable that he recruited a partner, Robert Finn. Finn was a twenty-six-year-old Irishman and former messenger for the bank of Page, Bacon & Co., in San Francisco. He had been a leading member of the YMCA until he was caught "in flagrante delicto with the lawfully wedded but not contented wife of a Sunday school teacher." Finn had served two terms in San Quentin for grand larceny and had escaped several months earlier, on January 15. He was working as a miner in the New Eureka shaft when he fell in with Shanks.[10]

At five o'clock in the morning, May 8, Shanks and Finn stopped the stagecoach from North San Juan, three miles above Nevada City.

Two Chinese were the only passengers. One of them put up a struggle before the two brigands could remove his money belt, which held four hundred dollars. The robbers ordered driver John Majors to throw down the express box and began pounding on the lock with a sledge-hammer. The lock refused to open, and Shanks allowed the stage to proceed. Later that day the pair attempted to stop the upbound Washington stage, near Six Mile House. The driver and a passenger pulled pistols and whipped up the team, and the coach was soon out of danger. The down stage came along shortly after this and was not so lucky. The outlaws halted it and relieved a passenger of forty dollars.

The editors of local newspapers decried the repeated holdups and urged citizens to start a reward fund. The *Nevada Daily Gazette* reported that several hundred persons had been stopped and robbed on Nevada County roads in the previous five months.[11]

But George Shanks continued his operations. For his next raid he took on a second partner, George W. Moore, an escaped convict whom Finn had known in San Quentin. Moore was a forty-year-old Canadian who had left a wife and two children "in the States." He had served two sentences at San Quentin and had broken out only a month before.[12]

A Telegraph Company stage left North San Juan in the early-morning hours of May 15, 1866, with six passengers aboard and Cal Olmstead at the reins. The coach had crossed Black's Bridge (now Purdon's Bridge) over the South Yuba River and had started up the grade out of the canyon when Shanks and his men, each armed with a revolver, stepped into the road and ordered Olmstead to halt. The passengers were ordered out and searched for guns; Frank McKee had a pistol, and the robbers removed the caps and handed it back to him. The passengers were marched to the side of the road, and one bandit went to work on the Wells Fargo box with a sledgehammer and a crowbar. Once again the box would not open, but this time Shanks was better prepared. Olmstead was ordered to unhitch his team and walk the horses one hundred yards up the road. Then one brigand poured a charge of black powder into the padlock's keyhole and touched a match to it, but the powder burned off without opening the lock. A second charge was placed in the keyhole and tamped down with mud and leaves. The explosion blew the door off the box. Olmstead was then ordered to hitch up his team and move on.

The holdup had taken place at 4:30 A.M., and by 6:00 A.M., Sheriff

Gentry and his men were racing toward Black's Bridge. The posse consisted of Venard; Al Gentry, the sheriff's brother; Frank McKee, the passenger from the stagecoach; and A. W. Potter and Jim Lee, deputy sheriffs. The six riders galloped out East Broad Street and up the steep slope to the base of Sugar Loaf Hill. From the summit of the ridge above Selby Flat it was downhill to the bridge, about four miles distant, and the posse let their horses fly. At the holdup scene they carefully examined the roadbed but were unable to find the robbers' tracks. Then Sheriff Gentry divided his posse. He took Al Gentry, McKee, and Potter off the right, or north, side of the wagon road to beat the thick brush for the bandits' sign. Steve Venard later explained what happened next:

> Lee and myself went down to the left side of the road. We struck their, the robbers, tracks and followed them down to Rock Creek. Then Lee went back at my request to bring the rest of our party 'round on the Holt's Road, about three-fourths of a mile from where we parted. I came on to the men at the mouth of Myer's Ravine. The first intimation I had of their being there was a noise of some kind. Looking up, I saw two men grab their pistols. I immediately fired at one. He fell back and the other drew his pistol and jumped behind a rock and almost instantly after I saw the pistol come over the top of the rock, and then the man's head appeared above the rock when I fired and he fell behind the rock, making a noise that sounded like "Oh" or "don't." I then sprang up to where the men that I had shot laid to see if I could see the other man. Not seeing any other man, I grabbed two sacks of bullion and gold dust—it proved to be—and the pistols of the men, one being cocked, and jumped below the rocks and buried them by throwing leaves, etc., over them. I then ran across a stream on to a point and about fifty yards up the point, from which place I saw a man about one hundred yards up the ravine answering the description of one of the men that were said to have robbed the stage. I fired at him. He fell on his hands and knees and kept on up the hill, looking back over his right shoulder. I fired again. He appeared to sink down, looking toward me. I held my gun on him from a half to one minute. His head then dropped down. Then I went up until I got above him and satisfied myself that he was dead.[13]

Venard picked up the sacks of bullion, shouldered his Henry rifle, and walked back to meet Sheriff Gentry and the posse, announcing quietly, "I got them all, Sheriff."

When Steve returned the sacks of bullion to Wells Fargo Agent A. D. Tower, in Nevada City, he learned for the first time that the express company had offered a $3,000 reward for the bandits. Venard refused to accept the entire amount, saying he wanted to divide it

"VENARD SENT A BALL CRASHING THROUGH HIS BRAIN."

Harper's Weekly published this somewhat romanticized version of Steve Venard's remarkable exploit in the South Yuba gorge. From author's collection.

equally with the rest of the posse. It was finally settled that he would receive half.

Steve Venard became a celebrity overnight. The story of how he had slain three outlaws with four bullets was published in newspapers throughout the country. Said *Harper's Weekly,* "No romance could depict greater bravery." Governor Frederick Low appointed Venard to his staff, with the rank of lieutenant colonel in the National Guard, "for meritorious services in the field." Wells Fargo presented him with a new Henry rifle, gold-mounted and specially inscribed, that can be seen today in the Wells Fargo Bank History Room, in San Francisco.[14]

In June, Sheriff Gentry appointed Steve resident deputy sheriff at Meadow Lake City, a rip-roaring boomtown located at the crest of the high Sierra, northwest of Donner Pass. Gold had been discovered a year before, setting off a huge stampede. The town soon had a population of five thousand, with a stock exchange, banks, thirteen hotels, doctors' and lawyers' offices, restaurants, billiard saloons, and the usual assortment of gambling halls and brothels. Steve was soon appointed city marshal, with his office on A Street. Ever popular, he became a leading member of the "Meadow Lake Yachting Club." The "yacht" was an old iron lumber scow, without mast, that was rigged with four sets of oars. The "yachtsmen" practiced every evening to learn how to control the unwieldy craft. Then, with Venard at the helm, they would cruise the waters of Meadow Lake, loaded with passengers.[15]

If any doubt remained about Steve's remarkable skill with a rifle, he quickly put it to rest. In August, while on a hunt five miles north of Meadow Lake with two friends, Fisher and Stephens, a huge grizzly bear confronted the trio. It rushed toward Stephens, who fired and missed. Venard's Henry rifle cracked once, and the grizzly tumbled over dead. A month later Steve was invited to participate in a shooting contest sponsored by the Nevada City and Grass Valley volunteer fire companies. To no one's surprise, he won top prize, the company medal, as the best rifle shot.[16]

The ore from Meadow Lake's gold veins was soon found to be "rebellious," making it difficult and too expensive to remove the gold from the rock. Within a year Meadow Lake City was a ghost town. Steve Venard moved on and became a shotgun messenger for Wells Fargo, riding atop Concord coaches and mud wagons, guarding the company's treasure. In 1869, Wells Fargo sent him to guard their express coaches on the Central Pacific Railroad, and he served in the Mountain Division for two years. In 1871 he was back in Nevada City, working as a police officer. It was not long before Wells Fargo was again requesting his services, this time to round up one of the worst gangs of outlaws that ever plagued the North Coast.

Earlier that year a daring series of stagecoach robberies was perpetrated in Sonoma and Mendocino counties. Within six months the Cloverdale-Healdsburg stage was "stood up" eight times; the coach between Ukiah and Cloverdale was also stopped regularly. The holdups generally took place at night on an upgrade where the driver was compelled to walk or jog his horses. Passengers and mail were never disturbed; the road agents preferred to loot the Wells Fargo boxes. The biggest haul made in these raids was $1500 but Wells Fargo's total loss was many times that amount.

The leader in these holdups was John L. Houx, a hardcase from Missouri who lived in Cloverdale. His lieutenant was Elisha William Andrus, a twenty-nine-year-old native of Warsaw, Illinois, who had worked as a butcher in Round Valley and was nicknamed "Bigfoot" because of the oversize shoes he wore to confuse trackers. The other members of the gang included Johnny and Lodi Brown, the young sons of a stock rancher in Sanel (now Hopland); Tom Jones, who lived with his wife and children in Cloverdale; and Billy Curtis, a young teamster from a respectable Cloverdale family. Jones and Curtis had always enjoyed good reputations, but John Houx, Bigfoot Andrus, and Lodi Brown were all desperate men. Bigfoot had killed a man on the Salmon River, and Lodi had several shooting and cutting scrapes to his discredit.[17]

Local officers suspected that Houx was one of the masked robbers, and he was arrested several times and lodged in jail at Ukiah, only to be released owing to lack of evidence. The outlaws threatened to kill anyone who gave testimony against them, and the holdups continued with impunity. Reported the *Mendocino Democrat,* "The road was considered so unsafe that people hesitated to travel it, and those who did were on the constant lookout when passing near the particular points where assaults had been made."[18]

On August 12, 1871, Houx and his men stopped the stage between Cloverdale and Healdsburg, only to discover that the passengers were four well-armed San Francisco men on a hunting trip.

"You can't get anything out of this crowd," the driver told the bandits. "They're hunters."

Houx thought twice about robbing the stage, and his gang rode away empty-handed. But just four days later, Houx was ready for another strike. On the evening of the sixteenth the down stage left Cloverdale for Healdsburg, sixteen miles to the south. At the ribbons was C. L. ("Sandy") Woodworth, and atop the coach sat Charles D. Upton, the Cloverdale Wells Fargo agent, armed with a rifle and determined to safeguard the express box. The stage held fourteen passengers, nine inside the coach and five on top. Several of the passengers had also armed themselves in anticipation of another holdup.

At nine o'clock, as the team slowed on an upgrade near what is now the Italian Swiss Colony in Asti, four masked men suddenly appeared from the side of the road. The bandits were John Houx, Bigfoot Andrus, Lodi Brown, and another ruffian who was never identified. Brandishing rifles, shotguns, and pistols, they called for the driver to halt, at the same time firing a shot into the air. Sandy Woodworth responded to the order by cracking his whip over the leaders, and the team plunged forward. The robbers opened fire on the fleeing stage. Woodworth, hit in the cheek by buckshot and with his whiplash shot off, urged on his frantic horses. From his perch on top of the coach, Wells Fargo Agent Upton returned the fire, while a passenger, Myers F. Truett, shoved his shotgun out a window and emptied both barrels. Lodi Brown received a slight wound in his chest, and the unidentified robber let out a scream and dropped, riddled with shot. Another passenger, B. S. Coffman, sitting next to the driver, tried to draw his pistol, but a ball smacked into his arm, and the weapon fell to the ground. By this time the stage was charging up the hill, but the bandits kept up a hot fire. Coffman, slumping against Woodworth, was struck by eighteen buckshot in his face and side, and Henry P. Benton, another passenger on top of the coach, was shot through the intestines by a rifle ball.

The stage was now out of range, so Houx and his men mounted their horses and fled. After riding a short distance, their badly wounded companion told his pals that he was dying and asked them to kill him. They complied and, tying a rope around his neck to make it appear that he had been lynched, threw his body into the Russian River.

The stagecoach stopped at a nearby ranch, and the wounded passengers were taken inside. Henry Benton died the following morning, but Coffman, who was expected to die, underwent painful surgery and eventually recovered. The news of the tragedy aroused widespread indignation. The state offered $1,000 for the arrest and conviction of each of the killers. Wells Fargo offered an additional $3500 reward and sent Steve Venard into Sonoma County to work up the case.[19]

Venard met with Deputy Sheriff William B. Reynolds, of Healdsburg, a shrewd detective and criminal catcher. Reynolds had achieved local fame a year earlier by tracking down the notorious outlaws Hal Brown and Bill Oiler. He knew John Houx and his comrades and suspected them of the latest outrage, but, as usual, there was insufficient evidence to arrest them. Since Venard was a stranger in Sonoma County, it was decided that he would work undercover and try to secretly gather evidence against the murderers. For two months Steve rode on horseback through the rough country of northern Sonoma and southern Mendocino counties. He adopted the name of Jones and told local settlers that he wanted to buy a hog ranch. He spent most of his time, however, in saloons and gambling places, rubbing elbows with the rough element of Ukiah, Cloverdale, and Healdsburg. Whenever a crowd of toughs was collected around a saloon, "Jones" would be at the center, treating, drinking, and staggering. No one seemed to notice that he frequently missed the spot where liquor goes down. It would be spilled on the floor, or with a hiccup his stomach would refuse the potion, and he would indignantly throw it away.

Venard met Houx and several other members of the gang. When drunk the outlaws were inclined to talk too freely, and he soon learned that Billy Curtis had deserted the gang before the killing of Benton. Venard and Reynolds met quietly with Curtis. He agreed, under a promise of immunity and a share of the reward, to act as a stool pigeon for the officers. Curtis provided the names of the gang members and agreed to rejoin the band.

On October 10, Houx, Curtis, and several other gang members held up a stagecoach at McDonald's Hotel, eight miles north of Cloverdale, taking $925 from the Wells Fargo box. Early in November Curtis informed Venard of Houx's latest and most reckless plan: to rob Sheriff D. C. Crockett, of Mendocino County, while he was on his way to Ukiah after collecting taxes on the coast. Venard realized that something had to be done soon before another killing took place. He and Reynolds met with Barclay Henley, district attorney of Sonoma County, and presented the evidence they had collected. Henley advised them that a conviction for the murder of Benton could not be obtained unless they could get one of the outlaws present at the killing to turn state's evidence and testify against his comrades. Venard decided to arrest the entire band as soon as Houx made a move to carry out his conspiracy to rob Sheriff Crockett.

On November 9, 1871, John Houx rode down from Cloverdale to Healdsburg to check on the movements of Deputy Reynolds, of whom he was both suspicious and fearful. But when Houx found Reynolds at home with his family, apparently unconcerned and off guard, he turned back toward Cloverdale, intending to join up with his gang and proceed on to Mendocino to rob the sheriff. As soon as Houx left town, Reynolds telegraphed Venard in Cloverdale that the outlaw was on his way. Then the deputy and his brother, Hedge T. Reynolds, mounted up and started north.

When Houx rode into town, he was met by Venard and Curtis, who invited the bandit into the Cloverdale Saloon to take a drink. They stepped up to the bar, and Curtis raised his glass and called for all hands to drink. As Houx lifted a whiskey to his mouth, he found himself looking down the barrel of Steve Venard's six-gun.

"You are arrested!" Venard barked. "Throw up your hands or you're a dead man!"

Houx was too surprised to resist. His hands shot up over his head, and Steve removed three pistols from his belt. A few minutes later the Reynolds brothers rode up. Venard placed guards on all roads leading out of town to keep Houx's friends from warning the rest of the gang. Steve then advised Houx of the evidence they had collected against him, particularly the holdup at McDonald's, and offered him immunity if he would reveal the names of Benton's killers. As Venard had hoped, Houx thought of his own neck first and named Lodi Brown and Bigfoot Andrus, but he refused to reveal the name of the dead robber they had thrown into the Russian River. He also admitted that Johnny Brown and Tom Jones had been involved in the other holdups.

John Houx had a former wife living in Cloverdale, and he told the officers that Bigfoot was sleeping with her. While Venard guarded Houx, Billy Curtis and the Reynolds brothers rode out to Tom Jones's place and arrested him without trouble. Placing Houx and Jones under care of a citizen guard, the posse rode to the house owned by the bandit chief's former wife, arriving at ten o'clock. They surrounded the place, with Venard and Curtis at the rear and the Reynolds brothers in front. Afraid to lose their quarry in the dark, Venard decided to wait for daylight. But at dawn, when Deputy Reynolds kicked in the front door, they found that Andrus was gone. The woman told Reynolds that Bigfoot and Lodi Brown were at a cabin in an isolated, almost inaccessible canyon on the headwaters of Dry Creek, ten miles northwest of Cloverdale, and that Johnny Brown could be found at the house of Old Man Houx, father of the bandit leader.

Billy Curtis led Venard and the Reynolds brothers to the Houx place. As the officers surrounded the house, a large dog began barking, and Johnny Brown appeared in the doorway, armed with a double-barreled shotgun, a six-shooter, a derringer, and a Bowie knife. Deputy Reynolds walked slowly toward Brown, warning, "I'll have to disarm you."

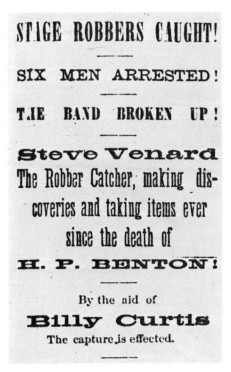

STAGE ROBBERS CAUGHT!

SIX MEN ARRESTED!

THE BAND BROKEN UP!

Steve Venard

The Robber Catcher, making dis-

coveries and taking items ever

since the death of

H. P. BENTON!

By the aid of

Billy Curtis

The capture is effected.

Headlines in the *Ukiah Mendocino Press* announce Venard's capture of the Houx gang. From author's collection.

"You need not be scared," Brown replied sarcastically. Clutching his shotgun tightly, the bandit stepped back.

"Stand still!" ordered Hedge Reynolds. "Nobody is afraid."

He lunged forward and snatched the shotgun from Brown's grasp. The officers ironed the outlaw and took him into Cloverdale. Then Hedge Reynolds and Charles Cook, former Wells Fargo agent at Cloverdale, loaded Houx, Jones, and Brown into a four-horse stage wagon and took them to McDonald's, while Venard, Curtis, and Deputy Reynolds started for Bigfoot's canyon hideout. They met a rancher named Knowles, who guided them to within a mile of the canyon. Tying up their horses, they proceeded along the creek about three hundred yards, then took off their shoes and walked silently another mile up the canyon until they came upon a small cave in the bank with a spring and a pool of water nearby. Seeing fresh horse tracks on the ground and hearing voices farther up the canyon, Venard and Reynolds decided to duck into the cave and wait for the outlaws to water their horses at the spring. Five minutes later Lodi Brown came walking down the canyon trail, rifle in one hand and leading his horse with the other.

"Hold!" Venard ordered, and Lodi turned to see three shotguns trained on him.

He dropped his rifle, and the officers tied his hands behind him.

"Where is Bigfoot?" Venard asked.

"He's up the canyon about three hundred yards at the camp, getting dinner," the outlaw replied, and added, "You'll never take him unless you kill him."

Venard and Reynolds held a quick consultation and hit upon a clever plan. While they took up positions behind the creek bank, Billy Curtis walked Brown back down the canyon. Then Curtis fired Lodi's rifle into the air and, pressing his pistol against the outlaw's head, forced him to yell, "Bill, I've killed a big buck! Come and help me pack him in!"

As expected, Bigfoot soon came down the trail. When he was ten steps from Venard and Reynolds, they stood up and yelled, "Halt!"

Bigfoot froze in his tracks.

"Unbuckle your pistol!" Venard commanded. "Drop it and step back!"

Bigfoot had the good sense to comply instantly. Then Venard's little posse took the prisoners up the canyon and searched the cabin, finding an ax that had been used to open the Wells Fargo boxes, Bigfoot's oversize shoes, and a mask made of oilcloth with eyeholes and a tie string. Taking the items as evidence, they started for the McDonald's road. The place where the outlaws were captured is still known as Bigfoot Canyon.

They met Hedge Reynolds at McDonald's, then took the five bandits to jail in Ukiah, arriving at eleven thirty that night. Venard and his companions, exhausted from lack of sleep, crawled into bed. In a little more than twenty-four hours they had rounded up the entire gang. Not a man had been injured nor a hostile shot fired.[20]

Unfortunately, the aftermath of the case was not as successful as the manhunt had been. The outlaws were removed to jail in Santa Rosa, where Bigfoot Andrus and Lodi Brown were charged with the murder of Henry Benton. Johnny Brown was indicted for robbing Wells Fargo during holdups in February and July, and Tom Jones was charged as an accomplice for keeping the band posted when valuable express shipments were sent out of Cloverdale. The evidence against Jones was weak, and he was released after his preliminary hearing. Bigfoot and Lodi, after learning that Houx had turned state's evidence and betrayed them, pleaded guilty to second-degree murder, and each was sentenced to thirty years in San Quentin. Johnny Brown pleaded guilty to robbery and received three years in prison. John Houx was released, which created a public uproar. He was rearrested and taken to Ukiah, where the Mendocino County grand jury indicted him for two stage robberies in that county. The district attorney dismissed the charges for lack of evidence, and the bandit chief was again set free. Complained the *San Francisco Alta,* "The deepest dyed villain of them all, John Houx, is now at large again."[21]

Henry Benton's widow was also dissatisfied with the outcome of the case. She sued the stage company for $25,000, claiming that if Sandy Woodworth had not tried to flee from the robbers her husband would not have been killed. Billy Curtis was unhappy with his share of the reward money, and he had a falling out with Hedge Reynolds. On the night of May 9, 1872, in a Cloverdale restaurant, the pair got into an argument over the rewards, and both went for their guns. Ten shots were exchanged at close range. Reynolds escaped with only a bullet hole in his coat, but Curtis was struck by one ball that grazed his head and another that pierced his chest, a serious, but not fatal, wound.[22]

Steve Venard ignored the squabbling and returned to his home in Nevada City, where he received generous praise from the newspapers for his skillful detective work. In time he learned that each of the killers met a just punishment. John Houx returned to his native Missouri and a few years later died of smallpox. In 1879, Bigfoot Andrus was slain in San Quentin by his cellmate, Tim McGrath, who cut his throat from ear to ear with a shoe knife. The next year Lodi Brown received a pardon, on condition that he leave the state. He went to New Mexico, where he was killed in a fight.[23]

In the meantime Steve Venard remained active as a bandit hunter. Early in 1876, Wells Fargo's chief detective, James B. Hume, called on him to help run to earth Charlie Pratt, "Old Jim" Smith, and "Texas George" Wilson, three stage-robbing hardcases recently released from prison. Pratt was a veteran of five terms at San Quentin; Smith had served three sentences; and Wilson had served two. On January 10 they stopped the Fiddletown-Latrobe stage near Plymouth, in

Old Jim Smith, *left,* and Texas George Wilson, *right,* both captured by Steve Venard in 1876. Courtesy Wells Fargo Bank History Room.

Amador County, and made off with the Wells Fargo shipment. Seven days later, just west of Greenwood, in El Dorado county, they held up the coach from Georgetown to Auburn. The three passengers were not bothered, and the highwaymen got only $105 from the Wells Fargo box.

Venard, Hume, and Len Harris (a Sacramento police detective) made a ten-day search for the robbers. They finally discovered that the outlaws were holed up in a house near Folsom and were being harbored by some black people. On January 27, Hume wired Judge Pawling in Jackson requesting an arrest warrant. The judge sent back a telegraphic warrant, and the next morning Hume, Venard, Harris, and Constable I. W. Kimble (of Folsom) surrounded the house. The officers had been informed that the outlaws were wary, desperate, and always armed.

While Venard and Kimble guarded the front of the house, Hume and Harris made a rush for the back door. Old Jim and Texas George heard them coming, and as the detectives burst inside, the two outlaws snatched up their Colt navy revolvers and fled out the front door. They ran head on into the cocked six-shooters of Venard and Kimble. Wilson and Smith threw up their pistols and were in the act of cocking them when Hume and Harris appeared behind them with drawn revolvers. Harris pointed his self-cocker at Old Jim and yelled, "Don't make a move, or I'll turn you into a lead mine!"

For a moment there was a deadly standoff. But in the face of four guns, Old Jim and Texas George lost their nerve. While Venard and Kimble covered the pair, Harris seized Smith's pistol, and Hume grabbed Wilson's. Both outlaws were much disheartened by their capture, and Smith told Venard that he was sorry he had not made a fight and declared that he would much rather be killed than return to San Quentin. Sent to Placerville to stand trial for the Greenwood robbery, they were convicted and sentenced to twelve years each. Charlie Pratt was arrested in February and was also sent across the bay for twelve years.[24]

Venard was galled when a minor dispute arose over the arrests. Constable Kimble, apparently miffed that the *Sacramento Daily Record* gave most of the credit for the captures to Venard, Hume, and Harris, complained to his hometown paper, the *Folsom Telegraph*. On February 5 the *Telegraph* ran a story claiming that

> [Kimble] almost unaided, disarmed and captured James Smith and George Wilson. . . . If Kimble and others who should know speak the truth, to Officer Kimble belongs almost the entire credit of relieving Folsom of these dangerous men.

Perhaps Steve got a chuckle out of Kimble's story, but such petty jealousy must have proved at least slightly annoying to the easygoing lawman.

Venard continued to make his home in Nevada City, serving as a deputy constable and a police officer. Although immensely popular, he still had enemies. The worst of these was Joe Lawrence, the most dangerous man in Nevada County. Lawrence was a muscular, thickset miner, who possessed tremendous physical strength and when drunk was a terror. In 1867 he had stabbed a man to death in a Grass Valley saloon and had been sentenced to San Quentin for ten years. He was pardoned after serving three years and returned to his old haunts, where he held sway as Nevada County's most-feared bully. Much to the disgust of law-abiding citizens, Lawrence was rarely arrested, and when he was, the courts treated him leniently.

While few men in the county were willing to tangle with Joe Lawrence, Steve Venard was more than a match for him in courage and
physical strength. On one occasion, while serving as night watch officer, Steve placed Lawrence under arrest, and the desperado put up a
violent fight. Venard clubbed Lawrence down and dragged him off to
the calaboose. Upon his release Joe Lawrence vowed repeatedly to
kill Venard the first chance he got.

Lawrence lived with his wife, four young children, and a fourteen-
year-old stepdaughter, Rosario, on a ranch in Willow Valley, just east
of Nevada City. On March 19, 1883, while on a drunken binge, Lawrence attempted to rape his stepdaughter. His wife interfered to protect the girl, and Lawrence beat her and drove both of them from the
house with a shotgun. He warned the pair to keep quiet about his
attack on Rosario, or he would kill them both. Mrs. Lawrence went
into Nevada City and swore out a warrant for her husband's arrest,
charging him with committing battery upon her. He was brought
into the justice court, pleaded guilty, and was fined thirty dollars.
Mrs. Lawrence was reluctant to reveal the attack on her daughter,
but this slap on the wrist left her no choice. She feared that, unless
her husband was locked up, he would surely kill her. The next morning, March 21, she filed a complaint against him for assault to commit
rape. That evening Lawrence rode into town looking for her.

Officer Fields spotted the desperado in front of the San Francisco
Saloon on Main Street and placed him under arrest. He took him to
Justice Blakely's courtroom, where Constable Steve Venard took
custody of the prisoner. Then Fields went down the street to see
Mrs. Lawrence, leaving Venard alone to guard Lawrence. Justice
Blakely set Lawrence's bail at $3500 and granted him permission to
go out and see if he could obtain bondsmen. Venard searched Lawrence's pockets for weapons and, finding none, started down the
courthouse stairs with him. As they neared the landing at the street,
Lawrence quick as a flash whipped a large knife from his sleeve and
stabbed Venard twice in the face and once in the back of the neck.
Venard reeled, stunned and bleeding heavily. But although he was almost sixty (twenty years older than his assailant), Steve Venard possessed the strength and power of a much younger man. Yanking his
six-gun, he struck Lawrence several terrific blows, finally knocking
the knife into the street. Lawrence broke loose and fled up Pine
Street with Venard close behind. As they raced up Courthouse Hill,
Steve fired three times at Lawrence, who staggered as if hit but kept

running. When he reached the top of the hill, Venard was so weak from loss of blood that he was forced to give up the chase.[25]

Several bystanders took up the pursuit, but Lawrence managed to escape. A few days later a letter from the fugitive was received through the post office, addressed "To the people of Nevada City and especially my wife and Venard." Wrote the desperado:

> If they can forgive me, and let me come home to my family, I will take a solemn oath there shall never, never, one drop of intoxicating liquor enter my mouth again as long as I live. If they cannot forgive I shall never be taken alive. I have a shot-gun and plenty of ammunition.[26]

Lawrence remained in hiding near Nevada City, sheltered by friends, and was finally captured at Clipper Mills, in Butte County, on June 26. His trial was set for September, and he later posted bond and was released. A week before trial Lawrence skipped out and evidently was not recaptured; he never served a state prison term for his attack on Venard.[27]

Venard's wounds eventually healed, and he returned to his badge and his duties. On the night of March 14, 1886, three men attempted to steal gold ore from the sluices of the Nivens Brothers' drift mine at Selby Hill, near Nevada City. They were surprised by a guard, who fired on them with a shotgun, and the sluice robbers fled. Venard took to the trail like a bloodhound, and after a search of four days he captured a suspect, Messaro Año. The next day the old manhunter picked up Telecena Bajer, who promptly "squealed" on the leader, a notorious ex-convict, Abyon Salvador. That evening Venard and two other lawmen rounded up Salvador at an Indian encampment near Rough and Ready; his back was peppered with seventy-two buckshot from the guard's gun.[28]

Venard was now suffering severely from chronic rheumatism, which, coupled with advancing age, soon convinced him that he must hang up his gun. He built a cabin on isolated Wet Hill Ridge and lived quietly, panning for gold in the Sierra streams and hunting in the pine forests. He never married, but perhaps he still enjoyed the "solitude of a mountain life" that he had written his sister about when he was a young man. Always kindly and charitable, he never refused requests to appear before local clubs and societies to speak about his colorful work as a pioneer lawman.[29]

Venard retained his interest in mining, and in 1888, with four partners, he opened the Detective Mine in the Cement Hill district, but the venture was apparently not a success. In 1891, Steve contracted a kidney ailment and entered the Nevada County Hospital, where he died on May 20. He was penniless, and his friends donated seventy dollars for a respectable burial. He was laid to rest in the Pioneer Cemetery in Nevada City, only a few feet from the unmarked graves of Shanks, Finn, and Moore.[30]

To this day Steve Venard remains something of an enigma. Virtually nothing is known of his personal life, and although he was among the best-known lawmen of his day, he died alone and impoverished. He never achieved wealth or political success, and even after winning prominence as a detective and manhunter, he spent most of his subsequent years working as an obscure, poorly paid police officer and deputy constable.

Nonetheless, although Steve Venard, the man, has long been forgotten, his legend lives on. His encounter with Shanks's gang is considered one of the classic gun duels of the Old West. The dramatic image of a solitary westerner pitted alone against multiple evils is entrenched in our folklore and epitomized by his cool nerve and deadly marksmanship in the granite gorge of the South Yuba so many years ago.

CHAPTER 3

Six-Gun Sheriff: Ben K. Thorn

IF you visit the sleepy gold town of San Andreas in the Sierra foot-hills, you may notice the beautifully preserved white brick mansion just off Highway 49, half a block from the old courthouse. Few real-ize that they are gazing at one of the oldest and finest houses in the mother lode, built by Calaveras County Sheriff Ben Thorn for his young bride in 1860. The house is authentically restored and conjures up thoughts of what life must have been like in the gold country a century ago.

If you are a more imaginative visitor, you might close your eyes and let your mind wander back through the years. Concentrate just a bit harder and you can almost make out the heavy tramping of horses' hooves. Can you hear them clearly? The hoofbeats gradually increase in volume to a thundering crescendo. Muffled shouts ring out in the night. You can see the dull glint of rifles and six-guns as riders' mounts plunge and rear excitedly in front of the old house. Hounds are bay-ing as a burly man, half-dressed and chomping on a huge cigar, steps onto the front porch. His horse, a fast charger named Cash, is quickly brought around, and the man swings lithely into the saddle. Leaning down, he pecks his wife gently on the cheek and in a moment is gone, galloping into the dust-filled darkness with his posse, in hot pursuit of a stage robber, a horse thief, or a murderer.

This scene was repeated again and again during the near half cen-tury that Ben Thorn was the "Law of Calaveras County." His record as a frontier sheriff is almost without parallel. He tracked down and captured some of California's most notorious outlaws, among them "Longhair" Sam Brown, Joaquín Olivera, and Tommy Brown. He hanged—or assisted in the hanging of—five murderers on the gal-lows at Mokelumne Hill and San Andreas. No mob ever took a pris-oner away from him, although three different attempts were made. He took part in numerous hair-raising gun battles, and superstitious

Mexicans and Indians came to believe that he led a charmed life and that no knife or bullet could kill him.

During the 1880s and 1890s, Ben Thorn was, next to his friend Tom Cunningham, the most famous sheriff in California. For over thirty years he was the political boss of Calaveras County, a controversial figure whose extraordinary feats of bravery and tenacity were at times overshadowed by the specter of scandal and corruption.

Benjamin Kent Thorn was born in Plattsburg, New York, on December 22, 1829, the son of Platt Thorn and Elizabeth Platt. His mother's family, for whom the town was named, had been early settlers. When Ben was four, his parents moved west to Chicago, Illinois, then a small, muddy village with a population of three or four thousand, half of them Potawatomi Indians. The Thorns soon moved to Ottawa, Illinois, where Ben grew up. The family home was a small log cabin. It had one window containing a single pane of glass and several rifle loopholes in the walls so that the cabin could be defended against Indian attack. A hundred feet distant lay a mass grave of sixteen white settlers who had been slain by Indians only a few months before.[1]

Young Ben worked on the family farm and attended school in Ottawa. When he was sixteen, he began teaching school in Plattville, and in 1849, at the age of twenty, he crossed the plains to California in search of gold, an arduous trip that left several members of Thorn's party dead from cholera. In September he began mining on the Yuba River, but met with little success. Thorn was fired with gold fever, however, and his interest in mining remained with him throughout his life. The following February he arrived in Mokelumne Hill, in Calaveras County, and worked a claim at nearby Upper Rich Gulch. Soon after, he moved to San Antonio camp, purchased two claims on San Antonio and Calaveritas creeks, and employed several miners to work for him.[2]

"San Antone" was a very wealthy but extremely wild camp in the early 1850s. Like many other mother lode towns, it was flooded with cutthroats and renegades of every type: Yankees, Frenchmen, Indians, Mexicans, Californios, and Chileños. The Chileños, in particular, bore a high profile. Although expert miners, they were quick-tempered and singularly unafraid of the Americans. They were ready to fight at the drop of a hat.

Ben Thorn, barely out of his teens and sowing his wild oats, was a daring, reckless youth. He was not a stranger to trouble. One day a

Chileño became convinced that Thorn was paying too much attention to his wife. The Chileño gathered several compadres around him and declared he would "do up" the young Americano without delay. They had been drinking and were in an ugly temper. Thorn had been drinking, too, and as soon as he heard the threats of the Chileño, he got an American flag, wrapped it around himself, and, with a six-shooter in each hand, paraded up the street in front of the Chileños, singing "The Star Spangled Banner" at the top of his lungs. The Chileños looked on in wonderment. Finally, admiring his nerve, they stepped into the street, shook Thorn's hand, and invited him into a saloon for a drink.[3]

Most difficulties did not end so amicably. Shootings, knifings, and brawls were commonplace. During the mid-1850s, Calaveras County newspapers frequently reported one or two killings a week. Many murderers managed to elude arrest and escape punishment altogether; one such murder Ben Thorn witnessed personally. One night in June, 1854, he heard two gunshots ring out inside a house of prostitution, just above San Antone. Thorn and several bystanders rushed into the house and found a Mexican gambler named Antonio lying dead on the floor with a bullet hole in his forehead. In a back room, Thorn found a woman, Juana, desperately wounded with a pistol ball in her abdomen. Before she died, Juana told Ben that her former lover, Pedro Ybarra, had shot them both in a jealous rage. Other witnesses told Thorn that Ybarra had mounted a horse and fled into the night. A hunt was made for the killer, but he could not be found.[4]

This rampant lawlessness seems to have sobered young Thorn. On April 15, 1855, the newly elected sheriff, Charles A. Clarke, appointed him a deputy so that he might have authority to do what he could to rid the county of its many gangs of ruffians and desperadoes. Ben Thorn was ably fit for the job. At five feet, eight inches tall, he was well-knit and possessed of superb strength, the result of years of hard labor in the placer mines. A deadly pistol shot, Ben had keen insight into human nature and seemed a stranger to fear.[5]

Only a few months passed before the young deputy tackled the worst band of toughs in Calaveras. This gang was led by Jess Miller and "Longhair" Sam Brown, both notorious hardcases. Its members included Hugh ("Bunty") Owens, John Hicks, Alfred Richardson, John ("Kentuck") Chambers, and Lafayette ("Punch") Choisser. All gamblers and fine-looking young men, each wore a Mexican sash and enjoyed fighting with knives and guns. Longhair Sam Brown was by

Ben K. Thorn, the six-gun
sheriff of Calaveras County.
Courtesy Calaveras County
Museum.

far the worst of the lot, especially when drunk. A two-hundred-
pound Texan, twenty-five years old, he wore his coarse red hair long
and brushed back. He had already killed a number of men and bragged
that he did not bother to count Mexicans, Chileños, or Chinese.

On July 8, 1855, Sam Brown was dealing monte in a gambling place
in Upper Calaveritas. Bunty Owens was with him, as well as most of
the other members of the gang. A crowd of Chileños was gambling
at Brown's table when another Chileño, Lorenzo, picked up some
money from the table and demanded to bet it. Brown ordered Lorenzo to put the money back and told him he could not place a bet at
his table. Another Chileño, Domingo, told Brown, "Then you won't
deal for anyone!"

Domingo grabbed the blanket stretched over the table and jerked
it away. Instantly the fight was on. Longhair Sam and Bunty Owens
stabbed two Chileños to death and wounded a third and then fled
the camp, closely pursued by the Chileños' infuriated friends. Brown
and Owens fired into the crowd, mortally wounding yet another
Chileño with a rifle ball through his body, which promptly ended the
pursuit.[6]

A bystander, E. R. Purple, raced to San Antone and informed
Deputy Thorn of the killings. Thorn, accompanied by one of his

miners, Ed Hopkins, took Purple to the sawmill on San Antonio Creek. The sawmill was run by Orrin Spencer, who was also justice of the peace of Township No. 5. Purple swore out a complaint against Owens and Brown, and Spencer handed Thorn a warrant for their arrest. Thorn and Hopkins started after the killers and rode all night in search of them. Finally, at daybreak, Ben learned that they were holed up with four other members of the gang in John Hicks's cabin on O'Neill Creek.

As Thorn approached the cabin on horseback, Sam Brown appeared in the doorway, rifle in hand, and took careful aim. The cabin was set back from the road some distance, and the space between had been cleared of trees. Ben dismounted and began walking slowly through the clearing toward the cabin. Hopkins, favoring discretion, remained on the road. By now, six cocked guns were trained on the young deputy, but he kept on, a cigar clenched in his teeth and his gun hand well away from his holstered pistol. Thorn could see the muzzles of six-shooters and rifles protruding from the windows and between the logs. When he had walked half the distance, Longhair Brown lowered his rifle, and Ben breathed a huge sigh of relief. He stepped up to the door and called on Brown and Owens to surrender. They came outside and after a brief parley submitted peacefully to arrest.

Many years later a newspaper reporter asked Thorn whether he had been afraid.

"Afraid!" the sheriff exclaimed, with an emphatic nod of his head. "You bet I was afraid. That two hundred yards from the road to the cabin seemed like ten miles!"

"Then what did you do it for?" the reporter asked.

"Oh, I knew what sort of man Brown was, and I knew that if we rode up to the cabin there would be a fight, and we would be at a disadvantage. But I didn't think he'd shoot me if I went up alone. I asked him afterward why he didn't shoot me and he said he knew I would be square about it and that he would probably get taken anyway before long and that he wouldn't get a better chance to surrender after that. He said he figured it out that I was trusting him to be as square as I meant to be myself and he didn't like to be any less than I was thinking him to be. His men wanted to shoot, but he ordered them not to as long as I didn't make any move toward my gun."[7]

Before Thorn started back with his two prisoners, Longhair Sam asked that he be allowed to pack his rifle with him for self-protection.

The deputy, realizing that they might be attacked by Chileños along the way, granted him this favor. Thorn and Hopkins took the pair to Judge Spencer's sawmill for their preliminary hearing. The examination was one of the most exciting that ever occurred in the county. One hundred angry Chileños gathered about the place, while over forty of Brown's friends were also present. Ill feelings were at a fever pitch between the two factions, and Ben had his hands full trying to prevent a bloody war.

The hearing lasted for two days, and seventeen witnesses to the killings were called. It was no secret that Brown's companions planned to take him away from Thorn. Ben called on some of his friends to help him guard the prisoners during the night, but all quickly found that they had business elsewhere. The hearing was held in a saloon near the sawmill. Thorn ordered the barkeeper not to sell or give away any liquor. He put his prisoners in a corner, sat down next to them on a box, and, with his six-gun in hand, waited alone for daylight.

The forty friends of Brown and Owens gathered around, glowering and swearing at the deputy. But the six-shooter in Thorn's fist and the determined glint in his eye cowed them. In the morning the hearing continued, and both desperadoes were held to answer. By now, Brown's friends were becoming desperate. Punch Choisser lunged forward and handed Brown a loaded revolver, calling on him to shoot Thorn. Ben snatched the pistol and felled Choisser with a blow to the jaw. Then another of Brown's gang, Alf Richardson, decided on a new tactic. He swore out arrest warrants before Judge Spencer against two notorious Chileño gunmen in the crowd, believing that they would kill Thorn rather than submit to arrest. Ben knew that the charges were false, but the warrants had been issued, and it was his duty to serve them. Much to the chagrin of Brown's gang, the two Chileños did not resist the nervy young officer and submitted quietly to the arrest.[8]

Ben Thorn then took Sam Brown, Bunty Owens, and the two Chileños to the county jail in Mokelumne Hill. The charges against Owens were dropped, but Longhair Brown stood trial for murder three months later. He claimed self-defense, but the jury convicted him of manslaughter on October 3, and he was sentenced to two years in San Quentin. Upon his release he returned to Calaveras County. Brown claimed that Frank Ness, one of the witnesses to the fight, had testified falsely against him. Longhair Sam found Ness in a fandango house in Calaveritas and flogged him with a cowhide whip. Ben Thorn had a talk with Brown. He told him that the atmosphere in Calaveras was not healthy and suggested that he leave the county. Brown took Thorn's advice and departed for the Comstock Lode, where he quickly ran up one of the worst records of any western "chief." He boasted that he had killed eleven men during his lifetime and, according to legend, coined the phrase, "I want a man for supper." On July 7, 1861, he met his death at the hands of Henry Van Sickle, a peaceable innkeeper who filled the mankiller with buckshot.[9]

In the fall of 1855, Ben Thorn ran for constable of Township No. 5 and was elected. Constables in those days were paid fees for serving subpoenas and civil papers, attaching and selling property subject to liens and judgments, and acting as court officers for the townships' justices of the peace. Thorn had early realized that an astute officer could earn a good salary, and years later he admitted frankly that he had run for constable "in order to secure the official business of the justice's court, which in those days reached a considerable amount."[10]

Ben Thorn also retained his position as deputy sheriff. During the 1850s, sheriffs in California were charged with collecting the foreign miners license tax, an outrageously racist and discriminatory tax of six dollars a quarter. The tax was levied against all foreigners, especially Chinese, and even included Indians. Tax collectors were paid a commission of about 20 percent of what they collected. Ben Thorn was aggressive and effective in enforcing this tax. One Calaveras pioneer, Wade Johnston, recorded this story about Thorn in his memoirs:

> I first met Ben Thorn in 1856. I was alone at our cabin in Yaqui Camp when Ben Thorn brought in a big Yaqui Indian that weighed 200 pounds. The Indian's head was bleeding and a white handkerchief was tied around it.
> Ben Thorn said to me, "Here's a man that owes me two licenses. I asked him for it and he asked me if I wanted to fight. So he showed fight, and I hit him over the head two or three times with the six-shooter."
> Thorn then pulled a goose quill from his pocket and said, "Here's the gold he has collected in this quill." I took the quill and weighed the gold dust for him. There was $5.75.
> "Now," Thorn said, "I'll take this gold and give him credit for one license, and when he pays the rest I'll give credit for the other license." I never saw the big Yaqui again.[11]

But if Ben Thorn was successful as a tax collector, he was even more so as a manhunter. Immediately following his appointment as deputy sheriff, he began to hunt down the fugitive killers who had previously committed murders in San Antonio Township. Ben ran to earth a ruffian named Bratton who had slain Thomas Titcomb, and he arrested four Mexicans who had murdered a German on Indian Creek for his gold. In March, 1857, he captured John Phillips, who had killed a Mexican named Morales with an ax in San Antone in 1854. Phillips was later hanged for his crime in Mokelumne Hill. In October, 1857, Ben tracked down Howard ("Pike") Maupin, who had shot James Dill to death in San Antone on August 24, 1855. Thorn found Maupin in a dance house in Marysville and brought him back to Calaveras, where he was convicted of manslaughter and sentenced to three years' imprisonment.[12]

One of the most dangerous ruffians that Thorn ran down was Santiago Molino, a Chileño who was reported to have slain six men. Molino brought a group of fifty peons to the mines near San Andreas in 1849 and worked them for all they were worth. He later moved his operations to Greenwood Valley, in El Dorado County. Molino hired a blacksmith, Daniel Andrews, to make a huge dagger (it was two feet long and weighed eight and a half pounds). It was the kind of weapon the Chileño of that day liked to carry in his bootleg. On the night of December 14, 1856, Molino and a fellow countryman got into a quarrel with Andrews. While Andrews and the Chileño were struggling on the ground, clinched together, Molino, with one plunge, drove his dagger through the blacksmith and his own compadre, killing both of them. Molino escaped, and the Americans arose in wrath and burned the Chileño quarter. Miners at Greenwood Valley and Georgetown offered a one-thousand-dollar reward for Molino, dead or alive, and notices were sent to officers throughout the state.

Ben Thorn worked diligently to locate the killer and finally, in January, 1859, learned that he was in Colorado, a small mining camp in Mariposa County. With another officer, Fred Wesson, he struck out for Colorado, arriving after a two-day ride. They found Molino and another Chileño in a cabin a short distance from the camp. When Thorn told Molino that he was under arrest, the outlaw seized his six-shooter and tried to throw down on the lawmen, but they wrestled the gun away. Then Ben took charge of Molino, Wesson took the other Chileño, and they started from the cabin. But Molino, desperate for his freedom, broke loose from Thorn and ran for the woods, with the deputy close behind, yelling in Spanish for the badman to halt. It was pitch dark, but Molino's white trousers stood out in the blackness. Ben, realizing that he could not catch the outlaw, drew his six-gun and fired three times. Molino dropped, mortally wounded.

At Thorn's request, Wesson went into Colorado to obtain assistance from the only three Americans in the camp, while Ben remained with Molino's body. They then carried the corpse into Colorado, and a coroner's jury was summoned. A crowd of more than fifty Chileños poured into the little camp, angered at the killing of their countryman, but, although they looked daggers at the lawmen, they made no trouble. The coroner's jury exonerated Thorn. He never claimed the one-thousand-dollar reward, nor was it ever offered to him.[13]

Ben Thorn owed much of his success in catching criminals to a wide network of friends and criminal informants who kept him posted on the activities of the various thieves, robbers, and other lawbreakers of Calaveras. Thorn continually kept his ear to this grapevine, and in October, 1858, he got wind that the long-missed Pedro Ybarra had been living for the last eighteen months with one American and three Mexicans in a cave in the Tuolumne River canyon, five miles above LaGrange (now covered by Don Pedro Reservoir). With Undersheriff Bob Paul and Deputy Gordon Sloss, Thorn rode to the hideout. They found Ybarra and his companions on the south bank, unarmed. Seeing the officers approach, the six splashed across the river for the cave to get their guns, but Thorn and his posse headed them off. Ben immediately recognized Ybarra and seized him, but one of the Mexicans, Simone, managed to grab his pistol, and he pointed it at Thorn's head. Paul and Sloss pounced on Simone and brought him down with a well-aimed blow to the skull. At that, the rest of the gang took to the hills pell-mell.

Thorn took Pedro into the cave to get the fugitive's valise. Ybarra bolted and grabbed his six-shooter, but Ben muscled it away from him. The lawmen took him to Mokelumne Hill for trial, and he was convicted of murder. His case was appealed to the California Supreme Court, which, in October, 1860, granted him a new trial. Pedro Ybarra was then either acquitted or succeeded in having the case dismissed, for he never served a prison term for the double murder in San Antone.[14]

The busy Thorn managed to find time to woo young Anna Meeks, who lived in San Antone with her mother and sister. Shy and retiring

Ben K. Thorn's badge.
Courtesy Fred Kern, Cala-
veras County Sheriff's Department.

but strikingly beautiful, Anna was attracted to the rough-and-tumble deputy, and they were married on October 30, 1859. As a wedding present Ben presented his bride with a magnificent home in San Andreas. Completed in 1860, it was constructed of bricks hauled by mule team from Stockton. It had three floors, thirteen rooms, plastered walls, a winding staircase, and a marble fireplace in the back parlor. Ben Thorn filled the house with luxurious furnishings, including a seven-foot Weber grand piano which had been shipped around the Horn.

Thorn's neighbors were much stupefied that a deputy sheriff could afford such a mansion. It was by far the largest and most costly residence in the county. Most people in Calaveras were then living in simple, wood-frame buildings; many miners lived in tents and huts. It was widely believed in the county that Ben Thorn had embezzled part of the proceeds of the taxes he collected. Said Wade Johnston of Thorn, "It was said that some collectors got away with a lot of money, and I guess they did."[15]

In fairness to Thorn it must be said that he owned several mining claims from which he may have earned enough money to build his home. But this is unlikely, for the Calaveras County Assessment List of 1859 shows that he owned personal property only, worth $300; in 1861 the list indicates both real and personal property valued at $2,800, a substantial and unexplained jump. The rumors of Thorn's mysterious wealth failed to put a dent in his political career, however. In 1861 the office of tax collector was separated from the sheriff's office, and Ben was elected for three consecutive two-year terms as tax collector and assessor of San Antonio Township. He also served as undersheriff for Sheriff Bob Paul from 1860 to 1864 and as deputy sheriff under James Oliphant from 1866 to 1868.

Thorn's questionable financial activities were almost completely obscured by his continued remarkable success in ferreting out the most dangerous outlaws in the mother lode. On March 6, 1860, he arrested Charles O'Connor, an American black, who had killed Joshua Anderson by crushing his skull with a club. On April 14 he captured Jose Carasca, a notorious horse thief who had previously given "leg bail" and escaped from a constable in Lancha Plana, in Amador County.[16]

Three months later, on July 23, Constable Miles Huntsman and a posseman, Matthew Howard, attempted to recover a stolen horse at a grand Indian fandango in Lancha Plana. One Indian, Momosa, shot and killed the constable. Other Indians in the crowd of one thousand opened fire on Howard, who, although hit several times, managed to return the fire and kill one Indian, wound another, and rout the rest. The white men who were present carried Howard to Campo Seco and sent word to Ben Thorn, who recruited Constable W. M. Denig and three citizens and set off after Momosa. They found him seven days later in El Dorado camp, lying in his hut with a loaded rifle by his side and a long knife under his head. Momosa tried to run, but Thorn jumped him and quickly had the killer in handcuffs.[17]

A month earlier, on the night of June 29, 1860, an exceptionally brutal robbery had occurred. Two bandits crept up on the tollhouse at the Indian Ladder bridge, on the North Fork of the Mokelumne River, near West Point. Seated inside was the tollhouse keeper, John McDonough, and his friend Gwin Raymond. The robbers leveled their pistols through an open window and opened fire at point-blank range. One ball tore through Raymond's shoulder and lodged in his cheek; McDonough was wounded in the right arm. Then the bandits entered and, ignoring their bleeding victims, took three hundred dollars in toll receipts and fled. The West Point constable trailed the outlaws and caught one, but the other escaped. The captured bandit confessed to the crime and named his partner as Charles Williams (alias Bill Green), a notorious twenty-eight-year-old desperado.

Ben Thorn, at the head of a twenty-man posse, scoured the hills for Williams, but not a trace of him was to be found. Thorn and Sheriff Bob Paul kept up a "still hunt" for the outlaw and five months later they received information that Williams was at Princeton (now Mount Bullion), six miles from Mariposa. Thorn and Paul rode to Mariposa County, where they were joined by Constable Benbrooke, of Hornitos. On December 6, 1860, at a cabin located between Princeton and Bear Mountain, the three officers found two men chopping wood some distance apart. Thorn rode down toward one man, while Paul and Benbrooke rode toward the other. Ben recognized his man as Williams and, pulling his revolver, ordered, "Stand!"

Thorn then called to Sheriff Paul, "Come down, I have the right man!"

Like a flash, Williams snatched up his ax, raised it above his head, and rushed headlong at the mounted deputy, who cocked and aimed his six-shooter. Throwing down the ax, Williams turned and raced for a dense thicket of chaparral.

"Stop, or I'll shoot!" Thorn called twice, but the outlaw only ran faster. Ben fired once and missed, and Williams plunged into the thicket and disappeared. The brush was too thick to follow on horseback, so Thorn and his companions galloped around to cut him off. Williams burst out of the underbrush with a large knife clutched in his hand. At a distance of fifty feet, Ben Thorn fired a single pistol shot from horseback at the running bandit. The ball struck Williams in the left shoulder and ranged downward toward his lungs. The desperado ran another thirty feet before he dropped.

"I give up! You have killed me!" he gasped, and threw away his knife.[18]

Thorn and Sheriff Paul loaded Williams into a spring wagon and drove him to the jail in Mariposa, where a doctor tended his wound. Several newspapers lambasted Thorn for shooting a fleeing fugitive. Said the *Mariposa News*, "We are inclined to think that Thorn fired rather too quick." The *San Francisco Bulletin* added that Thorn "seemed not to be very scrupulous" in using his pistol. But the *San*

Andreas Independent came quickly to Thorn's defense, its editor commenting:

> . . . had he ridden up to [Williams] without shooting him, Thorn would have been knifed, the *Mariposa News* would have gained a better sensation article, and the State would have lost an admirable citizen and one of her most efficient officers.[19]

Williams remained in the Mariposa jail for six weeks while he recovered from his wound, then was brought to Mokelumne Hill and sentenced to twelve years in prison. In February, however, with four other prisoners, he cut a hole in the jail floor and escaped. One prisoner in the jail who did not take part in this break was Jesus Bealoba [this was the Yankee version; the proper spelling is undoubtedly Villalobo]. He had been convicted of killing Judge Roberts, who had attempted to arrest him for horse theft, at Jenny Lind. He was sentenced to death, and his case was appealed to the California Supreme Court, which upheld the conviction. Bealoba was then sentenced to be hanged on March 19, 1861. Four days before the execution date, at the request of his mother, Bealoba was taken out of the jail to a nearby daguerreotypist's gallery to be photographed. A man of huge size and strength, he was accompanied by Ben Thorn and another officer.

On the way back to the jail the other officer told Thorn that he had forgotten something and left Ben alone with the unironed prisoner. Thorn continued on, keeping Bealoba eight feet ahead of him. As they neared the jail, Bealoba whirled around, crouched low, and charged Thorn. Grabbing him in a bear hug, Bealoba pulled Thorn's pistol from its holster. The two struggled desperately for the weapon, but the burly desperado managed to wrest it from Thorn. Now the officer was fighting for his life. Mustering his strength, he threw his assailant to the ground and straddled him, but Bealoba cocked the pistol and shoved it into Thorn's belly. Ben knew he had not a second to lose. With a lightning-fast movement he knocked the pistol away with his left hand and rammed the forefinger of his right hand as far up the outlaw's nostril as it would go. It caused such instant and excruciating pain that Bealoba's grip relaxed, and he dropped the pistol, screaming in agony. Thorn held his prisoner securely and yelled for help. Soon several friends appeared and helped him return Bealoba to his cell, where the killer showed great remorse and apologized profusely to Thorn. Bealoba's lawyers had been fighting vigorously to save his neck, and two days later he received a reprieve from the governor, who commuted his sentence to life imprisonment. On April 8, Thorn transported him to San Quentin.[20]

Ben Thorn's many conflicts with the tough element earned him a wide reputation for firmness and courage. His work as tax collector had brought him into contact with people throughout the county. He was a very popular man with a marked ability to make and keep friends, and it was only natural that, in 1867, the Democratic party chose him as its candidate for sheriff. Thorn's campaign was an uphill battle, however, for skeletons rattled loudly in the lawman's closet. In August both the *Calaveras Chronicle* and the *San Andreas Register* published stories that strongly implied that Thorn had embezzled tax monies during the previous year. It was revealed that as the collector for San Andreas Township, which polled 600 votes and had a return of $350,000 in taxable property, he had reported only $2,892 in tax receipts. By comparison the collector for Jenny Lind Township, which had a vote of only 123 and a return of $127,000 in taxable property, reported $2,900 in tax receipts. Thus Thorn's township, with three times the taxable property and over four times the number of voters, paid less tax than Jenny Lind Township.

The newspapers also pointed out that Thorn had reported that he had collected only 204 state poll taxes. The road overseer for Thorn's township had collected 795 road tax receipts. By law, whoever was liable for the road tax also had to pay the poll tax. Therefore, Thorn was shy 591 poll tax receipts worth about $1,040. "How is this, Mr. Thorn?" asked the editor of the *Chronicle*. He offered a hint, writing that Thorn "has built himself a costly residence, and disported himself in a style of living that has puzzled his neighbors."[21]

It was evident that the percentage fees allowed tax collectors were not enough for Thorn; he appears to have simply kept much of the tax money he collected. Such graft was commonplace in that era. In neighboring Amador County, the office of sheriff during the 1860s was reputed to be worth $15,000 to $20,000 a year, far more than the tax-collecting fees and the $4,000 salary could possibly provide. But many of the voters of Calaveras seemed willing to overlook Ben Thorn's pecuniary peccadillos, for on September 4 they elected him sheriff by a narrow majority of 158 votes. Thorn's term began on March 2, 1868, and he appointed his brother Abbot and his old friend Fred Wesson as deputies. He devoted all his customary energy and

Calaveras County officials, 1890. Ben Thorn is standing, center. His brother Abbot is at far right. Courtesy Calaveras County Museum.

diligence to his new duties, but his prowess as a detective and a man-hunter was soon to be severely tested.[22]

On the afternoon of September 30, Elkanah ("Kinney") Said, superintendent of the Petticoat Mine at Railroad Flat, started for Mokelumne Hill with a large shipment of gold bullion. He drove a buggy and was accompanied by two employees, E. L. Meek and Daniel Keese. They had traveled about three miles when four masked men armed with double-barreled shotguns suddenly arose from the thick roadside brush.

"Whoa!" one of the robbers yelled, at the same time firing a blast from his shotgun. Kinney Said was killed instantly, with buckshot in his jaw, neck, and sternum. Meek jumped from the buggy, but was captured by the bandits. Keese, however, leaped into the front seat. The horses, spooked by the shot, had started to run, and Keese took up the reins and whip and urged them on. The robbers fired at the horses, slightly wounding them, but Keese was soon out of range and brought the buggy into Mokelumne Hill.[23]

Kinney Said had been a popular man, and his brutal murder electrified the citizens. The owner of the Petticoat Mine offered a two-thousand-dollar reward, dead or alive, for the killers. Ben Thorn spared nothing in his efforts to track them down. He and his deputies made an extensive search of the murder scene and found a hat and a sack of provisions nearby. They showed these articles to shopkeepers throughout the county and finally learned that a man named Rodesino, who owned a store in El Dorado, had sold the hat to a Chileño, José Coyado, and the provisions to a Frenchman just before the murder. Thorn learned that Coyado's constant companions were two Frenchmen and another Chileño, Andreas Molino.

The sheriff continued his search for the killers with unremitting zeal and soon found that Molino and one of the Frenchmen were in Mariposa County. With Constable Lee Mathews, Thorn rode south, stopping that evening, October 27, 1868, at Fallon's Hotel, in Columbia. They ate supper at the hotel, and Thorn, not anticipating trouble, handed Owen Fallon his weapons to keep overnight. After the meal, Thorn, Mathews, and Constable Smith, of Columbia, stepped outside and noticed three armed, well-mounted, and elegantly dressed Mexicans ride up to Kelly's Livery Stable. Sheriff Thorn immediately recognized them as men wanted by the sheriff of Santa Cruz County for highway robbery.

It had always been Thorn's favorite method to take his man by surprise, if possible. He quickly crossed the street and seized the bridle of one Mexican's horse.

"You are my prisoner!" Thorn barked, and ordered him to dismount. The man refused, and Ben yanked him from the saddle. At the same time, Kelly, the liveryman, snatched the bridle of another rider named Rodríguez, who was trying to escape. The third Mexican, who had dismounted, was seized by Constable Smith. While Thorn and his man struggled violently for possession of the Mexican's pistols, Rodríguez fired at Kelly, slightly grazing his neck. Lee Mathews returned the fire, shooting Rodríguez in the side. Rodríguez jumped from his horse and fled into the livery stable, taking refuge behind a pile of harness.

The third desperado broke loose from Constable Smith, pulled his pistol, and fired three shots at Ben Thorn at close range. One bullet tore a hole through the sheriff's hat, and another wounded him slightly in the armpit. A citizen, T. J. Evans, rushed to Thorn's aid and emptied his pistol at the Mexican, who took to his heels. Evans hurled his six-shooter at the fleeing desperado, striking him in the back, but he escaped in the darkness.

Ben secured his man and handed him over to Mathews, then went into the livery stable after Rodríguez. The wounded Mexican fought like a tiger. The sheriff finally managed to grab him by the hair and drag him outside, where Mathews helped wrestle Rodríguez into submission.[24]

Thorn and Mathews guarded the prisoners during the night in Fallon's Hotel, and the next morning, Mathews took them to San Andreas. Thorn continued on alone to Mariposa after the Kinney Said murderers, but despite a patient and diligent hunt, he was unable to find the men. He gave a minute description to the Mariposa officers, however, and two months later, in January, 1869, they arrested Andreas Molino at Bear Valley. Thorn lodged Molino in the San Andreas jail and soon extracted a complete confession from him. Molino admitted that his partners had been José Coyado, Paul Tibeaux, and Baptiste Dueny and that Tibeaux had fired the fatal shot.

Sheriff Thorn continued his hunt for the killers and finally arrested Jose Coyado near Fiddletown, in April. Coyado confessed, and in June he was indicted for first-degree murder. Molino turned state's evidence and was allowed to plead guilty to second-degree murder in exchange for a life term. The legal machinations of Coyado's case lasted three years and help illustrate that, contrary to the claims of revisionist historians, due process was available to Hispanics in frontier California. Several continuances were obtained by Coyado's defense counsel, with a trial date eventually set for April, 1870. At that time the defense demurred to the indictment, which was sustained by the Calaveras District Court. In June, Coyado was reindicted, and in October he was tried and convicted. Coyado's attorney appealed to the California Supreme Court, which overturned the conviction on two grounds. First, the jurors who heard the case were found to be tainted by bias. Ben Thorn, as sheriff, was charged with selecting the panel of jurors. At trial, Coyado's attorney had placed the sheriff on the witness stand and asked him whether he had formed an absolute opinion about Coyado's guilt. Thorn, of course, testified that he believed Coyado to be guilty. The Supreme Court ruled that, since Thorn was biased, as a matter of law all jurors he selected were presumed to be biased also. Otherwise, a sheriff could simply choose jurors who he knew beforehand would convict the defendant. Second, Coyado had been indicted for aiding and abetting Paul Tibeaux in the murder. At trial, Molino testified that "a Frenchman named Paul" had shot Kinney Said. By "a mere oversight" the district attorney had neglected to show that it was Paul Tibeaux, and not just "a Frenchman named Paul," who had done the killing. This violated a basic rule of law: that the indictment must conform exactly to the proof, or evidence, offered at trial.

The case was sent back to Calaveras for retrial. In compliance with the Supreme Court's ruling, the entire panel of jurors was quashed, and the trial was continued until the next term of court so there would be time to draw up a new jury panel. In July, 1871, the district attorney had the faulty indictment dismissed. It then took six months to find an unbiased panel of grand jurors to reindict Coyado. Finally, in April, 1872, he was brought to trial, convicted, and sentenced to be hanged. At noon on June 21, 1872, in the San Andreas jail yard, Ben Thorn yanked the gallows lever, Coyado plunged through the trap, and the headline of the *Calaveras Chronicle* screamed: "The Fatal Noose! Patibulary Expiation!"[25]

Ben Thorn had expended fourteen hundred dollars of his personal funds in hunting the Said killers. The reward that had been offered was withdrawn when the Petticoat owner met with business reverses. Eventually a bill was introduced in the state assembly to repay the sheriff. He kept up his search for Paul Tibeaux and Baptiste Dueny, but they were never captured.[26]

During these years, Ben was very active politically and established himself as the leader of the Democratic party in Calaveras. But some of his methods of currying votes were suspect. The *Calaveras Weekly Citizen* stated that the sheriff did not collect business licenses from those he favored and reported that R. W. Russell, owner of the largest livery stable in San Andreas, had not paid for a license in years. Said the editor, "The Under Sheriff, A. G. Thorn, informs us that Russell has not paid a license since B. K. Thorn has been sheriff, and that he has reported him delinquent till he got tired of it."[27]

Thorn, however, managed to maintain his popularity. Modest and retiring, he was gentle to the weak and stern to the evil, a fine combination of kindness and valor. Many people sought him out for guidance and help in their personal affairs. Calaveras County had a large Italian population that regarded the sheriff highly. They brought many of their troubles between themselves and outsiders to Thorn, who invariably settled them to the satisfaction of all and without recourse to the courts. On one occasion he accompanied an Italian friend to court in order to obtain naturalization papers. Thorn testified that the man was honest, peaceful, and would make a good citizen. The judge was very particular about granting citizenship and severely tested all applicants brought before him. He asked the man about his willingness to forswear allegiance to all foreign powers, princes, and potentates, and if he understood the forms and workings of a republican government. All the questions were answered satisfactorily. The judge then asked the would-be citizen if he knew who was president of the United States.

"Why, of course I do," the Italian replied with a grin. "It's Ben Thorn."

The papers were promptly delivered, amid roars of laughter from the judge, attorneys, and spectators.[28]

Although Ben Thorn was widely known as an expert with a six-gun, most of his arrests were made without resort to firearms. On at least one occasion, however, he shot first and asked questions later. Thorn kept a hen house at the rear of his home, and early in 1875 he found that his chickens were being stolen. Convinced that local Chinese were responsible, he "vowed to set up a night vigil to see if a little pistol practice might cure the wayward cravings of the Celestial stomach." Late in the evening of January 31, A. H. Coulter, a former county supervisor who resided behind Thorn's house, passed through the sheriff's yard on his way home. Unaware of Thorn's night watch, Coulter stopped for a moment near the hen house to light a cigar. It was very dark, and Thorn, thinking that the match was being used to mesmerize the fowls, let fly two shots from his six-gun. The first bullet passed through Coulter's clothes, and the second hit him in the wrist, fracturing the bone.[29]

Thorn was mortified by this incident. It certainly affected his popularity among the voters. Additionally, rumors of the sheriff's questionable financial activities continued to plague him. This was an election year, and at the Democratic county convention on June 24, Thorn was accused of being "too damned extravagant" and failed to receive his party's nomination for sheriff. In later years, Thorn claimed that he "did not want the office," but it is clear that his party dropped its support of him.[30]

Thorn left the sheriff's office and did not return for four years. By now he owned a quartz mine in Calaveras valued at $80,000 and busied himself in this enterprise. His old friend James B. Hume employed him from time to time as a Wells Fargo detective, and Thorn remained active as a bandit hunter.

On August 3, 1877, the stage from Milton to Sonora was held up four miles from Copperopolis by Dave Parks, John Benson, and Ab Bryant. On August 31 the stage was robbed in the same spot by John Benson, his brother Jim, and Ab Bryant. Jim Hume and Undersheriff Garvey quickly rounded up Bryant and the Bensons, but they found that Dave Parks had fled to Missouri. On September 18, Hume sent Ben Thorn after him. Thorn trailed the outlaw to Saint Louis and arrested him in the house of Parks's sister. Ben returned Parks to San Andreas, where he was convicted and sentenced to eighteen years in prison.[31]

A few months later, Thorn and Hume ran down another gang of dangerous desperadoes. During the previous two years, Tuolumne County had suffered so many stage holdups that Wells Fargo's losses outweighed its profits by $18,000, and the express company threatened to withdraw its services from the county. On January 16, 1878, four masked men held up the Sonora stage and removed $4,600 from the Wells Fargo box. Thorn and Hume worked energetically on the case and soon fastened their suspicions on Pedro Ybarra, who twenty years earlier had escaped punishment for the double murder at San Antone. The break in the case came from Fabiana Soto, a Mexican prostitute, who admitted that the robbers were Ybarra, Dick Bolter, Charles Barnwell, and her paramour, Josh Thayer. Thorn and Hume rounded up the four. They dug up $1,200 in coin that had been buried behind Fabiana's house and uncovered another $2,000 under the steps of Ybarra's house. Bolter turned states's evidence and was freed; the others were sentenced to state prison, with Pedro Ybarra receiving a life term. The citizens of Sonora were so grateful to Thorn and Hume that a banquet was given in their honor.[32]

In September, 1879, Ben Thorn again ran for sheriff of Calaveras. He was unable to obtain the Democratic nomination for sheriff and ran instead as an Independent, winning by an overwhelming margin. Ben remained in office continuously for the next twenty-three years. In 1883 he played a major part in the hunt for Black Bart, the poet stage robber, and was instrumental in obtaining a confession from him, saving Calaveras County the expense of a trial. In June, 1886, Thorn single-handedly tracked down Tommy Brown, one of Califor-

Jim Hume, Wells Fargo's chief detective, in 1879. He was a close friend of Ben Thorn's until the two lawmen became embroiled in a bitter dispute over the Evans case. Courtesy California State Library.

nia's most notorious bandits, who had broken out of Folsom prison. Ben trailed the fugitive to a hotel near Big Trees, and when Brown put up a fight, the sheriff slugged him over the head with a pair of handcuffs and clapped him behind bars.[33]

Without question the most controversial case Ben Thorn tackled was the murder of Mike Tovey, one of the Old West's most famous shotgun messengers. Tovey had been a mail-rider for Ben Holladay and had served as a Wells Fargo guard for more than twenty years. His most famous exploit took place in 1880, when Milt Sharp and W. C. Jones held up his stage near Bodie. In an exchange of shots with the outlaws, Tovey was wounded, but not before he dropped Jones with a fatal load of buckshot.

On April 30, 1892, a lone gunman opened fire on Tovey's stage between San Andreas and Sheep Ranch (an old mining camp). Tovey and the driver, "Babe" Raggio, were wounded and a fifteen-year-old passenger, Johanna Rodesino, was killed. Sheriff Thorn, at the head of a 150-man posse, scoured the hills, but no trace of the killer could be found. A year later, on June 15, 1893, the bloody scene was repeated in exactly the same manner. Tovey was riding guard on a stage midway between Ione and Jackson when a man standing behind a buckeye tree and armed with a rifle opened fire without warning. Mike Tovey died instantly, and the driver, D. C. Radcliffe, was wounded. Once again the killer departed without making an attempt to rob the coach.[34]

Although the murder had occurred in Amador County, Ben Thorn immediately assumed control of the manhunt. He was certain that the man who had slain the Rodesino girl was also the man who had killed Mike Tovey. On July 12, Thorn and his undersheriff, George C. Graves, arrested William Evans, an exconvict, at Frank Rooks's ranch near Cat Camp, in western Calaveras County. Evans subsequently confessed and then recanted his confession and was eventually convicted under circumstances that raised grave doubts about his guilt. Thorn became embroiled in a bitter dispute over the case with his old friend Jim Hume, Wells Fargo's chief detective, who championed Evans's cause and accused Thorn of persecuting an innocent man.

Evans was a laborer who had served three terms in San Quentin for larceny and burglary. He had escaped from the Stockton Insane Asylum in 1887, but it was generally acknowledged that he was perfectly sane, though not very intelligent. Evans was lodged in jail at San Andreas, and Thorn and his deputies, including his brother Abbot, worked diligently to gather evidence against Evans. It took Thorn three weeks to obtain a confession from Evans, and the methods he used raised eyebrows even in that wide-open era of freewheeling police investigations. First, Thorn placed Constable Masterson in jail in the guise of a woodchopper, hoping that Evans would make incriminating statements. Next the sheriff showed Evans false newspaper clippings in which members of the Rooks family were quoted as saying that Evans was not at their ranch on June 15. When this failed, Thorn fabricated a letter from Rooks's daughter, telling Evans they would not back him up. Thorn had a blacksmith fasten leg-irons on Evans in his cell and plied him with whiskey and opium. He promised Evans that he would not hang if he cooperated. Finally, on August 1, Evans broke down and made a detailed confession to Thorn and Amador County District Attorney Richard C. Rust.

Evans was brought to Jackson for his preliminary hearing on August 5. In open court he stated that he had killed Tovey, but that Frank Rooks had put him up to it. "I did not know Messenger Tovey and did not want to kill him," Evans said. "I wanted to stop the stage and secure the treasure." Shortly after this, however, Evans learned that he had been tricked and that the Rookses would still give him an alibi. On August 8 he reappeared in court, retracted his confession, and pleaded not guilty.[35]

Evans's trial began on October 16, but when two jurors became ill and were unable to attend, a mistrial was declared. He was retried in March, 1894, before Judge John F. Davis. The judge threw out the confession, ruling that it was unreliable, but other strong evidence against Evans was introduced. Radcliffe, the stage driver, identified Evans as the killer. Another witness testified that before the killing of Tovey, Evans had referred to the killing of the Rodesino girl. Evans had stated that the man who had shot her did not intend to and was very sorry that she had died; the man had meant to kill Tovey and he vowed that "he would have him before he stopped." Another witness said that he had seen Evans hiding in the grass about half a mile from the fatal spot the day before the shooting and had later found Evans's pipe in the same spot. John Sapanor, a prisoner in the San Andreas jail, testified that Evans had told him that Sheriff Thorn would not let up until he had enough evidence to hang him. According to Sapanor, Evans declared, "Thorn can do nothing if the Rookses stand pat." Other evidence was introduced to show that Evans's clothes, walk, and general appearance were similar to the killer's. It was also shown that Evans had left Calaveras County three days after the murder and had changed his name, but that he continually talked about the killing of Tovey to people he met.

The defense brought out that Radcliffe had previously stated that he could not identify the murderer and that when he first saw Evans, he said he was the wrong man. A passenger in the stage testified that he had got a good look at the gunman and that he was positive that he was not Evans. Members of the Rooks family, which admittedly bore a bad reputation, swore that Evans was at their ranch all day on June 15. Mrs. Rooks said that Sheriff Thorn had offered her five hundred dollars if she would testify that Evans was gone from the ranch that day; she admitted that Thorn had also asked her to tell the truth. Other witnesses also swore that the sheriff had offered them money for testimony against Evans. "The testimony of money overtures produced a painful impression," reported the *San Francisco Chronicle*.[36]

On March 18, 1894, after deliberating for only three hours, the jury

William Evans, alleged slayer of Mike Tovey. Did Ben Thorn railroad an innocent man into prison? Courtesy California State Archives.

convicted Evans of first-degree murder, and he was sentenced to life imprisonment. His attorneys appealed to the state Supreme Court, which upheld the conviction on August 29, 1895. In its opinion, the court reviewed the facts in detail, stating that although the case presented "a sharp conflict of evidence on every material point," there was satisfactory proof of Evans's guilt. "Under these circumstances," the court said, "we cannot assume to overrule the verdict of the jurors, who saw and heard the witnesses."[37]

Evans served his time in San Quentin, and the affair eventually passed from public attention. Then, on September 16, 1907, almost two years after Ben Thorn's death, the *San Francisco Call* ran a front-page story, claiming that Evans had been railroaded to prison. The story was vague and garbled, but it claimed that "one of his prosecutors died a short time ago. Nothing definite was known, but it was rumored that he had confessed on his deathbed" to a frame-up of Evans in order to collect the reward. This "prosecutor" was evidently Ben's brother Abbot, who committed suicide by poison in the old Thorn house on May 1, 1907. He left no suicide note, and the exact nature of any statements he may have made about Evans's case is unknown.[38]

Wells Fargo Detective John Thacker had interested himself in the case because the express company still believed in Evans's innocence. Thacker collected evidence and appealed to the state board of prison directors, which appointed a committee to examine the facts. On October 19 the directors reviewed letters from Judge John Davis, who had tried the case, and Judge Richard Rust, who had prosecuted Evans, that asserted the convict's innocence, as well as an affidavit of the "deathbed confession." Unfortunately these papers have long since been lost.[39]

The documents apparently were not convincing. The directors failed to recommend Evans for a pardon, and he was not paroled for another two years. The *Calaveras Prospect* of October 26, 1907, dismissed the *Call's* account, saying, "the story was so distorted that we were in some doubt as to there being anything in it." The *Prospect*, however, said nothing about the mysterious deathbed confession, nor did it mention that two prominent judges now believed that Evans was innocent.

The truth about this case may never be known. Did Ben Thorn act in good faith and send the right man to prison? Could he have been honestly mistaken or simply overzealous? Or did he deliberately frame an innocent man? Perhaps the best answer was given by Wells Fargo's Jim Hume during Evans's trial. A newspaper reporter said to Hume, "Sheriff Thorn is an officer who stands very high. Why should he do all this to convict a man who is innocent?" To which Hume had replied "Sheriff Thorn has been my friend for thirty-five years. He is an honest man, and I never knew of his doing anything of this sort before. It is my idea he believes Evans to be guilty and feels he is justified in going even to these extremes to convict him."

"How much reward is contingent on Evans's conviction?" the reporter asked.

"Only $1,600. But I do not think for an instant that any such sordid motive is at the bottom of Ben Thorn's persistence in this matter."[40]

Although Thorn and Hume had engaged in a running battle of words in the newspapers over the Evans case, Ben emerged slightly tarnished, but unscathed. Despite advancing age he remained energetic in his efforts to track down lawbreakers. In October, 1897, he led the hunt for two highwaymen who pulled off a triple stage robbery and shot two passengers near Angels Camp. As late as March, 1901, he directed the manhunt for Fred Braun and Louis Biddle, two bandits who killed one of Thorn's deputies, Sam Holman, in a shootout near Wallace. This hunt resulted in the killing of Braun and the capture of his partner. In November, Ben was stricken with paralysis, but served out his term of office, retiring on January 5, 1903, at the age of seventy-three. His undersheriff, George Graves, succeeded him.[41]

Ben Thorn's beloved wife, Anna, died in 1904, and from that point on, he began to fail, finally passing away at his daughter's San Francisco home on November 15, 1905. The *San Francisco Call* eulogized him thusly:

> During his half century of service the former sheriff guarded the lives and the property of Calaveras County as few men could have stood against evil doers. In the days when the laws were loose, when the bandit, the stage robber, and the horse thief abounded, when life was cheap and men lived in the frontier stage of existence, Thorn's name was a terror to the criminal.[42]

Ben Thorn was no Old West legend, but a real man with human failings. And in the final evaluation it must be said that his good deeds vastly outweighed the bad. He richly deserves recognition as one of the great lawmen of the American frontier.

CHAPTER 4

The Iron Man of Mendocino: Doc Standley

YOU will not find any monuments to Doc Standley in Mendocino County. The memory of the man and his deeds is gone, as vanished as the rutted, dirt streets and clapboard, false-front buildings of Ukiah, Willits, and Fort Bragg. Yet the exploits of this remarkable sheriff are etched indelibly into the history of the North Coast, and they cry out for the telling. During his thirty years of public service, Doc Standley established himself as one of the great lawmen of the Old West. He broke up the Coates-Frost feud and sent Isom Frost to prison for eighteen years. He trailed the notorious Mendocino Outlaws a thousand miles across the state, killing one and capturing the rest. He braved lynch mobs and outlaws' bullets, ran to earth stage robbers, murderers, and escaped convicts, and time and again risked his life and political career to protect the weak and the oppressed.

The son of Harrison and Elizabeth Standley, he was born August 20, 1845, in Andrew County, Missouri, and was christened Jeremiah. When he was eight his parents crossed the plains to California by oxteam, first settling in Petaluma, but moving to Ukiah in 1858. Young Jeremiah worked on his father's cattle ranch and also in the family's hotel, the Ukiah House. While still a boy he doctored a sick cow back to health, and from that day on he was known to all as "Doc."[1]

At the age of sixteen he struck out on his own, leasing a ranch and raising cattle, and later entered the Ukiah schools to complete his education. In 1864 the nineteen-year-old Standley was appointed a deputy under Mendocino County Sheriff Lew M. Warden. He served three years and in 1866 achieved local repute as a manhunter by tracking down Jerry Bailey, a notorious ruffian. The next year he began teaching, which he followed for five years, at the same time courting young Sarah Clay, a comely brunette from Missouri. They were married in 1868, and to the couple were born three daughters and a son,

William Harrison Standley, who achieved prominence as an admiral in the U.S. Navy and as an ambassador to the Soviet Union.[2]

In 1872, Doc was sworn in as a deputy by the newly elected sheriff, S. J. Chalfant, who felt that Standley's talents were behind a silver star and in the saddle, not in the schoolhouse. Doc did not prove him wrong. On Feburary 25, 1873, Bill Burke shot and killed his brother-in-law at his ranch on Robinson Creek, three miles below Ukiah. Burke's wife had given birth exactly nine months after they were married, and he became convinced that the child was not his. When his wife's twenty-four-year-old brother, John Owens, insisted that the baby was legitimate, Burke chased him down on horseback and blew his head apart with a double-barreled shotgun. Doc Standley and Sheriff Chalfant, leading a thirty-five man posse, hunted the killer for three days in the mountains west of Ukiah before they ran him down. Burke received a life term in San Quentin for this cold-blooded murder.[3]

It was his investigation of the mysterious murder of Catherine Strong that firmly established Doc Standley's reputation. Mrs. Strong and her husband, George, lived on a 160-acre ranch on a ridge above Sherwood Valley, fifteen miles north of Willits, at what is now called Strong Mountain. In 1873, George Strong was convicted of stealing and killing a cow, and he was sentenced to San Quentin for six years, leaving his wife to look after their ranch and livestock. Catherine Strong was a hardy woman, fifty-five years old, and on horseback, with the help of a single dog, she worked her herd of cattle and sheep, which were commonly grazed together on the same range in Mendocino.

About the first of February, 1874, Mrs. Strong mysteriously disappeared. For four or five days she was not missed, but neighboring ranchers soon became curious. Their suspicions were first aroused when a stage driver, Ed Saunders, reported that on the last day of January Mrs. Strong had given him an order for a sack of flour, telling him not to forget it. The next day on his return trip he brought the flour and, finding Mrs. Strong not at home, left it on a stump in front of her cabin, where it still remained four days later. A neighbor named Wolf searched the Strong ranch and found a starving cow and calf in the corral. Her horse and dog were missing, but her saddle, gloves, bonnet, and dress, which she always wore, were in the house, as well as her jewelry and her money. A hunt was conducted by local men, and the country was searched thoroughly for miles around, but not a trace of the missing woman was found. While some suspected foul play, others believed that she had lost her mind and wandered off.

Sheriff Chalfant sent Doc Standley to work up the case. Standley put Indians out to search for Mrs. Strong and began making a careful investigation. Since her jewelry and her cash were not taken, he was certain that the motive was not robbery, if indeed she had been killed. Doc learned that two men who owned a neighboring ranch, James Alexander and D. H. Geiger, were not friendly to Mrs. Strong. Her husband had been convicted and imprisoned primarily from their testimony.

Doc talked with Charles Traber, owner of a mill in Sherwood Valley, who related that three months earlier Geiger had proposed forming a vigilance committee. Geiger told Traber that Alexander had visited Healdsburg, where there was a vigilance committee, and had obtained a copy of the committee's constitution and bylaws. Geiger claimed that Mrs. Strong had attacked his wife and children on the road, and he told Traber, "I don't feel safe to let her live any longer in the neighborhood. There ought to be an example made of her."

Another local man, H. T. Hatch, told Standley that the previous August he had talked with Geiger and Alexander, telling them that the imprisoned George Strong had applied for a new trial. Geiger had replied, "His wife ought to be with him, and if she does not look out, she'll be taken care of."

Another Sherwood Valley settler, W. J. Blair, informed Doc that a month before Mrs. Strong's disappearance Alexander had said of her, "We can't turn any sheep outside without her running, dogging, and killing them. I don't think it is any more harm to kill such a damned old bitch than a dog. She's not fit to live among white people."[4]

Doc's suspicions became fixed when he discovered that Geiger had filed a complaint against Mrs. Strong for killing sheep more than a week after the search had begun. As there was no evidence that any of Geiger's sheep had been killed, Standley was certain that this was just a ruse to direct suspicion elsewhere by making it appear that Geiger believed that she was still alive. Shortly thereafter Doc learned further that Geiger had told a neighbor that he had seen Mrs. Strong leave her ranch on horseback, disguised in a man's clothing, supposedly to escape arrest on the warrant he had sworn out. Geiger claimed that he had observed this three days after Mrs. Strong had been seen by anyone else.

By now Doc was ready to arrest Geiger and Alexander, but without the body of Mrs. Strong, he could not prove murder. He kept the Indians on the hunt, and finally, on February 18, they found her horse in a deep ravine, four miles west of Sherwood Valley. It had been shot through the head and pushed off an overhanging cliff. Nearby were the tracks of two horses that appeared to have been tied to a tree, and four hundred yards distant a lock of hair, some blood, and Mrs. Strong's comb were found. This discovery sent waves of shock through Sherwood Valley, and large parties of men turned out to search for Mrs. Strong, who everyone now was certain had been foully murdered.

On February 22 an Indian came to Doc Standley and said, "Me fine him woman. You go see. Me no go."

He told the deputy how to find the spot, half a mile from where her horse had been discovered. Doc rode to the scene, deep in a heavily forested ravine where a creek plunged over a small waterfall into a pool ringed by rotting tree trunks. He found Mrs. Strong's body at the bottom of the pool, weighted down by a two-hundred-pound rock. She had been shot in the back of the head and was clad only in her nightgown. It was evident that she had been abducted at night, taken to the ravine, and murdered.

Doc Standley promptly placed Geiger and Alexander under arrest. The community was thoroughly aroused, and plans were quickly made to lynch the two before Doc could get them to jail in Ukiah. But Standley had other ideas. He deputized B. P. Son to act as a guard and hid the prisoners in the house of a rancher named Tuttle, where they spent the night. In the morning Doc started for Ukiah with his men handcuffed and tied to their saddles. Word spread quickly, and a mounted lynch mob of twenty men was soon close behind. Standley urged their horses into a run, and the deadly chase was on. Doc's horses were fast and strong, and for twenty miles he managed to keep ahead of the pursuers. Finally he thundered into Ukiah, just in time to lodge his men in the county jail.

"I never saw men so glad to get into jail," Doc said later with a laugh.[5]

Sheriff Chalfant summoned a large posse to defend the jail, which effectively discouraged the mob. The citizens petitioned the gover-

Jeremiah M. ("Doc") Standley, the once legendary sheriff of Mendocino County. Courtesy California State Library.

nor to pardon George Strong, and he was released from San Quentin a month later. Strong returned to Mendocino County, and Standley took him out to the ravine where his wife's body had been found. Years later Doc recalled:

> He was a mean looking fellow and I didn't much relish his company. When I showed him the pool he said coolly, "So that's where they stuck the ole gal, is it?"
>
> The next moment he declared he was powerful hungry, and guessed we could eat lunch while he was talking. So we sat down, and he ate greedily, cutting his beef and bread with his old tobacco stained jack-knife, and all the time asking questions about the murder. When he was through he got up and stretched himself, and said, "Well, I guess I'll take a drink out o' the hole where the ole gal laid." He got flat down on his stomach to suck up the water, but I turned so sick at the sight that I lit out of there without waiting for him."[6]

Geiger procured the legal services of the fire-eating David S. Terry, former chief justice of the California Supreme Court. Due to the intense feeling against them in Mendocino, Geiger and Alexander were granted a change of venue to Sonoma County. Geiger was tried first, found guilty, and sentenced to life imprisonment, but Terry appealed the conviction to the California Supreme Court, which in April, 1875, upheld the verdict. Geiger had been prepared for this, however. With the assistance of friends he escaped the Sonoma County jail on May 25, 1875, and was never recaptured. The charge against Alexander was subsequently dismissed when the district attorney decided that there was not enough evidence to prove that a conspiracy to kill Mrs. Strong had existed between the two.[7]

Less than three weeks after arresting Geiger and Alexander, Doc Standley experienced one of the vagaries of service as a frontier lawman. The sheriff's budget was cut back, and Doc was laid off. He leased a sheep ranch in Sherwood Valley, but volunteered his services as a deputy whenever he was needed. Doc was an expert trailer and one of the deadliest rifleshots of his time. On one occasion he accompanied a hunting party into Trinity County after bears that had been preying on sheep. Wandering away from camp, Standley suddenly found himself face-to-face with five black bears. Two were old bears, and three were yearlings weighing two hundred pounds each. Swinging up his Winchester, Doc opened fire at a range of thirty yards. Two bears dropped; then Standley climbed a nearby tree and killed the other three in less than one minute. His companions ran up and, seeing the results of his deadly rifle work, asked Doc why he had bothered to climb the tree.

"My aim was getting bad from nervousness on the ground," he replied with a grin.[8]

These skills catapulted Doc Standley to the forefront of the Mendocino Outlaws' case, one of frontier California's most famous manhunts. The Mendocino Outlaws were a band of former convicts and murderers led by John Wheeler and Hal Brown.

Wheeler was a slippery customer and a criminal mastermind who claimed that he had once been a deputy sheriff at Boise City, Idaho. In June, 1868, with John Billings and several other bandits, he robbed a stagecoach in Oregon. He and Billings were arrested and sent to San Quentin as U.S. prisoners since there was no federal penitentiary on the Pacific Coast in those days. While in prison Wheeler learned dentistry and, upon his release in 1877, opened an office in San Rafael. By year's end he had moved to the boomtown of Bodie and had quickly made himself known as one of its more prominent badmen. In December he shot a Mexican and then opened fire on a crowd of other Mexicans who came after him. Two weeks later he shot it out with another ruffian over possession of a town lot.

The following August Wheeler settled in Mendocino City, opening another dental office. He was now married. His suave manners and dental skill made him many friends, and he did a thriving business. He was known to all as "Doc the Dentist," and no one suspected his true nature, even though he still used his real name. It was the custom in those days never to ask a man about his background.[9]

Hal Brown, the gang's other leader, was notorious on the North Coast. In the 1860s he had run with a pair of reckless desperadoes, Al Courtright and Bill Oiler. The trio robbed the Seawell ranch, west of Healdsburg, and stole one hundred head of horses. Tracked down by Sonoma County's ace bandit catcher, Deputy Sheriff William B. Reynolds, Brown in 1870 entered San Quentin, where he met Wheeler and Billings. These three, as well as Al Courtright, who had entered the prison in 1874, were all released from San Quentin in January and February of 1877.[10]

Hal Brown visited Doc Wheeler in Mendocino, and in August, 1879, they made plans to hold up the sheriff of Mendocino County when he was returning from the coast after collecting taxes. This was identical to the robbery that had been planned by the Houx gang and thwarted by Steve Venard, and it is not unlikely that Wheeler and Brown got the idea in San Quentin from Lodi Brown and Bigfoot Andrus. Wheeler sent the following letter to John Billings in Bodie:

> I have here in Mendocino a rich claim worth about $15,000. It can be worked in about two weeks if I have good men. The claim is the sheriff of Mendocino County. I have one good man with me. Come yourself and bring anyone you know and can depend on.[11]

Billings arrived in Mendocino City on September 10, bringing with him Sam Carr, a fellow San Quentin alumnus, and George Gaunce, a former railroad brakeman and the son of a good family from Oakland. Hal Brown led Billings, Gaunce, and Carr twenty miles up the coast to Al Courtright's cabin in the redwoods, east of Westport. Wheeler purchased guns, ammunition, and other supplies for the gang, who were busily collecting provisions and jerking beef for their anticipated flight from Mendocino. They agreed among

The notorious Hal Brown, captain of the Mendocino Outlaws. Courtesy California State Archives.

themselves never to submit to arrest, for as Sam Carr later said, "We heard that they hung people in Mendocino County for stealing chickens" (a reference to the triple lynching in Willits a month earlier, described in chapter 11).[12]

On October 10 the outlaws set up camp on the Big River, four miles east of Mendocino City. Wheeler rode out of town several times to the camp to keep them posted. They killed a steer that belonged to the Mendocino Lumber Company and hung it up to cure, burying the entrails nearby. Three days later Constable William Host, passing through the woods, discovered the buried entrails and reported his find to the Mendocino Lumber Company, where he learned that the steer had been stolen. The next morning, with two employees of the lumber company, Thomas Dollard and William Wright, Host returned to the spot and followed some tracks a quarter mile to what is now called Outlaw Spring. Four strangers were cooking breakfast, their rifles stacked up by a tree and the stolen beef hanging from another tree. Host noted their white hands and high-heeled boots and knew that these men did not make their living by hard work. Realizing that his little posse was outnumbered and off guard, the constable told the strangers that he was looking for a place to locate a tie camp and quickly returned to Mendocino City. He swore out a warrant and with a larger posse rode to the spring, but the birds had flown.

The next morning, October 15, Host started out again with a posse that included Dollard; Wright; Jim Nichols; Archibald Yell, later district attorney and warden of Folsom prison; and three other citizens. From the deserted camp they followed a ridge one mile north to the headwaters of Russian Gulch, where they found a warm campfire in the ravine bottom. Wright and Yell, in the lead, had bent over the fire to feel the ashes when a furious barrage of rifle fire sliced into the posse. Hal Brown, John Billings, Sam Carr, and George Gaunce had heard them coming and had taken cover behind the trees on the opposite side of the gulch. Wright pitched backward, one bullet in his neck and another near his heart. Dollard was wounded in the thigh, and another shot tore into Nichols's left shoulder. The other possemen leaped for cover and returned the fire, but the outlaws were so well hidden that they could only catch a glimpse of them. Two of the posse managed to reach their horses and race back to Mendocino City, where they spread the alarm. A second posse raced to Russian Gulch only to find that Dollard was dead, and the outlaws had escaped. They brought the dead and wounded to town, where Wright died that night.

A public meeting was held, and a committee of public safety was organized to map out a plan of action. John Wheeler attended this meeting and had the gall to deliver a speech, advising the citizens not to pursue the murderers, as it was too dangerous. Wheeler managed to have himself appointed to the committee. Suspicion soon fastened on the smooth-talking dentist, however. Deputy Sheriff Jerry Donohoe arrived in town that evening, and one of his possemen recognized Wheeler as a former San Quentin convict. Checking further, it was learned that a tin cup and a frying pan found in the outlaws' camp had been purchased by Wheeler a short time earlier. Hoofprints found at the camp were made by a horse with a broken shoe and matched those from a horse Wheeler had rented at a local livery stable. He was arrested and brought to jail in Ukiah.[13]

On October 17, at Little Lake, Doc Standley received a message from Sheriff James R. Moore, asking him to join his posse in the search for the Mendocino Outlaws. Standley saddled his horse at once and set out for the scene of the murder. And so began one of the most relentless, extraordinary manhunts ever undertaken by a California peace officer.

Doc rode alone to Mendocino City, where he learned that Wheeler had received numerous visits from Al Courtright. He checked Courtright's cabin and, finding it empty, rode on to the Noyo River and met up with Sheriff Moore's posse. They continued searching for Courtright and on October 21 returned to his cabin, where they found Sam Carr. He was tired and sick, with his ankles sore and wrapped up, and he had thrown his rifle away. Carr had fallen behind his partners, and they had abandoned him. In a spirit of revenge he agreed to turn state's evidence and testify against the others. Standley and Moore sent Carr to Ukiah, under guard of two constables.

They spent the next two days searching the backcountry between Westport and Ten Mile River. Finally a messenger told them that the three outlaws had been spotted on foot near Dutch Charley's, between Cahto and Ten Mile. Standley and the posse rushed to the area, forming an ambush at Uncle Tommy Damien's cabin, where they waited in vain for the outlaws until the next day.

By now at least a hundred men, encouraged by a reward of five hundred dollars each offered by the governor, were scouring the rugged hills and redwood forests for the fugitives. Al Courtright was picked up and brought to Ukiah. In exchange for his freedom he admitted harboring the outlaws and gave full descriptions of them.[14]

Doc Standley received a report that the three killers, Brown, Billings, and Gaunce, were heading north toward the South Fork of the Eel River. Standley sent word to Laytonville for twenty-two-year-old Andy Bowman to join the posse with pack animals. Andy, an expert hunter, and his brother Boag met up with Doc's posse, which included Mart and Old Jim Frost, who were taking a respite from the Little Lake Vendetta. Mart, fresh from presiding at the lynching of his nephew Elijah and two other young rowdies in Willits, was evidently anxious for a little more deadly work.

On October 29 the posse split in half, with Sheriff Moore continuing on to Sam Pearce's ranch in an attempt to cut off the fugitives. Doc Standley, with the Bowman brothers and Calib Wilson, struck out for Rattlesnake Creek, which parallels today's U.S. Highway 101, near Leggett. They followed the creek to its mouth, where it empties into the Eel River. Here Doc discovered the tracks of three men heading downriver. They had followed them for 150 yards along the bluff above the river when they were startled by a noise between them and the river bottom. Running to the edge of the bluff, Standley saw three men rush together and pick up their guns.

"Surrender!" Standley shouted, but the trio started to run. Doc and his men opened fire at the fleeing outlaws, who jumped over the riverbank and disappeared into the brush. The posse followed, but soon lost the trail in the thick undergrowth. Returning to the outlaws' camp, Doc found that they had captured virtually all of their supplies, including blankets, clothing, twenty pounds of jerked meat, thirty pounds of flour, five hundred rounds of ammunition, and two six-shooters. Doc's clothes had become badly torn from twelve days of riding and crawling through heavy brush, and he donned a pair of captured pants, plus a coat and an overcoat. Then he carefully examined the tracks left by the fugitives. Said Doc later:

> I found that the tracks differed greatly, one of them being made by a small-heeled boot, the heel projecting under the foot. Another was a little larger, having a square toe and round, flat heel. The third was still larger and longer, and having two large round-headed tacks, running diagonally across one heel, the other heel having a large tack at its front edge next to the center.[15]

Standley knew that his ability to recognize and follow these tracks would spell success or failure in the hunt. His posse had followed the footprints a quarter of a mile when a rider brought word that the outlaws had taken breakfast at William Rae's cabin, eight miles distant. Doc followed the tracks from Rae's to Blue Rock, where he lost the trail. He sent messengers to the outlying ranches and learned that the outlaws had been spotted in Round Valley, where they told a rancher they were hunters.

While Doc and his men, who had been rejoined by Sheriff Moore, struck for Round Valley, a sixteen-man posse, from Covelo, led by the notorious mankiller "Wylackie John" Wathen, was close behind the fugitives. That night the Covelo posse surrounded the outlaws in camp in a deep gulch south of the Mad River, in Trinity County. Wathen decided to wait until daylight to attack the camp, but by morning Hal Brown and his partners had slipped away.

Meanwhile Standley and Moore joined the Covelo posse and picked up the trail with the help of "Buckshot," a local Indian guide. The next morning the Indian found the remains of a small campfire and grouse bones containing a little meat. He told the posse that white men had been there; if Indians had made the camp, the bones would have been stripped bare.

For six days the chase had led the posse through what is to this day some of the roughest backcountry in California. The outlaws, still on foot, would follow a trail for five or six miles and then suddenly abandon it for the hills and gulches. From the Mad River they turned south again to the Middle Fork of the Eel and then climbed over Yolla Bolly Mountain in snow, sleet, and rain. By now Standley's posse was near starvation, with their only food being thirty pounds of flour, and they had no feed for their horses. He and Moore sent most of the posse back to Covelo. They kept Andy Bowman, Wylackie John, and three others.

Bringing food, supplies, and fresh horses, Deputy Sheriff Donohoe joined the posse in the Yolla Bolly country. They trailed the three outlaws across the seven-thousand-foot-high mountains to Pettyjohn's, on Cold Fork of Cottonwood Creek, where they met a posse, from Red Bluff, that had been warned that the killers were headed toward the Sacramento Valley. Sheriff Moore and Doc Standley decided to again split the posse. Standley, Moore, Andy Bowman, and another posseman stuck to the desperadoes' trail, while Donohoe and the rest rode toward the Sacramento Valley to try to cut off their flight.

Doc trailed the outlaws south across Cottonwood and Redbank creeks and along an old Indian trail to Vale Gulch, where their footprints were found not far from a small, abandoned cabin. Unknown to the officers, Brown, Billings, and Gaunce were hiding in the brush near the cabin. Doc Standley, leading one of Andy Bowman's pack mules, rode up to the cabin, looked it over, and then started up the canyon directly toward the spot where the outlaws were concealed. They recognized Standley as the leader of the posse that had been dogging them for more than a week. John Billings drew a bead on Standley with his rifle, but at that instant Doc's pack mule balked and refused to follow. Standley turned back after the mule, and Billings held his fire. Standley got the mule and headed back up the canyon, and as Billings again took aim, the stubborn mule once more turned back, with an exasperated Doc following. Billings told his partners that he would fire anyway, but Brown and Gaunce stopped him, saying that the lawman was too far off for a good shot. Standley then led the mule around by another route, inadvertently avoiding the lair of his would-be killers.

George Gaunce, captured by Doc Standley after one of the longest manhunts in California history. Courtesy California State Archives.

The three fugitives crawled on their bellies to a ravine and, keeping out of sight of the posse, waited for dark. Then they walked thirty-five miles down the coastal foothills to the Sacramento River. By moonlight Standley and his posse trailed them to the river, but it began to rain and washed away the tracks. Hal Brown and his partners made several attempts to cross the Sacramento River, but it was too cold and too deep. On November 7 they crossed over the river on the railroad bridge, at Tehama. Doc Standley and the other officers spent ten days trying to cut the outlaws' sign. They separated into two groups and searched all of the country from Yolla Bolly to the Sierra foothills. Finally, flat broke and without a clue, they returned to Ukiah.[16]

Although it was generally believed that there was now no chance of catching the killers, Doc Standley was not ready to give up. The manhunt had been a severe strain on the county treasury, but he found a spare two hundred dollars and with Moore and Donohoe set off again. While Donohoe took the train for Nevada to spread the word that the outlaws might try to cross the Sierra, Standley visited

San Quentin to see what he could learn about Brown and Billings. Moore went to Oakland to pick up points on Gaunce. Both officers found that Hal Brown had a brother-in-law, Fred Striker, living in Butte County. As this was very near the spot where the trail had been lost and lay in the direction the outlaws had been fleeing, Standley and Moore departed immediately for Oroville. Here they learned that Striker lived in Nimshew, in the mountains, some fifteen miles northeast of Chico.

The two lawmen boarded a stagecoach to Helltown and then walked the remaining seven miles to Nimshew, arriving late on the night of December 3. Making inquiries, they learned that three men matching the killers' descriptions had been in town nineteen days earlier. The officers spent the next day searching Nimshew and discovered that Fred Striker had recently bought a Winchester rifle. At eleven o'clock that night a local man informed Standley that he had seen Striker's son riding toward an old cabin owned by a man named McClellan and located a mile from town. The boy appeared to be carrying a loaf of bread in a sack.

It was a hopeful sign. Standley and Moore attempted to raise a posse, but they had little success. A stage driver named Messer agreed to join, and he supplied Doc with a Winchester and Moore with a shotgun, as the officers had been armed only with six-shooters. The only other posseman they could find was Clarence A. White. Formerly of Mendocino County, White was a fearless young man and a dead shot. Eight years later he killed Wylackie John Wathen in one of the North Coast's most-celebrated shootings.

McClellan's cabin was situated in a deep canyon that ran from Nimshew to Butte Creek. The canyon walls were covered with a thick growth of chaparral. It was raining heavily when the small posse surrounded the cabin at dawn on December 5. Standley and Moore took up positions thirty yards from the front of the cabin, while White and Messer covered the rear. At that moment John Billings, intending to chop firewood, came out the front door carrying a rifle and an ax.

"Throw up your hands!" Standley barked, but Billings turned and bolted for the cabin.

Doc squeezed off a round from his Winchester, and Billings staggered through the doorway with a bullet in his shoulder. At the same instant Hal Brown and George Gaunce snatched up their guns and ran for the rear door. Standley and Moore, firing as fast as they could, sent fifteen shots into the cabin. As Brown and Gaunce fled out the back door Clarence White shot four times at them with his Winchester, but the pair disappeared into the brush. Then Billings appeared in the rear doorway and raised his rifle to fire at White, but he quickly ducked back inside. Balls from Standley's rifle and Moore's revolver ripped through the cabin's flimsy walls and slammed into Billings, who burst back through the rear door, desperately wounded. White also fired at the running outlaw, and he dropped thirty feet from the cabin, sieved by bullets. He lay face down on his rifle, and Standley rolled him over. Billings gasped once and was dead.

They carried the body into the cabin and sent for the coroner. After giving testimony before the coroner's jury, Sheriff Moore took Billings's body to Nimshew and then to Chico, while Doc Standley and Clarence White set off after Brown and Gaunce. By now it was dark, and with the aid of a lantern they tracked the outlaws a hundred yards to Butte Creek, where they found that the two had split up; Brown headed up the creek, and Gaunce went downstream. Following Brown's track for a mile and a half, Doc saw that his steps were not equal in length and concluded that the outlaw was lame and could not go far. Standley turned around and struck out after Gaunce, trailing him down the creek for four miles and then back north to within two hundred yards of Nimshew, where he lost the track. It was now two o'clock in the morning, and as they had not slept in more than twenty-four hours, the exhausted manhunters put up in the hotel for some much-needed rest.

At the crack of dawn Doc was on the scout once again, certain that Gaunce was nearby. He learned that during the night a buggy robe had been stolen from a shed next to an abandoned cabin, near the hotel. Standley and White made a room-by-room search of the cabin. In the last room Doc noticed an old cupboard that looked as if it had recently been moved. Pointing his gun behind it, Doc ordered, "Come out!"

Out crawled George Gaunce. He was worn-out and broken-down in spirit and body. Doc took his prisoner by buggy to Chico and turned him over to Sheriff Moore, who took Gaunce and Billings's corpse to Ukiah.

Now Standley set off like a bloodhound after Hal Brown, the last of the Mendocino Outlaws. Returning to Nimshew, he was again joined by Clarence White with two good horses. They spent four days trailing the killer through soft, foot-deep snow that forced them to abandon the horses. Brown made several attempts to cross the Sierra, but each time he was turned back by heavy snow. Doc tracked him through Concow Valley and across both the North Fork of the Feather River and French Creek to Mountain House, on the Oroville-Susanville Road. From here Brown took the main road to Bidwell's Bar and then cut across the foothills to Wyandotte, southeast of Oroville.

Standley and White borrowed fresh horses and pressed on, just three miles behind the desperado. They were joined by Sheriff Sprague of Butte County. The lawmen alerted everyone they met to watch for Brown, and a general hue and cry was raised. They had followed his tracks two miles from Wyandotte when they came upon a pair of local men, George Thatcher and Thomas Moran, who had heard of the manhunt for Brown. They were loading the exhausted, freezing badman into a wagon. He was clad in an old quilt and looked like a common tramp.

Doc rode up to the wagon and said cheerily, "Hello, Hal!"

"God damn it, Doc! Won't you ever quit?" the outlaw chief exclaimed. Then, recognizing his overcoat that Standley had captured at Rattlesnake Creek and was still wearing, Brown said, "Give me my coat. I am nearly froze!"

Standley placed Hal Brown under arrest and returned with him to Ukiah, arriving on December 14. The town was overcome with excitement, and a crowd of three hundred greeted Doc's arrival. Anvils were fired, and speeches of welcome and congratulations were made, capped off by a grand celebration and dance that night. Doc Standley had been hunting his men for eight weeks and had covered more than a thousand miles in the pursuit.

Doc Wheeler was convicted of murder and sentenced to death, but two days later he committed suicide in his jail cell. George Gaunce was handed a life term, while Hal Brown was sentenced to hang, which was later commuted by the governor to life imprisonment.[17]

Doc Standley achieved such fame from his success in the manhunt that he easily won the office of sheriff at the next election, a position he held from 1882 to 1892. In 1886 he was defeated by Sheriff Ornbaum, who soon died in office, and Doc was appointed to fill out his term. His record as sheriff was nothing short of remarkable. Between 1887 and 1892 there were fourteen stagecoach robberies in Mendocino County, and Standley tracked down, arrested, and convicted the culprits in thirteen of them.[18]

Doc Standley's six-gun, a double-action Colt .44-40, serial no. 11366, manufactured in 1883, "J. M. Standley" engraved on trigger guard. Courtesy Vivian Standley Wincote.

Among this group of ill-fated stage robbers was Harry Miller, a young escapee from the Oregon state prison. Standley tracked Miller for thirteen days before catching him in Santa Rosa on November 28, 1891. At first Doc thought this was just another routine arrest, but it soon became front-page news across the country when Standley discovered that the bandit was the wayward son of Joaquín Miller, the famed "Poet of the Sierras." Young Miller was sent to San Quentin for two years.[19]

Two stage robbers whom Doc ran to earth in 1889 were H. W. Hanlon and Charles Manning. They were each sentenced to San Quentin for seventeen years, but on August 11, 1890, while working on a building outside the prison walls, they grabbed two Winchesters and several pistols that had been concealed by Manning's cousin and made a run for a nearby thicket, accompanied by Abe Turcott, a convicted murderer. Three Gatling guns poured a hail of lead after them, and a posse of fifty guards started in pursuit. Guard Bowen was in the lead, unaware that the convicts were armed. A shot rang out, and he dropped with a bullet in his forearm, which was amputated the next day. When another guard, Porter, tried to head off the convicts, Hanlon, an expert rifleman, shot his horse out from under him.

The convicts ran three miles to Larkspur and then climbed the wooded ridge above Laurel Grove. Here the posse of guards caught up and surrounded them. Realizing that they could not escape, the three convicts threw up a fortress of fallen pine logs, dug trenches behind them, and held off the guards with rifle and pistol fire. Warden John McComb tried to parley with the trio, but they distrusted the prison officers and refused to talk with anyone except Doc Standley. A wire was sent to the Mendocino sheriff, and he responded promptly, arriving by train that night.

The three convicts were in no mood to surrender yet, and they tried several times to slip through the picket lines in the darkness, but were driven back by gunfire from the guards. Throughout the night shots were exchanged, and at daybreak Hanlon yelled out defiantly, "You think you've got us, don't you? But you haven't, damn you! We'll never surrender. We'll make this spot our grave first!"

"You'd better give up, boys," one of the guards shouted back. "We've got you surrounded, and you can't get away."

"Then take our dead bodies!" And Hanlon punctuated his cry with a rifleshot.

More gunfire erupted as guards pumped lead into the log fortress, and the convicts returned it, shot for shot. Finally Hanlon called out, "Let up, boys. Don't shoot any more. We want to have a talk."

"All right," a guard replied. "Who do you want to talk to?"

"Is Sheriff Standley there?"

"Yes."

"Then send him up. We'll talk to him."

"All right, boys," Standley shouted. "Don't shoot and I'll come up."

Doc climbed up the ridge and found the escapees concealed in their makeshift barricade in a clump of pine trees. It commanded a clear view of the entire mountainside, and Doc realized that any attempt to storm it would result in heavy casualties among the guards. The convicts asked Doc if they had killed any of the guards, and he assured them that they had not. They insisted that Standley give his word of honor that they would not be shot down by the guards if they surrendered. Then the convicts began to negotiate the amount of punishment they would receive, but as Doc had no authority to dictate prison policy he made two trips down the ridge to meet with Warden McComb. Finally he returned to the fortress with Sheriff Healey, of Marin County, and told the convicts that they would receive ten days' solitary confinement in the dungeon on bread and water. This Hanlon and his partners agreed to. Standley shouted to the guards, "I say, boys, they have surrendered and are coming down with us. So don't get frisky with your guns!"

In a moment Doc appeared walking down the trail, carrying the convicts' two Winchesters. Behind him walked the three convicts, with Sheriff Healey bringing up the rear. Each shook hands with the warden, and then Standley accompanied them back to San Quentin in the prison van. Secure in his dungeon cell, a dejected Hanlon told reporters, "I am sorry that we did not take the advice of Sheriff Standley when he arrested us and told Manning and myself to act square."[20]

Doc Standley's duties involved more than running down dangerous stage robbers and escaped convicts. In August, 1891 the Union Lumber Company, of Fort Bragg, began making plans to extend its two-mile length of railroad track on Pudding Creek into the Noyo River canyon. To do so, a quarter-mile-long tunnel would have to be bored through the mountain divide that separated Pudding Creek from the Noyo River. The company, unable to find local men experienced in tunnel digging, recruited Chinese, who had dug the great railroad and mining tunnels of the Sierra and Comstock.

Anti-Chinese sentiment was then widespread in California. "The Chinese must go!" (the slogan of Denis Kearney's Workingmen's Party) was still a common cry in the 1880s. The Mendocino lumber industry was beginning to feel the first effects of the depression of 1893–94, and local loggers believed that the Chinese had been hired because they worked for lower wages than white men. Rabble-rousers whipped up feelings against the Chinese tunnel men, and a mob of whites drove them from the Pudding Creek tunnel.

A dispatch was quickly sent to Doc Standley, in Ukiah, and he mounted his horse and raced to Fort Bragg, where he learned that the mob had driven the Chinese south. Doc caught up with them at Mendocino. Riding in front of the mob, with the Chinese at his back, Doc dismounted and faced the crowd of white men alone. Every man in the county knew Standley, either personally or by reputation, and they listened to him carefully. Doc explained that he would not allow them to break the law and described how dangerous tunnel digging was.

"How many of you," Doc asked, "are willing to go over to Pudding Creek and volunteer to dig this tunnel?"

Not a man spoke up.

"Very well. It is just as I suspected," said Doc. "You men aren't willing to do this hard and dangerous work, and for that I'm not blaming you. But in that case you certainly should not try to prevent these Chinamen from doing it. Now, I know you are fair-minded men, so I suggest you disperse and go home, so that these China boys, who know how to do this kind of work, can go back and do it."

For a few moments there was silence. Then one of the leaders of the crowd stepped forward, shook Standley's hand, and said, "You're right, Sheriff, and we'll do what you say."

The Chinese finished the tunnel without further trouble, and eventually the railroad was extended east to Willits. Today tourists, not lumber, are carried on its famous "skunk trains."[21]

Eighteen ninety-two was an election year and Standley's action on behalf of the Chinese was not popular with some voters. In addition, he became embroiled in a family squabble over his dead father's estate. Doc, as executor, reported that the assets in the estate totaled $408, but his sister, Mrs. Emma Roller, charged that the proper figure should have been $5,927 and that Doc had mismanaged the funds. Standley's political foes made a great deal of hay out of this dispute, and although Doc was completely exonerated by Judge Robert McGarvey, he was defeated by J. R. Johnson in the election that fall. Doc, however, had the last laugh. In December, 1897, Sheriff Johnson absconded with $6,000 from the county treasury and was removed from office.[22]

Standley continued to raise sheep at his Sherwood Valley ranch, served as a deputy sheriff, and worked intermittently as a special detective for Wells Fargo. On December 31, 1895, a lone highwayman held up Spud Howard's southbound stage at Sewards, ten miles north of Ukiah, taking the U.S. mail and Wells Fargo shipments. Wells Fargo retained Doc Standley to work up the case, and John N. Thacker arrived to assist him, but neither they nor local officers were able to locate the bandit. On January 15, 1896, the same stage was held up at Robbers Pass, not far from the scene of the first robbery. Spud Howard recognized the bandit as the same one who had stood him up two weeks before. The road agent, armed with two six-guns, ordered Howard to throw out the express box and then sent the stage on. Sheriff Johnson and his deputies tried to trail the bandit, but heavy rains wiped out his tracks. Doc Standley began his own hunt for the robber, spending the night of the sixteenth in Calpella. The next morning he resumed his search, accompanied by John Starkey.

Stage robber John Schneider, who shot and wounded Doc Standley on January 17, 1896. Courtesy California State Archives.

Doc got his first break when a rancher named Arnold Ford told him that a suspicious-looking character, who matched the bandit's description, had taken a noonday meal at his place, three miles north of Ukiah. Doc and Starkey rode with Ford to his ranch and spotted the stranger crossing the fields on foot, half a mile from the house.

Doc, followed by Starkey, galloped after the stranger and quickly overtook him. Leveling his Winchester, Standley yelled, "Halt, and throw up your hands!"

Doc's reply was a blast from a six-shooter that the outlaw had drawn with lightning speed. The slug slammed into Standley's left arm, breaking the bone, and the impact knocked him out of the saddle. At the first fire Starkey put spurs to his horse and lit out for the tall timber like a scared rabbit.

Doc tried to bring his Winchester into play, but the gunman fired again, hitting the lawman in the right leg. The outlaw jumped behind a tree, fired once more without effect, and fled. Arnold Ford and his wife loaded the badly wounded lawman into a buggy and took him into Ukiah. Doc, in great pain, was carried into his mother's house, where a doctor surgically removed the bullets.

Doc's youngest daughter, Jessie Hildreth (at this writing alive and residing in Ukiah, at more than one hundred years of age), still recalls holding a lantern while the doctor operated on her father. All the adults present were too nervous and shaken to keep the lamp steady, so the job fell to twelve-year-old Jessie.

Three days later, after an exhaustive hunt, Sheriff Johnson and three of his deputies captured the bandit near Seven Mile House, north of Ukiah. He was armed with two Colt double-action revolvers and gave his name as John Schneider. The officers lodged him in the county jail, and many threats were made of lynching the prisoner. When it became apparent that Standley's wounds were not fatal, the lynching talk died out, and in April, Schneider was sentenced to twenty years in San Quentin for the two stage holdups.[23]

Doc's wounds quickly healed, and the next year he joined the gold rush to the Klondike. He settled in Nome, Alaska, engaged in mining and freighting, and served as a deputy sheriff. His wife, Sarah, soon followed him, and the couple remained in Alaska until 1902, when they returned to Ukiah. When the "Big Break" at Folsom prison in 1903 forced Warden Thomas Wilkinson to resign, Standley became a prime candidate for the job. In October the *San Francisco Call* headlined a story "Standley Will Be New Warden" and reported that he was favored for the position by the board of prison directors. Wells Fargo threw all of its influence behind Standley, but the job went instead to Doc's old friend Archibald Yell, former district attorney of Mendocino County.[24]

Doc returned to Alaska with his wife and daughter Jessie. In May, 1908, he fell on a staircase and injured his spine. This gradually paralyzed him and caused him to lose his eyesight. Sarah and Jessie started home with him, stopping to rest a few days in Seattle. They stopped again in Portland, Oregon, but here Doc breathed his last on July 8, 1908.

He was buried in the Masonic Cemetery, in Ukiah. Wrote the editor of the *Ukiah Dispatch Democrat*, "Doc Standley was one of the best men this country has ever produced."[25]

But how quickly are heroes forgotten. Not even the wind, as it blows in from the Pacific through Mendocino's majestic redwood forests, whispers the name of Jeremiah Standley.

CHAPTER 5

The Thief Taker: Tom Cunningham

THE sun beat down mercilessly as Tom Cunningham and five of his deputies rode onto the Bailey ranch, on the old Moquelemos grant, in San Joaquin County. Cunningham squinted and mopped his brow in the blistering 110-degree heat. He did not like what he saw. In front of him sixty settlers squatted on a huge mound of recently threshed grain. Each was armed with a six-shooter, and a few feet away three dozen Winchester rifles were neatly stacked. The sheriff carefully surveyed their grim, defiant faces. He realized instinctively that one wrong move on his part would make this bitter, twenty-year-old land dispute explode into bloodshed.

For what seemed like an eternity the lawmen and settlers squared off. Finally the tension was cracked by a hostile yell.

"We're going to hold this grain!"

Fingering his gun, the leader of the settlers added ominously, "You can begin arresting us as soon as you wish."

Tom Cunningham had once vowed that he would never kill a man unless he had absolutely no other choice, and now he feared that the "Moquelemos War," as the newspapers had dubbed it, would turn into another tragedy like the one at Mussel Slough four years earlier when, in an identical confrontation, a shoot-out had erupted that left seven men dead. The sheriff chose his words carefully.

"I don't see why I should arrest you now. You are doing nothing except sitting on that stack of grain, and if I were to take you in I would have no case against you."

"We have to die sometime. We might as well die here and now!" cried another settler.

Ignoring the challenge, Cunningham wheeled his horse and headed back to Stockton. He knew that his actions during the next twenty-four hours would inflame or quell the Moquelemos War. "It was the most critical period in the history of San Joaquin County," historian George Tinkham would write years later.[1]

But for Tom Cunningham it was but one of innumerable tense episodes during his long tenure as sheriff of San Joaquin. Time and again his extraordinary talents of tact, diplomacy, and unflinching courage preserved the peace in countless public emergencies, while his kindness, nobility, and dogged devotion to duty made him a legendary figure during his lifetime.

Born in County Longford, Ireland, on August 17, 1838, at the age of ten he was sent to Brooklyn, New York, to work as an apprentice in a harness maker's shop owned by his brother-in-law. Young Tom devoted his spare time to study and, when he had the chance, attended school at night. At sixteen he struck out on his own, taking a steamer to California, via Panama, and arriving in San Francisco in June, 1855. He settled in Stockton, where he worked for a succession of harness makers. In 1860, Cunningham opened his own shop, and a year later he married Catherine Burke, who bore him three daughters. From the start Tom had been active in civic affairs, serving as a volunteer fireman from 1857 to 1865, when he was chosen chief of the fire department. That same year he won election to the Stockton city council and was reelected in 1870. In 1871 the Republican party nominated him as its candidate for sheriff, and he was elected by a handsome majority, taking office in March, 1872.[2]

Cunningham was a popular man, but utterly inexperienced as an officer of the law. In addition, he was markedly gentle and retiring in personality and did not at all fit the mold of an iron-willed frontier sheriff. Pessimists on all sides shook their heads and predicted that the harness maker would prove a dismal failure. The sensitive Cunningham was deeply stung by this criticism, but it aroused within him a tremendous resolve. From that day onward he devoted all his boundless enthusiasm and energy toward his new duties, and soon any doubts of his competence were completely buried. For the next twenty-seven years Tom Cunningham was at the forefront of the manhunts for many of California's most-notorious outlaws: Tiburcio Vasquez, Black Bart, Bill Miner, Isador Padillo, Evans and Sontag, Jack Brady, and Sam Browning. So many desperadoes were run to earth by the tireless sheriff that he came to be known as the "Thief Taker of San Joaquin."

A pioneer in the infant science of criminology, he made a systematic study of the habits, methods, and motivations of criminals and compiled volume after volume of newspaper clippings and other data on American crime. He put together one of the largest rogues' gal-

Sheriff Tom Cunningham, the "Thief Taker of San Joaquin." Courtesy R. Tod Ruse, Historian, Stockton Police Department.

leries in the United States, which at the time of his retirement had cost him personally $20,000 and held some 42,000 photographs. He kept a stable of fast horses for his deputies and imported blood-hounds from Cuba for use in outlaw hunting. He personally de-signed the San Joaquin County jail, considered to be a model of its kind, which was known as "Cunningham's Castle" because of its dis-tinctive pointed towers. And over the years he painstakingly put to-gether a museum that once occupied four rooms in the old court-house. It held more than 1,000 weapons and other curios connected with the state's criminal history, each carefully tagged and displayed in glass cases, among them the rifle that California Ranger J. W. Chiles carried in the manhunt for Joaquín Murrieta and the hand-kerchief that led to the capture of Black Bart, the poet highwayman.[3]

Before Tom Cunningham's election, San Joaquin County had been known as the favorite stomping ground of escaped convicts and fugitives from other parts of the state. Harry N. Morse, the famed sheriff of Alameda County, liked to remark sarcastically to captured criminals, "Why the devil didn't you go to San Joaquin? You would be safe enough there!" But Cunningham was so successful at driving the thieves from his bailiwick that just two years after taking office Morse chose him as second-in-command of his handpicked posse, funded by the state legislature to track down Tiburcio Vasquez. The story of this posse's hunt for Vasquez and his gang has been told many times. Said Tom later of the manhunt, "It was the hardest riding I ever saw. We covered 2,709 miles, an average of forty-five and one-half miles per day, during the sixty days we were out. The chase led us through Fresno, Monterey, Tulare, San Luis Obispo, Kern, and Los Angeles counties, and we covered them all closely."[4]

Vasquez was pressed so hard that he took refuge in what is now the Hollywood hills. Acting on a tip from Morse, the Los Angeles sheriff captured Vasquez in his hideout in May, 1874; he was later tried and hanged at San José.

One member of the Vasquez gang who managed to elude Cunningham and Morse was the notorious Isador Padillo. Born and raised at Marysville, he had first come into prominence as a suspect in the infamous Medina murder case of 1869, when five men were bound, gagged, and shot to death during the robbery of a store in San Joaquin County. Isador Padillo, Jesus Tejada, and Antonio García were arrested for the brutal crime six months later. Padillo was convicted of first-degree murder and sentenced to death, but in January, 1872, the California Supreme Court reversed his conviction and granted him a new trial. During the long delay important witnesses moved away and could not be located, and upon retrial Padillo was found not guilty and released. He promptly joined the Vasquez band, and after Tiburcio's arrest he formed his own gang, which included such desperadoes as Joaquín Olivera (alias Antone Savage), Ramon Ruíz, Trinidad Rodríguez, José María (alias Coquimbo), Mitchell ("Little Mitch") Brown, and Antonio Valacca (known as Red Antone because he had reportedly spilled the blood of some twenty Chinese). This well-organized gang was divided into two bands. One, led by Padillo, operated in the Northern Mines and had a hideout in the "Spanish settlement" in Doty's Flat, five miles west of Auburn. The other, headed by Joaquín Olivera, was headquartered in a cabin three miles below Jackson, in Amador County.[5]

Padillo's gang was responsible for numerous stagecoach holdups in the mother lode, as well as the robberies of many Chinese mining camps. They stopped the Sonora-Milton stage in November, 1874, on March 23, 1875, and again on October 12, 1875. Padillo personally led raids on the Laporte-Oroville stage on August 3, 1875, and the Marysville-Downieville stage on October 5. In these and other hold-ups the gang was reported to have stolen $20,000 from Wells Fargo, who in December responded by suspending its operations in several of the northern counties.[6]

Tom Cunningham, with Sheriff Ben Thorn and Detective Jim Hume, of Wells Fargo, labored diligently to apprehend the culprits. They had long suspected Padillo and his compadres but were unable to secure enough evidence to convict them. On December 9 they got their first break when Ramon Ruíz was picked up for a holdup of the Chinese Camp–Copperopolis stage. Ruíz confessed and identified the members of the gang, as well as the locations of their two hide-outs. The officers carefully drew up plans to make lightning-fast raids on both bandit lairs at the same time. Cunningham was to lead the attack on the gang in Doty's Flat, while Ben Thorn would lead the raid near Jackson.

In such raids Cunningham always employed extremely large posses (sometimes twenty officers or more) in the belief that the outlaws would be so overwhelmed at the show of force that they would not even think of resisting, thus avoiding bloodshed. Thorn, on the other hand, preferred to use small posses (just a few men) that could travel more freely without attracting attention. The roundup of the Padillo gang illustrated the comparative effectiveness of these two techniques.

At four o'clock on the morning of December 22, 1875, Tom Cun-ningham left Auburn with a heavily armed group of lawmen, includ-ing Jerome Myers, chief of police in Stockton; Placer County Sheriff James McCormick; Butte County Sheriff S. L. Daniels; plus some fifteen deputies and constables. Arriving in Doty's Flat, they split into two groups and cordoned off the settlement. As Cunningham and several other officers surrounded the house of Antonio Seriacco, Isador Padillo and Red Antone tried to flee out the back door. Con-fronted by half a dozen shotguns, they promptly surrendered. Then the possemen made a house-by-house search, herding all the male oc-cupants together in the center of Doty's Flat. From this group Cun-ningham picked out Trinidad Rodríguez and another fugitive, and the four prisoners were lodged in the Auburn jail.[7]

Meanwhile, Ben Thorn, Jim Hume, and two possemen descended upon the gang's other hideout, near Jackson. Joaquín Olivera saw them coming, leaped out a back window, exchanged gunfire with a deputy, and escaped into the chaparral. The officers entered the cabin

The notorious Isador Pa-
dillo, captured by Tom Cunningham at Doty's Flat, December 22, 1875. Courtesy
Wells Fargo Bank History
Room.

and arrested Little Mitch. The next day they picked up Coquimbo
near Fiddletown. Thorn was much chagrined by the escape of Olivera, but he kept up his search for the brigand, finally capturing him
three months later.[8]

The members of the gang "crossed the bay" to serve long prison
terms. Isador Padillo was convicted of the Marysville stage robbery
and sentenced to twenty years in San Quentin. He served less than
six months, dying in the prison on May 7, 1877.[9]

Such exploits made Tom Cunningham's name a terror to evildoers,
not because he was quick on the trigger, but simply because he was
unflinching in his duty and smarter and wiser than the men he arrested. On one occasion a naïve country boy, who had managed to
save three years' wages laboring on a San Joaquin ranch, took the
train to San Francisco to deposit his savings in the Hibernia Bank.
He took the funds in a check, but once in the city the youth was
inveigled into a game of chance, made to endorse the check, and

soon had lost every cent. He returned home heartbroken. In due time the cancelled check came back with the name of a notorious gambler endorsed on it. When Tom learned of the young man's plight he obtained the check and took it with him on his next visit to the city. Calling on his friend, Isaiah W. Lees, captain of detectives of the San Francisco police, Cunningham related the story.

"Come along with me up the street," said Lees. "We will see what we can do."

Arriving at the gambler's place of business, Lees went inside, while Cunningham remained on the sidewalk. Lees showed the check to the gambler, who became indignant.

"It was his own fault. He took a chance at the game and lost his money," the gambler declared.

"He knew nothing about your game," replied Lees. "You have robbed the man of his three years' savings, and I want the money back."

"Where is your evidence?" the gambler haughtily demanded.

"Tom Cunningham is waiting outside. He has come down especially on this thing. You know he generally gets what he is after. I guess I'll call him in."

Like a shot the gambler was at the door, peering out stealthily. He returned a moment later, visibly shaken.

"What are you going to do?" demanded Lees.

"Well," the gambler quavered, "Don't make any disturbance and I'll dig up this time." And he did, promptly paying the full amount in gold coin.[10]

Despite this fearsome reputation, Tom Cunningham was an exceedingly modest man who seldom spoke of his exploits. Of the hundreds of arrests he made during his long career, one of the few he could be coaxed into relating was of his capture of the noted highwayman Pete Dalton, "The Mountain Spirit." During 1878 and 1879, Dalton was hunted doggedly by lawmen throughout the mother lode. Called by newspapers "one of the most daring road agents in the state" and "one of the most desperate criminals unhung," he had threatened to kill any officer who attempted to bring him in.

Dalton was an old convict with a long history of misdeeds. He had first entered San Quentin in 1860 for a robbery in Mariposa County. Released after four years, he landed behind bars again in 1866 with a twenty-year sentence for a Sacramento holdup. With credits, or "coppers," for good behavior, he gained his freedom in 1878 and soon was wanted for robbery in Sierra, Nevada, Yuba, and Mariposa counties. In between holdups Dalton stayed with a married sister who lived in Stockton, and no one in the neighborhood suspected him of being the noted outlaw. He made himself quite popular with the local children, carving for them small toys out of wood and bone, a skill he acquired in state prison.

On Saturday afternoon, November 22, 1879, Dalton went downtown to take in the district fair. Sheriff Cunningham spotted him watching a game in front of Malone's store in Hunter Square, opposite the courthouse. Cunningham had an almost photographic memory of faces, and though he had never seen Dalton before, he recognized the highwayman instantly from wanted circular photos. Without hesitation, Tom stepped close to the fugitive. Resting his hand on the butt of his holstered revolver, the sheriff said quietly, "Don't move."

The Mountain Spirit obeyed. Cunningham had a bystander remove a large Colt six-shooter and a knife from the bandit, and then he led him across the square to jail. So quickly was the arrest made that few on the street even noticed it. Pete Dalton was sent to Nevada County, convicted of robbery, and sentenced to thirty-four years in prison.[11]

Tom Cunningham was always amused that the "man-eater" had surrendered so docilely.

Although most peace officers become hardened and cynical from contact with crime and vice, Cunningham never lost his faith in the value of his fellowman, and tales of his kindliness and humanity were legion. When transporting a prisoner to the penitentiary, he always treated him with consideration, keeping all evidence of the man's condition out of sight on the cars and in the streets. He never failed to pay out of his own pocket for whatever small luxury the convict might want. Cunningham's truthfulness and forthright dealing with the men he captured earned him the respect and trust of a large portion of the criminal element, and he became known as a "father confessor" in the jails. Many an arrested criminal, upon being interrogated unsuccessfully, told his captors, "If you want me to talk, send for Tom Cunningham and I will talk with him."[12]

The sheriff was easily touched by a tale of trouble, and no charitable undertaking or request for aid from any quarter ever failed with him. His pocket was a well from which money flowed constantly to the poor and needy. Even vagrants could be certain of a free meal at the county jail, although Cunningham's political foes accused him of running a hotel for hoboes and tramps.[13]

One of his most outspoken enemies was a poor man with a large family living in Stockton. One day the family was stricken with smallpox, and the entire household was quarantined. Cunningham heard of the man's plight, and at nightfall he quietly carried an abundant supply of food and medicine to the rear of the house. It proved a godsend, for the family was destitute and starving. From that day onward his former enemy was one of the sheriff's staunchest supporters, telling all who would listen, "Tom Cunningham has a heart as big as an ox."[14]

Cunningham took great pride in the fact that he never once took a human life, although he came close many times. On one occasion he was notified that an escaped convict riding a stolen horse was headed toward San Joaquin. Taking a young man as a driver, the sheriff got into a spring wagon and trailed the convict into the Livermore Valley. He carefully instructed the youth that, should they encounter the outlaw, he was to turn the buggy to the right, so that Cunningham could jump out and cover him with his shotgun. Almost before realizing it, they came face-to-face with the desperado on the road. Cunningham tried to leap out of the buggy, but the driver turned the wrong way, and the sheriff was sent sprawling to the ground. As the convict drew his gun, Cunningham, quick as lightning, rolled over and let drive with his shotgun, killing the fugitive's horse. Animal and rider collapsed in a heap, and a moment later Cunningham had his man in handcuffs.[15]

But it was the Moquelemos War that most severely tested Tom Cunningham, and it was without question his finest hour. One of the longest and most bitterly contested land disputes in California's history, it had its origins under Mexican rule in 1846, when Governor Pio Pico granted to his brother Andrés Pico a tract of land eleven leagues square, south of the Mokelumne River, in what is now Calaveras and San Joaquin counties. It was known as the Moquelemos grant and was but one of eighty-seven grants made that year by Governor Pico, many of them ill-defined and of questionable validity. The grant was later ruled invalid by the U.S. Land Commission, thus beginning many years of legal wrangling over the title. In 1862, Congress granted to the Western Pacific Railroad Company (later the Central Pacific) certain odd-numbered sections of land along the railroad right-of-way, the sale of which was to help finance construction

Two of Tom Cunningham's six-shooters. *Top,* a Colt 1851 Navy Model, and *bottom,* a Colt .44-40 Frontier Model, manufactured in 1882. Courtesy R. Tod Ruse, Historian, Stockton Police Department.

of a route to Southern California. Many of the sections were located in the Moquelemos grant and had already been settled by farmers who claimed that the Mexican grant was valid, that the land was not public, and that Congress could not grant private land to the railroad. Long and expensive litigation ensued, and a number of clashes occurred between the settlers, or squatters, as some called them, and those who purchased the land from the Western Pacific and held what was known as "railroad title." In one incident, a purchaser's agent, Patrick Breen, was slain in a fight with settlers, and his alleged killer, Sam Markey, was later acquitted of murder by a sympathetic jury, in Stockton.[16]

The small wheat ranchers of the Moquelemos grant banded together and formed a Settlers' League to combat any attempts to remove them from their land. One man who opposed the settlers was a wheat grower named Charles K. Bailey. He purchased "railroad title" to a parcel of land, located four miles northeast of Linden, that was also claimed by four members of the League. Bailey sued for possession and won, and the U.S. marshal evicted the four on June 25, 1884.

The settlers had already planted four hundred acres of wheat on the disputed land, and they were determined to harvest it. Bailey was just as determined to get it himself, but he was afraid to tangle with the settlers. Bailey hit upon a clever plan to force Tom Cunningham to get the crop for him. He had a friend sue him on a promissory note for $2400. Bailey intentionally defaulted, and his friend was granted a court-ordered attachment against the disputed grain, in satisfaction of the $2400 supposedly owed on the note. He then put up a $10,000 bond to indemnify Sheriff Cunningham and handed him the attachment to serve. Now Tom found himself smack in the middle of a hornet's nest. Although his personal sympathies were with the settlers and he was fully aware of the collusive nature of the claim, especially since Bailey had other property that could be more easily attached, the sheriff had the utmost respect for the courts and never failed to serve any legal process placed in his hands.

On July 7, two of the leaders of the Settlers' League, Joseph Lynch and George Hurlbut, came into Stockton and advised Cunningham that on the morrow the settlers would begin to cut and thresh the grain. Cunningham and his deputies rode out the next day to serve the attachment papers and seize the grain, and therein ensued the confrontation with sixty heavily armed farmers. Returning to Stockton, Tom arranged a meeting that evening between Lynch, Hurlbut, and Bailey, but they were unable to reach a compromise.

For Cunningham it was a matter of principle that the law prevail and the attachment be served, but the thought of the bloodshed that was certain to follow abhorred him. He decided to employ the method that he had so successfully used to corner dangerous outlaws. At ten o'clock that night he served a requisition on General James A. Shepherd, requesting him to order out two companies of the National Guard. By three o'clock the next morning the Stockton and Emmet Guards had assembled, ninety-two strong, each man armed with rifle, bayonet, and forty rounds of ammunition. An hour later, with Cunningham in the lead, on horseback, they started for the Moquelemos grant in wagons. Tom hoped fervently that the show of force would prove too much for the settlers.

Meanwhile, one hundred settlers had gathered on the Bailey ranch, all armed and ready to resist any attempt to dislodge them. A messenger brought word of the militia's advance, and the settlers held a heated debate over whether or not they should fight the soldiers. At six-thirty, Sheriff Cunningham rode alone onto the ranch. He advised the crowd, most of whom he knew personally, that the soldiers would soon arrive and then read to them the provisions of the Riot Act, ordering them to disperse.

At that point, one of the settlers, Colonel Hyde, an old Union Army man and Civil War veteran, climbed onto a threshing machine and said, "I have not spoken until now, but now I say that we have gone far enough. We cannot fight the whole state, and if we got the best of these fellows there would be others on the march for us within six hours. We would be hunted down, without any stopping. If anyone is killed I would be an outlaw. I have a family in Stockton and I want to be able to return to it."

Cries of approval and disapproval greeted the speech. When the blue uniforms of the soldiers appeared over a ridge to the west, another of the settlers exclaimed, "Boys, it won't do to fire upon the flag. We must give up!"

The settlers realized the folly of resistance and, shouldering their rifles, gradually drifted back to their homes. Cunningham took possession of the grain, and the soldiers remained for nine days while the harvesting was completed. The dispute over the Moquelemos grant was not resolved until 1888, when the U.S. Supreme Court ruled in favor of those who held "railroad title." Many of the settlers lost their land, houses, and other improvements, but not their lives, thanks to Cunningham's judgment and foresight.[17]

Much of the sheriff's time was devoted to mundane tasks, paperwork, and run-of-the-mill arrests. But even a routine stage holdup might demand the exercise of an officer's best detective skills. On December 12, 1884, just months after Cunningham had defused the Moquelemos War, a pair of masked brigands wielding shotguns halted the Sonora-Milton stagecoach, in Salt Spring Valley. They hacked at the Wells Fargo box with a hatchet, but were unable to force it open. The robbers fled when a group of sheepherders approached, but not before one highwayman dropped his shotgun, the stage wheel running over the barrel before he could retrieve it.

Tom Cunningham got descriptions of the two bandits and rode out to Salt Spring Valley with Wells Fargo Detective John Thacker, Special Officer Orrin Langmaid, and Constable Carroll. Searching the scene carefully, they found the robbers' hatchet in the roadside brush. It still had flecks of green paint from the express box on its blade. Next to it was an oyster can and inside the can Cunningham and Thacker found the broken tip of a knife blade that had been used to open it.

Making inquiries among residents of the valley, Cunningham learned that three strangers had been seen on the evening before the holdup. They had been leading their horses by the bridles, and two had carried shotguns on their shoulders. As was often the case in those horseback days, the witnesses were able to give better descriptions of the mounts than of their riders, and Tom managed to learn that two hardcase brothers, Lon and Bert Aldridge, had recently purchased similar horses on Roberts Island, in the delta west of Stockton. The Aldridges owned a farm eight miles from Milton, and Cunningham discovered that they had a motive for robbery: their farm was about to be foreclosed.

Armed with a search warrant, Sheriff Cunningham, Thacker, Langmaid, and Carroll surrounded the Aldridge farm on the morning of December 16. Tom banged on the front door, and Lon Aldridge's wife opened it.

"Does Mr. Aldridge live here? I want to see him," the sheriff announced.

Both brothers came to the door. Lon, chewing tobacco, was known as a local bully, but when he spotted Cunningham he turned ghost white. Tom noticed immediately that Bert Aldridge was wearing blue overalls and a blue shirt, the same type of clothing worn by one of the stage robbers. He ordered the brothers and a third man, Billy Lynch, outside. While they were guarded by Langmaid and Carroll, he and Thacker made a thorough search of the house, and when he found a penknife with the blade tip broken off that matched the piece from the oyster can, Cunningham knew he had the right men. In a back room they discovered two shotguns, and sure enough, one had a fresh scar across the barrel, a mark made by the stagecoach's wheel.

Outside the house, Lon demanded of Cunningham, "Why are you here?"

"To arrest you for robbing the Wells Fargo stage," the sheriff responded.

"Well, if you can prove it on me, that's all right!" Aldridge grunted, angrily.

"Where are you taking us?" Bert Aldridge asked Cunningham.

"To Milton."

Tom Cunningham (center, with cigar) and his deputies on the day he retired, January 3, 1899. At far left is George Black, and standing at Cunningham's right is Billy Wall. Undersheriff Joe Long (seated, with beard)
was the first lawman to arrest Bill Miner. Courtesy R. Tod Ruse, Historian,
Stockton Police Department.

"Hold on then. Let me change my clothes first."

"Not much!" Tom exclaimed, eyeing the telltale shirt and overalls.
"You don't come by that game on me!"

The three prisoners were taken to San Andreas for their preliminary hearing, for the holdup had taken place in Calaveras County.
The evidence was not strong enough against Lynch, and he was released, but the Aldridge boys were held to answer. At their trial a
month later the brothers asserted their innocence, but they could not
explain away the knife blade or the scarred shotgun. The jury convicted them of attempted robbery, and both served six years in San
Quentin.[18]

Tom Cunningham's unshakable faith in the legal process and his refusal to shirk any duty, no matter how personally disagreeable, was to be again sorely tested a few years later, when it fell upon him to become the first and only peace officer ever to arrest a justice of the U.S. Supreme Court. This incident, the most famous of his career, was an outgrowth of the long-standing feud between David S. Terry, former chief justice of the California Supreme Court, and Stephen J. Field, also a former chief justice of the California court, but at that time a U.S. Supreme Court justice. Terry was a noted fire-eater; in 1859 he had slain U.S. Senator David Broderick in one of America's most-celebrated duels. In 1884 he had been retained to represent the beautiful Sarah Althea Hill in her sensational divorce suit against U.S. Senator William Sharon. Terry became infatuated with the former mistress, and in 1888 they were married.

The Sharon divorce case had dragged on for years in both state and federal courts. Things came to a head when Justice Field, riding circuit in California, delivered a ruling unfavorable to the Terrys, who started a brawl with deputy marshals in the courtroom. Judge Terry was sentenced to a six-month jail term, and from his cell he threatened to kill Justice Field. The next summer Field returned to California for circuit duty. Because of Terry's threats he was assigned a bodyguard, Deputy U.S. Marshal Dave Neagle, a diminutive gunfighter and former chief of police of Tombstone, Arizona.

On August 14, 1889, Field and Neagle, enroute by train from Los Angeles to San Francisco, stopped for breakfast in Lathrop, south of Stockton. The Terrys, who by chance happened to be on the same train, entered the depot's restaurant. David Terry spotted Field seated at a dining table, walked quickly behind him, and slapped the justice twice in the face. Neagle's reaction was instantaneous. Jerking out a triggerless belly gun, he thumbed two shots so quickly that they sounded like a single explosion. Terry fell dead to the floor.[19]

Neagle was placed under arrest at the scene by a constable. Sarah Terry went before a justice of the peace in Stockton and swore out a warrant for the arrest of Justice Field, charging him with murder. Terry had lived in Stockton for many years and was extremely popular there, so even though Field was absolutely innocent, the warrant was issued and handed to Tom Cunningham for service.

Cunningham found this duty most distasteful. He nonetheless took a train the next day to San Francisco, where Field had gone, arriving in the evening at the Palace Hotel, which he found packed with judges, lawyers, police officers, and newspaper reporters. Accompanied by Police Chief Patrick Crowley, he called on Justice Field in his suite. Cunningham, who had known Field for many years, apologized profusely for his visit and explained that the arrest warrant was at present incomplete and would have to be endorsed by a local magistrate. It was arranged that the warrant would be served at one o'clock the following afternoon, August 16.

At the agreed-upon time, Cunningham appeared at the federal building, this time with Chief Crowley and Captain Isaiah Lees. Hordes of spectators jammed the hallways, anxious to see the arrest of the noted jurist. They were disappointed, for Cunningham was ushered into the elevator and taken to Justice Field's private, third-floor chambers, which were packed shoulder-to-shoulder with lawyers and reporters. When Cunningham entered the room, Field arose from his chair and said with a pleasant smile, "I'm glad to see you."

The sheriff, extremely uncomfortable, made an inarticulate reply and then asked, "Do you wish me to proceed?"

"Yes, you may perform your duty," answered Justice Field.

Cunningham sighed, removed the warrant from his breast pocket, and intoned in a hoarse voice, "I am here to arrest you on a charge of murder. The warrant is in proper form. Do you wish it read?"

"No," Field responded. "I waive the reading of the warrant and submit to arrest."

A writ of habeas corpus had already been prepared and was presented to the U.S. Circuit Court, which immediately released Field on $5,000 bond, sparing him the indignity of a trip to jail. Ultimately the murder charge against him was withdrawn at the direction of Governor Robert Waterman. Neagle's case went to the U.S. Supreme Court, which in a landmark decision held that local authorities could not prosecute him for an act performed as a federal officer in the line of duty.

Public sentiment generally rested on the side of Field and Neagle. The authorities in Stockton were roundly criticized for their efforts to prosecute the pair, especially Field, who had not even lifted a finger against Terry. The warrant for Field had been the spite-work of a vengeful widow, and the prosecution of Neagle had been engineered by Terry's friends. Tom Cunningham's gentlemanly and tactful handling of the incident spared him public criticism, for it was recognized that he had no other choice than to serve the warrant.[20]

It was this same tact and foresight that served San Joaquin well during the severe depression of 1894. In that year Jacob S. Coxey led an "Industrial Army" of unemployed workers from the Midwest in a march on Washington, D.C., to demand jobs and food for their families. In California several similar marches were organized. One large group of unemployed men gathered at Sacramento and remained for months, taxing the city's resources and exhausting its hospitality. Eventually they were ordered to move on, and they began making preparations to descend upon Stockton, whose citizens became greatly alarmed.

Tom Cunningham, anticipating the unwelcome visit, appeared before the board of supervisors, presented his plan of action, and was granted a relatively small amount of money to put it into effect. The army arrived at the San Joaquin County line, fully expecting to meet with a hostile reception, but instead they found Sheriff Cunningham, smiling broadly and filled with sympathy for their plight. He directed them to load their bedrolls onto wagons and then invited them to partake of a lunch he had brought along. After the meal, Cunningham led the band on a march to Banner Island, on the San Joaquin River, just outside Stockton. Here a grand feast awaited them, consisting of all the delicacies of the season, and they ate as only hungry men can. Then a tugboat towing two barges pulled up to the landing, and Cunningham told the crowd that he wanted to help speed them on their journey. The Industrial Army embarked with loud cheers for the friendly sheriff of San Joaquin.[21]

While other sheriffs had met these men with clubs, Tom Cunningham, through diplomacy and generosity, had preserved their human dignity while sparing his county a great expense.

During the 1890s, Tom was kept busy hunting the many train robbers who raided the Southern Pacific, in the San Joaquin Valley. Best-recalled of these was his relentless pursuit of the Morrano Switch outlaws.

On the night of September 4, 1897, a bold attempt was made to halt the Los Angeles Express at Morrano Switch, an isolated side-track, fifteen miles south of Stockton. A large pile of railroad ties was placed on the track and set afire. The night was unusually clear, and Engineer Joe Openshaw spotted the fire two miles from the switch. Openshaw slowed his locomotive and stopped a few feet from the flames. Brakeman E. N. Whitney borrowed a pistol from the express

George Williams, *left,* and George Schlagal, *right,* the Morrano Switch Outlaws, both captured by Tom Cunningham in 1897. Courtesy California State Archives.

messenger and made a quick search, looking for bandits. He found none, the crew removed the ties, and the train proceeded on its way.

The incident was immediately reported to Sheriff Cunningham, who sent his crack deputies, George Black and Billy Wall, to Morrano to work up the case. Several days later Cunningham was paid a visit by George Cook, a Stockton youth, who informed the sheriff that the would-be robbers were two local toughs, George Williams and George Schlagal. Williams had asked Cook to join in a second train holdup, and when Cook refused, Williams had threatened to kill him if he divulged the scheme.[22]

Tom knew George Williams well. He was an intelligent young man from Banta, near Tracy, who had invented a railroad car coupler and a type of smokeless gunpowder. For the past few months he had experimented with the smokeless powder, receiving quite a bit of local attention, as well as money from investors. In 1892, when still a boy, Williams had held up the railroad depot at Banta, stolen a horse from his father, and ridden to Sonora, where he was captured by Cunningham and later sentenced to two years in the State Reformatory at Whittier. There he met George Schlagal, and upon their release, the pair returned to Williams's home in Banta. Shortly afterward, Schlagal stole a horse, but after a hard chase Cunningham nabbed him in San Joaquin City. He had served three years in San Quentin and had been released a year earlier, hooking up again with his pal, Williams.[23]

Tom knew that Williams and Schlagal were rooming at the Vermont lodging house, in Stockton. His deputies shadowed the two, and on the evening of September 8, they reported that the suspects, in the company of a third man, had left town, heading south. Cunningham put Deputy Sheriffs Wall and Black on the next southbound train; then he climbed into a buggy and started after the trio.

At nine o'clock, Southern Pacific Train No. 17 was forced to a halt by a blazing pile of ties on the track at Morrano Switch. Wall and Black, carrying sawed-off shotguns, walked forward to investigate. Williams and Schlagal were hidden behind a fence with James Roup (alias "Brock the Plumber"), an ex-convict whom Williams had recruited for their latest job. They opened fire on the deputies with a shotgun, a .32-caliber Winchester, and a six-shooter. The officers dived for cover and returned the fire. During the exchange of shots, a tramp, who was stealing a ride on top of a car, was wounded in the thigh.

The desperadoes, seeing that their plans had been thwarted, bolted from their hiding place and fled on foot across a large field, toward the San Joaquin River. Wall and Black kept up a hot fire until the outlaws were out of sight. They attempted to follow the trio, but lost their trail in the darkness. Several of the badmen's bullets had hit the train, but none of the passengers were injured. They were so badly frightened that the crew was able to persuade only a few to help remove the ties. The train pulled into Ripon a few minutes later, where the deputies telegraphed word of the attack to Cunningham, in Lathrop. At daybreak he began a hunt for the fugitives, but a strong wind had removed their tracks from the sandy soil.

Tom knew that Williams was familiar with the San Joaquin River bottoms. A wild, marshlike country of dense thickets of scrub oak, willows, and tules, it was then sparsely settled and an excellent hiding place for bandits. A $1400 reward was posted for the desperadoes, and the Southern Pacific sent Detectives C. C. Crowley and Jim

Meade to help hunt them. Wells Fargo Detective John Thacker arrived in Stockton and joined Cunningham and several of his deputies. They could find no trace of Roup, but learned that Williams and
Schlagal had held up a woodchopper near the river and had stolen
his supply of provisions.

Cunningham picked up their trail and began one of the most
tireless manhunts of his career. For the next six days he and Thacker
barely took time to eat or sleep. Following the footprints of the two
young fugitives, the sheriff trailed them south along the river, past
San Joaquin City, and into Stanislaus County, where he and Thacker
were joined by Sheriff Richard B. Purvis. Tracking was difficult in
the rough bottomlands, and the lawmen frequently lost the trail and
were forced to backtrack or circle widely to find the footprints. They
sent word to the isolated farmhouses and woodchoppers' camps to
be on the lookout for the outlaws.

On the night of the twelfth Sheriff Cunningham received a report
that Williams and Schlagal had appeared at a religious camp meeting
grounds, near the San Joaquin River bridge, and while there had
eaten supper. By the time the officers arrived the pair had fled. Cunningham trailed them west toward Grayson. He later learned that they
had taken refuge in a barn and earlier that day had slipped unnoticed
into Modesto to read newspaper accounts of the train holdup.[24]

The next day Cunningham and his posse searched both sides of
the river, and the following morning he returned to his home in
Stockton to get some much-needed rest. The sheriff was at his house
only a few hours when he was notified that a rancher's wife had
spotted the fugitives on the west bank of the river, near Carpenter's
Ferry. Cunningham caught the first train to Modesto, where he
joined Purvis and Thacker, and the trio raced to the bottomlands
near Crow's Landing. Unable to find any tracks of the outlaws, the
posse drove into Newman in the evening and spent the night with a
farmer, near Hill's Ferry. The sheriff suspected that Williams and
Schlagal might have recognized their buggy, so he exchanged it for
the farmer's spring wagon. In Hill's Ferry Cunningham was joined
by three local men: Ed and Will Newsome and Monroe Rogers. Said
Cunningham later:

> We were not successful in finding anything of them but we were
> confident they were not far away. In the morning we found the track
> made by Williams' left shoe, which has been a guide to us throughout
> our search. We found where they had supper the night before, but

could not get any trace of any morning movement. We crossed the river once, but could find nothing and coming back ran across the same tell-tale track.

Just about that time the farmer with whom we had talked the night before came running toward us to tell that the fellows were just waking up and crawling out of a strawstack some distance away from the protection of the river undergrowth. We started toward them and in a short time they started toward the river. I sent Thacker and Newsome around one way and with another Newsome boy and Sheriff Purvis I drove into a gate, while Rogers went back a little way into another field. We could see the two fellows making their way toward the river bottom through an alfalfa field and drove to head them off. Had we thought to take a hatchet with us we could have cut them off easily but as we came to a wire fence we had to tie up and make the rest of the chase on foot.[25]

Although he was almost sixty years old, Cunningham, with Purvis and Newsome, chased the young outlaws two miles across the fields toward the river. Williams and Schlagal, seeing that they were being surrounded, turned and ran back toward the road. The officers were rapidly closing in, and as the two desperadoes climbed over a fence onto the road, they found Thacker and Newsome almost on top of them.

"Throw up your hands!" Thacker shouted.

Schlagal dropped his shotgun, but Williams clutched his Winchester and turned toward Sheriff Cunningham, who was now close behind.

"Drop the gun, Williams," Cunningham said evenly, covering the young outlaw with a sawed-off shotgun.

Williams wisely threw down the rifle. Both prisoners were ironed and driven into Newman, where the officers boarded the noon train for Stockton and lodged them in the county jail. They claimed innocence, and Williams told Cunningham, "We were not connected with the alleged train robbery and will be able to prove that we were at least ten miles away from the place when the attempt was made to hold up the train. We were out hunting, and kept on our way up the river."[26]

Williams's story convinced neither his captor nor the jury who heard his case a month later. On October 20, after a three-day trial, he was convicted of attempted train wrecking and sentenced to life imprisonment. The next day George Schlagal pleaded guilty and also received a life sentence. He told Cunningham that Roup had been their partner in the second job. For a time it seemed that Roup had escaped the sheriff's clutches, but two months later, on December 29, the ever-vigilant Cunningham picked up a copy of the *San Francisco Call* and spotted a picture of Brock the Plumber, who had been arrested by police in Napa, following a house burglary. Cunningham rushed to Napa the next day and made arrangements to return Roup to Stockton for trial. However, on January 6, he pleaded guilty to the Napa burglary, was handed a life term, and was taken immediately to San Quentin, making it unnecessary to prosecute him for the Morrano Switch attack.[27]

During his many years in office, Tom Cunningham had taken but one week-long vacation, and by age sixty he was ready to retire. On September 1, 1898, he donated his museum and rogues' gallery to San Joaquin County, with the board of supervisors as trustees. On his last day in harness, January 3, 1899, Cunningham was surprised to receive a summons to appear in the courtroom of Judge Joseph H. Budd. Stepping inside, the sheriff found the room filled with judges, lawyers, county officials, and prominent citizens. Judge Budd ordered him before the bench, announcing cryptically, "The penalty is to be imposed."

An indictment had been drawn up and was read aloud by the clerk, charging Cunningham with "being true to the trust of the people." Judge Budd promptly found him guilty. Then gifts were presented and speeches were made. A pleased and surprised Cunningham thanked all those present and then, with tears in his eyes, unbuckled his gunbelt and placed it around the waist of the new sheriff, Walter Sibley, saying simply, "Never use this pistol to shoot down a man unless you find it absolutely necessary to the welfare of the people. Always protect a prisoner with your life, if need be."[28]

Less than two years later, Tom Cunningham was dead. On November 26, 1900, while campaigning for the Republican party, he suffered a fatal heart attack in Tuttletown, in Tuolumne County. The Stockton newspapers eulogized him for six days. Declared the *Stockton Daily Record,* "His best praises were sounded by his life's deeds, which live after him."[29]

But today Tom Cunningham is largely forgotten. One can visit Stockton and search in vain for any trace of her once-revered sheriff. His home and the jail he designed have been torn down. His museum collection has vanished and is believed to be in private hands in Stockton. When the old courthouse was razed, Cunningham's rogues' gallery met a similar fate. Scores of the sheriff's prized mug books were dumped ignominiously onto the sidewalk and carted off by souvenir collectors.

Perhaps one day the lifework of this extraordinary man will be properly recognized, but until then Tom Cunningham, like lost heroes and forgotten warriors, lingers in Valhalla.

PART TWO

With Force and Fear: The Outlaws

Robbery defined. Robbery is the felonious taking of personal property in the possession of another, from his person or immediate presence, and against his will, accomplished by means of force or fear. Section 211, California Penal Code, enacted 1872.

CHAPTER 6

Confederate Guerrillas in California:
Captain Ingram's Rangers

ALTHOUGH California remained loyal during the Civil War, the sympathies of her citizens were sharply divided. The state had been settled by men and women from every corner of the nation. Those from the North supported the Union, while southerners favored the Confederacy. Of California's total population, then about 400,000, an estimated 40,000 were rebel sympathizers. The legislature passed emergency laws making it illegal to display rebel flags or to endorse, defend, or cheer the subversion of the United States. Nonetheless, Secessionist feeling ran high, particularly in Los Angeles, San Bernardino, El Monte, Visalia, and San José. Although greatly outnumbered, "Secesh" men, or Copperheads, were active in espousing their cause, and isolated, unrelated incidents of violence occurred frequently.

The more fervent Confederate sympathizers joined the Knights of the Golden Circle, a clandestine organization that had been founded in the South in 1859 for the purpose of conquering Mexico, establishing slavery there, and annexing it to the Union as a new slave state. While few took the scheme seriously, by the outbreak of war in 1861 the Knights of the Golden Circle was firmly established in California and was believed to have a membership of sixteen thousand. Its members met secretly in small groups to escape detection and adopted an elaborate system of secret signs and passwords. Some raised money to support the Confederacy, and others plotted to overthrow the state government in Sacramento. But without question the most daring and desperate undertaking by any members of California's Secessionist movement was the organization of a band of Confederate guerrillas by Captain Rufus Ingram, C.S.A., and Tom Poole, former undersheriff of Monterey County. Both men had had long, checkered careers before Ingram recruited the band in the Santa Clara Valley in 1864.[1]

Thomas Bell Poole was a six-foot, rough-looking Kentucky widower who had raised several children on his ranch in the Pajaro River

Valley, near Watsonville. In 1858, Henry DeGraw, sheriff of Monterey County, appointed the forty-year-old Poole his undersheriff, a position he held for a two-year term. Poole, a strong-willed and popular officer, soon took over many of DeGraw's duties, becoming, in effect, acting sheriff. One of his first acts was to prepare for the legal execution of José Anastasio, an Indian who had been convicted of cutting a man's throat and robbing him of nine dollars on the Carmel road. Anastasio was sentenced to be hanged on February 12, 1858. By law, the sentencing judge was required to forward to the governor a statement of the facts of the case and a copy of the judgment. This statute had rarely been obeyed, and Governor John Weller a few weeks earlier had announced his intention to enforce it. When Weller received no copy of the judgment from the Monterey court, he sent a reprieve to Sheriff DeGraw, ordering the execution delayed until March 5. DeGraw, upon reading the order, saw that the reprieve had been issued for Anastasio Jesús instead of José Anastasio. The sheriff realized that this was only a misspelling and decided to obey the governor's order. Tom Poole had other ideas. He showed the reprieve to Judge Hester, of the Monterey district court, and to several lawyers who, unbelievably, advised him that the improper spelling invalidated the order and that the original sentence must be carried out, even though it would have been a simple matter to have the governor correct the mistake.

On February 12, before a large crowd on the hill between Carmel and Monterey (the scene of the murder), Tom Poole hanged José Anastasio on a temporary gallows. News of the execution created a public furor. The outraged governor fired off a scathing letter to Poole. "You are guilty of judicial murder," Weller charged, and he added, somewhat prophetically, "Your name ought to be consigned to eternal infamy."

Poole's response to the governor included a number of lame excuses, among them that if he did not hang Anastasio "in all probability the citizens would." Declared Poole, "My duty was plain; a ministerial officer has no duty to correct the errors of process, nor to shield even the Governor from the legal results of a blunder." The undersheriff concluded by blasting Governor Weller: "If there be difficulty and wrong in this matter, you are the culpable party. . . . Not all your pompous but puerile ebulitions, nor the vapid slang of a few slimy and venal journals which essay to be your mouthpieces, have shaken confidence in the rectitude of my course."

Tom Poole. He was hanged at Placerville in 1865 for the murder of Deputy Sheriff Joe Staples. Courtesy Wells Fargo Bank History Room.

Although Poole's attack on the governor was a masterpiece of consummate gall, he received strong support from the citizens of Monterey, who sent letters in his behalf to Weller. The *Pacific Sentinel*, of Santa Cruz, pointed out that in the previous three years more than forty murders had been committed in Monterey County and that this had been the first legal hanging since the county had been formed. Even influential newspapers like the *Sacramento Bee* stuck up for Poole, its editor commenting that the undersheriff and his Monterey friends "thus far have decidedly had the best of the argument."[2]

Tom Poole's role in this unsavory episode was but a portent of misadventures to come. After his term expired he located in San Francisco and became a partner in the What Cheer stables on Sansome Street. An ardent Democrat and Copperhead, he was quick to join the Knights of the Golden Circle when the Civil War broke out. Through the society's clandestine meetings he became friendly with Asbury Harpending, a twenty-three-year-old fellow Kentuckian from a wealthy family. Harpending had secured a commission as a captain in the Confederate navy and had concocted a daring plan to aid the South. With two friends, Ridgely Greathouse, a nephew of millionaire Lloyd Tevis, and Alfred Rubery, a rich young Briton, he purchased the *J. M. Chapman,* a ninety-ton schooner that was moored at the waterfront in San Francisco. The ship was secretly outfitted with two twelve-pound cannons. A large assortment of rifles, revolvers, and cutlasses was smuggled aboard in boxes marked "machinery," and twenty handpicked men, of proven courage and ready to die for the South, were recruited to man the ship. Tom Poole was asked to join the little band, and he did so eagerly.

Harpending's plan was simple, but risky in the extreme. The *Chapman* would pose as a cargo ship bound for Mexico, but once clear of the Golden Gate her cargo would be tossed overboard and the ship armed as a privateer. They would sail to Mexico, waylay the first three eastbound Pacific Mail steamers laden with gold and silver treasure and then circle the Horn and deliver their booty to the Confederacy.

On the night of March 14, 1863, Tom Poole and the other would-be pirates quietly assembled in a dark alley behind the American Exchange Hotel where they met Harpending and Rubery. Dividing into three groups, they slipped past the Embarcadero's roaring saloons and sailors' boardinghouses and boarded the *Chapman.* They cast the ship free from the wharf and anchored in the bay in preparation of sailing at daybreak, and then all hands went below to sleep. At dawn the privateers were awakened by a shout from their lookout. Harpending ran to the deck and saw the U.S. sloop of war *Cyane* two hundred yards off, her guns trained on the *Chapman.* A tugboat filled with San Francisco police led by Captain Isaiah W. Lees was making fast for the pirate ship, and in moments the *Chapman* was swarming with Marines and police. Harpending, Greathouse, and Rubery were captured on deck; Tom Poole and the rest were surprised in the hold. Poole and his companions soon learned that they had been betrayed by their navigator, William Law, who had lost his nerve at the last moment.[3]

Tom Poole and the other crewmen were charged with treason and imprisoned at Alcatraz to await trial. For seven months they languished behind bars, but in October they were released on condition that they take the oath of allegiance and post a $3,000 bond. Tom Poole took the oath, but he had little intention of keeping it, for he was as ready as ever to join in any scheme to aid the Confederacy. He soon showed up in San José and joined the local chapter of the Knights of the Golden Circle, which held regular meetings at night in two secret hideouts. One was located in the Arroyo Hondo, in the hills east of San José, near the ranch of a prominent farmer, Preston C. Hodges, and the other was in the mountains west of San Jose, not far from Saratoga.

Early in 1864 a new face appeared at the secret meetings: Rufus Henry Ingram, a thirty-year-old former member of William C. Quantrill's guerrilla band. A medium-sized, heavily bearded, well-educated man, with suave manners and magnetic personality, Ingram had been notorious in Missouri as the "Red Fox." On August 21, 1863, he had taken part in Quantrill's infamous raid on Lawrence, Kansas. The guerrillas killed every man in town and burned 185 buildings in one of the Civil War's most ghastly atrocities. Following the Lawrence raid Ingram fled to Mexico where he met George Baker, a young farmer from San José who was on his way to join the Confederate army. Ingram, whose brother John also lived in San José, learned from Baker that there were more good men in the Santa Clara Valley ready to fight for the South, but they lacked an experienced military leader. Ingram convinced Baker to return with him to California to recruit soldiers for the Confederacy.[4]

Ingram and Baker first met with the Knights of the Golden Circle in their camp west of San José. Ingram presented his commission as a captain in the Confederate army and explained that he wanted to lead a party of men to the southern states to fight. Many of the Knights agreed to join his band, and Ingram picked Tom Poole as his lieutenant. The others included the captain's brother, John Ingram; John and Wallace Clendenning; John Creal Bouldware, a San José carpenter; James Wilson, a young blacksmith from Missouri; Henry I. Jarboe; Joseph W. Gamble; Washington Jordan; John Gately; Thomas and James Frear; and George Cross, a well-known pioneer who had come to California with Frémont, taken part in the Bear Flag revolt, and made a small fortune panning for gold in 1848. Preston Hodges allowed members of the band to camp near his ranch, and he provided them with food and horses. John A. Robinson, a San José storekeeper, also agreed to join the group and in turn recruited his eighteen-year-old clerk, Alban H. Glasby, who had arrived in California from Missouri a year before. The only criminal in the entire bunch was Jim Grant, described by the *Sacramento Union* as "about as thorough a scoundrel as ever stretched hemp." Born in Ireland and raised in Tennesseee, Grant had once been caught stealing horses in Oregon, and a lynch court had sentenced him to a terrible flogging. After killing two men in a drunken brawl, he drifted south to San José. Small and wiry, twenty-six years old, with a pleasing countenance and an affection for women and whiskey, Grant looked little like the desperado he was.

These men formed the nucleus of a band that the *Sacramento Union* would soon dub "Captain Ingram's Partisan Rangers." In all, some fifty San José Copperheads became familiar with Captain Ingram and his plans. Ingram appeared frequently at the meetings of the Knights and attempted to raise funds to equip his men for the long trip to the South. But money was scarce, and he was unable to obtain the needed financing. Ingram knew that large shipments of silver were being sent over the road from the Comstock Lode to Sacramento and decided that if he and his men could not raise the money honestly, they would steal it.[5]

In March, 1864, while Captain Ingram was busy recruiting his band, a new sheriff took office in Santa Clara County. He was Captain John Hicks Adams, a burly, rough-and-ready veteran of the Mexican War. Adams became one of California's most famous pioneer sheriffs and in 1878 was murdered by bandits while serving as a deputy U.S. marshal in Arizona. Adams and his undersheriff, R. B. Hall, also an energetic and daring officer, became suspicious of the late-night comings and goings of San José's Copperheads and determined to find out what they were up to. Hall managed to locate the secret society's meeting place in the mountains, near Saratoga, and one night he set out to spy on them. Years later he described his experience in a colorful story written for the *San Francisco Post*:

> They had selected an unusually secluded spot, the spur of the mountain protecting them on one side from the view of the village, while the thick pines and chaparral hid them completely on the other. I settled myself in a comfortable position, from whence I could command a view of the whole company, grasped my sixshooter and waited. Pretty soon they began to gather by twos and threes, until quite a crowd had collected, and, sure enough, it was just as I had suspected, the Knights of the Golden Circle, and among them some of the most prominent men in San Jose! They soon began discussing ways and means. Money was to be distributed in the South and a company of horsemen formed, with Ingram as Captain. The company was to be sent to Texas. The money or life of no Union man was to be considered sacred! For once impulse got the better of me. I cocked my pistol, and pointed it at the leader, thinking how easily I could silence

his boastful words, and, inwardly much excited, I scrutinized the band. They were from all climes and conditions, and with all grades of intelligence from the swarthy, low-browed man, with his massive frame, the perfect embodiment of brute force, up to the slender, well formed and polished gentleman, with his broad, high brow and low, full voice. . . .

I lay there for a full minute, with my pistol cocked, hesitating whether to shoot or not; then discretion overcame my valor, for I could not hope to war successfully against such odds, and I attempted to uncock my weapon, but as I did so it went off in the air, and you never saw such a stampede! Some sprang to their feet and looked wildly around; some crawled on all fours toward the brush; others lay flat on their stomachs in paralyzed fear; but finally all made their way to their horses, which were tied in an opposite direction from where I was. It was all I could do to keep from laughing at the absurd appearance they presented; but my own case was hazardous, for had but one come in my direction and discovered me this story would probably never have been told or my fate known. But Providence and their own fear protected me.

In half an hour all was still, and I made my way home, but it was this surprise that made them change their place of meeting to the east of San José, and not their intention of raiding the town, as the newspapers stated at the time. For sanitary reasons I kept silent about the scare I had given them.[6]

But it is more likely that Hall and Sheriff Adams did not act against the band because the rebels had as yet broken no laws. This was soon to change. On May 1, 1864, James Wilson and Jim Grant started from Preston Hodges's ranch for Placerville, arriving three days later. Captain Ingram and George Baker were already in town, and the little band loitered about for two more days, picking up information on Wells Fargo's silver shipments. But on May 6, Jim Grant got drunk and tried to recruit a local man into the gang. Captain Ingram was furious and, afraid that their plans might become known, ordered his men back to San José.[7]

Most of the band now made their headquarters at Hodges's ranch, dividing their time between the house and their camp, two miles distant. Captain Ingram, apprehensive about returning to Placerville, began planning a grand raid on San José to rob and loot the banks and stores, much like the attack on Lawrence. Meanwhile, Jim Grant and George Cross got into a quarrel over a local girl named Katie Kincade, and Grant threatened to kill Cross. Fearing for his life, Cross took refuge at the farm of a man named Hogan and told the farmer his troubles and also about the planned raid on San José.

Hogan brought the story to Undersheriff Hall, who later recalled, "I quietly made preparations to give them a warm reception. They must have had spies around, however, for quietly as it was managed, they received a note of warning from some direction and changed their plans."[8]

Jim Grant next quarreled with Henry Jarboe and threatened to murder him also. Jarboe was unafraid of Grant and, with Cross, who had regained his courage, spent two days hunting Grant in order to kill him. Realizing that Grant would ruin his entire operation, Captain Ingram got Hodges to give Grant a horse and some money and ordered the diminutive desperado to leave camp. Grant departed grudgingly, but it was not the last that was to be heard from him.[9]

In mid-June Captain Ingram decided to make another trip to Placerville. His plan was to hold up a stagecoach from the Comstock, bury the bullion nearby, and then return quietly to San José. When the hue and cry had died down, Jarboe would go to El Dorado County, dig up the treasure, and take it to the firm of Roundtree Brothers, in San Francisco, exchanging it for currency. Said Tom Poole later, "We were determined to raise funds to go South, and if we could not go peaceably we intended to raise an insurrection in the State of California."[10]

On the night of June 21, Captain Ingram, Tom Poole, George Baker, John Bouldware, John Clendenning, and Al Glasby assembled at Hodges's ranch. Jim Wilson was sleeping in the ranch house, and Ingram asked him to join them, but Wilson got cold feet and declined. In the morning Captain Ingram and his little band, well armed, mounted up and started the long ride to Placerville. They rode north through Calaveras Valley, over Livermore Pass, and spent the night at the Mountain House, fourteen miles west of Livermore, a popular stopping place for travelers bound for the mines. The next day they continued on to Stockton, registering under false names that night at the Pacific Hotel. On this trip Captain Ingram took his time, riding leisurely up the road to Mokelumne Hill, staying overnight at Jim Coe's place and the next two nights at Jackson and Fiddletown. From here they rode on to the Somerset House, thirteen miles south of Placerville, arriving at four o'clock on the afternoon of June 27 and introducing themselves as a party of miners on their way to the Reese River in Nevada. Maria Reynolds, a young grass widow who was staying with the landlady, showed them to their rooms and took special note of Poole, the oldest of the group, and Glasby, the youngest. But she paid little attention when the strangers walked off into the brush a few hours later for a little target practice.

In the morning Captain Ingram and his men rode to the Mountain View House, but found that no stages traveled on that road. Staying overnight, they then went on to the main highway, stopping first at Bartram's Hotel, ten miles east of Placerville, where they passed the morning. Charley Watson, driving a Pioneer line stagecoach bound for Virginia City from Placerville, noticed the six strangers lounging in front of the hotel, but paid them little heed.[11]

The Placerville toll road over the Sierra was then one of the most heavily used highways in California. By day a continuous string of teams stretched from Placerville to Lake Tahoe, carrying freight to Virginia City and other Nevada mining camps. Each night nearly every station on the road fed three or four hundred horses and mules and dozens of teamsters, who would curl up and sleep underneath their wagons. The six-horse Concord coaches of the Pioneer Stage Company carried much of the silver bullion across from the Comstock, treasure which helped greatly to finance the Union's war effort. Few but the Pioneer stages traveled the road after nightfall.

Captain Ingram, Tom Poole, and the rest slept that night at the Six Mile House, and the next day, June 30, they rode to a bend in the highway, about eleven miles east of Placerville, not far from Bartram's Hotel. The band hid in the brush until dark, checking their weapons and talking over their plans. Tom Poole later recalled, "It was agreed that we were to fight to the last if attacked, and never be taken. We were determined to resist anybody that undertook to arrest us. We expected Captain Ingram would receipt for the treasure as Captain, and then the military authorities would take it up."[12]

That morning two Pioneer stagecoaches had rolled out of Virginia City, each loaded with fourteen passengers and several sacks of gold and silver bullion. In the lead was driver Ned Blair, followed a short distance behind by Charley Watson's coach. They stopped briefly at Gold Hill, two miles out of Virginia City, and picked up more silver bars and gold dust. Each driver was now carrying four bags of bullion weighing a total of 250 pounds and valued at $26,000. The coaches continued on through Carson City to Genoa, where Watson picked up a Wells Fargo express box containing some $700 in coin. They then made the long climb up the east side of the Sierra, past

Lake Tahoe, and over the summit. It was ten o'clock that night when the first coach, its journey nearly completed, approached the bend where Captain Ingram and his followers lay in wait.

Ingram had assigned each man a position on the roadbed. They were masked and armed with fourteen six-shooters; Clendenning also had a shotgun. When Captain Ingram heard the stagecoaches approaching, he cautioned his men, "Keep cool, but if they resist, empty all your shots."

Then he snatched up the shotgun and stepped out in front of Ned Blair's coach, which was a few hundred yards in the lead.

"Hold on, or I'll fire!" Ingram warned, and Blair reined his team to a halt.

Tom Poole ran to the head of the team and grabbed the lead horse to keep the animals from bolting, and the rest of the band, six-guns cocked, encircled the coach. Ingram ordered Blair to throw down the bullion, to which the driver hotly replied, "Come and get it!"

Two of the bandits clambered into the stage and tossed down the four sacks of treasure. At that moment Charley Watson's coach rumbled into sight. Seeing the other stage blocking the road, Watson jumped down and walked forward to investigate. Suddenly Captain Ingram stepped out of the darkness with his shotgun leveled at the driver.

"Stop, or I'll put a hole through you damned quick!" the guerrilla leader barked.

While Al Glasby covered him with a pair of pistols, Watson returned to his stage. Then Ingram ordered Ned Blair to move on. As Blair released his brake, one of his passengers, a Virginia City police officer named McDougall, shoved his pistol out a window and unloosed one shot. Blair's spooked horses bolted into a run, and the coach careened around the bend and out of sight. The guerrillas, hopping mad, turned their attentions to Watson's stage.

"We ought to shoot them all!" yelled one bandit, waving his gun at the terrified passengers in the coach.

"Don't harm my passengers for what someone else has done," Watson pleaded.

Captain Ingram addressed them in a reassuring manner. "Gentlemen, I will tell you who we are. We are not robbers, but a company of Confederate soldiers. Don't act foolish. We don't want anything of the passengers. All we want is Wells, Fargo and Company's treasure, to assist us to recruit for the Confederate Army."

Al Glasby, the youngest of
Captain Ingram's Rangers.
Courtesy Wells Fargo Bank
History Room.

Watson threw down the sacks of treasure, and Ingram asked him,
"Is that all the bullion?"

"Yes," Watson lied.

"He can go," remarked another of the guerrillas.

"No," Ingram replied. "I want to see if he has it all out."

Then the captain reached into the boot and removed the Wells
Fargo box. The passengers, eleven men and three ladies, watched the
proceedings nervously. Two of the men carried derringers and another a revolver, but they wisely made no move to draw them. A
seventeen-year-old girl inside the coach, however, displayed more
nerve and cool than any of the others. Addressing Captain Ingram,
she asked, "Do you have a flag?"

Ingram replied in the affirmative, and she remarked, "I would like
to see it."

"It's not convenient to show it," the captain replied with a wry
grin. "We are busy just now."

The nervy young traveler drew Al Glasby and several of the others
into her conversation, asking them numerous questions about how
much bullion they were taking, how they would carry it, and what

they planned to do with it. When one of the guerrillas' pistols approached her face she asked him to lower it, explaining, "It might go off accidentally."

The robber immediately lowered his six-shooter and declared, "We are Southern gentlemen, and prefer to protect rather than injure ladies."

When Captain Ingram asked if anyone in the coach would like to contribute a few dollars to the Confederate cause, the plucky young lady exclaimed, "I have a five cent postal currency in my pocket, but I won't give it up without a fight!"

None of the other passengers seemed inclined to make a donation, and Ingram then gave Charley Watson a handwritten note, telling him that it was a receipt for the bullion. It read:

> June, 1864
> This is to certify that I have received from Wells, Fargo, & Co. the sum of $_____ cash, for the purpose of outfitting recruits in California for the Confederate States Army.
> R. Henry Ingram, Captain, Commanding Co., C.S.A.

The guerrillas then waved the stage on. As it rounded the bend one passenger, a correspondent for the *San Francisco Alta*, asked the young lady why she had asked the robbers so many questions. She replied that since they were masked she wanted to hear their natural voices so that they might later be identified. Wrote the *Alta*'s reporter, "She was smarter than we men were, at any rate—and, I might add, considerably more self-possessed."[13]

The holdup spot was ever after known as Bullion Bend. Captain Ingram and his guerrillas buried their booty at a nearby spring, taking with them the coin, some gold dust, and two silver bars. Then they rode the ten miles to the Somerset House, arriving at daybreak.

The two stagecoaches arrived in Placerville at one A.M., and El Dorado County Sheriff William Rogers was quickly notified. Rogers sent for his deputies and then rushed to the courthouse and organized a posse of citizens. The sheriff sent Deputies John Van Eaton and Joseph Staples and Constable George Ranney south toward Diamond Springs, while he and eight citizens rode up to Bullion Bend, hoping to cut the robbers' trail. Van Eaton, Staples, and Ranney rode four miles over the hill to Diamond Springs and then east for ten miles, arriving at Pleasant Valley at dawn. Dismounting, they searched the road for hoofprints and found that six riders had passed going south toward the Somerset House, five miles distant.

The Somerset House, scene of the gun battle between lawmen and Captain
Ingram's guerrillas. Courtesy California State Library.

A few weeks earlier Van Eaton, Staples, and Undersheriff Jim
Hume had engaged in a shoot-out with the Ike McCollum gang, and
Van Eaton had been wounded. The deputy had not yet fully recovered, and he told his companions that he did not feel able to stand a
long ride. It was decided that Staples and Ranney would stick to the
trail, and Van Eaton would ride to the holdup scene and notify Sheriff
Rogers.

Meanwhile, the guerrillas, upon arriving at the Somerset House,
again met Maria Reynolds, who happened to be up early. They told
her that they had met friends from the Reese River and had been
advised that the diggings were played out and now were returning
home. Captain Ingram asked for breakfast for his men, and Mrs.
Reynolds went inside to wake up the lady of the house, Mrs. Davis.
The guerrillas put their horses up in the stable, where they hid one
silver bar, and then walked down to the spring to wash. Baker and
Clendenning walked up the road for a little pistol practice, firing off
ten or fifteen shots, and the rest returned to the hotel. While Mrs.
Reynolds and Mrs. Davis prepared breakfast in the kitchen, Ingram,
Poole, and Glasby went to sleep in a ground-floor bedroom on the

east side of the house, leaving Clendenning's shotgun leaning against the front wall.

An hour later Bouldware rushed into the room and cried, "Get up! Someone is after us!"

Staples and Ranney had just dismounted in front of the house and hitched their horses to a tree. Four roads joined together at Somerset, and the officers were checking the ground for the robbers' tracks when Ranney spotted the shotgun standing on the porch. Staples walked into the kitchen and asked the two women if any strangers had passed by, and after receiving an affirmative reply, he picked up the shotgun and saw that it was loaded. At the same time Ranney walked to the east bedroom and stepped into the doorway. Captain Ingram was reclining on a lounge, and Poole and Glasby were on the bed. Bouldware was standing in the doorway of an adjoining room, while Baker and Clendenning were still a short distance down the road.

The guerrillas in the room were as surprised as Ranney, for he had appeared almost immediately after Bouldware had sounded the warning, and all instinctively dropped their hands to their gun butts. The constable knew instantly that one false move would mean his life, and he threw the outlaws off guard by greeting them pleasantly: "Good morning. Have you heard or seen any horsemen pass last night?"

His answer was a gruff "No," and Ranney quickly ducked out of the room. He met Staples coming down the porch, cocking the shotgun. Ranney put his hand on the deputy's shoulder and said in a low tone, "We are right upon them. Hold on!"

But Staples ignored Ranney and, brushing past him, continued on toward the robbers' lair. During the fight with the McCollum gang, Staples's horse had been spooked by the gunfire and had galloped off with him. Later, in a Placerville saloon, the deputy had overheard a saloon lounger remark, "Staples took damned good care to keep out of danger!"

Angered, Staples had vowed, "The next time I go I'll be brought back dead or I'll bring back my man!"

Now the officer put words into action and leaped inside the room, yelling, "You are my prisoners. Surrender!"

Captain Ingram started to draw his pistols, but Staples covered him with the shotgun, and the guerrilla leader put up his hands. Then Poole and Glasby, on the bed directly in front of Staples, pulled

CONFEDERATE GUERRILLAS IN CALIFORNIA

their guns, and the deputy swung his shotgun toward them. At that instant Captain Ingram jerked both six-guns and opened fire, as did Glasby and Bouldware. One ball sliced through Staples's body at the left nipple, and another entered his right side, passed around the breastbone, and lodged in his left side. Staples fired once with the shotgun, and Tom Poole clapped his hands to his face and collapsed on the bed, his left cheek shot away.

Ranney was at Staples's side when the deputy staggered back out the door and fell dead on the porch. A veritable hail of lead was now pouring out the door at the two officers, and Ranney backed down the steps, fired twice, and then turned to run. A ball slammed into his side, coming to rest in the muscles of his lower back. Ranney bolted for cover behind a nearby pine tree, while the guerrillas sprang out of the room, six-guns spitting fire. They spread out and advanced on Ranney, driving him from the tree. The constable made a wild dash toward an outbuilding fifty yards away, turning sideways and shooting as he ran. He took cover behind the building, but the guerrillas kept after him, and Ranney fled up a ravine amidst a rain of bullets. A pistol ball plowed into his right side and exited through his breast, and blood gushed from his mouth, choking him. Ranney dropped, gasping for breath, and told the advancing guerillas, "I'm killed. Don't fire any more."

Ingram and his men quickly surrounded the fallen officer.

"How in hell did you find us so soon?" asked one, incredulously.

"Do you suppose a Confederate officer is going to surrender to a damned Yankee?" Captain Ingram bellowed. "We are Missouri bushwhackers!"

Al Glasby asked Ranney if he had any money and took three twenty-dollar gold pieces from the wounded constable, who managed to hobble back to the Somerset House, followed by the guerrillas. Bleeding profusely, Ranney sank into a chair. George Baker put his six-shooter against his head and snarled, "God damn you, you have killed Poole! I'll blow your brains out!"

At that, Maria Reynolds ran forward, shoving two of the outlaws aside, and, in a voice filled with scorn, cried, "Ain't you ashamed! Shooting a dead man!"

Baker lowered his pistol, evidently believing that Ranney was too far gone to offer any more fight. Then Baker, Glasby, and another guerrilla walked over to Staples's body and one remarked, "There's one Union officer less."

They kicked the corpse and rolled it over with their feet.

"Maybe he has some money about him," said another, searching the body and taking Staples's pistol and watch.

Ingram and his men mounted up to leave. Tom Poole staggered out of the room, badly wounded, and begged them to take him away. Ingram refused and told Poole that they would get a buggy at Fiddletown and return for him. He sent Glasby into the house after Poole's pistols. Glasby handed them to Ingram, and the guerrillas galloped off, leaving Poole, as the *San Francisco Alta* reported, "to test the quality of hemp." [14]

Meanwhile, Sheriff Rogers had arrested two strangers, Thomas Finney and William Belcher, at Sportsman's Hall, on the Placerville road. Both were entirely innocent, but Ned Blair mistakenly identified them as two of the robbers. When Deputy Van Eaton arrived, bringing news that the bandits' trail had been found, Sheriff Rogers lingered at the Hall with his posse and the prisoners, an act for which he later came under harsh public criticism. Van Eaton finally managed to convince the sheriff that the real robbers were heading toward the Somerset House, but by the time Rogers and his posse arrived there it was noon and the guerrillas had a six-hour head start.

Word of the shoot-out had also been sent to Undersheriff Jim Hume in Placerville, who had been out of the county on official business and had just returned to town. He reached the Somerset House shortly after Rogers's posse, bringing with him Dr. H. W. A. Worthen. Hume had been a close friend of Joe Staples, and when he saw the dead body of the deputy he was frantic with grief and rage and swore that he would capture the men responsible. Constable Ranney was half dead, but Dr. Worthen administered to his wounds and saved his life. Sheriff Rogers placed Tom Poole under arrest. Poole told Rogers that he was the former sheriff of Monterey County and denied any knowledge of the holdup, claiming that he had met the others that morning at the house. Poole was taken to the Placerville jail, where he quickly recovered from his wound. [15]

Sheriff Rogers, Undersheriff Hume, and their posse started in pursuit of the outlaws, who had left the road and struck south across the mountainous country between the Cosumnes and Mokelumne rivers. While crossing the mountain ridges Ingram and his men could look back and see the posse on their trail. They continued south for two days, riding slowly, and crossed the North Fork of the Mokelumne River into Calaveras County, where Rogers and Hume lost their trail near West Point. Unaware that they were just a few miles behind the guerrillas, Rogers and Hume gave up the hunt and returned to Placerville.

Captain Ingram and his men rode south from West Point for several miles, and at dusk on July 2 they climbed a craggy mountain on the South Fork of the Mokelumne, near Railroad Flat. The exhausted outlaws picketed their horses near the summit, posted a guard, and fell asleep. At midnight they were jarred awake by a shout from the lookout. A party of horsemen was riding up the mountainside in the direction of their camp. Certain that it was the posse, Ingram and his followers rushed about in wild, madcap confusion, grabbing weapons, loot, and supplies. Some of the guerrillas wanted to stand and fight, but their captain overruled them. Thinking that they had no time to saddle their horses, the outlaws fled on foot down the other side of the mountain, leaving behind their mounts, blankets, saddles, and one bar of bullion. The intruders were not lawmen, but a gang of horsethieves who had stolen a dozen horses nearby and was headed toward the same hideout!

Captain Ingram's band struck out on foot for the Valley, crossing the San Joaquin by ferry and forcing the ferryman to land them downriver from the wharf to avoid detection. They crossed Livermore Pass and finally arrived at Hodges's ranch a week later. Ingram hoped he would be able to get fresh horses and escape south to Cherry's Ranch, on the Kings River, in Fresno County, where they would be resupplied by sympathetic Copperheads.[16]

Back in Placerville Tom Poole made a full confession to Deputy Van Eaton, identifying his fellow guerrillas and revealing where the bullion was buried. He also told Van Eaton that the gang would most likely return to San José. Van Eaton and Jim Hume left immediately for San José, where they notified Sheriff Adams and began a quiet search for the outlaws. They learned that their quarry had been seen in town, but they were unable to find them and returned to Placerville.[17]

By now Captain Ingram had come up with a new scheme to finance his band. Through friends in San José he learned that the agent of the New Almaden Mines would pick up a large payroll in San José on the afternoon of July 15 and transport it to the mines on the evening stagecoach. On the evening of July 14, Ingram, Baker, Clendenning, Bouldware, and Glasby showed up at the ranch house of Edward Hill, on the Almaden road, a mile and a half from town.

They told Hill that they were looking for friends that they expected to pass by on the road and asked him to put them up for the night. Hill led them to an empty building on his ranch, where the five Confederates remained until morning. They loitered about all of the next day, causing Hill to become increasingly suspicious. That afternoon the guerrillas carelessly told the rancher of their plan to steal the payroll. Making the excuse that he had to water his stock, Hill managed to slip away and inform a neighbor, who quickly took word to Sheriff Adams.

Adams raised a posse that included Deputy Sheriffs J. M. Brownlee, G. W. Reynolds, and Fred Morris, City Marshal J. C. Potter, Constable Robert Scott, A. Bowman, and three other citizens. Armed with six-shooters and shotguns, the posse left town at six o'clock and reached Hill's place just at sunset. The guerrillas' lair was a small whitewashed house, set well back from the road and surrounded by dense thickets and clusters of willow trees. After his men had encircled the house, Sheriff Adams called, "Come out and deliver yourselves up!"

Without hesitation, the Confederates sprang outside, each with two blazing six-shooters in his hands. The posse closed in on the outlaws, firing as they went. Forty shots were exchanged at close range. Deputy Sheriff Brownlee dropped with two bullets in his leg. John Clendenning fired twice point-blank at Sheriff Adams. One ball slammed into a watch in the sheriff's vest pocket and glanced off, cutting flesh and bruising his rib. He staggered, but swung up his shotgun toward Clendenning, who was now running at top speed for a nearby fence. The sheriff's shotgun roared, and Clendenning reeled, his back riddled with buckshot. The outlaw kept on, vaulted the fence, and disappeared into the willows.

Bowman fired a blast from his shotgun at Al Glasby. Several other possemen concentrated their fire on the young guerrilla, who ran backwards trying to fire. One of his pistols jammed, and the other had its butt shot off. Glasby, his clothing pierced by seven bullets, threw up his hands and surrendered.

John Bouldware traded fire with Bowman and Deputy Sheriff Reynolds, who pursued the outlaw across an open field below the house. The two possemen closed on Bouldware, pistols barking, and the bandit fired back as he ran. A high fence stood at the west end of the field and beyond it the woods. As Bouldware raced up to the

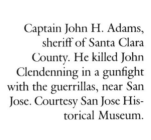

Captain John H. Adams, sheriff of Santa Clara County. He killed John Clendenning in a gunfight with the guerrillas, near San Jose. Courtesy San Jose Historical Museum.

fence, Bowman stopped, shoved his six-gun into his belt, and took dead aim with his double-barreled shotgun.

"When he climbs that fence I'll stop him on one side or the other!" Bowman told Reynolds.

Bouldware mounted the fence and turned to give his pursuers another shot. As he did so his form came into full view, silhouetted against the setting sun, and Bowman squeezed the trigger. His shotgun was loaded with pistol balls, and Bouldware let out a scream and dropped over the opposite side of the fence. Bowman and Reynolds vaulted the fence to find Bouldware sprawled on the ground, writhing in agony. Plucky to the last, the carpenter-turned-guerrilla raised his pistols and blazed away at the two possemen. They leaped forward and tried to wrestle the guns from him, but Bouldware continued to struggle. Bowman put his revolver up to the outlaw's ear and barked, "Give up your pistols or I'll blow your brains out!"

Bouldware relaxed his grip, and the officers snatched the guns away and then examined his wounds. He was shot in both hands, and another ball had entered his right side and passed out near the heart. Bouldware was dead in half an hour.

Captain Ingram and George Baker had escaped into the thickets. Adams's posse returned to San José with Glasby and Bouldware's corpse. Adams told Undersheriff Hall about the fight and instructed him to ride out to Hill's place and look for Clendenning, who the sheriff believed was badly wounded. At one A.M. Hall found Clendenning lying in the willow thicket in a dying condition. Hall took from the outlaw two pistols, a bag of stolen gold dust, and Deputy Staples's watch and then took him to the San José jail in a wagon. Later that morning, knowing that he had only a few hours to live, he made a clean breast of the affair, telling all he knew about Ingram's band. Clendenning was visited by several Copperhead friends who became uneasy when they learned that he had confessed. One said to him in a low voice, "Why don't you die like a man, and not make a calf of yourself?"[18]

Clendenning breathed his last at ten o'clock. Al Glasby was badly frightened, and he, too, confessed, implicating Preston Hodges and the other members of the gang. He was taken to Placerville, where he testified before the grand jury, which returned indictments against the entire band, charging them with being accessories to the murder of Joe Staples. On July 29, Jim Hume and John Van Eaton arrived in San José, carrying arrest warrants for the Confederates. With the assistance of Sheriff Adams and his deputies and backed by four companies of infantry, they arrested Preston Hodges, John Ingram, Wallace Clendenning, George Cross, Henry Jarboe, Joseph Gamble, John Gately, John Robinson, and the Frear brothers. Hume, Van Eaton, and Undersheriff Hall took the prisoners by riverboat to Sacramento and then overland to Placerville, where they joined Poole and Glasby in jail.[19]

Undersheriff Hall returned to Santa Clara County to hunt for Jim Grant, who had embarked on guerrilla raids of his own. On July 6, Grant and Washington Jordan had stopped the Los Angeles–bound stage on the Salinas Plain, twenty-two miles south of San Juan Bautista, relieved its passengers of sixty dollars, and escaped. Grant made his headquarters at the ranch of R. F. Hall, a Copperhead who lived on the Salinas River, fifteen miles south of San Juan. He was a prosperous, well-educated stockman with several hundred head of cattle, but bore a bad reputation among his neighbors, who called him "Thief" Hall.[20]

Jim Grant was not satisfied with the poor haul from his first holdup. He borrowed a hatchet and another gun from Hall and, assisted by Jordan, stopped the northbound stage at the same spot three days later. This time the coach held eight men and one woman. Grant pulled open the side curtain and said, "Come out with your money, men."

One passenger forked over $10, but the rest hid their valuables behind the seats and told him they had no money. Grant ordered a man named Goldstein out of the coach and searched his pockets, finding only $2.50 in silver.

"You have no business to travel on this road without more money," Grant complained.

The Confederate robbers broke open the Wells Fargo box with the hatchet and then handed it back to the driver, who asked if they had found any money in it.

"Not a damned cent!" Grant snapped.

By way of condolence, the driver offered the bandits a drink of whiskey from his flask, which both accepted. Then Grant waved his six-gun at the stage.

"Boys, you can go ahead now. We won't trouble you any more. It don't pay us to come here—you carry too poor a crowd."[21]

On August 5, Grant and Jordan tried a new road, halting the Visalia stage, near Pacheco Pass, and taking $113 from the passengers. Undersheriff Hall investigated the robbery, which, unlike the previous two, had occurred in his bailiwick. Although the bandits had been masked, he was certain that Jim Grant had had a hand in the job. Hall remembered that Grant and Cross had quarreled over Katie Kincade, and he learned that she lived with her family near Forbes Mill, in Los Gatos. The undersheriff suspected that Grant would try to visit Katie, who was, as Hall described her, "pretty as a picture, with a slight figure, skin like milk, and great grey eyes—just the sort of girl to devour chalk and poetry, and dote on brigands."[22]

Hall, disguised as a German laborer, obtained work at the Kincade farm, and it was not long before he found what he was looking for. He later recalled, "I saw Katie under an old apple tree with a copy of Byron's *Corsair* in her hand, pretending to read, for she didn't turn a leaf, and by and by went into the house, leaving the book on the grass." Hall picked up the book, and inside was a letter from Jim Grant, saying that he would visit her in a few days and would stay overnight with a neighbor named Leigh. Hall described the rest of the letter as "a lot more lovers' nonsense that robbers know how to use as well as anybody else, with the assurance that she should yet have the finest dresses and diamonds of any woman in the land."[23]

The Leigh ranch was located in a canyon at the head of Portentia Creek, a spot the *Alta* called "one of the most notorious rendezvous of thieves and murderers in California." Hall; San José City Marshal Potter; and a posseman, John Ward, hid in the brush and watched the roads to Forbes Mill for two days and nights. On the night of August 8, Jim Grant rode up, spent the evening with Katie, and at midnight went to the Leigh ranch to sleep. Hall, Potter, and Ward surrounded the ranch house and at daybreak silently crept into Grant's bedroom. The outlaw was sound asleep. Hall rested his shotgun against the wall and pinioned Grant's arms, and his companions snatched two pistols and a Bowie knife from underneath his pillow. Then Grant was ordered to dress, and his hands were ironed in front of him.

As they were preparing to leave, Jim Grant grabbed the unattended shotgun and bolted out of the bedroom. Hall snatched another shotgun from one of his possemen and jumped after the escaping outlaw. The house had a long inner hallway with an outside door at one end. As Grant fled down the hall, he cocked the shotgun in his manacled hands and pointed it back over his shoulder at Hall. Three times Hall knocked the muzzle of the weapon into the air, and as Grant reached the door the undersheriff fired both barrels of his shotgun simultaneously. Grant dropped instantly, his lower back filled with buckshot.

The officers loaded their prisoner into a buggy and took him to a doctor in San José. At first his wounds were thought to be fatal, but the outlaw began to recover, and Katie Kincade visited him in the San José jail. Said Undersheriff Hall, "She would have married him, sick and in prison, had not the jailer and I prevented her." In a month Grant had healed almost completely and was sent to Placerville to join his former comrades.[24]

On August 19, Sheriff Adams and Undersheriff Hall arrested R. F. Hall at his ranch on the Salinas River on a charge of harboring Grant and Jordan. He readily admitted his guilt, but his wife pleaded with Adams: "Suppose you, Mr. Sheriff, knew of a band of two hundred and fifty desperate men, bound together by the most solemn oaths, sworn to take the life of any person who should disclose their purposes, or betray any of their number into the hands of the officers of the law; and suppose two of their number should seek the shelter of

Jim Grant, described by the *Sacramento Union* as "about as thorough a scoundrel as ever stretched hemp." Courtesy San Jose Historical Museum.

your roof, as did those men who robbed the stages. What would you do in the premises?"[25]

Unimpressed, the officers lodged Hall in jail at Monterey, but the charges against the rancher were soon dismissed. Undersheriff Hall arrested Jim Wilson at the Seven Mile House on the Monterey road, and on September 3 he captured Washington Jordan in a billiard saloon at Half Moon Bay. Now each member of the band had been captured or killed, with the exception of Captain Ingram and George Baker, who were believed to have fled to Missouri. Neither was ever captured.[26]

Tom Poole's trial for murder began in Placerville on August 24, less than two months after the crime. Although he had not pulled the trigger, by law he was a principal in Staples's murder and equally at fault. Al Glasby turned state's evidence and testified against his fellow guerrilla. The trial lasted just three days, and the jury deliberated only fifteen minutes before returning a verdict of guilty. Poole was sentenced to be hanged in October, but his execution was delayed while his attorneys brought an appeal to the California Supreme Court.[27]

Preston Hodges was the next to go on trial. Al Glasby and Jim Wilson testified against him in return for their freedom. Hodges was charged with being an accessory to the murder of Staples, as he had harbored the band and provided them with assistance. He was convicted of second-degree murder and on September 10 was sentenced to twenty years in San Quentin. Hodges's case was also appealed to the Supreme Court, and the proceedings against him and the rest of the band dragged on for a year. They were granted a change of venue to Sacramento County. The Supreme Court then threw out Hodges's conviction on the grounds that he should have been tried in Santa Clara County, where his acts as an accessory had taken place, and not in El Dorado County, where the murder had occurred. Pursuant to this ruling, Hodges and the rest were sent to San José, where in March, 1865, the grand jury indicted Hodges for murder and treason and also found treason indictments against Jim Grant, Robinson, and Wilson. Grant was instead convicted of grand larceny and on April 3 entered San Quentin to serve a two-year sentence. Washington Jordan, Wallace Clendenning, John Ingram, and Cross, Gamble, and Gately were all released when the district attorney decided that he lacked sufficient evidence to convict them.[28]

Meanwhile the Supreme Court had upheld Tom Poole's conviction. The likeable rogue made many friends while in the Placerville jail, and they began working to secure a pardon from Governor Frederick Low. Nonetheless, his execution date was set for September 29, 1865. Ten days before the scheduled hanging Poole's comrades who were still in jail in San José were all set free. They had been charged in state court with treason, a federal crime; only a federal court had jurisdiction over treason. The remaining charges of murder were also dismissed. District Attorney F. E. Spencer reported that the evidence against them "was of a vague and untenable nature," and he dropped the charges "rather than subject the county to the expense of a bootless trial."[29]

As the date for Tom Poole's execution approached, a flurry of letters on his behalf was sent to Governor Low. Many prominent citizens of Monterey and El Dorado counties requested clemency, including Sheriff Rogers, Jim Hume, John Van Eaton, and seven members of the jury that convicted him. Former Judge James Johnson, a friend of Poole's, pleaded with the governor: "Do not the hundreds of thousands of southern men slain sufficiently atone for the southern rebellion? Has not enough blood been shed? . . . Shall Poole be executed and Lee, Bragg, and Joe Johnston go at large?"[30]

Governor Low was unmoved. Of the six men involved in the killing of Joe Staples, two had been shot to death, two had fled the state, and one had turned state's evidence, leaving Poole alone to atone for the deputy's murder. Perhaps, too, the governor considered Poole's action when another prisoner had been granted a reprieve seven years earlier.

On September 29, five months after Appomattox, Poole calmly ascended the Placerville gallows. Smiling and cordial, he shook hands with Sheriff Rogers and his deputies and then took his place on the scaffold. He stood perfectly composed while the black cap was placed over his head and his arms and legs secured with straps. Precisely at noon Tom Poole plunged through the trap, the fall breaking his neck. In seconds he was dead.[31]

Poole had never expected that he would be treated as a common criminal. "We did not think of being arrested by the civil authorities," he had once said. "We expected it would be a regular fight—the same as we had back in the Atlantic States, and if we were taken we would be treated as prisoners of war."[32]

In more ways than one, fate had dealt an ironic hand to the last of Captain Ingram's Partisan Rangers.

CHAPTER 7

The Gentleman Bandit: Bill Miner

BILL Miner was a western original. He was a gentleman bandit who, according to the Pinkertons, coined the command "Hands up!" and robbed trains and stagecoaches in five states and Canada during a criminal career that spanned almost fifty years, from 1865 to 1913, making him one of the last of the frontier outlaws. A newspaper reporter who had once met Miner described him as a "handsome and graceful fellow, fluent of tongue and captivating in style." He was a ladies' man with a penchant for gold watches and large diamonds, but underneath his expensive and fashionable clothes were numerous crude prison tattoos typical of an old convict who had spent most of his adult life behind bars.[1]

Bill Miner's career as a train robber in the Pacific Northwest is well documented and was dramatized in a charming 1983 film, *The Grey Fox*. Little, however, has been written about his early days of banditry and jailbreaking in California, and much of what has appeared in print has been false or inaccurate. Miner loved to spin tall tales and fed interviewers and reporters wild but fictional accounts of his adventures. As an old man, serving a prison term for train robbery in Georgia, he dictated a thirty-thousand-word manuscript of his life and adventures to a guard. This account has also been the source of much misinformation.

Miner claimed to have been born in 1847, running away to Texas at the age of thirteen. In 1863, Bill said, he was with General George Wright, of the Department of the Pacific, in San Diego, California, when the general offered him $100 to ride through hostile Apache country to deliver a message to a fort on the Gila River. He rode all night, stopping briefly for rest at the Tejon Ranch, near Salt Lake. He then swam his horse across the Colorado to the fort and returned to San Diego the next morning. Cashing in on the notoriety he earned from this adventure, Miner claimed he began a Pony Express—

style mail service, but quickly squandered all the money he earned and soon turned to a life of crime.[2]

There are a few things wrong with Bill's story. There were no Apache Indians in California. Rancho El Tejon is in the Tehachapi Mountains, over a hundred miles north of San Diego, far from his supposed route. The only "Salt Lake" in Southern California is the Salton Sea, which did not exist until 1905. The Gila River is 350 miles round trip from San Diego, and no horse could possibly make this distance in one day. Over the years this tale has been repeated by a number of writers, but it is most improbable, to say the least.

Bill Miner's saga needs no such embellishment. With a little sleuthing in old newspapers and court records, his story has emerged, true and unvarnished. He was born in Clinton, Michigan, in 1846. His father's name is unknown, but his mother was Harriet J. Miner. Bill had an older brother who died in Tennessee while serving in the U.S. Army during the Civil War. He also had several sisters. One, Mary Jane, four years his senior, married a mine owner named Wellman and settled in Colorado Springs, Colorado. Bill's father died when he was a boy, and in 1860 he and his mother settled in Yankee Jim's, a small gold camp in Placer County. The youth evidently received a decent schooling, for numerous letters that he wrote while in San Quentin and preserved in the California State Archives show him to have been both intelligent and literate.

At Yankee Jim's, Bill worked as a common laborer but soon tired of it. On April 26, 1864, he enlisted as a private in the California Cavalry, Second Regiment, Company L, and was stationed at Camp Union, just outside Sacramento. He deserted on July 22, 1864. According to C. A. Tweed, the Placer County deputy district attorney who prosecuted Bill for his first offense, young Miner "bore an exemplary character at Yankee Jim's" and was not a criminal until "he made the acquaintance of a woman of bad character" and had "fallen under her influence."[3]

On December 28, 1865, the nineteen-year-old Miner boarded a westbound train on the recently constructed Central Pacific Railroad, in Colfax, eight miles from Yankee Jim's. He rode down to Newcastle and walked to A. H. Smith's livery stable, where he hired a mare, telling Smith he wanted to make a short trip to Auburn, and promised to return soon. Bill rode the three miles to Auburn and at 8:30 that evening entered Houser's Clothing Store on Main Street. In what

Young Bill Miner in a rare
photograph, 1864. Courtesy
San Jose Historical Museum.

was to become a habit over the years, he picked out an extremely
expensive suit, valued at ninety dollars, and told the clerk to wrap it
up. Then Bill's sense of humor took over. He explained that he had
no money, but could obtain some from Mr. Dickerson, the Placer
County treasurer, who lived a short distance up the street. The unsuspecting clerk agreed to accompany Miner to Dickerson's house.
They hadn't gone far when Miner drew a revolver on the clerk.

"I'm on the rob," Bill declared. "Come out with your money."

The clerk had no cash, so Miner relieved him of a $50 watch and
then warned, "Stand where you are for twenty minutes or you'll lose
the top of your head."[4]

The youthful bandit mounted up and leisurely rode out of town,
not bothering to take back his rented horse. He returned to Yankee
Jim's unsuspected, and a week later, on January 4, 1866, he stole a bay
horse worth seventy-five dollars from John Elson, in Forest Hill, two
miles east of Bill's home. Now well-mounted and gorgeously attired,
young Bill Miner set off to find his fortune in that city of sin and
excitement, San Francisco. Enroute he met a fifteen-year-old youth
from Petaluma, John Sinclair, who was also anxious for high adventure. Together they continued on to the city, where they disposed of

the horses, but soon ran out of money. On January 19 the boys took the ferry to Oakland and rented two more horses and riding rigs, assuring the livery man that they would come back shortly. Instead they rode east into San Joaquin County. On January 22 they encountered a ranch hand named Porter at Johnson's Ferry, on the San Joaquin River, south of Stockton. Porter was driving a wagon, heading toward town, when Miner and Sinclair covered him with pistols and demanded his money. Porter told them that he had none.

"You're a damned liar," Miner snapped. "Shell out."

Porter shelled out to the tune of eighty dollars, telling them that it was all the money he had. He showed the robbers his wornout boots with the toes protruding and asked to be allowed to keep enough money for a new pair. Miner magnanimously handed back ten dollars and allowed Porter to drive on. He reached town that evening and reported the holdup to Officer Jerome Myers and Deputy Sheriff Joe Long. Making a quick investigation, the officers learned that two boys matching the robbers' descriptions had been seen on the road to Woodbridge, fifteen miles north. Myers and Long left Stockton at eleven o'clock, but the roads were flooded, and they didn't reach Woodbridge until daylight. They found the young desperadoes asleep in a hotel and arrested them without trouble, relieving each of them of a Colt navy revolver and a Bowie knife. The boys were crestfallen, and Miner indignantly told his captors, "You fellows think you've done a smart thing, arresting us while we were asleep. If you had met us on the road and attempted to arrest us, you wouldn't have found yourselves quite so smart."[5]

Bill Miner and his partner were lodged in the county jail in Stockton to await trial. They occupied the same cell, and Miner immediately began plotting to escape. He and Sinclair removed two bolts from their cell window and used them to gouge a hole in the wall. Gradually they burrowed deeper, removing the bricks and hiding some under their beds. Other pieces of brick and mortar were placed in their toilet buckets and carried out and emptied each morning by a friendly trusty. In the daytime the hole was covered by a box. The jail wall was well constructed, however, and the prisoners were halted by an iron plate inside the wall. Desperate, Miner landed on a new plan. On the night of February 21 he and Sinclair knocked over one of their buckets and yelled loudly for Jailer Conklin to clean up the mess. Conklin, his suspicions aroused, refused to enter the cell. In the morning, with Sheriff Hook and Deputy Long, he searched the cell and found the hole, as well as a slungshot made of a piece of brick bound up in the end of a torn towel. Bill and his friend had intended to lure the jailer into the cell, fell him with the slungshot, and make their escape. Conklin placed the pair in separate cells and put them under constant watch.[6]

A month later Miner and Sinclair were brought to trial. Each was defended by J. H. Budd, an expert criminal attorney. They were convicted and sentenced to three years apiece, but neither seemed fazed by the prospect of a term in state prison. The *Stockton Daily Independent* chronicled their departure from town:

> John Sinclair and William Miner were taken off, in charge of Deputy Sheriff J. M. Long, on the steamer *Julia* yesterday, en route for San Quentin to serve a term of three years for highway robbery. The prisoners were chained together, and stood on the upper deck until the steamer left the wharf. They were jovial and appeared unconcerned. When the steamer moved off they threw apples into the crowd on the wharf, and waved their pocket handkerchiefs, as if bidding adieu to friends. A more thorough evidence of perverted nature we never saw.[7]

Bill Miner entered San Quentin for the first time on April 5, 1866. It was to be his home for much of the next thirty-five years. On March 7, while he had been in the Stockton jail, the Placer County grand jury had indicted him on two counts of grand larceny for stealing the horses at Newcastle and Forest Hill. On June 7, Judge Fellows, of the Placer County Court, ordered that Miner be sent to Auburn for trial. The youth pleaded guilty and was sentenced to one year for each count. For some reason Bill was not charged with robbing Houser's Store. He reentered San Quentin on July 3 as convict no. 3313 with a new term of five years.[8]

Conditions in the prison were nothing short of barbaric. Typical offenses by convicts included "insolence and disobedience," refusing to work, "idling time away," stealing, gambling, and impertinence. Punishments ranged from loss of credits for good behavior to flogging, imprisonment in the dungeon, and "showering," a form of water torture in which a high pressure hose was directed onto the prisoner's face. Faced with such punishments, Bill Miner was a model prisoner, served his time uneventfully, and was released on July 12, 1870.

Bill lost no time in looking up an old pal from San Quentin, "Alkali Jim" Harrington, who was living with a Mexican woman at

Mayfield (now part of Palo Alto). Brother of a wealthy Cincinnati banker, Alkali Jim was notorious in San Francisco as a Barbary Coast ranger. It was not long before the crooked duo became thorns in the sides of all the officers between San Francisco and San José, who suspected them of assorted holdups and burglaries.

But Bill Miner was interested in bigger game, and in January, 1871, he began planning to stop one of the stagecoaches that carried gold bullion from the mines to Stockton. He and Alkali Jim burglarized Hickman's hardware store, in Stockton, and stole two double-barreled shotguns, two six-shooters, one seven-shooter, and a pair of derringers. Then they paid a visit to a friend, Charlie Cooper, who was at work strapping rails on the Stockton and Copperopolis Railroad, and persuaded him to join them. Cooper, who had lately fallen into bad company, was a well-educated young man from a good family back East. He drew his pay and the trio set off on foot for Mokelumne Hill. They loitered about San Andreas for several days without attracting the attention of her ever-vigilant sheriff, Ben Thorn. Miner watched the outgoing stages and spent the nights with his partners in a deserted cabin just outside town.

Early in the morning of January 23 they walked to the crossing at Murray Creek, on the road to Stockton, a mile and a half from San Andreas. At five o'clock the down stage hove into sight, with Driver William Cutler at the ribbons. Bill Miner stepped into the road, while his companions remained concealed in the bush.

"Hello, stranger. Stop a minute," Miner called.

"Do you want a ride?" Cutler asked, to which Bill answered in the affirmative.

"Just unbuckle those straps and jump in," the driver said.

Miner began fumbling with the leather curtain on the stage door, and Cutler, growing impatient, asked if he was ready.

"No, not quite yet," Bill replied. "You had better not go any farther. You better stop here a little longer."

Cutler suddenly discovered Cooper and Alkali Jim standing in front of the team, shotguns pointed at his head.

"Now, gentlemen, you have got me," Cutler gulped. "You better drop those guns, as there are no passengers."

They lowered the shotguns, and Miner drew a pistol and hatchet and demanded the Wells Fargo box, which Cutler pulled out and tossed to the ground. Miner went to work on it with the hatchet, but the box would not open. Then Bill pointed to Cutler's boots and demanded, "Haul 'em off. One of my boys out here wants a pair of boots."

"Look here, gentlemen. This is pretty rough, to make a fellow take off his boots and drive all the way barefooted," Cutler complained, but he handed them over.

Alkali Jim tried the boots on, but they did not fit, and he passed them back.

"What else have you got about you?" Bill asked, and the hapless driver handed over a five-dollar gold piece.

"Have you got a watch?" Miner asked.

"Yes."

"Then come out."

"Look here, boys. Take my coat, take anything, but don't take my watch. It is a keepsake from my mother, who is dead."

"If that is so," Cooper broke in, "keep the watch. I respect a keepsake from a dead mother."

Miner waved the coach on, and as it rolled down the road, Cutler yelled back, "I wish I had a bottle of cocktails! I'd like to treat you fellows!"

Alkali Jim picked up the hatchet, and in a few minutes the strongbox door flew off. After removing $2600 in coin and gold dust, they walked north to Mokelumne Hill, crossed over the hills to Jackson, and sank the shotguns in a creek. They continued on to Ione, hid the loot under a shed, and took a room in the hotel for the night.

This had been Bill Miner's first stage robbery, and he had not worn a mask. Sheriff Ben Thorn sent descriptions over the wire to all police and sheriffs, and San Francisco Chief of Police Patrick Crowley recognized Bill Miner and Alkali Jim. Crowley sent several of his detectives who knew the bandits by sight to Stockton to assist in the hunt.

The next morning after the robbery the three highwaymen walked to Brighton and boarded the southbound train, getting off fourteen miles from Stockton. They continued on foot, stopping at the outskirts of town. First Cooper strolled in and brought back some food; then Miner went in and bought a new suit of clothes, his first priority after making a good haul. Finally Alkali Jim started downtown, but he spotted two San Francisco police detectives and quickly returned to his comrades. Jim gave Cooper two dollars and, since he was unknown to the police, instructed him to go into town to buy a shirt. Cooper did so, but when he returned Alkali Jim, Miner, and

Alkali Jim Harrington, stage
robber and jail breaker.
Courtesy San Jose Historical
Museum.

the gold dust were gone. The dejected Cooper hunted in vain for the pair and then boarded the train for San Francisco with just eighty dollars in his pockets.[9]

Bill and Alkali Jim had already arrived in the city. They rented a room and sold some of the gold dust, but believing San Francisco to be too hot for them, they departed for San José. At six o'clock in the morning, January 27, San José Policeman Mitch Bellew came on duty at the police office and was notified by the night watch officer that he had seen "two state prison birds prowling around" during the night. He identified them as Miner and Alkali Jim, whom Bellew knew well and suspected of having burglarized several homes in San José a few weeks earlier. Bellew set out to find them and an hour later spotted the pair near a box factory, not far from the San Pedro train depot.

"Stop!" the officer ordered, but the outlaws went for their guns. Alkali Jim drew a derringer, and Miner pulled a heavy navy revolver. Bellew's holster had swung behind him on his gunbelt, and he fumbled frantically for the weapon while Miner took careful aim at him.

Just as the officer got his pistol out, Bill Miner pulled the trigger. But fortune favored Bellew, for Miner's six-gun misfired. At the same instant Alkali Jim tried to fire his derringer, but the hammer would not fall, being only at half cock.

Bellew fired twice at Alkali Jim, who turned and fled. Miner leaped for cover behind a telegraph pole, and Bellew fired at his exposed shoulder. The bullet grazed Bill's coat, and he started running in the opposite direction. Both managed to make good their escape in dense morning fog.[10]

The outlaws returned to San Francisco, where Alkali Jim rented a fast livery team and drove back down to his girl's place, in Mayfield, intending to flee with her to Mexico the next morning. At the same time San Francisco police picked up Charlie Cooper, who readily admitted his guilt and identified Miner and Harrington as his partners. Chief Crowley sent a wire to Redwood City to Sheriff Tom Lathrop, who had been hunting the pair for three days. Crowley instructed him to arrest Alkali Jim if he could. That night, January 31, Deputy Sheriffs Freeman and Whitlock and Constable Walker hauled Alkali Jim out of bed at the Mayfield house and relieved him of two derringers and an "Arkansas toothpick," a heavy knife with a razor-sharp, fourteen-inch blade. They turned him over to the San Francisco police.

The next day Captain Henry Ellis and three detectives broke into Miner's room in the southern part of the city and captured him. Bill tried to pull a gun, but the officers wrestled it away from him, and he joined his partners in the city prison.[11]

On February 7, Chief Crowley and several of his men took the prisoners to San Andreas. They stopped overnight in Stockton and were visited in the jail by Jerome Myers and Joe Long. Miner recognized them and joked good-naturedly about his arrest five years before. The following day, while en route to San Andreas, they stopped for a meal, and Miner slipped a steel table knife into his sleeve, but it was found when he was searched. Lodged in the Calaveras County jail to await the June term of court, Sheriff Thorn ironed Bill and Alkali Jim to their cell floors with chains that weighed forty pounds each.[12]

On March 5 the jailer, G. W. Smith, was aroused by an unusually loud noise from the prisoners and suspected it was a diversion for an escape attempt. His office was next to Alkali's cell, and Smith crept to the door and distinctly heard a file working on metal. He found that

Jim had completely cut through his irons with a smuggled case knife and was working on the bolt that secured Bill Miner's chain in the adjoining cell. Alkali Jim was secured with a new forty-pound chain, but he later managed to cut it nearly off with the bale from a water bucket. Commented the editor of the *Calaveras Chronicle*, "A forty pound steel chain ought to form an alkalimeter of sufficient capacity to test the strength of any alkali." Miner's partner, no doubt, was not amused.[13]

Charlie Cooper turned state's evidence to get revenge on his treacherous companions, who stood trial on June 22. Ben Thorn, rightly concerned that they might try to escape, kept them in irons in the courtroom. The trial lasted just four and a half hours, and both were sentenced to ten years in prison. They were taken to San Quentin, but their case was appealed to the California Supreme Court, which reversed the conviction on the grounds that they had been tried in chains, prejudicing the jury and depriving them of a fair trial. On February 9, 1872, they were returned to San Andreas for a new trial. Ben Thorn, always alert, searched the pair thoroughly and found a small, four-inch saw in the waistband of Harrington's trousers. Alkali Jim was a good actor and appeared more astonished than anyone else present.

"By God," he exclaimed. "Them chaps in San Quentin would play anything on a feller!"

Thorn, unamused, turned his attentions to Bill Miner and found another saw concealed in the sole of his boot.

They were retried and convicted on March 21. The wrathful judge sentenced each to thirteen years, not including the year they had already served. Thus by appealing their case they had lengthened their sentences by four years, a result that is not permitted in a modern court.[14]

A week later Bill Miner was returned to San Quentin as convict no. 5206. On May 7, 1874, he staged a fight with a fellow prisoner, John Wheelan, and attempted to escape. Wheelan received two days in the dungeon for this escapade, but Miner, the ringleader, was sentenced to twenty lashes, lost all his "coppers," or credits, and was thrown in the dungeon for nine days. The dungeon was a dismal hole, pitch dark, with no windows, no beds, and no ventilation. Prisoners slept on the stone floor and ate bread and water. Bill Miner, for the rest of his term, made no further attempts to escape. He did, on occasion, run afoul of the prison rules. On August 13, 1879, he was charged with beating a fellow convict and was sentenced by the state board of prison directors to twelve lashes.

During the 1870s prison reform was slowly accepted by San Quentin officials. The Goodwin Act of 1864 gave convicts time off their sentences for good behavior. Flogging was abandoned in 1880, and "showering" in 1882, although sentences in the dungeon remained common for another twenty years. Eventually Bill's credits were restored, and he was released on July 14, 1880, having served nine years.[15]

He took the train to Colorado Springs to visit his sister Mary Jane Wellman and may have worked for a time in Wellman's mines in Leadville. But Bill Miner was a dyed-in-the-wool bandit, and an honest life held no attraction for him. On the morning of September 22, 1880, a lone highwayman wearing a white mask and carrying a shotgun and revolver held up the Auburn–Forest Hill stage, eight miles above Auburn. He made two unsuccessful attempts to blow open the Wells Fargo box and then took $40 from the passengers. A few minutes later Congressman H. F. Page came along in a buggy and was forced to donate $280 and a valuable gold watch.

Wells Fargo's chief detective, James B. Hume, investigated this double holdup and found that the bandit had gone to Colfax that night and had paid a brakeman five dollars to stow him away in a boxcar. The robber got off at Reno and bought a ticket to Denver, where he pawned the watch for five dollars. Hume identified the bandit as Bill Miner, but subsequent events show that this was extremely unlikely.[16]

In the middle of September, 1880, Miner was aboard a train bound from Denver to Colorado Springs when he chanced to meet a young farmhand from West Liberty, Iowa, named Arthur Pond. They struck up a conversation, and young Pond was much taken with California Bill, as Miner was known in Colorado. Pond had arrived in the Rockies only a few months before and had been unable to find steady work. Bill's tales of quick riches and beautiful women were too much for him, and he readily agreed to become a stage robber. The two lost no time. They continued on to Canon City, got off the train, and beat their way to the South Arkansas. From there they walked over Marshall Pass, and on the night of September 23, 1880, they held up the Barlow & Sanderson Company buckboard, near Ohio City, getting fifty dollars and two mail pouches. This was Gunnison County's

Bill Miner at the time of his
arrest for stage robbery, 1881.
Courtesy Wells Fargo Bank
History Room.

first stage holdup. It was also just one day after the California robbery, making it impossible for Miner to have done both.[17]

On October 7 they stopped the Lake City stage at Slumgullion
Pass, but obtained very little booty. A week later, October 14, they
struck it rich when they halted a mail coach between Alamosa and
Del Norte, obtaining $4,000. Stage robberies were much less com-
mon in Colorado than in California and these three holdups, coming
so close together, created much excitement. Miner and his partner,
who now adopted the alias of Billy LeRoy, boarded a train in Fort
Garland and went east to Chicago. Miner, with his share of the loot,
filled two Saratoga trunks with clothes of the latest fashion and departed alone for Onondaga, a village in Michigan. Calling himself
William A. Morgan, he posed as a wealthy gentleman from California on a business trip.

Miner created a stir in society circles of the town. Handsome, well
dressed, and charming, with a ready wit and jocular nature, he bowled

over the ladies, filling them with stories of his gold mines and houses in Sacramento and San Francisco. One particularly smitten girl, a daughter of one of Onondaga's best families, became engaged to marry him. But Bill soon ran out of money, and late in February, 1881, he told his new friends that his aged mother was in feeble health and that he had to return to California to take her on an ocean voyage. Part of this was true enough. His mother was living in poverty on Ninth Street in Sacramento, while he squandered his ill-gotten gold in Michigan. On the eve of Bill's departure the prominent citizens of Onondaga gave him a banquet at which the mayor presided and acted as toastmaster. Bill promised his sweetheart that he would soon return.[18]

Miner went to Denver, where he learned that Billy LeRoy had been arrested at a ten-pin alley on January 14. He had been sentenced to ten years at the federal House of Corrections, in Detroit, Michigan, but on March 27, while en route and guarded by a deputy U.S. marshal, he jumped from the train and escaped, near Fort Hays, Kansas. LeRoy returned to Colorado, this time with his brother Silas Pond, and quickly hooked up with Bill Miner. By now state and federal officers throughout Colorado and Kansas were on the lookout for them. On May 15 they made an unsuccessful attempt to rob the Lake City–Del Norte stage. Three days later they held up the same coach, near Clear Creek, wounded a passenger, and took the mail bags and express box.

These brazen holdups had thoroughly aroused the citizens of Del Norte. Lew Armstrong, deputy U.S. marshal and sheriff of Rio Grande County, at the head of a large posse, overhauled the gang, near Powder Horn station. Bill Miner had gone into Lake City for supplies, but the brothers were captured, Sheriff Armstrong putting a bullet into LeRoy's leg. The two prisoners were taken to Del Norte, but on the night of May 22 a mob broke into the jail and lynched them both. Billy LeRoy remains something of a legend in Colorado and is one of the best known of all Rocky Mountain bandits.

Bill Miner, unfazed by his narrow escape from the noose, joined up with another young ruffian, Stanton T. Jones, and in July held up a stage in Saguache County. They were pursued for three hundred miles by Sheriff William A. Bronaugh and a deputy and were finally captured in the San Juans. The lawmen had been in the saddle for forty-eight hours without sleep, and they stopped to rest at a deserted prospector's cabin, near Wagon Wheel Gap. Two bunks were formed, and the prisoners' hands were tied with small leather straps. Then Bronaugh and his deputy each bedded down with a prisoner. At one A.M., while the officers were sound asleep, Bill Miner got loose, grabbed a gun, and fired four times, wounding the deputy and breaking Bronaugh's arm.[19]

Miner and Jones fled on horseback into New Mexico, held up a stage between Silver City and Deming, and then returned to California on the Southern Pacific Railroad. Bill lost no time in looking up an old compatriot from San Quentin, Jim Crum, who the *San Francisco Examiner* described as "the most noted horse thief in the state of California, and a tale of his adventures would fill many a dime novel." Crum was the head of a well-organized gang that had stolen at least two hundred horses in the previous eighteen months. The members of his band included Bill Miller, an ex-convict who owned a ranch near Woodland; Ben Frazee, who lived in Cacheville (now Yolo); and William Todhunter, the errant son of a good Yolo County family. They operated as far north as Tehama County and as far south as Tuolumne, pasturing the horses at Miller's ranch and also at "The Pocket" (a notorious rendezvous for thieves and fugitives), in Stanislaus County.

In October, Bill Miner came down with chills and fever and was laid up in Chinese Camp for some time. While there he made many friends, who knew him as William Anderson. To celebrate his recovery he attended a country ball in Angel's Camp on the evening of November 6. As usual the ladies were much taken with the dashing stranger, and Bill promised one young girl he would send her some sheet music on his next visit to San Francisco.[20]

At 5:30 the next morning, Miner, Jim Crum, Bill Miller, and Stanton Jones stopped the down stage from Sonora, near the Garibaldi Mine, ten miles south of Angel's Camp. The bandits were masked, each armed with a shotgun. With military precision, Miner called his men by numbers and ordered them to take positions surrounding the coach. The three passengers were ordered out and told to turn around with their hands behind them.

"Do I have anything you want?" asked the driver, Clark Stringham.

"No," Miner told him. "The drivers on this line are all damned good fellows, and we would rather give them something than take anything from them."

Then Bill, reconsidering, instructed one of his men to search the driver for a pistol.

"He might get mad and use it," Miner explained with a grin.

Then Bill took a sledgehammer and broke open two wooden Wells Fargo boxes, as well as an iron safe that was bolted to the floor of the stage, and removed $3300 in gold. Next the bandits turned their attentions to the passengers. One, John Mundorf, a Sonora merchant, had slipped his lunch and a $500 pouch of gold dust into a gunnysack in the bottom of the coach. Miner found it and tossed it to one of the gang.

"This lunch will suit us at this time of day," he chuckled.

By now Stringham was growing impatient.

"Hurry up," he grumbled. "I don't want to miss the train at Milton."

"All right," Bill responded. "What time is it?"

Stringham told him, and then Miner shook his hand and waved the stage on.

"Ta-ta, my boy!" Bill yelled gaily as the coach rumbled off.[21]

Wells Fargo Detective Charles Aull and Sheriff Ben Thorn investigated the holdup and immediately suspected that the humorous highwayman was Bill Miner, although they had thought he was still in Colorado. Officers from Stockton, Sacramento, and San Francisco were placed on the lookout, but Miner and his gang managed to elude them for several weeks. Traveling by night, Miner and Crum rode to San Francisco, where Bill attired himself in the height of fashion, buying an $85 suit and a $50 double-breasted Chinchilla frock coat, black beaver pants, and a silk plush vest, topping it all off with a gold watch and chain. And true to his word, he sent the girl in Angels Camp some sheet music.

Detective Aull had learned of Miner's dalliance in Angels, and the sheet music was intercepted, giving the first clue that the robbers were in San Francisco. Miner and Crum left the city and started for Angels Camp so Bill could resume his courtship. Halfway back they learned that the officers were hunting them and changed direction, riding north to Bill Miller's ranch, near Woodland. By this time Wells Fargo Detective John Thacker and Tuolumne County Sheriff George McQuade were just twelve hours behind them.

A huge posse of lawmen from five counties descended on Yolo County to trap the outlaws. On the morning of December 6, Yolo County Sheriff Frank Rahm, Yuba County Sheriff Henry McCoy, and John Thacker drove out to search Ben Frazee's house, in Cacheville. Miner, Miller, and Crum were holed up inside, armed to the

Stage robbers Jim Crum, *left,* and Bill Miller, *right,* partners of Bill Miner.
Courtesy Wells Fargo Bank History Room.

teeth. When the officers were still three hundred yards away, the wary
outlaws spotted them and fled out the back door. They tried to reach
their horses, grazing in a field next to the house, but the lawmen cut
them off. Miner and Miller ran through the field, and as the officers
stopped to open a gate, they found Jim Crum blocking their path.
He was partly hidden behind a tree, with his double-barreled shotgun at full cock, covering his partners' escape.

Crum warned the lawmen to stay back, yelling, "I'll shoot your
heads off!"

"Don't you do it, Crum!" Thacker barked. He and Sheriff Rahm,
pistols drawn, slowly closed in on the outlaw from opposite direc-
tions, while Sheriff McCoy covered them with a rifle. Crum held his
fire, realizing that he had only two shots. He might kill two of the
officers, but the third would surely kill him. Thacker realized this,
too, and when Crum tried to pull his six-shooter with his left hand,
the detective lunged forward and grabbed his fist. At the same time

Rahm seized Crum's shotgun, and an instant later the desperado was in irons.

Miner and Miller had disappeared into the brush. Nearby, the officers found Jim Crum's favorite horse, Flora, which was already celebrated for endurance and speed. They proceeded to an adjoining ranch and arrested Ben Frazee and William Todhunter, who were taken with Crum to the Woodland jail. The next day, November 7, Charles Aull and Billy Arlington, a Sacramento police detective, left Woodland in a buggy and headed south toward the capitol. About eight miles above Sacramento they suddenly spotted two men climb the river levee and disappear behind it. Aull was armed with a sawed-off shotgun and Arlington with a single revolver. Leaving Arlington in the buggy, Aull climbed the levee to look for the men and was startled to find Miner and Miller thirty feet away, their shotguns covering him. Each man also wore a brace of self-cocking Smith & Wesson revolvers. Aull knew that he was at a dangerous disadvantage and that the situation called for some quick thinking. He greeted the pair cordially and told them that he was a duck hunter and had mistaken them for members of his party. Miner and Miller, who did not know the detective, were thrown off guard and allowed him to walk back to the buggy.

The detectives drove rapidly away, circled back, and managed to close within 125 yards of the fugitives before they were spotted. Bill Miner and his partner jumped over a fence and broke for the tules to the west. Aull fired several loads of buckshot at the running outlaws, and Miller finally threw up his hands and surrendered. Arlington put Miller in the buggy and started for Sacramento, while Aull continued on alone after Bill Miner. He chased the outlaw half a mile through the tules before Miner threw down his shotgun and surrendered.

Frazee and Todhunter were taken to Stockton by Sheriff Tom Cunningham to stand trial for horse theft, while Miner, Miller, and Crum were taken to Sonora and charged with the stage robbery. Jim Crum confessed to the holdup and was sentenced to twelve years. Confronted with Crum's confession, Miner and Miller both pleaded guilty, hoping for light sentences, but instead each was sentenced to twenty-five years.[22]

On December 21, 1881, Bill Miner reentered San Quentin's stone walls and was put to work as a leather cutter in the shoe shop. The prison officials were to find that Bill was almost as much trouble in prison as out. On April 17, 1884, with the help of a fellow stage robber, Burton Greeley, he attempted to escape. He rigged up a dummy in his cell and stowed away in the prison's door factory, but he was found by the guards. Bill was sentenced to one day in the dungeon and lost all of his time credits, nine years and nine months. Three years later, however, he helped put out a fire in the drying rooms of the main shop building, and as a reward, five years were taken off his sentence. In June, 1889, Miner was assaulted and stabbed by another prisoner, Bill Hicks, but the wounds were not fatal, and he recovered.[23]

The desire for freedom continued to burn strongly within the wily outlaw. In the early morning hours of November 29, 1892, Bill and his cell mate, Joe Marshall, using a smuggled ratchet drill, cut a hole through their cell door lock. The guards heard the boring and reported it to Captain J. F. Birlem. Instead of entering the cell and confiscating the tools, Birlem instructed Guards Waters and W. A. Alexander to take up positions behind a blanket hung in a window of the guards' dormitory building, which overlooked cell 47. The cell blocks were three stories high, and each story was surrounded by a balcony, or walkway. The cell doors opened up onto these walkways. Cell 47 was on the second tier, about fifty feet across the yard from the guards' dormitory.

At five A.M. Bill Miner and his cell mate finally cut through and stepped out onto the walkway. Just as they reached the stairs, Guard Alexander, without a warning, fired one barrel of his shotgun, and Joe Marshall dropped dead, with eleven buckshot in his head, neck, and right shoulder. Alexander let drive again, and a single buckshot sliced into Bill Miner's left cheek, tore out two teeth, and lodged in his jaw.

Miner, unconscious, was carried to the prison hospital, where he soon regained his senses. When told that his cell mate was dead, he said, dejectedly, "I wish I was in the morgue with him. Better there than here."

Bill's spirits improved after his wound was dressed, and by the time newspaper reporters arrived to interview him, he was downright talkative.

> Joe Marshall was the machinist of the jute mill, and he was working all the time in the machine shop. He was a good workman and made plenty of things for the convicts.
> About a month ago he proposed a plan to get away and took me into it. I was ready to go in because I am tired of this place and have

twenty five years' solid time to serve. They took 117 months' coppers away from me a while ago, and I saw no chance to get a show. Marshall told me how he would forge a climbing hook, and we could make a rope out of pieces of the baling rope that the jute bags are baled with. He said he could cut out of his cell in two hours, but it was a mistake. Joe took a big ratchet drill to pieces and we carried the pieces up to our cell in two trips, under our shirts, and we could have taken up as many as we liked. He made a hook and we worked in the cell plaiting rope until we got about forty feet of it that would hold a man's weight. It was rainy on Saturday and Sunday, and we stayed in the cell and finished getting ready to make a break.

There was nobody in with us . . . Sunday, after lockup at three o'clock, we decided to get out that night, but there was something the matter with the drill and we had to wait until Monday. Monday afternoon we began to drill, and we kept it going pretty steady all the time until near morning today. We had a couple of old oilskin coats and we put a couple of pairs of socks on over our shoes to deaden the noise. We hurried after we had drilled the door, and Joe took the hook and rope and I had a dark lantern that Joe got somewhere. He opened the door and looked out and nobody was to be seen. Then we slid out and started toward the steps. There was no guard in sight and we calculated to slip by one man in a guardhouse near where we had to go down the steps. Joe was ahead and I was close behind. Just as we got to the corner of the stone building and Joe had gone down a step or two the shot came and you bet it was a surprise when I heard that gun. Joe tumbled down and I started to run, but the guard sent in another shot and I did not know much for some time after . . . The guard did not call out or make any noise to let us know he was there. If he had we should have gotten back to 47, because it is no use to go up against buckshot.[24]

This cold-blooded shooting raised a public furor. Guard Alexander brazenly admitted that he had laid in wait and fired without warning, but insisted that he was merely following Captain Birlem's orders. Warden William Hale defended the act, stating that his men had acted properly to prevent an escape. On December 3, however, Alexander was arrested on a charge of manslaughter and, at his preliminary hearing a week later, was bound over for trial.[25]

Bill Miner's brush with death cured him of any desire to escape, and a new development began to attract his fancy. Train holdups had become extremely common during the 1890s, and a number of California train robbers ended up in San Quentin, among them Kid Thompson, Alva Johnson, and Harry Gordon. Subsequent events showed that Bill learned much from them about the art of train robbery.

In 1898, Miner wrote numerous letters to the governor, requesting executive clemency and restoration of his credits that had been revoked in 1884. On February 10, 1900, his lost credits were all restored in consideration of good behavior during the previous seven years. Bill Miner walked out the San Quentin gates for the final time on June 17, 1901. He promptly left California, and there is no evidence that he ever returned.[26]

He was then fifty-five, but while most old convicts retire at that age, Bill Miner's criminal career was just beginning. It would take a book to detail his later exploits. On September 23, 1903, with three gang members, he held up an Oregon Railroad and Navigation Company express train, near Portland, Oregon. The engineer and one of Bill's men were wounded in an exchange of shots with the messenger. On September 10, 1904, he and two companions pulled the first train holdup in Canada's history, stopping Canadian Pacific Train No. 1, at Mission Junction, British Columbia, and taking $7,000 in gold and currency. A year later, in November, 1905, Miner was the prime suspect in the robbery of a Great Northern train, near Seattle. On May 9, 1906, Bill stopped a Canadian Pacific train, near Kamloops, British Columbia. He and his men were tracked down by the Mounties, and Miner was sentenced to life imprisonment. A year later he escaped and on June 22, 1909, was believed to have been involved in the holdup of a train, near Ducks, B.C. Bill's last hurrah took place in Georgia, on February 22, 1911, when he led a raid on a Southern Express train at White Sulphur Springs. Captured a few days later, Bill was sentenced to twenty years in the state prison in Milledgeville.

But Bill Miner, tough and resourceful despite his years, broke out of prison on October 18, 1911. Recaptured and secured with a ball and chain, he escaped again on June 29, 1912. He was caught after a grueling flight through the swamps and returned to the prison, his health broken, but his sense of humor intact.

"I guess I'm getting too old for this sort of thing," he told his guards.

These breakouts had taken their toll on him, and he slowly weakened. On September 2, 1913, at the age of sixty-seven, he died in the prison hospital.[27]

It was Bill Miner's last escape.

CHAPTER 8

Terror on the Tracks:
Kid Thompson and Alva Johnson

THE rumbling of huge wheels, the hissing of released steam, and the wail of its locomotive whistle announced the arrival of Southern Pacific Train No. 20, the Los Angeles Express, at Burbank station shortly after eleven o'clock on the night of December 23, 1893. Constable H. P. Fawkes, on duty at the depot, spotted four tramps trying to climb onto the blind baggage, and he pulled them off. One of the four, a young man wearing a black slouch hat and an overcoat, bolted up the tracks, with Fawkes in pursuit. As the train started up, the young tramp swung aboard and climbed to the roof of the car, leaving the constable behind.

Engineer "Rocky Bill" Stewart was at the throttle as the train continued on its northbound journey through the San Fernando Valley. As it approached Roscoe station, about four miles north of Burbank in what is now the Sun Valley section of Los Angeles, the young tramp, with a six-shooter in each hand and a bandanna tied around his face, jumped down from the fruit car into the coal tender.

"Stop this train!" the robber shouted, and he fired six shots into the cab to punctuate his command.

Engineer Stewart set his brakes, but the train suddenly left the main track onto a blind siding. Someone had set the spur switch, sidetracking the train. As Stewart brought his engine to a halt, he saw a bonfire blaze up on the side of the track, and a second masked man stepped forward toward the cab. He was carrying a Winchester rifle and appeared to be heavier set and older than the first robber. The younger bandit acted as the leader, and as he ordered the engineer to get down from the cab, three tramps jumped down from the blind baggage and ran for the brush. The robber sent a volley of pistol shots flying after them.

Constable J. C. Villegas (a passenger), of San Fernando, heard the gunfire and, with brakeman J. T. Snyder, walked forward to investigate. As they approached the engine they heard the fireman say, "We will do what you want if you don't hurt us."

"Gentlemen, gentlemen," Villegas called out. "What is the meaning of all this?"

"Get back there, you son of a bitch!" was the decidedly unfriendly reply.

"I am an officer!" the constable protested lamely.

"You bastard! Get back now, will you!" one of the bandits roared, and he snapped a shot at the constable.

Snyder doused his lantern and dived under a car, while Villegas scampered back to the passenger coaches.

The robbers walked Stewart and his fireman back to the express car. They produced a tin can filled with black powder with a short fuse, placed it next to the sliding door, and ordered Engineer Stewart to light it. He did, but the fuse fizzled out. After two more tries, the bomb exploded and tore a large hole in the door. Wells Fargo Messenger Fred Potts, sound asleep in the car, was thrown out of his bunk by the blast. Before he could regain his senses, the two bandits were in the car, covering him with their weapons. Potts was instructed to open the way safe, and when he did so, the bandit leader remarked, "She's as full as a daisy, ain't she?"

"Yes, that's the way she is running now," said the messenger, and he handed over $150.

"Where is your through safe?" the robber asked, and Potts replied that his car did not carry one.

The second bandit pointed his Winchester at Potts and snarled, "Don't you remember reading about a messenger having his head blown off for not opening up his through safe?"

"Yes," Potts answered. "But that was back east, where they have lots of treasure to carry. We don't have it on the Coast."

The robbers seemed satisfied with Potts's explanation. They forced him out of the car and then ordered Engineer Stewart to "ditch the train" by driving off the end of the spur track and derailing it. Stewart pleaded with them not to do this, and the bandits, after a quick consultation, relented. They instructed Stewart, Potts, and the fireman to walk far up the tracks and not to return until the robbers had left. Then the two desperadoes mounted horses and fled northeast.

The crew returned to the engine and took the train into San Fernando, where news of the holdup was sent to all telegraph offices be-

Southern Pacific Train No. 20, in 1889, minus its passenger coaches. It was
held up twice, at Roscoe station, by Kid Thompson and Alva Johnson and
was wrecked in the second robbery. Courtesy California State Library.

tween Fresno, Santa Barbara, Needles, and Yuma. By four A.M.,
Southern Pacific Detective Will Smith was in the field with a posse,
but he could not cut the robbers' trail. Wells Fargo and the Southern
Pacific offered a sixteen-hundred-dollar reward for the holdup men,
but they managed to disappear without a trace.[1]

At that time the population of the city of Los Angeles was just over
50,000. The massive real-estate boom that was to boost the city's en-
virons to 2.3 million people in the next four decades was just beginning. The northern part of the San Fernando Valley was sparsely
settled, and most of the surrounding hills and a sizable part of the
valley were cattle range. Roscoe station was used mainly as a shipping
point for cattle and consisted of nothing more than a small depot
with a spur switch one hundred yards to the south. From the switch a
"blind" sidetrack ran north past the station house. Railroad ties were
piled at the end of the siding and just beyond was a six-foot ditch.

Seven weeks after the first holdup, on the night of February 15, 1894, Train No. 20 left the Arcade depot in Los Angeles with Engineer David W. Thomas in the cab. His fireman was Arthur Masters; a second fireman, Ben LaGrange, was also in the cab, "deadheading" a ride to his home in San Fernando. Stealing a ride to San Francisco, two tramps, Arthur Granger and James Pacey, were seated on the engine pilot, or cowcatcher. As the train neared Roscoe station, Engineer Thomas saw two men standing near the switch with a lighted torch. One of them threw the torch into the middle of the track as a signal to stop, and the other fired a rifle at the cab.

"Look out, boys. They're shooting!" yelled Thomas, and he threw the throttle wide open. The train, which had been running at thirty miles an hour, began to accelerate, and one of the bandits threw the switch. Train No. 20 suddenly swerved off the main track and careened at high speed down the spur line. Thomas tried to slow his engine, but it was too late. The big locomotive rammed through the pile of ties at the end of the spur, jumped off the rails, and slammed down at a sharp angle into the sand at the bottom of the ditch. The impact sent one of the tramps, Pacey, fifty feet through the air, knocking him unconscious. The other tramp, Granger, tried to jump free but was crushed to death by the locomotive cylinder. Escaping steam from the shattered boiler burned him beyond recognition.

Just before impact, Engineer Thomas and Fireman LaGrange leaped out of the cab and escaped injury. Arthur Masters was not so lucky. Two fruit cars loaded with oranges were just behind the tender. The force of the collision shattered the cars and slammed them forward into the engine cab, crushing Masters against the boiler. Desperately injured, the fireman screamed in agony and pleaded for help.

The two masked bandits ran up to the side of the train. One carried a Winchester rifle, and the other carried a pair of six-guns. They fired several shots up and down the coaches to keep the passengers inside, and one yelled, "The son of a bitch! I'll show him whether he'll stop or not!"

As the dust and steam began to clear, Ben LaGrange scrambled into the cab to assist Masters. Seeing that the fireman was pinned, LaGrange told him he would go to the passenger cars for help. As LaGrange jumped from the engine, the two robbers ordered him to put up his hands. Marching the fireman to the Wells Fargo car, they placed a dynamite bomb at one corner of the back door and commanded him to touch it off. The blast shattered the door into splinters and filled the express car with smoke. The bandits fired several shots into the car and yelled to the messenger, Harry Edgar, "Open quick or we'll blow you to hell!"

Edgar slid open the splintered door, and the robbers and LaGrange climbed in. While one bandit went through the express packages, the other stood at the door and fired his pistol down the side of the train.

"Open up your safe," one of the desperadoes ordered, and Edgar quickly complied.

The robber removed seven small sacks containing $100 in U.S. currency and about $1200 in Mexican silver coin. He hefted the sacks and exclaimed, "Jesus Christ! Is this all you've got?"

Then, placing the sacks into a larger bag, he remarked, "I'll be damned if I'll carry it," and ordered Edgar and LaGrange to carry the seventy-five pound bag toward a buckboard waiting two hundred yards away on an old dirt road. Halfway to the wagon the bandits instructed the trainmen to put down the sack to keep them from getting a close look at the buckboard and team. At that point LaGrange told them that the fireman was pinned in the engine cab.

"God damn the luck," one robber replied. "If I'd known this would happen I wouldn't have held up the train."

The bandits carried the booty to the wagon and raced away in the darkness. Then LaGrange and Edgar ran to the engine and met the tramp, Pacey, who had regained consciousness. They worked feverishly with axes to cut through the beam that crushed Masters, who suffered untold agony and pleaded with his rescuers to kill him. After an hour of frantic efforts they managed to remove the beam, but it was too late, for Masters was already dead.[2]

Meanwhile a brakeman ran to a nearby farmhouse, borrowed a horse, and rode to Burbank, where he reported the wrecking by telegraph to the sheriff in Los Angeles. Before daybreak a manhunt was under way, headed by U.S. Marshal George Gard, who had captured train robber John Sontag eight months before. Detectives Miles T. Bowler, of the Southern Pacific, and Walter Auble, of the Los Angeles police, checked the holdup scene and found a small campfire and wagon tracks two hundred yards southwest of the depot. The wagon appeared to have been drawn by two horses, one shod with mule shoes. The wagon wheels did not track perfectly, as if the axle was worn. After closely examining the tracks and manure, the detectives followed the trail south toward Los Angeles for four miles, when a heavy rain fell and obliterated the tracks. Along the trail they found a number of Wells Fargo tags that the robbers had removed from the sacks. The spot where the trail was lost was on the Lankershim Ranch, just north of the old Ventura road and northwest of Cahuenga Pass. The detectives sent word to Los Angeles that the robbers might be headed for the city, and armed guards were placed on the roads leading into town.

A group of five deputy sheriffs guarded the Arroyo Seco bridge, just outside Los Angeles. Shortly before daybreak the deputies saw a wagon approaching from the direction of the city and recognized the driver as Alva Johnson, a rancher from Big Tujunga Canyon who owned a feedstore in town. Seated next to him was his hired man, William H. ("Kid") Thompson, and in the wagon bed was a large box covered with canvas. This was the way nearby dairy ranchers delivered milk.

"Hello!" Johnson called to the deputies. "What's the matter?"

"What is that, a milk wagon?" the officers asked.

"Yes," was Johnson's quick reply. "What's the matter with you fellows, anyway?"

The deputies explained that there had been a train holdup, and then stepped back and let the wagon pass. They were on the lookout for robbers coming from the San Fernando Valley, and since Johnson's wagon was headed toward the Valley, they didn't bother to investigate further. As the wagon rumbled off, one of the deputies called, "Look out for robbers!"[3]

While Marshal Gard and the other officers continued to hunt the bandits, Wells Fargo and the Southern Pacific offered a reward of $1,000 for the arrest and conviction of each of the robbers, in addition to the standing reward of $300 offered by Wells Fargo in such cases and $300 by the state of California. News of this second holdup created a sensation, and deputy sheriffs, constables, and private detectives, eager for the big rewards, flocked into the valley. Declared the *San Francisco Examiner,* "It was the boldest train robbery that ever took place in Southern California, or, for that matter, in the State."[4]

A week later, on February 22, the sheriff of Los Angeles County received a visit from John Johnson, older brother of Alva Johnson. John was not on good terms with his brother, and he told the sheriff that he suspected Alva, Kid Thompson, and George Smith of committing the Roscoe wrecking and robbery. Alva had recently sued John over water rights to a stream near his ranch, and John now claimed that Alva had robbed the train to pay his legal expenses. But he had little hard evidence. On the morning of the train wrecking he had seen the tracks of his brother's wagon enter Big Tujunga Canyon and turn into Alva's ranch. And he had seen Alva and George Smith with twenty-dollar gold pieces, similar to those reported to have been taken in the two holdups.[5]

The sheriff relayed the information to the Southern Pacific and Wells Fargo detectives, who began a quiet investigation. They found that Alva Johnson bore a good reputation and was well known in Big Tujunga and Little Tujunga, two canyons in the San Gabriel Mountains, east of the San Fernando Valley and only a few miles from Roscoe station. Born in Gentry County, Missouri, in 1858, Alva had moved to California in 1875 and had settled in Big Tujunga Canyon eight years later. His parents, two brothers, and a sister also lived in the canyon. His sister, Olive, was married to George Trogdon and was on friendly terms with Alva. His two brothers, John, a bee-keeper and farmer, and Cornelius, a rancher, had, however, developed strong feelings against him because of the water dispute. A man of modest means, Alva divided his time between his ranch, where he raised cattle and poultry, and his feedstore, on the corner of Broadway and Franklin Streets, in Los Angeles. He was a typical stockman, thirty-six years old, with shaggy red hair and beard. Johnson was married and had two small children and two teenage stepdaughters.[6]

George Smith was an old-timer who was considered harmless and did odd jobs around Alva's ranch in exchange for room and board. Kid Thompson had worked for Johnson as a teamster and cowboy for about five months. He was a reckless youth of twenty-two, much given to drinking, gambling, and consorting with prostitutes. The detectives were unable to learn much about the Kid's background, but it later developed that his true name was David Boone and that he had been born in Iowa on November 3, 1871. He was raised with three brothers and a sister in Hill City, South Dakota, and, while still in his teens, drifted into Arizona, where he worked as a cowboy and a teamster and adopted the alias of William Thompson. In 1888 he drove a team for Marshall Miller, who owned a mine near Prescott, but the next year he fell in with two noted desperadoes, the Fox brothers. They engaged in cattle rustling in the Salt River Valley, and in one raid the trio had a running gunfight with a constable named Shankland, who shot and captured one of the Fox boys. The Kid and the other brother fled into New Mexico, where Thompson, with Fox and "Mysterious" Dave Taylor, was believed to have taken part in a bank robbery in San Pasqual. The Kid returned to Arizona, where he and another youth, John Long, were arrested for horse theft in Maricopa County and sentenced to three years each in the territorial prison in Yuma. Thompson entered the prison on November 2, 1889, and was released on March 20, 1892. The following year he drifted into California and worked on the Santa Anita Ranch. He then showed up in Los Angeles, where he temporarily "got religion" and paraded the streets with the Salvation Army. In October he met Alva Johnson at the latter's feedstore and Johnson gave him a job.[7]

The detectives continued their investigation and learned that Alva Johnson hated the Southern Pacific and had told his neighbors that the engineer was to blame for the Roscoe wreck because he had not stopped the train. Johnson's feelings about the SP were not uncommon, however, for the railroad was roundly disliked in California. Immensely powerful, for years it had controlled the state's political and economic life. Ranchers and farmers, in particular, despised the SP, accusing it of setting arbitrary and exorbitant shipping fees.

The detectives found other circumstantial evidence. A carpenter from Glendale reported that he had seen Kid Thompson board Train No. 20 in Los Angeles on the night of the first robbery. The Kid rode in the smoker and got off at Burbank. He had enough time to climb onto the blind baggage before being pulled off by Constable Fawkes. Also, after the second job, Alva Johnson could easily have driven his wagon into Los Angeles and then left the city at the time the deputies saw him at the Arroyo Seco bridge. The tracks of Johnson's wagon roughly matched those found at the scene of the train wreck. Alva fitted the physical description of the taller robber, and either Kid Thompson or George Smith was the same size as the other bandit.

Alva Johnson was interrogated several times by Southern Pacific Detective Will Smith and Wells Fargo Detective John Thacker. Johnson, an emotional man, became extremely nervous and agitated under questioning but insisted that he was innocent. The detectives became even more suspicious when they learned that Kid Thompson had suddenly disappeared about the first of March. On March 26, Johnson and Smith were placed under arrest by Constable Lester Rogers, who lacked solid evidence but hoped that Alva, while in jail, would break down and turn state's evidence. Johnson had a different idea, and he secured the services of two expert defense attorneys, D. K. Trask and C. C. Stephens.[8]

The preliminary hearing of Johnson and Smith began on March 31. All of the evidence against them was circumstantial. John and Cornelius Johnson testified that they had seen Alva's wagon tracks after the Roscoe wreck. A Los Angeles shopkeeper testified that George Smith had paid for goods with a twenty-dollar gold piece. There was also testimony that Kid Thompson had been seen aboard Train No. 20 before the first job. In all, the prosecution's case was weak in the extreme, and Justice Bartholomew refused to hold them to answer and dismissed the charges.[9]

This was a great blow to the railroad detectives. They continued to hunt for Kid Thompson and redoubled their efforts to apprehend the other guilty parties since they knew that at least two, if not more, men were involved. They were certain that if Alva Johnson had not taken part in the holdups, he at least knew who the culprits were. The detectives concentrated their investigation on the small farmers and ranchers of Big and Little Tujunga.

At that time Will Smith was the most active railroad detective in the state. A native of Scotland, he had been a deputy sheriff in Yuma, Arizona; a guard at the territorial prison; and a U.S. customs inspector. He had investigated the famous "Wham robbery case" and had also been a member of an eight-man posse that pursued a band of train robbers into Mexico in 1887. The posse had included three Papago Indian trailers and was led by U.S. Marshal W. K. Meade. Meade, Smith, and the rest of the posse were thrown into jail and charged with "armed invasion" and "bringing savage and hostile Indians into Mexico." In California, Will Smith had played a leading role in the attempts to capture the Dalton brothers and Evans and Sontag, but he had met with little success. His handling of these latter cases had been severely criticized by the press, and he was greatly disliked by fellow lawmen, who accused him of glory hunting and undermining their work.[10]

While other officers concentrated on Alva Johnson, Will Smith fastened his suspicions on three men who lived in Little Tujunga Canyon: John Comstock, Walter Thorne, and Pat Fitzsimmons. He learned that shortly before the train robberies Comstock and Thorne at a general store in San Fernando had bought bandanna handkerchiefs similar to those used by the bandits. Comstock had been seen in possession of Mexican coins. Also, William Rapp, a San Fernando farmer who had been aboard Train No. 20 on the night of the Roscoe wrecking, told Smith that he had looked out a window at the robbers, and one had told him, "Get back in there." Rapp said he recognized the voice as Walter Thorne's.

Smith had made plaster casts of the tracks left by the bandits after the second job. He compared these with the tracks of wagons and horses owned by the trio and found that they did not match. Smith concluded that Comstock, Thorne, and Fitzsimmons were the wrong men and reported this to Marshal Gard. To many Californians of the period, Will Smith epitomized the type of detective who would do anything to secure a conviction for the railroad, but it is to his credit that, at least in this case, he acted honorably.[11]

Marshal Gard was not satisfied with Smith's report. He sent a message to Visalia, and on March 9 a medium-sized, roly-poly stranger appeared in Little Tujunga Canyon. He told residents that his name was Frank Hudson, and he had all the appearance of a simpleton. Clad in threadbare clothes and muddy brogans, he was about fifty years old, with a slouching, foot-dragging gait and innocent blue eyes. He moved into a house near the mouth of the canyon, told his neighbors that he wanted to buy a mining claim, and soon became quite friendly with John Comstock. The stranger's real name was J. V. Brighton, the "Ferret of the Sierra." Virtually unknown today, Brighton was one of the shrewdest detectives of the Old West. He had been a detective for eighteen years and, among other exploits, claimed to have joined the James gang as an undercover agent after the death of Jesse James in 1882. In 1887 he had tracked down and killed the notorious Arizona cattle rustler, Ike Clanton, famous for his part in the gunfight at the O. K. Corral. During the manhunt for Evans and Sontag, Brighton and his wife had lived next door to the Evans family, in Visalia, taking care of the outlaw's children. Unknown to Evans, Brighton was in the employ of the Southern Pacific. Less than three weeks before his arrival in Little Tujunga he had skillfully laid a trap for Chris Evans, luring the outlaw home to be captured by a sheriff's posse.[12]

Brighton lived in the canyon for a month, gathering information. Comstock told him about the train wreck in great detail, saying that he had heard the story from the fireman, Ben LaGrange. Comstock confided to Brighton that he knew how to open a railroad switch lock and also expressed the opinion that the engineer was to blame for the wreck. Brighton engaged Thorne and Fitzsimmons in a number of conversations in which they, too, made damaging statements.

Meanwhile, E. L. Brown, the storekeeper from San Fernando who had sold Comstock and Thorne bandannas, had been collecting evidence against the trio. Eager to collect the large rewards, Brown swore out a complaint against the men, charging them with the first train robbery. This charge was quickly dismissed, but the Los Angeles County grand jury soon indicted Comstock, Thorne, and Fitzsimmons for the train wrecking, and all three were held for trial, which began on June 6. The prosecution's star witness was J. V. Brighton, and he testified about his undercover work and claimed that Comstock had told him that Thorne and Fitzsimmons had wrecked the train. He also testified that Fitzsimmons had said that detectives would never find the stolen loot. But there was little other evidence of substance. A black man, John Belt, claimed that he had seen Comstock in a Los Angeles saloon with a pocket full of Mexican coin. Numerous other witnesses took the stand against the defendants, but their stories, while pointing the finger of suspicion at the trio, fell short of actual proof. When the prosecution rested, many were surprised at how weak its case was.

The newspapers devoted much attention to the trial. Commented the *Los Angeles Herald:*

> It is very readily seen that . . . Marshal Gard spared neither time nor expense to thoroughly investigate the suspicious circumstances connecting the defendants with the robbery. The number of officers and persons paid to work upon the case is very unusual. The power of the officers has been exerted to an extraordinary degree to weld the chain which is now being exhibited in court.[13]

On June 11 the defense began putting on its case. Many witnesses were produced who attacked the credibility of the prosecution's witnesses, painting them as liars eager to share in the rewards. Others provided alibis for the three defendants. The trial lasted nine days, and 150 witnesses were called. On June 15 the case was submitted to the jury, which deliberated only three minutes before returning a verdict of not guilty. The jurors evidently believed that Brighton had committed perjury and had either invented or embellished the statements made by the defendants. Subsequent events proved that the trio had not been involved in the holdups at all. It is a marvel that they were ever brought to trial on such flimsy evidence and is a cogent illustration of the power the Southern Pacific could bring to bear in a California courtroom when its interests were at stake.[14]

Los Angeles County District Attorney Henry C. Dillon was much disgusted with the work of the railroad officers, and he hired a well-

Train Robber Alva Johnson, partner of Kid Thompson. Courtesy Dave Langerman, San Quentin.

known private detective, A. B. Lawson, to work up the case. Eight years previous Lawson had arrested Alva Johnson's brother-in-law, George Trogdon, for a murder in Trinity County. Lawson became convinced that Trogdon was innocent and procured his release and dismissal of the murder charge. Now, in gratitude, Olive Trogdon, Alva's sister, agreed to secretly cooperate with Lawson. She told the detective that both she and Alva's wife were convinced that he was guilty, and she agreed to try to persuade her brother to confess. Lawson, in return, promised to work for a pardon for Johnson. But neither of the women had any success with Alva, for he steadfastly denied to his family that he was involved in the holdups.[15]

The investigation came almost to a standstill. The officers continued to hunt for Kid Thompson, but he had disappeared without a trace. Finally, on October 10, Will Smith found the Kid in Phoenix, Arizona. He interrogated him several times but got nowhere. With no evidence and no warrant, Smith gave up in disgust and returned to Los Angeles. A few days later, Billy Breakenridge, the Southern Pacific's special officer in Phoenix, received a visit from an old rancher named Baker, from Tonto Creek. Baker had in tow a thirty-four-year-old teamster and cigar maker, Charles Etzler, who told Breakenridge a most interesting story. A month earlier Etzler, with a tramp named Mefford, had been stealing a ride in the blind baggage on a train from Bakersfield to Los Angeles. In Tehachapi a young man climbed down from the roof of the baggage car, and Mefford immediately recognized Kid Thompson, whom he had served time with in Yuma Prison.

"Here is one of the God damndest horse and cattle thieves in the country!" Mefford had exclaimed, and he introduced Thompson to Etzler.

Shortly thereafter the train crew ordered them off, and they started on foot for San Fernando. En route, the Kid told Etzler that Mefford had been a "snitch" in Yuma. They gave him the slip, and then walked to Alva Johnson's ranch, seven miles distant, where Thompson said he could get some money. Alva was not at home, so they climbed into a haymow to sleep. The Kid was talkative and told Etzler about the Roscoe holdups in detail. He admitted that he and Alva had planned and carried them out, and that Johnson had buried the Mexican coin on his ranch. When Alva returned that evening, the Kid and Etzler walked out to meet him.

"Hello, Alva," Thompson said.

Johnson seemed surprised to see the Kid and exclaimed, "What in the name of Jesus Christ are you back here for? You are not keeping your word."

"I know I promised not to come back so soon," Thompson replied. "But I got busted and had to come. This fellow is all right. He will be ready for another job."

The Kid asked for his share of the treasure, but Alva responded, "I ain't going to give you no Mexican money now. I'll give you some good money and a pistol and after you get to Arizona I'll send you some of the Mexican coin."

The next day they drove into Los Angeles, with Thompson covered with a blanket and hidden from view under the wagon seat. Alva and the Kid discussed the holdups freely and laughed uproariously when they told Etzler how they had fooled the deputies at the Arroyo Seco bridge by rigging up a chicken coop under a blanket to make Alva's buckboard look like a milk wagon. At Johnson's feed corral Alva gave Etzler $2.50 and a revolver wrapped up in a paper and said, "For God's sake get Thompson out of the country."

Will Smith, the controversial Southern Pacific Railroad detective who investigated the Roscoe holdups and claimed to have pursued Kid Thompson for four hundred miles, in Arizona. Courtesy Arizona Historical Society.

Johnson promised to ship the Kid's share of the loot to Arizona, and Thompson and Etzler left the next day for Yuma. A few weeks later the Kid received a wood crate that contained $600 in Mexican coin at the Wells Fargo office in Tempe. Etzler and a pal of the Kid's, H. L. Tupper, a nineteen-year-old cowboy with the facetious nickname of "Colonel," sold the silver coin to Chinese merchants in Phoenix at the rate of forty cents on the dollar. But when the Kid proposed that they hold up another train, Etzler lost his nerve and hunted up the Phoenix city marshal, telling him that Kid Thompson had robbed two trains and was in a nearby barbershop with a pocketful of Mexican money. The marshal paid no attention to Etzler's story and told him that his supper was getting cold.[16]

Etzler, fearful that the Kid would kill him if he found out that he had tried to give him away, slipped out of town and obtained work at Baker's ranch on Tonto Creek. He told his story to Baker, who immediately took Etzler to Special Officer Breakenridge, an astute lawman who had captured a number of notorious outlaws in the Southwest. That night Breakenridge took Etzler to Los Angeles and turned him over to the local officers. Then Breakenridge and Will Smith returned to Phoenix on the first train. They learned that the Kid was working on a nearby ranch and rode out to arrest him, but the ranchman told them that Thompson had gone into town. Much to Breakenridge's surprise, Smith said to the rancher, "Tell the Kid that Will Smith, the Southern Pacific detective, wants to see him to get some information, and for him to call at the Commercial Hotel."

As they left the ranch, Breakenridge told Smith, "It's all off. The Kid will get away unless we hide close by until he returns from town."

But Smith replied that he knew Thompson well, had talked with him several times about the train robberies, and that he would be glad to come and see him. The next day, October 15, when the ranchman gave him Will Smith's message, the Kid mounted his horse and left for parts unknown. Smith, with Deputy U.S. Marshal John Slankard, set off in search of the Kid. Smith later reported that they trailed Thompson, on horseback, for nine days and four hundred miles, first to Tempe, then to Arizona Canyon Dam, and finally to the Centipede River, where the tracks were lost.[17]

Billy Breakenridge knew that Kid Thompson had once worked on a ranch near Agua Caliente, on the Gila River, and had many friends in that vicinity. He called on Maricopa County Deputy Sheriff Billy Moore, who was visiting Phoenix and lived up the Salt River, at the gate to Tonto Basin. The detective asked Moore to be on the lookout for Thompson. On the morning of November 6, while stopping at the Crabtree ranch, thirty miles from Phoenix, Moore learned that two suspicious customers had taken breakfast there and had gone on over Reno Pass toward Tonto Basin. One of them matched the description of Kid Thompson and the other of his pal, Colonel Tupper. Moore and four cowboys went after the pair and caught up with them near Reno Pass. When called on to surrender and raise their hands, Tupper said with a laugh, "Well, you've got the drop on us."

But when they put their hands up, each held a six-gun spitting fire at Moore's posse. Then, with rifle bullets raining around them, the outlaws wheeled their horses and fled into a rocky side canyon. Abandoning their mounts, they took cover in a natural rock fortress and exchanged gunfire with the possemen all afternoon. At dark, in response to one of many commands to give up, the Kid shouted, "We'll die first!"

The night was bitterly cold, but Moore and his men kept up their watch, and at daybreak they began a systematic fire into the rocks. At last the Kid, realizing that they could not escape, called, "We've had enough!" and the two walked out with their hands in the air. Inside their fort were found two .44-caliber revolvers, dozens of spent cartridges, and two hundred rounds of unused ammunition. Thompson had only sixty cents in his pockets, and Tupper had but fifty cents.[18]

Moore took the two outlaws to Phoenix and turned them over to Breakenridge. Tupper was taken to Gila Bend and charged with resisting arrest. The Kid waived extradition, and Breakenridge took him to Los Angeles. He refused to talk about the holdups and told the district attorney, "I am not going to put a rope about my neck with my own hands. If you gentlemen will assure me of a life sentence I'll tell you all I know, otherwise I'll stand a trial and let you prove me guilty."[19]

In the meantime, Alva Johnson, still protesting his innocence, had been rearrested. His preliminary examination began on November 1, with Charles Etzler as the state's star witness, and Alva was bound over for trial. On November 8, Kid Thompson was lodged into the Los Angeles jail with Alva, who began to realize the likelihood that both of them would hang. His wife and sister continued to pressure him to confess, in hope that it would save his neck, and finally he made a deal with District Attorney Dillon: in exchange for a life term, he would plead guilty and testify against the Kid. He made a clean breast of the crime and revealed where the rest of the loot could be found. Will Smith and Miles Bowler drove out to Big Tujunga and dug up $576 in Mexican silver on Alva's ranch.[20]

Kid Thompson was charged with train wrecking, a capital offense, and his trial began on May 1, 1895. Although penniless, he was defended by three Los Angeles attorneys: Ben Goodrich, William A. Harris, and D. K. Trask. In a courtroom packed with spectators and reporters, Alva Johnson told the jury how he and the Kid had planned and carried out both robberies. Alva claimed that Thompson had thrown the switch and wrecked the train in the second job and said that when he saw the train go into the ditch, he lost his nerve and told the Kid, "For God's sake, let's get out of here." But Thompson had replied, "By God, let's not give up now. We have got them where they can't help themselves."

Charles Etzler then took the stand and corroborated Alva's confession. Old George Smith testified, too, and said that on the night of the train wrecking, Alva and the Kid were not at the ranch, and he had been in bed reading *Tom Sawyer;* he saw Alva and the Kid arrive home in the morning.

Among the defense witnesses was Detective F. B. Kennett, former chief of police of Saint Louis, Missouri, and a former partner of Detective Lawson. Kennett and Lawson had quarreled over the division of rewards offered in the case, and now, to get even, Kennett testified that Lawson had offered three hundred dollars to Alva's sister, Olive Trogdon, if she would testify against the Kid, implying that she was a paid perjurer.

Finally Kid Thompson took the stand. He denied any knowledge of the robberies and said that he had worked at Alva Johnson's ranch for five months, leaving on March 1, 1894. He had returned to Arizona and then had gone to visit his parents in Lawrence County, South Dakota. In June he had labored on a railroad in Wyoming, and then drifted through Washington and Oregon and back into California, hiring on to drive a herd of cattle south to Sacramento. From there he beat his way on the SP to San Fernando, meeting Etzler on the train. But the Kid claimed that it was Etzler who was the train robber, not he, and that Etzler had arranged with Johnson for the Mexican money to be sent to Arizona. When his lawyer asked about Will Smith's four-hundred-mile chase, the Kid howled with laughter and replied, "The reason Smith didn't find me was that he went east, while I was going west all the time!"

The trial lasted just five days, and on May 8, after deliberating for twenty hours, the jury found Kid Thompson guilty of train wrecking and affixed his punishment at death. He was formally sentenced a week later when Judge B. N. Smith ordered

> that within ten days from this day you be by the sheriff of this county conveyed to the state's prison at San Quentin and there delivered into the custody of the warden of said state's prison, and that you be, by him, upon a day and time to be hereafter fixed in the warrant of your execution, hanged by the neck until you are dead.[21]

But the Kid was a tough steer to rope. His attorneys immediately prepared an appeal to the California Supreme Court on the grounds that the charges against him had been improperly drafted in the pleadings. The Kid remained in the county jail while the appeal was pending. Just three weeks later, the case once again hit the front pages. On June 10, Detective F. B. Kennett bearded A. B. Lawson in the latter's office on New High Street, in Los Angeles. Their feud had reached a fever pitch, and Kennett, drunk, demanded his share of the reward money. When Lawson refused, Kennett whipped out a Smith & Wesson .38 and pumped three bullets into the unarmed detective, killing him instantly. Kennett claimed that Lawson had tried to grab a gun, but he was convicted of manslaughter and sentenced to ten years in prison.[22]

In February, 1896, the Supreme Court upheld Kid Thompson's conviction, and he was sent to San Quentin for execution. He was surprised to discover that his prison cell mate was his old Arizona employer, Marshall Miller, who was awaiting hanging for a brutal robbery and murder in Marysville. While taking his two hours' exercise in the yard a few days later, the Kid received another surprise in the form of his old sidekick, John Long, who, after his release from Yuma, had held up a stage and was now languishing "across the bay."

Interviewed at the prison, Thompson told a reporter:

> My folks write to me all the time. They wanted to come out here during the trial but I told them not to come near me. I can stand my troubles better alone than to have my folks here to sympathize with me. . . . My sister teaches school and has been sending money to pay my attorneys. My folks are poor people, and it comes pretty hard on them.
>
> I am ready to die, all right. The only thing is my family. This hanging business will be pretty hard on them. A man can only die once, though, and I'm ready to go now.[23]

The Kid's lawyers appealed a second time, and in November, 1896, the Supreme Court reversed his conviction on the grounds that the judge had given the jury an erroneous instruction. Despite the fact that the Kid had been charged with train wrecking, Judge Smith instructed the jurors that if they found that he had boarded the express car and robbed the messenger (a crime he was not charged with), they should find him guilty. Although there had been detailed testimony at the trial that Thompson had wrecked the train, the Supreme Court held that this instruction had misled the jury, a ruling that conveniently ignored the overwhelming evidence of the Kid's guilt.[24]

Kid Thompson's second trial began on April 13, 1897. Still claiming innocence, he wrote the editor of the *Los Angeles Times*:

> At the former trial of my case I was convicted solely on perjured testimony of witnesses who were accessories in the robbery, and I was railroaded to conviction to save the scalps of these same men. . . .
> I desire to say that if Alva Johnson, Etzler and others should tell the

Kid Thompson, 1897. He
narrowly escaped hanging
for the Roscoe train rob-
beries. Courtesy California
State Archives.

truth and nothing but the truth, I would be acquitted, and that is all I
want. . . . I am going into this trial without a dollar, and I have not
paid my lawyers a cent since the last trial, and in the face of all this
the fight for my life will be a hard one.[25]

Alva Johnson was once again the state's star witness, and he created
a sensation by refusing to testify, saying he had been threatened with
death in the prison if he did. The next day, at his wife's urging, Alva
changed his mind and retold the story of the train wrecking.

The Kid's pal, Colonel Tupper, had since been released from jail,
and he came from Arizona to testify on Thompson's behalf. But
Tupper had another type of aid in mind for the Kid. Shortly after
arriving in Los Angeles, he met with a friend of Thompson's named
Maggie Brown, a thirty-year-old prostitute and morphine addict.
The Kid had smuggled several letters out of jail to Maggie, asking her
to supply him with a gun and a horse and buggy. He told her that a
youth named Fay Harris would help in smuggling a six-shooter into
the jail, as would the jail trusty, Kramer.

Tupper had brought a Colt .44 with him from Arizona. He was
anxious to help the Kid, but he was then free on $5,000 bail on a

pending murder charge in Arizona and desired to conceal his involvement in the plot. Maggie Brown introduced Tupper to another pal of the Kid's, Harry Jenkins, and Tupper gave him the revolver. Jenkins, in turn, gave the weapon to Fay Harris. On April 16 the defense opened its case. That morning Fay Harris called at the jail to visit the trusty, Kramer. He managed to slip the revolver unnoticed to Kramer, but shortly thereafter the jailer, P. J. Kennedy, noticed that Kramer was acting nervously and casting furtive glances at him. Kennedy determined to keep a close watch on the trusty. At one o'clock, while the Kid was in jail during the midday court recess, Kennedy saw Kramer walk over toward the train robber's cell. Suddenly Kramer snatched the six-gun from under his coat and thrust it through the bars. Just as Kid Thompson reached to grab it, Kennedy lunged forward, threw the trusty down, and seized the pistol. The gun was fully loaded, and Kennedy found nine more cartridges in Kramer's pocket.

Upon being questioned, Kramer revealed the whole plot, and the other participants were quickly arrested, except for Tupper, who took the witness stand in the Kid's defense that afternoon, unaware that his plan had been foiled. He testified about his travels in Arizona with the Kid and claimed that the Mexican coin had been shipped to Etzler, not Thompson, thus implying that Etzler was the real train robber. When Tupper completed his testimony, the prosecutor asked him, "Is it true, Mr. Tupper, that you smuggled a pistol and nine cartridges to Kid Thompson in his cell in jail today through the assistance of a man named Harris and a woman by the name of Brown?"

A dead silence fell upon the courtroom. It was the first public mention of the plot. Tupper paled but answered at once, "No sir, it is not."

The young cowboy was placed under arrest as soon as he stepped down from the stand. He was later tried and sentenced to five years for trying to help the Kid escape, but his conviction was overturned by the California Supreme Court because the judge left the courtroom while the case was being argued to the jury and did not return for twenty minutes.[26]

On April 20, Kid Thompson was once again convicted of train wrecking, but this time was sentenced to a life term. He was sent to Folsom to keep him away from Alva, who was beginning to despair behind bars. At the time Alva confessed, Detective Lawson had promised to use his best efforts to secure him a pardon, but now Lawson was dead. Later Alva's wife divorced him. So it was no surprise when, early in the morning of July 19, 1900, Johnson made an ingenious attempt to escape San Quentin.

Alva and another lifer, Lucien Healy, were assigned to work in the prison hospital. For months they plaited a sixty-foot rope from bits of rags and string stolen from the jute mill. On one end of the rope they fastened a "S" shaped hook made from heavy steel wire. The hospital ceiling was constructed of wood and tin, and the convicts easily cut through it with a stolen knife and auger. Once on the roof Alva used his skill with a lasso to hurl the rope forty-seven feet across the yard to the outer wall. He drew in the slack, and the hook snagged on the guard railing. Then, tying the other end to the hospital chimney and hooking his arms and legs around the rope, Alva slid across the yard to the wall. He gave the rope a jerk to let Healy know the coast was clear, tied a window cord to the railing, and climbed down the twenty-eight-foot-high wall. It was 2:20 A.M. when Alva dropped to the ground and slipped off into the darkness. A minute later Guard Lee Carpenter, on patrol outside the prison, saw a dark figure crouching at the foot of the whitewashed wall and fired both barrels of his ten gauge shotgun. Healy dropped in his tracks, peppered with fourteen buckshot.

The two shots roused every guard in the prison, and in a few minutes a squad of eighty men was in hot pursuit of Alva Johnson. It was not long before Guard S. L. Randolph found the exhausted train robber in a clump of brush on the hill behind the prison. The long run up the hill had completely outwinded him. "It's all up," Alva gasped. "I knew it was when the shots were fired." [27]

Johnson served another seven years and through the efforts of his parents and friends, was paroled on October 20, 1907. The state board of pardons came under fire from the Los Angeles press for releasing him, but Alva proved he was a reformed man and, in 1910, was granted a full pardon. Kid Thompson seemed to have less interest in redeeming himself. He was paroled on December 14, 1909, but a year later violated his parole conditions and escaped. Recaptured in 1915, he served another year and was again released on parole to work in Imperial, California. Unable to make it on his own outside of prison, in 1921 he returned to San Quentin voluntarily. Released after three months, the Kid died in 1925, still on parole. [28]

More than a little effort is needed to realize that the story of Kid Thompson and Alva Johnson was not conjured up in the film and television studios of Burbank and Hollywood. Today's San Fernando Valley, with its sprawling tracts of cedar-shingled houses, its shopping malls, and its congested freeways, seems an unlikely stage for a western train robbery drama. It is a far cry from the stomping grounds of the Arizona cowboy and the Tujunga rancher who set Los Angeles on its ear almost a century ago.

CHAPTER 9

The Tulare Twins: Ben and
Dudley Johnson

THE decade following 1890 was the heyday of the American train robber. During those years trains were held up in numbers unmatched before or since. Between 1890 and 1903 there were 341 actual and attempted train robberies in the United States in which 99 men were killed. Tulare County, California bears the dubious distinction of probably having fostered more of these train robbers than any other county in the country. The Dalton brothers, Chris Evans, John and George Sontag, Dan McCall, and Jim Parker were among the Tulare train bandits who raided the railroad in the 1890s.[1]

Why so many men got mixed up in train robbery in Tulare has never been fully explained nor understood, but most of the bandits knew each other and were undoubtedly influenced by one another. The first Tulare train robbers were Chris Evans and John Sontag, who held up four trains in the San Joaquin Valley between 1889 and 1892. Although these robberies generated a tremendous amount of public excitement, Evans and Sontag were not accused until their final holdup. After a lengthy manhunt, Sontag was slain and Evans captured.

One of Chris Evans's friends was Grat Dalton, the roughneck son of a large Kansas family. During the summer of 1888 the two worked together at the Granger's Union warehouses in Pixley and Tipton. In the 1880s, Grat and his brothers Bob and Emmett made numerous trips to California with their father. Several of their older brothers settled in the San Joaquin Valley, and another brother, Bill, got married and leased a ranch near Paso Robles. Grat and Bob were commissioned deputy U.S. marshals in the Indian Territory, in 1888, and were later joined by Emmett, who worked for them as a posseman. While on duty as a deputy marshal, Grat made two extended trips to California. Bob and Emmett also made frequent trips to visit friends and relatives in Tulare and San Luis Obispo counties. These were the days of railroad fare wars, and, in 1887, a ticket from the Midwest to southern California could be purchased for as little as a dollar. Grat Dalton was well known as a gambler, brawler, and drinker in saloons and bordellos the length and breadth of the San Joaquin Valley. His drinking was his downfall. In 1890 he was fired by U.S. Marshal Jacob Yoes, and in June, Bob and Emmett also lost their badges. The three brothers quickly turned to horse theft, and in September, Grat was jailed in Fort Smith, but he was soon released for lack of evidence. A month later, Bob and Emmett, under indictment for stealing horses, fled to the West Coast, appearing at brother Bill's ranch, near Paso Robles, on October 15. Grat, at his mother's request, went to California to check up on his younger brothers. He arrived there on January 15, 1891.[2]

The Daltons were popular with the rough crowd of Tulare, Fresno, Merced, and San Luis Obispo counties, but their habit of going armed at all times now caused considerable talk among respectable people. Local officers were unaware that a $1,000 reward had been offered for Bob and Emmett in Oklahoma.[3]

Two young men from Traver, in particular, were much impressed with Grat, Bob, and Emmett Dalton. They were Ben and Dudley Johnson, a pair of hell-raising, eighteen-year-old twin brothers who had recently settled in Tulare County. They were born Dudley D. and Benjamin Babbitt Johnson in Whitesboro, New York, and were the sons of Chester L. Johnson, a skilled machinist, who later moved his family to Amsterdam, New York, where the boys and their several sisters were raised. On their father's death in 1890 the twins struck out for San Francisco to visit a married sister, Mrs. Heath. They stayed in that city and in Oakland for a time, looking for work. Hearing that they could find jobs in Tulare County, the Johnsons journeyed south and worked as laborers in the towns of Traver and Tulare. They became known as the "Tulare Twins."[4]

The brothers lionized the tough, hard-drinking Daltons. Bob and Emmett, only a few years older than the Johnsons, were dead shots and expert horsemen, ever ready with a tale of their adventures as lawmen in Indian Territory. They made a profound impression on the two young newcomers from the East. The friendship between the twins and the Daltons was shortlived, however. On the night of February 6, 1891, after drinking more than a quart of whiskey each to get their courage up, Bob and Emmett stopped Southern Pacific

Outlaw Ben Johnson, slain, in 1898, in a shoot-out with Florida lawmen. From author's collection.

Train No. 17, near Alila. In an exchange of gunfire with the Wells Fargo messenger, the fireman was killed, and the Daltons rode off empty-handed. Bob and Emmett escaped back to the Indian Territory, but Grat, who had helped plan the robbery, was arrested and lodged in the Tulare County jail in Visalia.[5]

The Johnson boys were working for a retired minister, F. H. Wales, who owned a fruit orchard near Tulare. On August 10 they got into a dispute with Wales over their wages. When he accused the brothers of laziness and refused to pay them, Ben and Dudley took two of his horses and rode into Tulare, where they bought a saddle. They then headed north for Oakland. They took turns riding the horse with the saddle (while the other rode bareback), but the animals got lame and sorebacked soon after they left Tulare. The brothers walked nearly

The notorious Dudley Johnson, one-half of the train-robbing Tulare Twins. From author's collection.

two hundred miles, leading the horses. When they reached San Leandro they put the horses out to pasture and went on to Oakland. Wales, however, had sworn out warrants for the twins, charging them with grand larceny. Their descriptions were telegraphed to the Oakland police, and on August 27, as they were walking down 14th Street to the post office to pick up their mail, they were spotted and arrested.

The brothers were returned to Visalia and, after a hearing, were sentenced to thirty days in jail. They admitted taking the horses but blamed the affair on Wales: "He did us up pretty hard. We worked for him all summer until he owed us $90. We told him we wanted the money, but he wouldn't pay us and said that we would have to wait until next summer. We told him that if he didn't pay us we would take two of his horses for our money and still he wouldn't settle, so we took the horses."[6]

In the Visalia jail the Johnsons met their friend Grat Dalton, who had been convicted of the Alila robbery and was awaiting sentencing. Five days later, on September 3, two masked bandits attempted to rob a Southern Pacific train, near Ceres, in Stanislaus County, but were driven off after a furious gun battle with two railroad detectives. Bob and Emmett Dalton were immediately suspected. Southern Pacific detectives believed that they would attempt to liberate Grat, and a heavy guard was thrown up around the jail. The detectives, however, were barking up the wrong tree, for the real bandits, Chris Evans and John Sontag, had escaped undetected.

Tulare County Sheriff Eugene Kay placed Bill Dalton under arrest for the holdup at Ceres. Bill was soon cleared of any complicity, but he had been indicted by the Tulare County grand jury as an accessory to the Alila holdup and was forced to languish in jail to await trial. There were eighteen prisoners in the jail, a two-level building located at Visalia's courthouse square. On the main floor the Johnsons, Grat Dalton, and other prisoners were kept in four cells inside a large locked cage. Each cell had an individual lock as well as a long safety bar that ran the length of the corridor. The bar was operated by a heavy lever in the jailer's office and simultaneously secured each cell door. Next to the cage was a long corridor with a staircase that led to the basement cells. Also in the basement was a room used to store firewood. It had a window covered by a hinged grate of metal bars that could be opened and closed so that the wood could be thrown inside. It was secured by a heavy lock.

Bill Dalton was locked in an isolated cell for insane prisoners upstairs, and the basement cells were filled with hoboes. At night the prisoners were locked in their cells, but during the day they were allowed free run of all the jail corridor, where they passed the time in idle conversation and card playing. Talk of train robbery was no doubt the topic of the day, and the Johnson boys drank it all in. Grat Dalton took the twins into his confidence, told them he was planning to escape, and asked for their help. They agreed but declined to take part in the actual break since their sentences were so short. Grat told them that he had a friend who was helping from the outside and showed them a wrench, a file, a knife blade filed into a saw, and a whetstone, all smuggled into the jail by a black trusty. Grat's friend who gave the tools to the trusty is reliably believed to have been Chris Evans. Sheriff Kay later investigated the plot and determined that Evans had provided the assistance; George and Perry Byrd, Evans's brothers-in-law, confirmed this.[7]

Two other prisoners were involved in the plot: W. B. Smith, a boxcar burglar, and Arvil Beck, a horse thief. Using the wrench, they attempted to loosen the long locking bolt, without success. They then tried to cut a hole in the outside wall but were stopped by a steel plate. Finally Grat decided to saw through one of the iron bars in the corridor. There was a large dry goods box, covered with a blanket that the prisoners used for a card table in the corridor. They placed it next to the bars and began working with the file and knife. While the Johnsons, Dalton, Smith, and Beck played cards and sang in loud voices, each took his turn hiding behind the box and sawing the bar, and after three days it was cut through. A broom handle stolen from the basement and blackened with soot was used to replace the missing bar.

J. W. Williams, the head jailer and not particularly vigilant, was in the habit of using a trusty to lock up. On the evening of September 27, 1891, Williams called to the prisoners, "Everybody inside!" Looking into the corridor, he saw no prisoners and assumed that they were all in their cells. Williams closed the bolt and sent the trusty into the corridor with the keys to lock each cell. Unknown to the jailer, Grat Dalton, Beck, and Smith were hiding behind the box in the corridor and the wall of the rear cell. On a prearranged signal the hoboes in the basement tanks began singing at the top of their lungs to cover up any noise. The three prisoners then removed the broomstick, crawled through the hole, and went downstairs to the wood room. Using the iron bar that had been cut from the cage, they pried open the grate window and crawled outside. They stole a buggy and left town unnoticed. Several guards were on duty in the jail, but the escape was not detected until twelve hours later.

The jailbreak stunned the Tulare public, and local newspapers ran facetious headlines: "Dalton Departs" and "Goodbye, Grat!" Reporters who toured the jail found the good-natured Bill Dalton strumming his guitar and singing, "You'll Never Miss My Brother Till He's Gone." Bill told them that one of the Johnson boys had crawled out of his cell by squeezing through an eight-by-ten-inch aperture at the bottom of the cell door and then freed the escapees with a skeleton key. The jailers made a careful search, found the blackened broom stick in the cage wall, and realized that Bill was lying.[8]

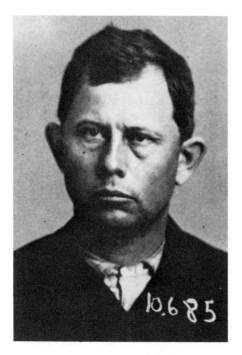

Police mug photo of Grat Dalton, taken, in 1891, at the time of his arrest for the Alila train robbery. Courtesy Special Collections, California State University at Fresno Library.

Grat Dalton eventually escaped back to Oklahoma Territory, where he rejoined Bob and Emmett. The Daltons became the most notorious outlaws in America until their demise on October 5, 1892, when they attempted to rob two banks at Coffeyville, Kansas. Eight men died in a pitched gun battle with the townfolk, and the Dalton gang was wiped out.

Although it was well known that they had assisted in the escape, the Johnsons went unpunished and were released after serving their term. For a few years they managed to keep out of trouble. Dudley worked on the Giant Oak orchard, near Farmersville, and later both worked at the Sequoia lumber mills. Ben Johnson purchased a small ranch in Kings County, adjacent to a piece of land owned by Sandy White. Ben paid White for the right to obtain water from his neighbor's flume, but Johnson soon lost his land and demanded that White buy back his interest in the flume. When White refused, Ben destroyed the flume. White swore out a complaint against Johnson, and on January 11, 1895, Constable Harry Bernstein placed him under arrest. Ben hired two lawyers, and in a trial three days later a jury acquitted him.[9]

The brothers then bought a five-acre plot of ranchland, six miles east of Traver and two miles southwest of Monson, and began building a ranch house, but they soon ran out of money and were unable to finish it. In October, 1895, their mother came to live with them. The twins were not suited for hard work, and their association with the Daltons had marked them indelibly. Already they had begun committing thefts at neighboring farms. They organized a gang of five local youths, stealing cattle and grain, and were also reported to have been members of the "Forty Thieves," a well-organized band captained by Joe Foster, a notorious burglar and robber from Fresno.[10]

The brothers, especially Dudley, took care not to be seen in public with their criminal friends and associated only with members of good families. Ben became engaged to marry a girl who lived nearby, but she learned of his lawless escapades and broke off the engagement. Embittered, Ben and his brother became increasingly bold. On August 25, 1895, they pulled a daring midnight burglary of the Porterville post office. The twins first entered the home of the postmaster by cutting a wire screen from a kitchen window. Then, creeping into the bedroom where the postmaster and his wife were sleeping, they took his pants, which contained the office and safe keys. Proceeding to the post office on Main Street, they managed to avoid two night watchmen and unlocked the back door. The boys used the keys to open the safe, removed $500 worth of stamps and $250 in coin, and then slipped out of town.[11]

On December 11 the Johnsons burglarized a Farmersville store owned by T. J. Brundage, who had befriended Dudley and employed him on several occasions. They used a ten-pound sledge hammer, a chisel, and a punch to crack the safe, taking $20, postage stamps, and a chain and locket. On February 6, 1896, they broke into Charles Rankin's store, in Lindsay, and stole an entire wagonload of merchandise. The Johnsons committed numerous other minor thefts in Kings and Tulare counties, and Dudley made several trips to Los Angeles and San Francisco to fence the loot. On the night of February 10 they stole eight sacks of barley from Charles Howard's ranch, near Hanford, and also took a harness belonging to a Mexican named Domingo, who soon discovered the theft and reported it to Constable Harry Bernstein. At daylight the officer and Domingo found the thieves' trail and followed it twenty-eight miles to the Johnson ranch.

When they rode up to the house the Mexican spotted his harness partially hidden in a haystack.

Bernstein hailed the house, and Mrs. Johnson came outside. Bernstein, who had never seen her before, asked her name, which she gave, and after further questioning she admitted that she had two sons but claimed that neither was at home. The constable heard a noise in the house and walked to the east wall.

"Johnson!" Bernstein called.

A young man stepped outside, and the constable recognized Dudley Johnson.

"What do you want?" Johnson asked.

"I have a warrant for your arrest," was Bernstein's reply.

"No officer will ever serve a warrant on me!" Dudley snarled. He snatched a Winchester rifle from inside the doorway and covered Bernstein.

Dudley ordered the officer to leave the ranch, and since he had the drop, Bernstein complied. As the constable and Domingo rode away, they saw both Johnsons saddle their horses and head toward the mountains. Bernstein raced back to Hanford and notified Kings County Sheriff William Van Buckner. With Constables Goodrich and Collins they returned to the Johnson ranch and watched the place all night, hoping that the twins would return. By daybreak the Johnsons had not appeared so the officers moved in and searched the house. They discovered a hoard of stolen property, a Winchester rifle, a shotgun, two hundred pounds of shot, two thousand rounds of ammunition, forty files, eighty keys, gunpowder, dynamite, caps, and fuse. Most of the merchandise stolen from the store in Lindsay was found under the house. The officers also discovered a collection of newspaper clippings about the Dalton gang. Mrs. Johnson was arrested for receiving stolen property and was taken to jail in Visalia. She admitted that her sons had been friends of the Daltons and were great admirers of Evans and Sontag.

Though they were spotted in the area several times during the next week, Ben and Dudley eluded lawmen sent to arrest them. They broke into a farm house and stocked up on provisions. They held up a rancher near Orosi and unharnessed two horses from his plow team, but after trying the animals out, they found them to be poor saddle horses and gave them back. The Johnsons then rode south toward the Tehachapi Mountains.[12]

From her jail cell Mrs. Johnson wrote a pleading letter to her fugitive sons, which was published in the Visalia newspapers:

Visalia, Cal., February 18, 1896—My Dear Children: This is your dear mother that you love more than your life. You know, dear boys, that you have done those things that you ought not to have done. That man that came to the house was, I think, the sheriff from Hanford, had a right to arrest you, and now every bad thing will be laid to you unless you come back and face it. Do, dear children, come back and face it; do, dear children, come, and all things may turn out for the best. Do it for my sake; come, they cannot kill or hang you. Trusting that this may reach you is the prayer of your Fond Mother.[13]

The Johnson boys had no intention of giving themselves up. The call of the outlaw trail was drawing them inexorably down its path. Ben and Dudley wanted to emulate the Daltons and rob a train in Tulare, but their plans were thwarted on March 19, when an attempt was made to hold up SP Train No. 19, at Tagus Switch. A. P. Merritt, sheriff of Tulare County, had gotten wind of the plot and had put deputies on both the north- and southbound trains. Bandit Dan McCall was shot dead. Si Lovren (a Visalia saloonkeeper and an old friend of Chris Evans's) and three accomplices were arrested.[14]

The twins continued to linger about their old haunts in Tulare County, undoubtedly harbored by members of the Forty Thieves. At two in the morning of April 26 they burglarized the office of the Puget Sound Lumber Company, in Visalia, blowing open the safe, which contained but fifteen dollars. To make their effort worthwhile they took a Yost typewriter, and then escaped in a buggy, leaving behind a half stick of giant powder and a size nine footprint.[15]

The Johnsons knew that things were too hot in Tulare for another train holdup, so they looked for a better location. They had heard of the big robbery, near Davis, two years earlier, when Jack Brady and Sam Browning had stopped the Omaha Overland and removed $52,000 from the Wells Fargo car. This had been the biggest haul in a California train robbery, and it was well known that the Overland still carried huge shipments of gold to the East. Ben and Dudley decided to try their hand at stopping it and teamed up with Frank J. Morgan, an itinerant laborer and thief, well known in the rookeries along Front Street, in Sacramento. A big man, thirty-five years old, Morgan had a reputation as a crack shot and always carried a Colt .41 army-model six-gun under his coat.

Frank J. Morgan, partner of the Johnson boys. He was shot to death in the Webster train holdup, near Sacramento, in 1896. Courtesy Pacific Center for Western Studies, University of the Pacific, Stockton.

On September 3, Morgan and the Johnson boys met in Henry's Saloon on East Street, near Market, in San Francisco, and laid plans for the holdup. The trio went to Sacramento the next day and broke into a hardware store, taking a large quantity of giant powder, caps, and fuse. The following day Morgan and one of the twins visited an opium den in Sacramento's Chinatown and smoked a pipe of "hop." They then headed west along the railroad tracks toward Davis. The spot they had chosen for the holdup was near Webster, about six miles west of Sacramento, in the great "Tule Basin" of Yolo County. At that time it was sparsely settled and flooded with water for miles.

At six that evening, September 5, 1896, eastbound Southern Pacific Train No. 3 left Oakland with Engineer Ed Ingles and Fireman Patrick Burns in the cab. Filled with passengers headed for the state fair in

Sacramento, it pulled into Davis at nine o'clock. When the train rolled out of the Davis depot, Frank Morgan swung aboard and concealed himself on the tender. As they passed Swingles station, near Webster, Engineer Ingles heard the sound of coal falling from the tender. He turned around in time to see a masked man jump down onto the gangplank.

"Throw up your hands!" Morgan shouted, pointing his Colt at the engineer's head, and both Ingles and Burns quickly complied.

"Now slow her down," Morgan ordered, and Ingles eased back the throttle.

The engineer and his fireman had each been in a previous train holdup, and Burns knew that Ingles had a pistol hung on the side of the engine, just ahead of the seat box. With this in mind Burns took the hose from the tender and washed off the deck of the engine, also turning the hose on the cinders from the firebox to create a cloud of steam in the cab and give Ingles a chance to grab his gun. But the robber kept his six-shooter within two feet of Ingles's head, and the engineer made no move for his pistol.

"Now stop her," Morgan instructed a moment later. Ingles set his brakes, and the train rumbled to a halt.

Morgan peered out of the locomotive cab, glanced up the tracks where the engine's headlight cut a swath through the darkness, and said, "Pull her up easy."

The train moved forward only two car lengths when Morgan again ordered Ingles to stop, leaving the passenger cars on a long trestle with only the engine and express car on solid ground. This was known as the "trestle method." It was an old trick to discourage passengers from leaving the coaches. If anyone in the cars wanted to interfere, he would have to walk on the trestle, risking a long fall or a bandit's bullet.

Just as the train halted, the Johnson boys clambered up the embankment and took up positions on each side of the engine, Dudley on the left and Ben on the right. Both were masked, and Dudley carried a large revolver, while Ben held a sawed-off shotgun.

"Well, how about it?" Morgan asked Ben Johnson. "Is everything all right?"

Ben answered that it was, and Morgan told Burns, "Get down off the engine."

Ben then walked the fireman back to the rear of the express car.

"Get between there and uncouple," Johnson ordered, and Burns climbed up between the express car and the smoker and began to work on the air brakes, hooks, and levers.

Meanwhile Frank Morgan was getting nervous. Dudley had walked back to the express car, leaving Morgan alone in the cab with Ingles. The robber kept glancing back, worried by the delay in uncoupling the car. Ingles told Morgan that he would have to open the injector valve to let more water into the boiler. He stooped down, grabbed his pistol, and, unnoticed by Morgan, slipped it into the waistband of his trousers. Once again Morgan looked out the cab, and Ingles saw his chance. He whipped out the pistol and, at a distance of two feet, fired two quick shots into Morgan's breast. The robber threw up both hands and pitched headfirst off the engine, discharging his Colt as he fell. Ingles then shoved the throttle open, and the train lurched forward.

At the sound of the shots, pandemonium broke loose in the passenger coaches. Women screamed in terror, and those in the front coaches made a wild rush for the rear of the train, while other passengers tried frantically to hide their money and jewelry by shoving them under the seats.

Ben Johnson, on hearing the gunfire, started back toward the engine, but Burns, thinking quickly, reassured him. "That's nothing. I guess your partner is scaring some hoboes away."

At that moment the train began moving, and Burns climbed onto the forward platform of the smoker. The Johnson boys both scrambled onto the rear platform of the express car. Burns felt certain that Ingles had shot the robber, but he coolly told the Johnsons that their partner must have thought that the express car had been uncoupled and was having the engineer pull the train forward. The ruse worked. The Johnsons jumped down onto the tracks, but the train, instead of slowing down, rapidly picked up speed, and the enraged brothers sent a volley of shots crashing into the passenger cars.

Ingles roared into Sacramento at full throttle. At the passenger depot he ran to the office of the superintendent to report the holdup, and within an hour a posse of deputy sheriffs and railroad detectives had raced back to the scene. They found the dead robber lying on his stomach near the tracks, with his face turned to one side and his arms outstretched. His six-gun, covered with blood, lay near his right hand. In his pocket was a memorandum book containing the inscription, "F. J. Morgan, Henry's Saloon, 307 East Street, San Francisco." Nearby, the officers found twenty-four pounds of dynamite, carefully wrapped into charges of one to four sticks, each fitted with a cap and fuse. "Enough to have scattered the express car over an acre of ground," one of the detectives said.[16]

An intensive hunt was made for the missing robbers, but without success. Morgan's body was taken to Sacramento on a freight train and placed in the city jail, where a huge crowd gathered and spilled out into the street. Hundreds of people viewed his remains before several of Morgan's friends identified the body. He was buried in a rough pine box in a pauper's grave in Helvetia Cemetery.

For his heroic action in thwarting the robbery, Ed Ingles was awarded an engraved gold watch and $250 by the grateful company, and Wells Fargo presented him with a reward of $300. Patrick Burns was also presented with a gold watch.

Captain Isaiah W. Lees, of the San Francisco police, sent Detectives Wren and Tom Gibson to Henry's Saloon to pick up points on Morgan. The bartender identified a postmortem photograph of the robber and said that Morgan had frequented the saloon for two years. Two days before the holdup he had visited the saloon with two young men; their descriptions generally tallied with those of the two missing train robbers. The detectives also learned that Morgan had stored a Yost typewriter in a back room of the saloon. Within a few days the officers had identified the typewriter as the machine that had been stolen from the Puget Sound Lumber Company. When Southern Pacific detectives found that the Johnson boys were wanted for the Visalia burglary, it became evident that the Tulare Twins had been Morgan's partners.[17]

The Johnson brothers dropped out of sight for more than a year. They surfaced but once, when Dudley appeared at the home of one of his sisters, Mrs. Nettie Clark, in Syracuse, New York. She later recalled:

> He spent much time at my house and left suddenly. Where he went I was never able to find out. He was well dressed and in talking with us told of many of his experiences. He would tell how he and his brother traveled all over the country, beating their way not only on freight but also on passenger trains. He never said anything about having committed any crimes or having been arrested.[18]

The killing of the twins' partner had been a sobering experience, but their desire for easy riches was overwhelming, and they decided to pull another train robbery. This time they chose more familiar territory. The spot they picked was Cross Creek, an isolated railroad siding located four miles north of Goshen, in Tulare County. Two trestles spanned the forks of the creek, and two miles downstream was an old, long-abandoned Butterfield stage station, a notorious hangout for robbers and cattle thieves. The Daltons had used the station as a hideout seven years earlier.

On February 28, 1898, the twins stole a horse and buggy from the ranch of J. C. Anderson, near Madera. Two weeks later they burglarized Barrett & Hick's powder house, near Fresno, and took a large amount of dynamite. On the night of March 22 they secreted the stolen rig in the brush next to the Cross Creek trestles and walked into Goshen. Train No. 18, northbound, pulled into Goshen at 10:30 P.M. for a brief stop. When it passed out of the depot ten minutes later, the Johnsons emerged from the darkness and jumped onto the blind baggage at the rear of the mail car. They found a black youth stealing a ride, searched him for weapons, and warned, "When the train stops, don't get off or we'll shoot you."

The twins climbed onto the roof of the car and walked forward to the tender. Fireman Dan McAuliffe spotted the pair crawling over the coal. Both were masked and wore slouch hats pulled down over their eyes. Dudley carried a Winchester, and Ben held a six-shooter in each fist. Covering McAuliffe and the engineer, Jimmy Moore, they climbed down into the cab and searched both trainmen for weapons. The Johnsons had learned their lesson from Ed Ingles and were not taking any chances. They ordered Moore to stop the train at Cross Creek bridge, leaving the passenger cars on the trestle. Most of the two hundred passengers aboard were asleep in the five Pullman coaches. Others, including Southern Pacific Detective Jim Meade, former sheriff of Fresno County, were playing cards in the smoker, near the front of the train.

The Johnson boys marched Moore and McAuliffe past the mail coach to the express car. After firing several shots down each side of the train to cow the passengers, the twins ordered McAuliffe to tell the Wells Fargo messenger to open the door. The messenger, Joseph Pease, did not answer, so Dudley Johnson removed a stick of dynamite from a sack under his coat, handed it to the fireman, and instructed him to place it under the side door. McAuliffe struck a match to the fuse, and the door was blown out of its frame. Dudley called for the messenger to come out, but Pease refused. The outlaw lit a second stick of dynamite and threw it inside the car, but the fuse sputtered out. A third stick was tossed in, but Pease had had enough.

Wells Fargo express car at Cross Creek, blown apart with dynamite by the Johnson boys in 1898. Courtesy Tulare County Historical Society.

"I'll come out," he called. "Let me throw out the bomb."

Pease threw the charge down the embankment, where it exploded harmlessly. Then he clambered out of the car. Dudley entered, placed a huge charge of dynamite under the through safe, and rushed back outside. The result was a terrific explosion that was plainly heard four miles away, in Goshen. The express car was blown to pieces, with only the floor and parts of the two ends left intact. Passengers in the smoker were thrown from their seats, the safe was rent and shattered, and crates of produce and chickens, as well as coins from the safe, were scattered up and down the railroad bed. Part of one chicken coop lodged in the telegraph wires overhead.

Back in the smoking car Detective Meade decided to take action. He loaded his pistol and said, "Boys, we are in for it. Out with your guns."

Not a man responded. They were too busy hiding money and jewelry in their shoes and under seat cushions. Meade stepped alone onto the front platform of the car and let drive three shots at the robbers. The Johnsons instantly replied with a barrage of Winchester and six-gun fire, and Meade, favoring discretion over valor, hastily ducked back into the smoker.

After removing a quantity of coin from the safe, the twins turned their attention to the mail car. Clerk George Nickell was ordered to open up, and he quickly complied. Ben Johnson climbed in and instructed Nickell and his two assistant clerks to put up their hands and march to the end of the car.

"Where is the registered pouch?" Ben demanded. "Get it quick." Nickell denied that the car held any registered mail, but the robber would not be fooled.

"Get it quick," Johnson snapped again.

An assistant clerk dragged the registered pouch to the other end of the car. Johnson ordered the fireman to cut it open and then placed twenty registered packages into a smaller pouch.

Dudley Johnson then turned to Moore and said, "Take out your watch, engineer, and tell us the time."

"Eleven-thirty," replied Moore.

"I do not want you to leave this place for one hour," warned Johnson. "If you do, I will blow you up."

The brothers sprinted off, jumped into their buggy, and headed north at a trot, leading a second horse behind them. Exactly how much money they took has never been satisfactorily determined. Since the through safe was opened, newspapers guessed that the sum was $75,000. Charles C. Crowley, the Southern Pacific's chief detective, stated that only $400 was taken from the safe. Since the robbers decided to rob the mail coach, and since most of the coin in the safe was destroyed or blown across the tracks, the smaller figure is probably more accurate.[19]

By daylight the sheriffs of Tulare, Kings, and Fresno counties were in the field with large posses, and before noon every important road and highway in the San Joaquin Valley was patrolled and guarded. Rewards totaling $2,300 were offered for each bandit. The officers learned that after the holdup two men were seen driving north through Traver at high speed in a buggy drawn by a sorrel horse and leading a black horse. For five days they hunted the outlaws in vain. Several suspects were arrested but soon released. Then, on March 27, two weather-beaten strangers in a buggy pulled up front in John Semorello's store at Indian Gulch, in the Mariposa County foothills, 150 miles north of Cross Creek. They bought canned goods, clothes, and a hat, and paid for them with eighteen silver dollars, all badly bent and scarred. Semorello recalled reading in the newspapers that coins taken in the Cross Creek job had been bent, and he sent a message to the Mariposa County sheriff. The manhunt swung into high gear again, with lawmen scouring the hills between Catheys Valley and Hornitos. Six miles from Indian Gulch they found the robbers' abandoned camp. Blankets, ammunition, and the black horse and buggy had been left behind.[20]

Sheriff Tom Cunningham was called into the manhunt, but he gave up the next day. He told a reporter:

> This thing has narrowed down to a still hunt. The men can never be caught while the hills are full of vehicles. The pursuers have been stumbling all over each other, and the chase has looked more like a funeral procession than anything else. I came here because I was informed that the men were surrounded in the hills, and that additional assistance was needed to take them.[21]

The Johnson boys made a clean getaway, leaving few traces behind. The sorrel horse was found a week later, wandering loose in a field near Fresno. The twins had abandoned the animal when it gave out. In June two boys playing in a ditch four miles east of Fresno found ten empty Southern Pacific money bags that had been part of the stolen shipment and a vest and hat worn by the robbers. The name of the store where the hat was purchased had been scratched off with a knife.[22]

A lengthy investigation of the Cross Creek holdup was conducted by Detective Crowley, of the SP, and Sheriff Merritt, of Tulare County. Exactly how they pinned the job on the Johnsons is unclear. Crowley would only say that he had "inside information." Historian Wallace Smith, in his book *Prodigal Sons,* states that Jim Lee, a member of the Forty Thieves, was interrogated and confessed that the Johnsons had robbed the train. The *Weekly Visalia Delta* reported that Deputy Sheriff D. O. Harrelson, while searching the train robbers' abandoned camp in Mariposa, had found a memorandum book filled with cryptic writing, which was turned over to the railroad detectives, who traced it to the Johnson brothers.[23]

Once again the Tulare Twins managed to disappear completely. In April another of their sisters, Ada, married James C. Johnston, in Portland, Oregon. Johnston was the son of a respectable New York family and the brother of a prominent U.S. army major and mathematics professor at West Point. He knew little about his bride's family and never dreamed that her brothers were notorious outlaws. Johnston and his new wife moved to Orange City, Florida, where he planned to go into the tobacco business. Their spacious home, known as the Shivers place, had long been owned by Johnston's family and was situated on West French Avenue, a mile west of town.

In the fall the twins' mother, suffering from heart disease and with her health failing, went to live with the Johnstons, in Orange City. Somehow Ben and Dudley learned of her plight and managed to make their way to Florida in time to see their mother pass away on November 15. The boys moved in with Ada and their new brother-in-law, and neighbors assumed that they intended to raise tobacco with Johnston. But, as the *Volusia County Record* reported, "Not many weeks rolled by before there was a cat and dog life at the Shivers house." 24

On December 10, 1898, Ben and Dudley got into a raging quarrel with their brother-in-law. He ordered them to leave, but his wife sided with the twins, and Johnston found himself ejected, half dressed, from his own house. He went into town and looked up City Marshal Sperry, who accompanied him to the county seat, Deland, where Johnston swore out warrants against the twins. Then they returned to Orange City with Chief Deputy Sheriff W. P. Edwards and Deputy Sheriff Will Kreamer, none of whom knew that the Johnson boys were dangerous desperadoes. They arrived at the house at six o'clock, and Johnston told the officers that he wanted to remain in their buggy, saying that he would be shot if he went inside.

The lawmen took up positions in the darkness around the house, with Sperry on one side, Kreamer on the other, and Edwards at the front door. His knock was answered by Ada Johnston, and when Edwards told her his errand, she snapped, "You can't come in here. There will be trouble!"

She slammed the door shut, and a moment later Marshal Sperry shouted that two men were coming out a side door. As Will Kreamer rushed around the house, Ben and Dudley opened fire on the lawmen with Winchesters. A bullet struck Kreamer above the left eye and tore through his head, killing him instantly. Sperry was trading shots with the Johnsons when their sister threw open the door, clapped her hands, and cried, "That's right, boys, go it! Give it to them!"

Deputy Edwards, six-gun in hand, leaped off the front porch and found himself face-to-face with the twins. They all fired at the same time, and Edwards reeled as a rifle bullet tore into his right breast, laying two ribs bare. The officer stayed on his feet and fired again, and Dudley Johnson dropped with a bullet in his heart. Ben Johnson kept shooting at Edwards as fast as he could work his rifle. The deputy staggered back toward the gate, emptying his six-shooter as he went. "Go, you son of a bitch!" Ben Johnson yelled. "I'll show you what kind of stuff we are made of!"

Edwards, bleeding freely, climbed into the buggy, and Marshal Sperry took the reins and rushed him to a doctor in town. Edwards's wounds were dressed; then, with Sperry and a large posse, he returned to the house. They found Dudley Johnson and Will Kreamer dead in the yard and placed the sister under arrest. In her brothers' room they found a grip containing a set of burglars' tools. Ben Johnson had managed to escape.[25]

Ada Johnston was taken to jail in DeLand and charged with aiding and abetting the murder of Deputy Kreamer, but the charges were evidently later dropped.

When Detective Crowley learned of the shootout, he wired information about the Johnsons to Orange City, and for the first time the Florida officers realized how notorious their quarry really was. Southern Pacific and Wells Fargo detectives sent reward notices for Ben Johnson throughout the South and Southwest, but he was never brought to justice for the train robberies in California or the murder in Florida. He disappeared completely, and his fate remains unknown.[26]

With his brother dead and the law hounding his trail, Ben Johnson's days were numbered. The twentieth century lay just around the corner, and time was fast running out for the train robbers of the Old West. The editor of the *Hanford Daily Journal* offered a fitting epitaph for the elusive outlaw: "The rule of Wells Fargo is to never let up on a robber, and the fate of Ben Johnson is only a question of time—death or capture."[26]

Either way, it was the end of the line for the Tulare Twins.

CHAPTER 10

Gunsmoke and Dynamite:
The Gates Boys

AT eight o'clock on Friday evening, April 11, 1902, Andrew Piccardo, his twenty-two-year-old son, Louie, and a half dozen customers were gathered in Piccardo's Saloon, in Jackson, Amador County, when a bandit suddenly burst through the front door, his face covered with a black mask, his clothes concealed by a long linen duster, and his hands filled with a pair of six-guns. He strode quickly into the center of the saloon, covering Andrew Piccardo with a Colt .45.

"Throw up your hands!" the robber barked, and sixteen arms stretched for the ceiling.

"Get into the cellar," he ordered, and herded the customers into the back room of the saloon. One, a newcomer from Italy, didn't understand the command, but a quick kick from the bandit's boot proved an ear-opening introduction to the English language. Then, directing the saloonkeeper and his son into the office, the outlaw demanded, "Open the safe, and be damned quick about it."

But Piccardo was in no hurry to find the keys, and after a few minutes of stalling, he told the bandit that he had left them at home. Nervous and impatient, the freebooter commanded Piccardo to hand over the cash in the till (about $25) and began backing toward the door. As soon as he turned his back, Louie Piccardo snatched up a double-barreled shotgun from one corner of the office. He slipped in two shells loaded with No. 7 birdshot and, at a distance of forty feet, pulled both triggers. The fine shot found its mark on the bandit's left hip and forearm, and he fell in the doorway, dropping one six-gun. But instantly he picked himself up and ran off into the darkness.[1]

This inauspicious beginning launched the criminal career of one of the boldest and certainly one of the last of California's "Old West" stage and train robbers. George Gates is unknown today, but he was once notorious as the leader of the Copely train bandits. He was wanted for robbery and murder in five states before he and his brother Vern met their inevitable fates at the muzzles of a posse's guns.

The Gates boys were born and raised in Amador County, where their father, George E. Gates, owned a quartz mine at Pine Grove. The family was highly respected, and the elder Gates was the inventor of a widely used mining process. George was the oldest of four children. His brother Edward Vernon was five years his junior, and the two youngest children were Lillian and Emery. The father saw to it that his children received good educations and, in 1897, moved his family to Alameda. George, big and muscular, became well known as an athlete and boxer in Alameda and Oakland. Vern attended Alameda High School and established a local reputation as a fine tenor singer.

In November, 1900, when George was twenty-two, he enrolled in a six-month course at the Van der Naillen School of Mining, in San Francisco. He was a good student but spent too much time betting at the races. He loved to read romantic Scottish novels (then quite popular) that depicted the adventures of fictional eighteenth-century highwaymen. The following year George was matched for a prize-fight at the Reliance Club, in Oakland, but he was defeated. Much disgusted, he gave up athletics and went to work in his father's mine, in Amador County. In March 1902 he worked a short stint at the Central Eureka Mine and roomed at Nixon's Hotel, in Sutter Creek, where he was quite popular and had many friends. But George was bright and imaginative, and a career as a miner held no attraction for him. He had a reckless streak that soon extinguished any desire to follow an honest occupation and led him on a downhill trail that culminated in his unfortunate encounter with Louie Piccardo's shotgun.[2]

Sheriff U. S. Gregory spared no effort to identify the perpetrator of the saloon holdup, which the *Amador Ledger* termed "one of the most daring attempts in the highwayman line that has occurred in this county for many years." The bandit's hat and an American Bulldog revolver were found at the spot where he had fallen. The sheriff carefully searched the area and found a shot-riddled gun belt, a Frontier Colt .45, and a linen duster in an old smelter on the Jackson Gate Road. The duster was splattered with blood, and a large hole had been shot through the left side, proving that the bandit had indeed been wounded. Gregory offered a $100 reward for the robber, but several weeks passed, and he was unable to find any further clues.

Two days after the holdup George Gates was at his usual haunts in Sutter Creek, not visibly injured, and drank with various friends in the mining town's saloons. He ran into Constable H. E. Kay, of Jackson, and, in an effort to find out if the officers suspected him, greeted the constable good-naturedly, "Well, I suppose you are after me."

Kay, unsuspecting, thought Gates was joking and shook hands with him. He was on the lookout for any man with a wounded left arm or a limp, and as Gates suffered from neither ailment, Kay thought nothing else of the encounter. The next day George, saying he planned to stay another month, paid his hotelkeeper a full month's board, but the following afternoon he disappeared from town, leaving all his belongings in his room. On the evening of April 22, George's father showed up at Nixon's Hotel, remained overnight in his son's room, and left on the morning stage. He took with him George's trunk and all the contents of the hotel room.

A few days later Sheriff Gregory learned of the elder Gates's brief visit to Sutter Creek and became suspicious because the visit seemed to have had no other purpose than to carry off George's effects. The sheriff learned that the bandit's pistols, gun belt, and duster had been stolen from the office of Dr. Endicott, in Jackson, and that George Gates was a frequent visitor to the doctor's office. Investigating further, Gregory found that Gates had appeared in his hotel room the morning after the robbery, that he had had his meals brought to his room, and that friends had secretly visited him and picked birdshot out of his hip and forearm. The wounds had been minor, and the next day he had been able to get about without trouble.

On May 1, Sheriff Gregory and an Alameda policeman went to the Gates home on Eagle Avenue, in Alameda. The father answered the door and told Gregory that both George and Vernon were gone. He allowed the sheriff to search the house, but Gregory was unable to find any bloodstained clothing or other evidence of the Piccardo robbery, and he returned to Jackson empty-handed.[3]

George Gates fled California and beat his way to Trinidad, Colorado, where he adopted the alias of Guy LeCroix and worked in the coal mines at Starkville, Sopris, Gray Creek, and Gardner. In Gray Creek, Gates rented a room at the house of Abraham L. Hudson and his common-law wife, Mary. Hudson was a fellow miner, and George told him that he was a fool for slaving in a mine when he could make a fortune in a train holdup. Gates convinced Hudson that it would be simple and boasted that he was an old hand at robbing trains and saloons.

While his wife sewed a red handkerchief around a lantern, Hudson borrowed a shotgun and a .38 Smith & Wesson revolver. On the night of November 18, 1902, using the red signal lamp, George Gates and Hudson flagged down Colorado & Southern Railway Train No. 8 at Beshoar Junction, seven miles east of Trinidad. After capturing the train crew, they forced the engineer to uncouple the express car from the passenger coaches and drive a short distance up the track. Hudson then climbed down the engine and walked back toward the express car.

Wells Fargo messenger Hollis W. Schriber slid the side door open a few inches and, poking his ten-gauge Remington shotgun through the crack, took dead aim and fired. The charge of buckshot caught Hudson full in the belly, and he fell dead in his tracks.

George Gates was unfazed. Using the engineer as a shield, he approached the end door of the express car and ordered Schriber to give up and come out.

"I'll die first," was the messenger's simple reply.

Gates fired several shots through the car door, breaking its window and splattering Schriber with glass. The messenger jumped for cover behind a big drummer's trunk and pumped three rounds back at the bandit. Gates then placed a dynamite bomb on the plate beneath the door and lit the fuse, but it failed to explode. The outlaw realized that he had met his match and fled.

A fruitless hunt for the robber was conducted by local lawmen and W. H. Reno, special officer for the railroad. They identified the dead bandit by letters found on his body and placed Mary Hudson under arrest. She made a full confession but said that she knew the missing bandit only as Guy LeCroix. A $550 reward was offered for the fugitive, but it was more than a year before his true identity was discovered.[4]

George Gates fled back to California and took up work in the mines in Trinity and Shasta counties. He was joined by his brother Vern, now twenty years old. Vern idolized his older brother and willingly followed him into a career of crime. He was a daredevil youth, a dead shot, and something of a dandy, always dressing in the height of fashion. Reward posters would soon note that he "has a feminine appearance" and "is a very good dresser and has nice smooth complexion; in his dress he often wears a white vest and low shoes."[5]

In the northern counties George Gates developed a reputation as a ladies' man and a gentleman. Intelligent and self-confident, he stood six feet tall, weighed two hundred pounds, and appeared to be much older than his twenty-five years. He continued to read romantic novels, taking from them assorted high-sounding aliases, and imagined himself a latter-day Dick Turpin. A diligent letter writer, he kept in frequent touch by mail with his parents in Alameda.[6]

On June 9, 1903, George and Vernon posted themselves on the Weaverville-Redding stage road, near Four Mile House, in Shasta County. At 4:30 P.M. the down stagecoach headed for Redding approached, and the brothers shouted for Jim Wilson to halt, but he didn't hear the command. They fired twenty shots into the air and also into the lead horses, effectively stopping the stage. The Gates boys were masked, with handkerchiefs covering their faces, and each was armed with two six-shooters and a rifle. They broke open the express boxes, lined up the eight passengers and relieved them of $400 and two gold watches, and then sent the coach on its way.

The *Trinity Journal* in reporting the affair called to mind the stage-robbing Ruggles boys who had been lynched in Redding eleven years before, saying: "This was the boldest holdup for many years. . . . It would seem that the memory of the Ruggles brothers had outlived its usefulness." Sheriff James Richardson used Indian trailers in a futile hunt for the bandits.[7]

The Gates boys now embarked on a prolific crime spree in California, Oregon, and Washington. How many holdups they pulled cannot be accurately determined. They were reliably believed, however, to have taken part in numerous holdups and burglaries in Seattle, as well as in a number of daring streetcar robberies in Portland. The worst of these occurred on July 14, 1903, when the Sellwood-bound electric car slowed for the Southern Pacific crossing, a half mile from East Portland. George and Vern Gates and four other masked desperadoes, never identified, swung aboard. Brandishing pistols, they took money, watches, and jewelry from the car's forty passengers. One passenger, Fred Day, did not turn over his valuables quickly enough and was shot in the abdomen. While one bandit propped up his fainting body, another rifled his pockets, ignoring Day's moans and the blood flowing from the gaping wound. They ordered the motorman to run the car two miles from town and then disembarked and es-

Outlaw Gates Boys
Killed by a Posse

Edward Vernon Gates, Who Was Killed by a Posse in New Mexico.

George Gates, Leader of the Outlaw Boys, Who Was Killed by a Posse of Citizens in New Mexico.

ROB SALOON AND ARE SHOT

Chased by Citizens Who Bring Back Their Dead Bodies

MURDER IS AVENGED.

Career of Crime Is Brought to Close and Officials Are Breathing Easier.

A T LAST the Gates boys — George, the elder, and Edward, the younger—have run out their string. Their ...

KIRKMAN'S FATE IN THE BALANCE

Court-Martial Which Tried the Captain Forwards Its Conclusions to Washington.

Special Dispatch to the "Chronicle."

OMAHA, April 10.—The court-martial proceedings against Captain George W. Kirkman of the Twenty-fifth Infantry are believed to have resulted in a decision decidedly unfavorable to the accused. The papers were received at Army headquarters here on Saturday from Fort Niobrara, where the trial has been in progress for three weeks, and were forwarded

FIRE THREATENS GREAT OIL TANKS

A Spectacular Conflagration at the Capital Which Looked Like a Lake of Flames.

Special Dispatch to the "Chronicle."

SACRAMENTO, April 10.—A picturesque conflagration, but one which fortunately caused almost no loss, occurred this afternoon. By the dropping of a red-hot rivet into a small lake that was covered with crude oil near the Southern Pacific depot the floating oil became ignited and burned over about three acres of oil-covered area.

A headline story in the *San Francisco Chronicle* describes the killing of George and Vern Gates by New Mexico lawmen in 1905. Courtesy San Francisco Academy of Comic Art.

caped into the timber. Although a $2,300 reward was posted, the robbers were not captured.[8]

The brothers returned to California and took up with two young prostitutes, Trixie Grey and Levon Baxter. They were well-heeled from their holdup spree and for several months traveled with the girls through Siskiyou and Trinity counties, visiting Henley, Hornbrook, Weaverville, and Detrick. They kept their weapons (two 30-30 "take down" Winchesters, a hammerless shotgun, and a .44 Colt) out of sight in a pair of dress suitcases and a telescope grip. The brothers told Trixie and Levon that they were mining men. George said his name was Guy Williams and Vernon was Ed Williams.

Trixie and Levon introduced the Gates boys to James ("Shorty") Arnett, a half-Mexican, foulmouthed miner and tinhorn gambler, well known in saloons and bordellos from Redding to southern Oregon. The girls moved into a brothel in Chico, where the Gates brothers and Arnett frequently visited them. J. A. Peck, a Chico policeman, became suspicious of the trio. Believing them to be "high class criminals," he shadowed them for several weeks. This spooked George Gates, and the three departed for Dunsmuir, Siskiyou County, in January, 1904, where George became known as Bruce Van Drake and his brother as Ed Lee.[9]

The Gates boys rented a room at the Riverside lodging house run by Bess Whiteman, whose husband, Thomas, was a painter in the Dunsmuir railroad shops. The strangers claimed to be mining contractors and said that they had an interest in the nearby Dewey Mine. Mrs. Whiteman, thirty years old, strikingly attractive, and the mother of two children, took more than a passing interest in George Gates. Silver-tongued, impeccably dressed, and incurably romantic, the young desperado made a fine appearance next to the rough miners and laborers of Dunsmuir. Mrs. Whiteman became infatuated with him, and he made her believe that he loved her.[10]

Shorty Arnett frequently joined the brothers at the lodging house, and they would often leave for a week at a time, telling Mrs. Whiteman that they were visiting their mine. On one such absence in February the three outlaws held up and robbed a saloon in Edgewood, twenty miles north of Dunsmuir. On March 20 they robbed Dave Endicott's saloon in Kennet, twenty miles north of Redding. Fifteen customers were lined up and relieved of their money.[11]

But George Gates wanted to make a big haul, and he decided to take a chance on a second train robbery. He made his plans carefully, picking an isolated water stop at Copley, in Shasta County, as the spot for the holdup. An abandoned cabin on Nigger Hill, five miles southwest, was chosen as their hideout. On March 29, George told Mrs. Whiteman that he was going to the Dewey Mine for a few days, and she bid good-bye to the Gates boys from her front porch. Two days later, at ten o'clock on the night of March 31, 1904, southbound Southern Pacific Train No. 15, the Oregon Express, pulled by two engines, slowed to a halt at Copley to take water. Copley, later called Motion, was a tiny settlement consisting of two or three scattered rows of houses, a general store, a saloon, a railroad depot, and a watering tank. It was located ten miles north of Redding, on the upper reaches of the Sacramento River. Surrounded on three sides by sparsely wooded foothills, its quietude was not disturbed except by occasional bursts of song or laughter from those waiting at the saloon for the evening train.

Train No. 15 had stopped with the engines near the water tank, but before the two firemen could open the valves, the Gates brothers and Shorty Arnett burst out of the brush that lined the riverbank a hundred yards away and charged toward the locomotives at a dead run. They had barley-sack masks covering their heads; all wore pistols, and George Gates and Arnett also carried Winchester rifles. Arnett had a gunny sack half filled with dynamite slung by a leather strap over his shoulder.

The bandits covered the train crew, and one, pointing his rifle at Fireman A. Raymond, who stood on top of the tender, barked, "Come down from there or I'll blow your head off!"

The two engineers and the firemen were stood up next to the engines. A brakeman, Dan Stone, walked up to see what the trouble was, and Arnett ordered him into line. Stone did not move quickly enough, and Arnett struck him over the head with the barrel of his rifle, cutting a deep scalp wound. The conductor, Jack Depanger, rushed forward and called out, "What is going on here?"

Arnett pressed the muzzle of his Winchester against the conductor's head and snapped, "I'll show you damned quick. Get in line with the others, you son of a bitch!"

The trainmen were then marched down to the baggage car. Arnett fired several shots along the side of the train to intimidate the passengers and then ducked under the cars and fired more shots down the other side. Depanger, Stone, and the two firemen were ordered to get into the smoking car and keep out of sight.

William J. O'Neill, the Wells
Fargo messenger who was
murdered by George Gates
during the Copley train
robbery in 1904. Courtesy
San Francisco Academy
of Comic Art.

Messenger L. O. Colford, inside the baggage car, heard the voices
outside and opened the door and peered out. Shorty Arnett pointed
his rifle at Colford and ordered him out, and the Gates brothers put
him into the smoker also. Inside the express car were Wells Fargo
Messenger William J. O'Neill and Frank Rockwell, an off-duty guard
who was "deadheading" a ride. O'Neill was a veteran of twenty-three
years in Wells Fargo's service, and his train had never been held up
before.

George Gates forced Engineer E. A. Bissell to knock on the side of
the express coach and call to O'Neill to open the door. O'Neill, thinking that the train crew was having trouble with tramps and needed his
help, slid the door open about ten inches. George Gates was not taking any chances with this messenger. He swung up his Winchester
and cold-bloodedly shot O'Neill through the heart. The messenger
slumped dead in the doorway.

Then George Gates ordered the other engineer, B. H. Joesink, to
enter the express car. Joesink obeyed and spotted Frank Rockwell
crouched in the far corner of the car, his rifle trained on the doorway.

Joesink quickly stepped to one side, and as George Gates climbed through the door, Rockwell pulled the trigger. The firing pin snapped on a dead cartridge. Rockwell levered another shell into the chamber, but Gates had already leaped out of the car. The bandits threatened to dynamite the express car, and Rockwell, after the engineers pleaded with him to surrender and avoid further bloodshed, handed over his rifle and climbed outside.

George Gates placed twenty sticks of quarter-inch dynamite on top of the big through safe and attached a two-foot length of fuse. He then instructed the engineers and Rockwell to hoist the smaller way safe and position it on top of the dynamite. Finally George had the three trainmen remove the dead messenger from the car. With his twisted romantic code, the outlaw leader had more respect for O'Neill's body dead than alive.

Gates touched a match to the fuse, and the robbers and train crew rushed forward to the engines. Moments later a massive explosion ripped through the express car. The roof and sides were blown into kindling, and the train was shaken throughout its length. The way safe was completely demolished, and shattered pieces of coin and shreds of currency were scattered in every direction. A deep, round hole was blown through the iron outer wall and the concrete inside wall of the big safe. A small dog that was being shipped in a crate near the safe escaped unharmed. The explosion shattered the crate, and the dog was blown through the roof of the car. He landed fifty feet away, unhurt, and ran yelping from the scene.

While Vern guarded the trainmen, Arnett and George climbed into the wreckage of the coach. George reached into the safe and cursed.

"Pal, there is nothing here for us," he told Arnett.

Unknown to the outlaws, deep at the bottom of the safe, covered by concrete debris from the inner wall, were sacks of golden treasure.

George Gates ordered Engineer Joesink to uncouple the forward locomotive, and the three robbers climbed into the cab. With the engineer at the throttle, they proceeded four miles south to Keswick and stopped two hundred yards past the depot, where a wagon bridge crossed the Sacramento River. The bandits jumped off the engine and vanished into the brush. They then walked a mile through the darkness to their hideout on Nigger Hill.

Joesink backed his engine into Keswick and telegraphed news of the holdup to Sheriff Richardson in Redding. Richardson instructed

Joesink to bring his engine into Redding as fast as he could. When the engineer arrived at the depot he was met by an excited crowd of a hundred people, among them Sheriff Richardson and Sheriff Tom Bergin, of Trinity County, who happened to be in town. The sheriffs and a dozen deputies boarded the engine and sped back to Keswick, where most started in pursuit of the robbers, and the rest continued on to Copley. The officers examined the holdup scene and found a mask made from a handkerchief with one corner torn off. They also found a sack with a leather strap containing thirty sticks of Hercules powder no. 2.

News of the robbery created a sensation, for this was the first major train holdup in California in several years. Said James B. Hume, Wells Fargo's veteran chief detective, "It was the most cold-blooded murder in connection with a train robbery of which I have any knowledge." [12]

Charles C. Crowley, chief special agent of the Southern Pacific, arrived in Redding the next day with two of his detectives and joined the hunt. He and Sheriff Richardson employed Indian trackers and for days scoured the hills and ran down every clue. Rewards of $850 each were offered for the bandits.

Two days after the holdup the Gates boys reappeared at their lodging house in Dunsmuir. George Gates asked Bess Whiteman to show him the *San Francisco Examiner* of April 1, and he read carefully the front-page stories of the robbery and murder. Said Mrs. Whiteman later, "He seemed nervous and exited. He told me that he had failed to keep his contract and had forfeited a great deal of money. He said he was going away for good. Before he left he told me to write to him and gave me names and addresses which he said I must use in order that the letters might reach him." [13]

George in turn promised to send her letters to the Dunsmuir post office under the name of Agnes Brown. Blinded by her infatuation for Gates, she did not question his motives. The brothers stayed in Dunsmuir two days, and then quietly left town.

Several days later a railroad lineman told Detective Crowley that he had seen three suspicious men in an abandoned cabin on Nigger Hill two days before the robbery. Crowley, Constable Crum, and Deputy Sheriff Cooper rode out to investigate. They found the cabin deserted but inside were several papers taken from the express car during the holdup and a number of romantic Scottish novels. Nearby, at the bottom of a fifty-foot mine shaft, they found masks and shirts that had been worn by the bandits and a leather strap matching the one on the dynamite sack. But most important, the officers discovered the corner that had been torn from the handkerchief mask left at the scene. This piece of linen bore a small laundry mark, which Crowley recognized as their most valuable clue. Checking the laundries in the area, he learned that the mark had come from the Redding Steam Laundry and was part of a bundle of washing sent from their agent in Dunsmuir. From the Dunsmuir agent, Crowley found that the handkerchief was the property of a young man known as Bruce Van Drake, who roomed at the Riverside lodging house.

Crowley made a quiet investigation and learned that Van Drake had a partner named Ed Lee. He also learned that Van Drake and Lee were not in Dunsmuir the day of the holdup but had returned a few days later and then had suddenly left town. Van Drake and Lee had frequently been seen in the company of Shorty Arnett. Crowley spoke with Mrs. Whiteman, who claimed to know nothing of the whereabouts of Van Drake. Crowley and other detectives searched Van Drake's room and found that he had left a trunk that contained a rifle, pistol, holsters, cartridges, and a pair of pincers used to pinch caps on dynamite fuse. A broken blade on the pincers left a peculiar mark that matched perfectly with marks on the caps in the sack that had been dropped by the robbers. Also found in the trunk was evidence that showed that Van Drake's real name was George Gates and that Ed Lee was his brother Vern.[14]

The detectives checked the post office and found that Mrs. Whiteman picked up two letters addressed to "Miss Agnes Brown." They intercepted a third letter and saw that it was signed "Bruce." Although dated "San Francisco, May 1, 1904," it had been postmarked in Portland, on April 30, an apparent attempt by Gates to conceal his whereabouts from Mrs. Whiteman, and read as follows:

> My Darling Bessie: Just a line to-day saying good-by and telling you what to do in my absence. I can never tell you, darling, what it costs me to go away and leave you, but as I think it is best, darling, I will do so for a time, but rest assured, dearest, that I will come back in about one year, and then we can sneak away together to a dear little place that I will have found by that time, and no one will bother us then. I was coming to San Francisco to see you, darling, when I received your letters. It was a good thing, because I would have died before giving up if the fools had tried to arrest me.
>
> Well, you saved my life perhaps, darling, and I will love you for it always. I suppose the old gossipers have lots to think of now about

Bess Whiteman, the married proprietress of the Riverside lodging house, in Dunsmuir. She had a secret love affair with George Gates and harbored the Gates boys after the Copley train robbery. From author's collection.

Van Drake. Well, they can talk, the fools; it won't hurt me. Always think of me, Bessie, and believe in my love for you as you believe in your God.

I do love you, dearest, now and to the last beat of my heart. When the year is up look for me or to hear from me, and we will fly together. Curses on Tom! So he is my enemy? Well, I will make him hate me worse, if I do not kill him, before I have done with him. Can't you fix him some way, Bessie? Give him some poison and swear that he took it accidentally from where you had it to poison rats. I know it is an awful thing to say, but I could kill a dozen to steal you away, my own precious.

If you are a widow when I return, darling, so much the better, eh? Remember, darling, if they catch me, I was in your house the night of March 31st—see? You will swear to it, darling, won't you?

If Lee comes tell him I have gone for good and do not let anyone see my trunk until you have taken some things out of it. I have lost the key, but some day when no one is around you can break the lock off and take out all you think is necessary.

First take out the pistol, holsters and the gun and cartridges; hide them, and some time you can throw them in the river. Will you, darling? There is nothing else I can say further. You can burn all the rest of them up. Give all the clothes away to some poor hobo or tramp—see? You can give both overcoats and everything away there. If they break into the trunk they will find it. Remember, darling, to break the lock or get some one to do so, telling him you lost the key to your trunk. Then take the rifle wrapped in a canvas case and the cartridges and pistol holsters, hide them and put them in the river piece by piece—see? I trust to you, darling; so do as I ask you. If you do not find what I tell you in the trunk they have broken into it while you were away, and Tom would likely help the sneaks.

Well, my own darling, I must say good-bye, as I am about to sail. I am leaving on a ship for Australia to-night, and, oh, Bessie, how I grieve to think an ocean will separate my little sweetheart from me in a couple of weeks!

Well, darling, I will return, so do not grieve, as it is all for the best, and I am doing as you asked me to do.

They may arrest Ed Lee, as I made a friend of him when he worked in the box factory in Dunsmuir. Well, they cannot prove anything wrong on him, as he was at your place that night, was he not?

Swear he was, darling, and save the poor boy. He may not come back, as he said he was going home to Arizona. But in case he does tell him all about it so he can go away and avoid trouble. What wouldn't I give to have you sail with me to-night, darling! To hold you in my arms and have you always near me! She is a lively vessel that will carry me away from here, but it makes me sad to think of leaving my little girl behind. Think of me always, darling, as I will think of you, and believe me, dear Bessie, that, come weal or come woe, you will always come first in my heart.

Kiss little Stephen for me, as I loved the little rat because he looked like you. Do all you can, love, and believe me now and forever yours,

BRUCE.

P.S. Tell Tom if he says anything against me you will leave him. He will shut up then. Get a divorce if you can. Burn this letter, darling; be sure.

I am in San Francisco and will sail to-night. Will send this letter to Portland to be mailed, so they will be fooled. If they watch you at the post-office remember Miss Brown's letter came from Portland.

Good-by, good-by, darling. And may God keep you until my return.[15]

Detective Crowley and Dunsmuir Constable L. H. Brown promptly placed Mrs. Whiteman under arrest and took her to District Attorney Thomas Dozier, in Redding. She said she knew neither Van Drake's true name nor of his involvement in the robbery, but she admitted sending him a letter addressed to "Jim Smith," in Ashland, Oregon, warning that the detectives had come to her house looking for him. She turned over the other two letters written by the outlaw. Dozier, convinced that Bess Whiteman was an unwitting dupe of George Gates, released her without charge.[16]

Wanted posters for the Gates brothers and Shorty Arnett were circulated throughout the western states. Newspapers had a field day with the story and quickly labeled George "a victim of the novel reading craze." The notoriety was a great blow to the Gates family, who refused to believe the boys' guilt.[17]

George's letter to Bess Whiteman was the last that was heard from either of the Gates boys for almost a year. Up and down the Pacific Coast and throughout the Southwest, law officers and railroad detectives kept up a hunt for the brothers. Many arrests were made, but the right men were never taken. Shorty Arnett was also hunted doggedly, but he was never apprehended. He reportedly died in Mississippi about 1920.[18]

At one o'clock in the morning, March 16, 1905, a medium-sized young man entered the front door of Mart Hardin's Gem Saloon, in Lordsburg, New Mexico, and walked through the barroom to the cardroom in the rear. A few of the patrons glanced over and recognized him as a stranger who had been about the place earlier in the day. He had "piked" a little at the roulette wheel and had entered into the general conversation of the crowd. He wore a heavy overcoat and had his hands in the side pockets.

"Gentlemen!" the stranger called out, and pulled a pair of .45's from his overcoat pockets. "I have to ask you to go into the front room. I must ask you first to hold up your hands and keep them up. Go quietly and arrange yourselves against the wall and face the wall, for there may be doings that you will not like to look at. Now hurry, and remember that the first man who turns or who tries to take his hands down will be shot."

The thirteen men in the saloon obeyed. The front door opened, and a larger man entered, a revolver in each hand, and announced, "We are here for the money and we mean business."

The smaller bandit then looted the cash register and safe. He was going through the pockets of the gamblers when the door opened and the two railroad men walked in.

"Hold up your hands," they were ordered.

Charlie Lee, an engineer, thought it was a joke and ignored the command. The big robber slammed the barrel of his pistol into Lee's face, laying open a large gash on his cheek.

"We don't intend to tolerate any trouble here," the bandit growled.

The other robber picked up three six-shooters from a shelf behind the bar and said, "Gentlemen, perhaps you would not appreciate if we expressed our thanks. Yet we do thank you and we would take a drink with you, but we never indulge. Now we are going. Do not be in too much of a hurry to come out. It may not be healthy outside for quite a little time."

The robbers backed out the door and vanished. Grant County Deputy Sheriff Herb McGrath was quickly notified, and at daybreak he circled the town on horseback, trying to cut the trail of the men if they left on foot or by horse. He also searched outgoing trains and sent word to nearby towns to be on the lookout for the desperadoes.

At four o'clock the next afternoon two strangers appeared at John Weems's lodging house, in Separ, twenty miles south of Lordsburg. Both wore overcoats with bulging pockets. They paid for a meal and room with nickels and dimes and asked Weems to wake them when the eastbound passenger train arrived. Weems suspected that the pair were the saloon robbers, and as soon as they had gone to bed, he telegraphed Herb McGrath. The deputy and two possemen, Joe Olney and Rube Gannon, caught the first freight train out of Lordsburg and arrived in Separ an hour later.

McGrath listened to Weems's description of the two strangers and was convinced that they were the wanted men. The room they occupied was at the rear of the house, and McGrath hoped to surprise the two in bed and take them alive. Since it was very dark, the deputy planned to have Weems carry a railroad lantern, while he, Olney, and Gannon threw down on the strangers.

The four walked silently to the bedroom, and McGrath opened the door, which swung in front of Weems and cut off the light from the lantern. McGrath snatched the lamp from Weems and, pointing his automatic shotgun with one hand, shouted, "Hands up! We have come to arrest you!"

Olney, wielding a pump shotgun, was at McGrath's side in an instant and cried out, "Turn up your hands! We have got the best of this!"

The strangers were lying on the bed awake, but neither moved. Both looked calmly at the officers. The smaller man had one foot

Veteran Wells Fargo Detective John N. Thacker, who
investigated the killing of
the Gates boys, in New Mexico. Courtesy Mrs. Ellen
Stout.

resting on the floor and his arms folded on his chest. The big man
also lay on his back, with his hands behind his head on the pillow.

"Hands up!" McGrath ordered again.

Suddenly their hands dived under the blanket, and the big man
jerked upright in the bed. McGrath did not waste a second. He fired
three blasts with his shotgun, and Olney fired once. The black powder smoke was so thick that McGrath could not see the bed. When it
finally cleared away he reentered the room and found that both men
were dead, riddled with buckshot. Each had been shot in the head,
and the larger man had wounds in his arm and breast.

McGrath lifted up the bloody blanket and found eight pistols in
the bed. The large man had a Colt automatic grasped tightly in his
right fist and a .45 in his left. The other man held a Smith & Wesson
hammerless .38 in his right hand, and his left was inches away from
another pistol. Each man wore four holsters, one on each hip and

one in each back pocket. The big man also had a holster slung under his left shoulder. Four hundred rounds of ammunition were found in the room. The linings of their overcoats were cut out so their guns could be drawn quickly through the pockets. One pistol taken in the saloon holdup was found in the bed. Most of the other six-guns had the hammer spurs filed down and the bent springs honed to a hair trigger. McGrath knew that only gunmen and killers doctored their weapons in such a manner.

There were no means of identifying the bodies. Even the labels in their hats and clothing had been cut out. In the pocket of the smaller outlaw, however, was found a photograph of an older woman and a girl. The bodies were photographed and shipped to Lordsburg for a coroner's inquest, where all thirteen witnesses from the Gem Saloon identified them as the robbers. A circular bearing their descriptions was sent to all police departments and detective agencies.[19]

Several weeks later Wells Fargo Detective John N. Thacker, upon receiving the circular, traveled to Lordsburg and viewed the post-mortem photographs. He identified the large man as George Gates. The birdshot scars inflicted by Louie Piccardo's shotgun could plainly be seen on his left hip and forearm. The smaller man was positively identified as Vern Gates. The women in the photograph taken from his pocket were Mrs. Gates and her daughter Lillian.[20]

Reported the *San Francisco Chronicle*, "In the detective department of the Wells Fargo Company and in a score or more sheriff's offices in the Coast States the officials are breathing easier. Two as desperate criminals as ever ran amuck in this or any other country have been run to earth."[21]

The parents of the Gates boys refused to believe that their sons had been killed and did not claim the bodies. The brothers were buried in a potter's field, in Lordsburg. The only legacy they left to their confused, grieving family was a letter George penned to his mother, in Alameda. "God help me! My fate is awful," he wrote. "Pity me, oh, pity me, my loved ones, and believe me now and until death."[22]

It was the timeless lament of an outlaw on the run.

PART THREE

Lawbreakers and Lynchers

CHAPTER 11

The Coates-Frost Feud

THEY called it the "Little Lake Vendetta," and it was California's bloodiest family feud, lasting over twenty years and resulting in the killing of fourteen men. The full story of this blood feud will probably never be told, for those with firsthand knowledge of the bitter war between and among the Coates and Frost clans have been dead for many years. Yet scraps of information gleaned from old newspaper files, court records, and written memoirs reveal a dramatic tale from an era when men settled disputes at gunpoint.

Little Lake Valley is located in Mendocino County, about twenty miles north of Ukiah. It was first settled in 1853, and two years later the Baechtel brothers established a cattle ranch at the southern end of the valley. The old county road, roughly paralleling what is now Highway 101, ran through the ranch. Around a cluster of widespreading oaks near the road, the tiny village of Little Lake sprang up. A saloon was built in 1859, a public social hall in 1860, then a schoolhouse, and in 1865 the first store was opened. About this time a rival town, Willitsville, was established one mile to the north. Today the two villages are incorporated into the city of Willits.[1]

Among the early settlers in the valley was the Frost clan, from Davis County, Missouri. Patriarch of the family was Elijah Frost, known by all as "Old Man" or "Pap" Frost. He was born in 1800 in Tennessee. His wife, Elizabeth, born in 1803, was a native of Kentucky. The couple raised nine children in Missouri: Elisha, James, Martin, Isom, Catherine, Phoebe, Elizabeth, Lavisa, and Polly. The Frosts moved to California in about 1858 and settled in Little Lake Valley. Two of their daughters, Phoebe and Polly, were married and remained in Missouri. Elisha (the oldest son) and his wife, Amanda, had seven young children. Catherine Frost, thirteen when the family left Missouri, later married Frank Duncan in Little Lake. A cousin, Benjamin F. Frost, also moved to Mendocino County, first living in Ukiah and later moving to Little Lake.[2]

The Frosts were a tough and wild breed. A hardworking but hot-tempered bunch, they engaged in hog and sheep raising. All were handy with firearms, but young Mart in particular was a deadly shot with a Colt navy revolver. Like many of their neighbors, they were rabid Secessionists and Democrats.

Another large family of early settlers in Little Lake Valley was the Coates clan. Old Abner, Thomas, and George Coates were brothers, originally from Philadelphia, Pennsylvania. In the 1840s they settled in Wisconsin and emigrated to California in the 1850s. Abner Coates started a farm in Rock Tree Valley, just east of Little Lake. He had two sons, John and Abraham, and five other children. George Coates opened a grist mill in Little Lake. He had three sons: Wesley, Henry, and James. In addition, there were numerous other relatives living in the valley. The Coateses were staunch Republicans and supported the Union. In Little Lake they established reputations as industrious, responsible citizens.[3]

During the Civil War, Little Lake, like the rest of California, was a divided camp, and the Coates and Frost families in particular were in sharp disagreement over the rebellion. It was in this atmosphere of political hatred that the Coates-Frost feud erupted. In about 1862 children from both the Frost and Coates clans attended the school in Little Lake. One of the Coates boys quarreled with a Frost, and the youths left the schoolhouse during intermission and attempted to settle the dispute in a fistfight. The schoolmaster broke it up and flogged both boys. The fathers of each boy went to the school and complained to the teacher about the flogging, each father siding with his son and claiming that his boy had been unjustly punished. The schoolmaster told them, "In order to maintain discipline of the school it is necessary to punish students for all infractions of the rules, and fighting on the school grounds is against the rules."

Coates was finally convinced that the teacher was right and was willing to let the matter drop. Frost, however, brought the affair before the school district board of trustees. During an emotional hearing arguments for and against the teacher were heard, and when the trustees voted to uphold the schoolmaster's actions, Frost was furious. Threats were made back and forth between the two families, and Frost removed his boy from the school. Elections for the school board were approaching, and Frost swore that no member of the old board would be reelected. He vowed that he would see to it that the new board would fire the schoolmaster. The Coates clan immediately sided with the current board, and before long this trivial affair had virtually every settler in the valley lining up in support with one or the other of the factions.[4]

Cool heads eventually prevailed, and the matter was settled, but the Frosts and Coateses were now deadly enemies. Threats of death were freely exchanged, especially between young Wesley Coates and Frank Duncan, who had developed an intense hatred for one another. The pair met, hot words followed, and they would likely have shot it out had not friends separated them. Duncan and Coates went their separate ways, each vowing vengeance.

During the next several years numerous brawls broke out between members of the two families. In the fall of 1866 twenty-two-year-old Mart Frost and twenty-year-old Abraham Coates had a fistfight in Little Lake. Several of the Coates boys joined in, and Frost was badly beaten. The Coates clan was to regret this incident. A year later, September 4, 1867 (a general election day), Elisha Frost and one of the Coateses got into a fierce argument at the polls. Other Frost and Coates boys present formed a ring, and the two squared off, but the sheriff arrived and separated the group.

As the men began to leave, Frank Duncan bragged in a loud voice, "I can whip any Abolitionist in Little Lake, or any Black Republican of the Coates name."[5]

Wesley Coates was not present, but when he heard of the boast, he took it as a personal challenge. It must have been uppermost in his mind when he and nine of his kinfolk drove into Little Lake in Abner Coates's big farm wagon on Wednesday afternoon, October 16, 1867, to vote at the social hall in the judicial election, which in those days was held six weeks after the general election.

Three of the Frosts had also come to the polls that day: Elisha, Mart, and their twenty-one-year-old brother, Isom. With them was their brother-in-law Frank Duncan. Each wore a Colt navy revolver in a holster on his hip, and Duncan also wore a knife. Most men at the time still carried six-guns tucked into their belts, but holsters had been popularized during the war and were becoming increasingly common.

The Coateses were not expecting trouble. Most of them were unarmed, except for Wesley and Abraham, who each carried a pistol. James Coates had a knife on his belt, and sixty-six-year-old Abner Coates had a double-barreled shotgun in his wagon, one barrel rifled and the other smooth bore for shot.

Scene of the big shoot-out in Little Lake as it appeared in the 1890s. The old county road passes the barns and outbuildings of the old Baechtel ranch. Directly across the road from this spot stood the Little Lake social hall, store, and saloon. Courtesy Rena Lynn Moore.

The three Frosts and Duncan were lounging inside Baechtel's store with several local men. Duncan was sitting on the counter when Henry Coates, his brother James, and his cousin John entered. When words were exchanged between Henry and the Frosts, George Coates entered and told his son, "Henry, it's time to leave."

Henry got up and walked out the door, saying, "I can't get any fight out of any damned big man."

Then Wesley Coates, upon hearing that the Frosts were in the store, entered. Spotting Duncan, he stepped up and said, "I hear you said you could whip any Republican at Little Lake."

"What I said, I said out there before all," Duncan replied. "I do not take anything back."

"Do you say it now?"

"If it comes in the way, I can," Duncan snapped back.

"I am your man," challenged Coates. "Just walk out and try it."

For a moment Duncan paused, as if to reconsider, and Coates jeered, "You can't do it."

"I can do it damned quick!" Duncan returned angrily, and jumped off the counter and headed out the door.

Wesley Coates followed him outside, as did the rest. James Coates drew his knife and declared, "I'll be damned if I don't see a fair fight."

Duncan walked about twenty feet, with his hand on his Colt. Wesley stopped, pulled off his coat, and began to lay it down when Duncan suddenly turned, pulled his pistol, and struck Coates over the head, knocking him to the ground. As Wesley started to rise, Duncan again slammed the gun over his head with such force that it broke the weapon in half. The two men grappled in the dirt, and the three Frosts and Abraham and Henry Coates joined the fray. Old Thomas Coates jumped into the middle and tried to break up the fighters, but it was useless. Years of hatred and anger exploded in unstoppable violence.

Wesley Coates, bleeding and stunned by Duncan's onslaught, managed to pull Duncan's own knife from his belt and stabbed him three times in the chest. Duncan broke loose and tried to run. Wesley followed and stabbed him again in the shoulder. At that, Mart Frost drew his pistol and shouted, "Stand back! Stand back!"

Suddenly the roar of gunfire drowned out the noise of the brawl. Who fired the first shot will never be known, but in an instant the dusty street became a smoke-filled, bullet-riddled deathtrap. The action took place so fast that it was almost impossible for bystanders to tell what happened.

Abraham Coates was the first to go down. A bullet plowed into his left side at the seventh rib and passed through his chest. He staggered to cover behind a large pine tree, and then fell to the ground.

Mart Frost shot Henry Coates, the .36-caliber ball passing through his rib cage and into his right lung. Coates collapsed, mortally wounded. Mart fired twice at Albert Coates, both rounds hitting the dirt at his feet. Albert, unarmed, fled toward the social hall. He had run about eighteen yards when Elisha Frost took aim and fired twice. The first ball slammed into his back and spun him around. The second ball tore into his left side and cleaved his heart.

"Oh, my God!" Albert gasped, and toppled over, instantly killed. These were the only words spoken during the shoot-out.

Wesley Coates, seeing his cousin fall, dropped Duncan's knife, pulled his revolver, and fired at Elisha, but missed. Old Abner Coates had better luck. Pulling his shotgun from the wagon, he let Elisha have both barrels. Frost dropped dead with thirty-eight pieces of shot in his chest, arms, and hips.

Isom Frost returned the fire and hit Abner in the shoulder. Abner turned and staggered back to the wagon. Mart Frost then spotted Wesley Coates aiming his six-gun for a second shot. Mart's Colt roared, and the slug tore completely through Wesley's body from left side to right, piercing both lungs and causing instant death.

At the same time Isom Frost opened fire on unarmed Thomas Coates, who had been trying to break up the fight. The elder Coates crumpled, fatally wounded by two bullets in his chest. A moment later a pistol ball slammed into James Coates's abdomen, and he dropped his knife and stumbled back into the store.

Abraham Coates, though desperately wounded, crawled around the pine tree and took a shot into Mart Frost. Mart fired back, and once again his aim was deadly. The ball hit Coates behind the left shoulder and entered his chest cavity. Abraham was game, however, and managed to raise up and fire again, but his aim was too high.

This was the last shot of the battle. It had lasted just fifteen seconds, and twenty shots had been fired. Six men were dead or dying, and three were badly wounded. The dead were Thomas, Wesley, Henry, and Albert Coates and Elisha Frost. Abraham Coates lasted until noon the next day, when he, too, died. James and Abner Coates and Frank Duncan eventually recovered from their wounds. Mart Frost had exacted his revenge for the beating he had suffered the year before—three Coateses had died before his deadly gun.[6]

The following afternoon the feudists were buried, and the *Mendocino Democrat* poignantly described the scene:

> They were taken outside the hall and placed in front of it, when they were removed to their graves. As the coffins lay in front of the hall, immediately before the funeral procession moved, the friends of the deceased came up to take a farewell glance at them. Then transpired a scene rarely witnessed. The parents, children, wives, brothers and sisters of the slayers and slain, mingled their tears together over those who a few short hours before were grappling in fierce combat, but now are cold and still, and lay peaceably side by side. The sobbing and wailing that rose from the numerous mourners were enough to melt a heart of flint. "My father!" "My brother!" "My husband!" "My son!" and similar expressions, were simultaneously ejaculated. Few eyes were dry in the large assemblage present.

The funeral procession was conducted with great order and judgment. The first wagon moved up and took off the oldest, Thomas Coates, and as it moved off five elderly gentleman, all about the same age as the deceased, served as pall-bearers, and walked along with the wagon to the grave. The next that followed was Elisha Frost, who was next in age. A like number of similar pall-bearers took charge of his remains. The same ceremony was observed in each case. The funeral procession was about three quarters of a mile in length. They were all buried in the same graveyard, a few feet only from each other.[7]

Today the graves can still be viewed in Little Lake Cemetery, located on a small knoll off East Hill Road, in the southern part of Willits.

The next day Justice of the Peace William Henry impaneled a coroner's jury and held an inquest into the killings. The jury found that Isom had slain Thomas Coates; that Mart had slain Wesley, Henry, and Abraham Coates; and that Abner Coates had killed Elisha Frost. Justice Henry issued coroner's warrants for the arrest of Isom, Mart, and Abner, and Sheriff Lew M. Warden arrested all three and brought them to be arraigned before Justice Henry. Each posted $2500 bond and was released. The case was sent to the Mendocino County grand jury, which refused to indict any of the trio. The charges were dismissed on October 29, 1867. According to one old account, "A preponderance of Democrats and fear of the Frosts were accountable for the laxity of the law."[8]

The hatred that exploded that October afternoon in Little Lake smoldered and spread over the years. In time, family loyalties blurred. Hate and fear twisted blood ties until family members began quarreling among themselves. The old reasons behind the feud were forgotten and supplanted by new ones. Political differences and quarrels over land only partly help to explain the tangled events that followed. Violent incidents became commonplace, especially for the Frosts. Their victory in the big shoot-out emboldened them, and the family became increasingly feared in the valley.

One night two of the Frost boys, probably Mart and Isom, rode into the Little Lake Indian rancheria and shot at "everything that moved." The Indians fled into the mountains and never returned. "The Frosts had terrorized the valley to such an extent that the settlers knew that it was as much as their lives were worth to attempt to bring them to justice, so not a hand was lifted in defense of the Indians," reported a writer of the day.[9]

Old Man Frost did his best to keep his boys in line. When they got into a dispute he would take down his gun and threaten to shoot the first one who made a move to draw a knife or pistol. But such threats were of no use. Mart and Isom had a falling-out with Frank Duncan, who was wise enough to sell his ranch and move out of the valley. Another family quarrel occurred when one of Old Man Frost's daughters eloped with her lover. Shots were fired, but none took effect.[10]

The Coates family, too, began fighting among themselves. Samuel Besse was married to Abner Coates's daughter Mary. Coates and Besse filed on adjoining land claims on Tomki Creek, in Scott's Valley, twelve miles east of Little Lake, and the two entered into a partnership to raise livestock together. On Abner's claim was a small but comfortable house, and since he already had a ranch nearby, he allowed the Besses and their six children to move into it. Besse was known as a desperate man with no control over his emotions, easily aroused into violence, and he had had many difficulties since he had lived in the county. On one occasion he had been indicted for assault with intent to commit murder. Abner Coates had trouble with his son-in-law and ordered him to move out of the house, but Besse refused.

On February 1, 1872, Abner sent his sons John and William to evict Besse. John Coates, who had been present but had not participated in the big shoot-out, was a forty-year-old farmer and "sporting man" who suffered severely from tuberculosis. Although not regarded as violent or dangerous, he harbored an intense dislike for Besse and had previously threatened to kill him. The Coates brothers found Besse in the woods a mile from the house, hauling log rails with his team. John Coates handed Besse a written notice to vacate signed by his father. Besse read the paper, tore it up, and told them that he would not leave the premises.

"I'll hold all the law will allow me to," Besse declared.

"Thieving bastard!" John Coates roared, and Besse, infuriated, pulled a butcher knife and started for his brother-in-law. Coates jerked his six-gun and fired three shots into Besse's chest. The first shot severed the main artery one inch above the heart, killing him instantly. Besse sank to the ground, and Coates pumped two more bullets into his prostrate body.

The brothers rode to the house, told their sister of the killing, and then returned home. Mary Besse, with several neighbors, brought her husband in and laid the body in the house to await the coroner.

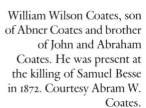

William Wilson Coates, son of Abner Coates and brother of John and Abraham Coates. He was present at the killing of Samuel Besse in 1872. Courtesy Abram W. Coates.

Two days later John Coates rode into Ukiah and surrendered, claiming self-defense. Nonetheless, he was indicted for murder by the grand jury. He was tried in Ukiah and on July 18, 1872, was convicted of manslaughter and sentenced to three years in the state prison.[11]

Coates was admitted into San Quentin on July 25 as convict no. 5337. Since he suffered so severely from consumption, his family began working to secure a pardon from the governor. His condition worsened in the prison, and on February 15, 1873, he wrote a plaintive note to his mother: "My health is such that I shall not be able to live but a short time hence. Therefore, what you do, do as quickly as possible. I am failing each day and cannot expect to hold out long." On March 4 he was pardoned by Governor Newton Booth and returned to Little Lake to spend his remaining days with his family.[12]

Elisha Frost's widow, Amanda, died in 1870, leaving behind two daughters and five sons: Elijah, Taylor, Asbury, David, and Jimmy. James McKindley, who married Elisha's older daughter, Sarah, was appointed as legal guardian of the four youngest, but he had no luck trying to control the boys, especially the eldest, twenty-one-year-old Elijah. He was a wild one, following fast in the footsteps of his gun-

FROST FAMILY TREE

Elijah "Old Man" Frost

- Polly
- Lavisa
- Elizabeth
  - Taylor
- Phoebe
  - Sarah (Mrs. James McKindley)
  - Elijah
- Elisha
  - Asbury
  - David
- James (Old Jim)
- Catherine (Mrs. Frank Duncan)
  - James (Little Jimmy)
  - Mary
- Martin
- Isom

fighting uncles. Encouraged by his family's fearsome reputation, he began engaging in all kinds of petty thievery. The old court records show that Elijah and a friend, Bob Reynolds, were arrested for stealing a two-thousand-pound wagonload of apples worth fifty dollars. The charges were later dropped for lack of evidence. Another time, Elijah, his brother Taylor, and Reynolds were indicted for stealing two hogs and altering their ear brands.[13]

Within a few years young Frost had graduated to horse theft. On September 10, 1875, Elijah; his young wife, Mary; and his fourteen-year-old brother, Jimmy, stole sixteen head of horses from Joseph Brock's ranch on the Pit River, in Shasta County. Brock, discovering the theft the next day, saddled up and started on their trail, which led south to Red Bluff. Brock rode into town on the twelfth and reported the theft to Tehama County Deputy Sheriff O. A. Lovett, who make a quick search and found that the horse thieves had crossed the Sacramento River the previous day. Lovett and Brock trailed them south to Oroville, where they were joined by Butte County Sheriff S. L. Daniels. On the morning of the fourteenth the little posse caught up with the Frosts on the Dogtown road, six miles from Oroville, and arrested all three. Only eight horses were left. Elijah had sold the rest.

The Frosts were returned to Shasta County and lodged in jail at Redding. Mary Frost was released, but Elijah and Jimmy were charged with grand larceny. There is no record that Jimmy was ever tried; he was probably released also, because of his age. Elijah stood trial alone in December. He claimed "to have bought the horses from a Spaniard, paying him one hundred and fifty dollars in coin, and a mare valued at fifty dollars." The jury deliberated for twenty-four hours and returned a guilty verdict. Judge Hopping sentenced him to four years in San Quentin, and Elijah was received at the prison on December 18, 1875. With time off for good behavior, he was released on August 18, 1878, having served two years and eight months.[14]

Elijah returned to Little Lake, where his neighbors soon discovered that his stay in prison had only made him worse. With two young friends, Abijah Gibson and Thomas McCracken, he embarked on a spree of minor thefts and vandalism. Barns, henroosts, and smokehouses were robbed nightly; harnesses were cut to pieces, and geese, chickens, and other livestock were stolen. On one occasion a flock of geese was found, all dead, with their heads fastened between the rails of a fence. Frost and his friends also enjoyed, as one newspaper put it, "getting drunk and rendering nights hideous and life dangerous with their shouts, yells and reckless use of firearms; and no one dare complain lest his life pay for the act." One man who did complain by having charges brought against the gang awoke the next morning and found his barn burned to the ground.

On the night of September 1, 1879, Frost, Gibson, and McCracken were caught in the act of stealing a set of harness. Since there was no jail in Little Lake Valley, they were handcuffed and placed under guard in a room in Brown's Hotel, in Willitsville. Their preliminary hearing before the justice of the peace was set for September 4. While awaiting their hearing, Elijah and his friends made numerous threats "that when they got at liberty they would make it hot for the persons who had them arrested."

At two o'clock in the morning, September 4, the prisoners were asleep in the hotel room, guarded by John Tatham and a man named Davis. Gibson and McCracken were handcuffed together in bed, and Frost was manacled alone. Without warning, a group of about thirty armed men, masked and with their feet muffled in sacks, entered the room and covered Tatham and Davis with guns. The guards were disarmed, tied, and gagged. Frost, McCracken, and Gibson were ordered out of bed and gagged and with the two guards were marched into the street and to the bridge just outside town, four hundred yards to the north. Well ropes were produced, nooses looped around their necks, and the ends tied to the bridge rails. At the last moment the three confessed where they had hidden many geese, chickens, and other stolen property. Then Gibson and McCracken were shoved off one side of the bridge, and Elijah was dropped off the opposite side. Frost died of a broken neck, and the other two slowly strangled to death. The members of the lynch mob released Tatham and Davis and silently disappeared into the night.

Although several Mendocino County newspapers ran editorials condemning the lynching, the actions of the mob met with general approval in Little Lake. An inquest was held, but the coroner's jury "found no one in particular guilty." Governor William Irwin offered a reward of $500 for the first arrest and conviction of one of the lynchers and $200 for each subsequent conviction, but no one seemed too interested in collecting it.[15]

As in any small rural community where nobody's business was private, the identities of the lynchers were no real secret, and it soon became widely rumored that the leader of the mob had been Elijah's

Main Street, Willits, 1888. At far right is Brown's Little Lake Hotel, from which Elijah Frost, Abijah Gibson, and Thomas McCracken were seized by a mob and lynched in 1879. Courtesy Rena Lynn Moore.

uncle, Mart Frost. Now a deadly enmity sprang up between Mart and Elijah's four brothers. The youngest, known as Little Jimmy to distinguish him from his uncle, Old Jim, was only eighteen, five and a half feet tall but aggressive in a fight and a deadly marksman. His oldest brother, Taylor, was also a dangerous man, while Asbury and Dave were known as gentlemen but never backed down from an enemy. None of them, however, were willing to tangle with Mart, whose reputation as a mankiller was widely acknowledged. Wrote one newspaperman of his day, "He was a man of mild unobtrusive manner, which gave no conception of the desperado he was when aroused. He was a deadly shot with a pistol or longarm, and hence, a very danger-ous person to encounter."[16]

Perhaps Mart's conscience weighed greatly upon him, for he drank heavily after the lynching. When drunk he could be counted on to raise trouble. One such incident occurred on October 22, 1880, and was graphically described in the *Ukiah Democratic Weekly Dispatch:*

Mart Frost, of Little Lake township, came to Ukiah, on Friday last, armed and equipped for a good time. He filled himself with "tarantula juice" that evening, and made considerable noise, but managed to get to bed without much trouble to himself or others. The next morning, however, he was not so successful. Not feeling well, after his spree of the night before, and believing that a little good whiskey would prove an antidote for all his ills, he took a little "for the stomach's sake," then more for a headache, and by nine o'clock in the morning he was very drunk. To impress those around him with his importance, he talked very loud and handled a pistol in a careless way. To prevent him from getting into trouble, his brother took the revolver from him, a large sized self-cocking English bull-dog, and retained it some time; but, on a promise from Mart that he would at once start for home, returned it to him. Shortly after regaining possession of the firearm he took up a position on the sidewalk in front of the People's Hotel, and, with pistol in hand, forced pedestrians, under threats, to take to the middle of the street. Some one, not liking this kind of fun, complained to Marshal Jamison of Frost's conduct, and that officer proceeded at once to the hotel to look into the matter, but before he arrived there Mr. Tanner and others had persuaded the belligerent individual to retire into the saloon attached to the hotel, where he was when the Marshal came upon the scene, engaged in very loud talk and other war-like demonstrations. The Marshal stepped up to the door and looked in, which seemed to enrage Frost, who grabbed the officer by his coat and jerked him into the middle of the room, at the same time charging him with having come to make an arrest, and declaring that if he made an attempt of that kind he would kill him. Mr. Jamison at once saw the condition Frost was in and tried to quiet him, and finally persuaded him to sit down and have a talk. He remained seated but a moment, when springing to his feet, he declared that no man could make him sit down, and then stepped back a few paces, put his hand to his hip pocket and ordered the official to remain seated. The Marshal, seeing there was likely to be trouble, in order to gain time and get nearer to Frost, rose up slowly, saying that he could not sit there without someone to talk to. Without further ceremony Frost drew his revolver and attempted to level it for the purpose of firing, when Jamison sprang upon him, grasping him around the body with his right arm, and with his left hand seizing the pistol. They had quite a scuffle, Frost endeavoring to get the pistol in position to shoot, and Jamison doing his utmost to frustrate him. Seeing that his life depended on disarming his antagonist, the officer pushed him backward toward the fireplace, in which there was a good fire burning at the time, intending to shove him into it and thus force him, by means of the fire, to give up the revolver. But just as the contestants reached the fender there was an explosion, and a moment later Frost relinquished his hold on the revolver and began to sink and would have fallen into the fire had the officer not prevented him. An examination showed that Frost had received a wound on the inside of his right foot. Dr. King was called and found the ball imbedded among the bones of the heel, from which he extracted the ball with considerable difficulty. The wound is a very serious one. . . .

Had not Frost accidentally shot himself there is no telling how many lives might have been lost, as Frost is known to be perfectly reckless when under the influence of liquor. The strangest part of the proceeding is that during the Marshal's fight for life no one attempted to render him any assistance, and there were several men standing around.

The injured limb is much swollen, and Frost suffers a great deal of pain. He says that he has no recollection of anything that he did that morning, which is undoubtedly true, as he was perfectly crazy with liquor.[17]

Mart's troubles were not only related to his drinking and his nephews. On March 12, 1882, he was involved in the killing of his cousin Ben Frost under suspicious circumstances. Mart and Ben had taken a drove of hogs from Little Lake over the Big River road to Mendocino, on the coast, and then south to Navarro Ridge. After selling the hogs, they spent the night in Mendocino and started the long ride back in the morning. Where the Caspar road meets the Big River road, they met a friend from Little Lake, John Robertson, who was on his way home after selling a load of turkeys on the coast, and the three rode on together.

What happened next is unclear, for Mart Frost and Robertson told one story to the newspapers and another at the coroner's inquest. According to the story printed by the *Mendocino Beacon,* Ben Frost was drunk and almost fell off his horse. Mart and Robertson attempted to keep him in the saddle, but Ben's horse was skittish and wild. In the scuffle that ensued in trying to keep him on his horse, a pistol in Robertson's pocket discharged accidentally. "Who fired that pistol?" Ben had gasped, and he fell over dead. Mart and Robertson then took the body to Ben's wife in Little Lake.[18]

At the inquest held before a coroner's jury in Little Lake, they gave a different account. Mart stated that Ben's hat fell off and he tried to pick it up without dismounting. The horse shied, and Ben fell off. Mart and Robertson were helping him back into the saddle when a pistol shot rang out. Ben turned straight in his saddle and fell forward. Mart testified that he thought that the shot had come from a pouch on Robertson's horse. "I believe the pistol was exploded by the horse shaking himself. No one had a pistol in his hand. Robertson said the

Isom Frost. He served eighteen years in Folsom prison
for the murder of his nephew
Little Jimmy Frost. Cour-
tesy William B. Secrest
Collection.

shot came from his pistol, at the same time pulling it out and throwing it into the brush by the roadside. I saw Robertson take the pistol
from the cantinas after the report of the pistol."

The coroner found that the bullet had pierced Frost's left biceps,
entered his left chest, crossed through the heart, and lodged under
the skin on his right side. The jury's verdict was that Ben Frost came
to his death "by a shot from a pistol in the cantinas on the saddle of
John Robertson's horse, accidentally discharged by the horse shaking
himself." [19]

This was perhaps the first and only time on record that a man had
been shot by a horse. If any members of the jury found Mart's story
hard to believe, they had enough common sense to keep their suspicions to themselves.

A few months later, on July 29, Isom Frost became involved in
a little family trouble of his own. A Ukiah newspaper reported,
"Last Saturday afternoon Isom Frost drew a Winchester on his sister, Mrs. Cox, and shot her in the finger of one hand. The shooting

happened at Old Man Frost's. It is understood that Isom has left the neighborhood."[20]

The following year the bad blood between Mart and Isom and the young Frost boys reached its boiling point. Mart had a business partner named Andreas Hamburg, a forty-five-year-old German immigrant who had a wife and three children and owned a sheep ranch in Scott's Valley. Hamburg was quiet, inoffensive, and well respected, but he and Mart quarreled with the young Frosts over ownership of a parcel of land, and Mart threatened to kill Little Jimmy.

Two weeks later Jimmy and Taylor went to Hamburg's house late at night and called him to come outside. Hamburg, his suspicions aroused, had his wife inquire from a window who was there. The reply was that Mart and Isom Frost wished to speak with him. Hamburg knew that Mart and Isom, who were his friends, would not take such an unusual method to see him. Fearing for his life, he instructed his wife to tell them to return at a more reasonable hour.

The Frost boys left, and the next morning, December 28, 1883, Hamburg rode over to Mart's place and told him what had occurred. Mart was furious and, accompanied by Alf McCabe and Charlie Bean (both enemies of the young Frosts), rode out in search of his nephews. He first checked Taylor's ranch and, not finding them, continued on ten miles from Little Lake to the ranch of James McKindley, brother-in-law of the young Frosts, arriving there at four in the afternoon. The trio rode up to the house, and Mart was greeted by his niece Sarah McKindley, with whom he was on good terms. Sarah was standing at the kitchen door, and Taylor and Jimmy were near the well, a few steps from the house. Mart dismounted and shook hands with Sarah, telling her that she was his friend, but her brothers were not.

"I hope you and the boys will not have any fuss here," Sarah told him.

Charlie Bean walked up behind the Frost boys, and Taylor pushed him back, saying, "Don't come up. I don't want any trouble."

At that, Mart began walking toward his nephews, and Jimmy called to his sister and her children to get back into the house, at the same time pulling his six-gun and holding it behind his back.

Mart stepped closer to Taylor and said, "You are the cause of all this trouble."

"No, Mart, I am not," Taylor replied, as he and his brother stepped back from the well.

"You are a damned lying son of a bitch!" Mart roared.

"By God, you are another!" Taylor yelled back, and at the same time Mart reached for his Colt.

Jimmy quickly threw up his revolver and fired. The ball slammed into Mart's head, entering the left ear and crossing completely through the head and exiting three inches behind the right ear. Mart slumped against the well platform, dead.

Gun in hand, Jimmy turned to Charlie Bean, shouting, "God dam you, you had better go home just as quick as you can!"

Jimmy then stepped over to Alf McCabe and snarled, "Get out of here. Don't you ever cross my path."

Then Jimmy mounted his horse and rode into Ukiah, where he surrendered at the county jail. When he was asked whether Mart had drawn his pistol, he replied, "No. If he had, I would not be here to tell it."

Jimmy was charged with first-degree murder and was released on $5,000 bail, pending trial, which began on July 8, 1884. His defense was that he had shot his uncle to protect Taylor, and the jury believed him, returing a verdict of not guilty. As Jimmy left the courthouse, one of the jurors told him, "You had a close shave. Straighten up and be a law abiding citizen."

"I won't stir up any more trouble," Jimmy replied, but added, "I won't be imposed on." [21]

Isom Frost was outraged by the verdict and swore revenge. But before he could do anything, he almost met Mart's fate. On July 16, a few days after the verdict, Isom drowned his grief in liquor and got roaring drunk at Old Jim's ranch, in Wheelbarrow Valley, eight miles north of Willitsville. With Isom were two of Old Jim's ranch hands, José Sicotte and Isaac Smith, who were also drinking heavily. Isom and Sicotte were on bad terms because Sicotte had preempted a section of land that Isom wanted.

The trio walked a half mile down the road to the cabin of Tom Gibson, an old friend of Isom's, from Davis County, Missouri, and brother-in-law of Andreas Hamburg. Here a fight broke out, with Isom and Gibson on one side and Sicotte and Smith on the other. While Gibson grabbed Sicotte's rifle, Isom pulled a Bowie knife and stabbed Smith once and Sicotte four times. The wounds were not serious, and the two ranch hands went back to Old Jim's, obtained rifles, and returned to Gibson's cabin. They fired twenty shots into the cabin, narrowly missing Gibson's wife and her sister. Isom and

Gibson returned the fire, and in the exchange Isom was wounded in the knee.[22]

Sicotte and Smith were arrested for assault to murder, tried, and sentenced to six years each in San Quentin. Isom's wound gradually healed, but it was months before he was well enough to exact vengeance on Jimmy Frost. Without Mart to aid him, Isom was reluctant to tangle head on with his nephews, and he told his friends that there were too many for him to handle alone. Isom's only remaining brother, Old Jim, also hated the young Frosts, but he was sixty years old and never took part in the family's gunplay.

Isom began looking for someone to help him kill Jimmy Frost. He first approached Tom Gibson. Isom told him, "Tom, by God, I will give you $500 if you will kill Jimmy for me."

"No, I won't do it," Gibson responded. "What do I want to kill Jimmy for? He never wronged me."[23]

Isom turned next to Tom's twenty-five-year-old brother, George Gibson. George had grown up with the young Frost boys, but, in 1882, he got into a brawl with Taylor and Jimmy at a dance at his brother's house. From that moment on, Gibson was a deadly enemy of Jimmy and his brothers. George had settled on a piece of public land east of Little Lake, and, in 1883, Jimmy and his brothers contested his claim and threatened to kill him if he didn't move out. One day Gibson rode into Little Lake and saw Jimmy Frost and Less Case riding toward his claim. Gibson, on his way home the next day, stopped at Hamburg's ranch and saw Jimmy and Case riding back from his claim. George mounted up and rode out to his place, only to find his cabin in ashes. Tacked to a small tree nearby he found a piece of paper bearing a crudely drawn coffin with his name in the center. There were twelve bullet holes fired into the tree, one on top of another. Gibson threw the paper down and rode back to Little Lake. He gave the land up and never returned to it. The Frost boys later "proved up" on the claim and got a deed to the property.

Gibson thought his trouble with the young Frosts was over, but they continued to threaten him and tried to drive him out of the valley. Isom and Old Jim knew of Gibson's troubles with their nephews, and they began to play upon his fears. They continually came to him with news of the latest threats made by the Frost boys, keeping him in a state of apprehension. Finally, Isom asked Gibson to help him kill Jimmy. He refused at first, but Isom and Old Jim kept working on him, and finally he consented.[24]

Isom told Gibson that there was going to be a sheep rodeo for several days at Hamburg's ranch in which all the sheepmen in Scott's Valley would round up their stock, marking them and separating the lambs from the ewes. Isom knew that his nephews would be there, and on the morning of April 9, 1885, he and Gibson rode out to the Rocktree road, which led from Little Lake to Scott's Valley, and prepared to ambush the boys as they rode up the grade. But the Frosts had already passed by, so Isom and George rode to Old Jim's place, the Wheelbarrow House, and ate their noon meal. George's nerve failed him, however, and, leaving Isom, he mounted up and rode the seven miles to Hamburg's corral, where he worked all afternoon helping to mark the lambs. There was a large number of sheepmen present, including Old Jim, Hamburg, and Jimmy and Dave Frost. The day passed uneventfully, and in the evening Gibson rode back toward Little Lake with Old Jim. At the point where the trail turned off to Wheelbarrow Valley, Old Jim urged George to come home with him, but he refused, saying his wife would be looking for him.

"No," said Old Jim. "Come and go over with me and go with Isom in the morning and kill them. Shoot them from the hill. I will see you are not hurt by the law. If you don't go they will kill you anyway. You'll never be hurt if you go."

Gibson turned his horse around and rode to Old Jim's place, where he spent the night with Isom and a friend, Ed Jewell. In the morning Old Jim went back to work at the rodeo, and a few hours later George and Isom rode to Scott's Valley, dismounted a mile and a half from Hamburg's corral, and proceeded the rest of the way on foot. Each carried a high-powered .45-70 Marlin rifle.

Hamburg's corral was located southwest of a low ridge and was divided into four sections, with a shearing pen behind it and a wool shed on the east. Old Jim, Hamburg, Jimmy and Dave Frost, Tom Lynch, W. H. Bedford, and nine other men were working in the corral. Jimmy and Dave wore six-guns on their belts; the others were all unarmed.

Isom and George positioned themselves under a fir tree on the ridge, 130 yards from the corral. They saw Jimmy Frost walk from the corral to the wool shed and disappear behind it.

"When he comes back I am going to kill him," Isom said. "You shoot Dave."

A moment later Jimmy returned, walking a sheep backwards by pulling a hind leg. Bedford opened the corral gate, and Jimmy put

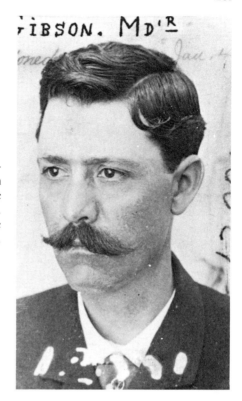

George Gibson. He was sentenced to seventeen years in prison for his part in the ambush at Scott's Valley. Courtesy California State Archives.

the sheep inside. He then stepped to the side of the gate and rested both hands on the fence. Isom Frost took careful aim and fired. The large slug tore through Jimmy's back near the right shoulder, exited through his chest, and lodged in the fence.

"Jesus Christ, I am shot!" Jimmy gasped, as blood spurted from his wound.

A moment later George Gibson fired at Dave Frost, but missed. As Dave ran toward the wool shed for cover, Gibson fired again, but his aim was poor. Dave saw the two puffs of smoke on the hill and fired twice at them, but he could not see his attackers, who were concealed in the brush.

Jimmy Frost, not knowing who had shot him, drew his Colt .44 and asked one of the men in the corral, "Did you shoot me?"

"No. I have nothing to shoot with," was the quick reply.

Jimmy then turned and, spotting Hamburg near the wool shed, snapped two shots at him. Hamburg fled behind the wool shed, and Jimmy followed, six-gun blazing. Dave Frost saw this and thought that Hamburg had shot his brother. He fired twice at Hamburg, who crumpled, mortally wounded. One shot struck him near the navel, passed through the right kidney, and came out near the lower spine. A second bullet entered his sternum and lodged in his spine. Within moments Hamburg was dead.

Still not sure who his attacker was, Jimmy turned his gun on the men in the shearing pen. He fired at Tom Lynch, who was fleeing through the pen, and Lynch dropped with a bullet in his right shoulder. Jimmy fired his last shot at Bedford, but the bullet passed over his head. Stumbling back to the wool shed, Jimmy collapsed while trying to remove the cartridges from his .44. He pleaded in vain for someone to reload his gun and died an hour later.

Dave Frost mounted one of Hamburg's horses and lit out for home. Isom and George Gibson rode quickly out of the valley, unnoticed by anyone.

"Don't you tell anybody about this," Isom warned. "If you do I'll blow the top of your head off."

Then Gibson went to his home in Little Lake, while Isom returned to Old Jim's place. Ed Jewell was there, and Isom asked him if anyone had been at the ranch that morning. Jewell told him that only a neighbor, Jake Dunn, had stopped by. Jewell noticed that Isom's horse was sweating and knew that there had been trouble. Isom foolishly told him what had happened, and Jewell agreed to swear that Isom had not left the ranch all morning. Isom then spoke with Dunn, an old friend, and he, too, agreed to supply an alibi.[25]

Word of the killings was sent to Ukiah, and Sheriff Doc Standley rode to Hamburg's ranch, arriving at ten the next morning. He was determined to put a stop to the feud and made a careful, deliberate investigation. Examining the bodies of Frost and Hamburg, he found a mysterious second bullet wound, smaller than the first, in Jimmy's abdomen. He questioned all the men who had been present. Most were certain that Dave Frost had killed Hamburg, but none had seen anyone fire shots from the hill. Dave, however, insisted that at least two shots had been fired from ambush.

Standley found the bullet that had killed Jimmy Frost lodged in the corral fence and noted that it was of large caliber. He placed a straight stick in the hole to determine the bullet's trajectory. The stick pointed toward a spot at the top of the ridge. Doc climbed up to the spot and found freshly broken twigs on the ground and a limb cut by a knife from a manzanita bush. He attended the funeral of Jimmy Frost that afternoon, and then placed Dave Frost under arrest for the murder of Hamburg and took him to Ukiah.

Standley had known Isom Frost for many years and was familiar with all the details of the feud. He was certain that Isom had killed Jimmy, but he had no evidence. Riding to Old Jim's place, he questioned the Frosts, Jewell, and Dunn, but all claimed ignorance of the affair. Standley examined their guns and saw that Isom's rifle was of large bore. He spent the night at Old Jim's, leaving the next day. Doc knew that the Frosts and Dunn would never talk, but he could see that Ed Jewell was afraid of Isom. He decided that Jewell was the key to solving the case. Doc kept a close watch on Jewell's movements, hoping to catch him away from the Frosts. Six weeks later Jewell disappeared, and it was a month before Doc learned that Old Jim and Jake Dunn had driven him down to Healdsburg in a covered wagon to get him away from the sheriff's prying eyes.

Standley was well known in Sonoma County, and he knew his presence there would excite suspicion, so he sent a deputy, George McMullen, who lived at Point Arena, down to Healdsburg to make a quiet investigation into Jewell's whereabouts. McMullen found that Jewell had again disappeared. After a lengthy search he managed to trace Jewell to Willows and then to Marysville, where he was reported to be working on a wharf on the Yuba River. Standley and McMullen went to Marysville and learned that Jewell was working for a man named Jacob Schimp. The officers took Schimp into their confidence and asked him to introduce McMullen to Jewell as a relative. Schimp did so and arranged for the two to work and share a room together. McMullen quickly became Jewell's friend and confidant, and it was not long before the deputy had learned the whole story of the killings.

On September 17, 1885, McMullen got his friend blind drunk, and, by arrangement with Officer Finn of the Marysville police, Jewell was arrested and lodged in jail. Standley visited Jewell in the jail and made a deal with him. Since Jewell had harbored and concealed the identities of the killers, he was an accessory after the fact. If he would testify in court against Frost and Gibson, Standley and the district attorney would request leniency, and he would receive no more than three years in prison. Jewell agreed, and Standley left immediately to arrest Isom Frost.

Doc knew that Isom had spent the summer herding sheep for a rancher named Tyler, in Tehama County, and that Isom had driven the sheep into the mountains, near the headwaters of Hayfork Creek, in Trinity County. The sheriff wasted no time. Taking the train to Red Bluff, he proceeded on horseback fifty miles up Cottonwood Creek, through the Bald Hills, and to the sheep camp on Hayfork Creek. Isom was not at the cabin, so Doc sat down to wait for him. An hour later Frost came walking up, carrying his rifle on his shoulder. He did not see the sheriff until he was a few feet from the cabin. Doc stood up, stepped toward Frost, and said casually, "What in the devil are you doing here, Isom?"

Frost was so startled that he did not know how to react. Instinctively he offered the sheriff his right hand. Standley grabbed it with his left, and with his right hand on his pistol, ordered, "Give me your gun."

Isom handed the rifle over, and Doc said, "You are under arrest for the murder of Jimmy Frost. Are you going to make any kick?"

"How can I kick?" Isom retorted. "I have nothing to kick with."[26]

Standley took his prisoner to Marysville and, with McMullen and Jewell, returned to Ukiah, arriving on the twenty-fifth. Doc hurried on to Little Lake, surprised George Gibson at midnight, and lodged him in jail at Ukiah. Both Jewell and Gibson turned state's evidence.

Dave Frost's trial for killing Andreas Hamburg began two weeks later. His defense was that it was his brother who had shot Hamburg. Ed Jewell testified that Isom Frost had told him that Hamburg had paid George Gibson $1,000 to kill Jimmy Frost. True or not, the jury could not agree on a verdict, with ten men voting for acquittal and two to convict. Dave Frost was freed.[27]

Isom Frost went on trial on January 5, 1886. Gibson and Jewell testified against him. His attorneys based their defense on the second bullet wound found on Jimmy's body, arguing that this shot had caused his death and had been accidentally fired by Dave Frost during the melee. The trial lasted five days, and Isom was convicted of first-degree murder and sentenced to life at Folsom prison. His attorneys were credited with saving him from the gallows.

Jewell pleaded guilty and was sentenced to two and a half years in San Quentin. Gibson pleaded guilty to second-degree murder and received seventeen years in San Quentin.[28]

Isom Frost proved a model convict, driving an oxteam at Folsom. He served eighteen years of his sentence and was paroled in 1904. He returned to Little Lake, lived quietly, and received a full pardon five years later.[29]

Isom lived to old age, a changed man, gentle and kindly. On February 11, 1928, suffering from arteriosclerosis, he was admitted to the Mendocino State Hospital, where he died on April 29.[30] He was buried in the hospital cemetery, in Talmage, and with him were laid to rest the last remnants of rivalry, revenge, and hatred that had ended so many lives in the Little Lake Vendetta.

CHAPTER 12

The Modoc Lynching

ON a fateful May morning in 1901, early risers in the isolated settlement of Lookout, in Modoc County, were treated to a ghastly sight few of them would ever forget. Dangling by ropes from the two wood bridges that spanned the Pit River, just east of town, were the bodies of five men, their necks stretched by hemp, their hands and feet bound with rope, and their features frozen grotesquely in death.

Although the hanging of the so-called "Hall gang" has long since faded into obscurity, it once created a statewide furor and resulted in the only serious attempt ever made in California to punish the members of a lynch mob. The Modoc lynching remains one of the best examples of frontier justice gone awry, for the five hanged men had been accused only of burglaries and minor thefts, none of which warranted the death penalty.

Vigilante activity was common in California during the gold rush period. In the first eight months of 1855 there were thirty-six lynchings in the state. As law became established, such hangings became less frequent, but they did not disappear completely. Between 1883 and 1901 there were thirty-one cases of lynching in California. Only one had ever taken place in Modoc County, when John McCoy, a murderer, was strung up in August, 1877. After 1895 vigilantism became increasingly rare. In the five years prior to 1901, California experienced but one lynching. By the turn of the century the state had made gigantic steps forward in agriculture, industry, commerce, and education, and its population had increased accordingly, attracted by the myriad of opportunities. But although California's spirit and soul were wholeheartedly in the twentieth century, it still had one foot firmly implanted in the nineteenth. Those brawling, blustering frontier habits were hard to shake, particularly in remote, rural areas like Modoc County.[1]

Located in the extreme northeast corner of California, Modoc County, in 1901, had some five thousand residents and was far from the state's centers of population and government. It had no rail service, and travelers were forced to take a train to Reno and then board a stagecoach for the 175-mile journey north to Alturas, the Modoc County seat. The town of Lookout lies in southwest Modoc County at the north end of Big Valley, and just west of the Pit River. In 1900 it had a population of about one hundred and was the social and commercial center for neighboring cattle ranchers. The nearest towns were Adin, located twelve miles due east, and Bieber, six miles south, in Lassen County. Alturas was fifty miles from Lookout, a full day's trip by buggy. A direct telephone line connected Lookout with the county seat.[2]

Lookout's main street boasted a few shops and businesses, among them William D. Morris's general merchandise store, the Leventon brothers' blacksmith shop, E. S. Trowbridge's general store, and James R. Myers's hotel. Myers served as justice of the peace, and his hotel was used when needed as the town jail. Law enforcement was provided by Myers's son-in-law Erv Carpenter, the thirty-year-old constable of Lookout Township.

The Big Valley was quiet and peaceful, but in the late 1890s its residents began to experience numerous incidents of livestock rustling, petty thievery, and vandalism. It was not long before the finger of suspicion was pointed at the sons of old Calvin Hall, who owned a small ranch and truck farm, nine miles northeast of Lookout, in a draw called Gouger Neck. An early pioneer of Modoc, Calvin Hall was well known throughout the county. Born in 1828, in Mayzodon, Ohio, he had come to California during the gold rush and worked in the mines. In 1861, nine months after the outbreak of the Civil War, he enlisted in Company C, 2d Regiment of the California Cavalry, and was stationed at Fort Crook, in the Fall River Valley, some thirty miles southeast of Lookout. Intelligent and educated, he was promoted to sergeant but soon was stripped back down to private for being drunk on duty. Working as a millhand and carpenter, Calvin served three years in the army and was discharged on September 20, 1864.[3]

During his service at Fort Crook, Calvin Hall had become an expert on the customs of the Achumawi, or Pit River, Indians, and later, in 1873, he dictated a detailed description of their way of life, which to this day remains an important source for the study of Achumawi culture. In 1865 he began living with a seventeen-year-old Pit River Indian, Mary Joe, and in time she became his common-law wife. The couple had four children: Mary Nevada, born in 1866;

Calvin and Mary Hall. He met his death in one of California's most infamous lynchings. Courtesy Modoc County Museum.

Dora, born in 1876; Charles, born in 1878; and James, born in 1881. In
1869, Mary Hall adopted a newborn Indian baby, whom they named
Frank and raised as their own.[4]

In the 1870s, Calvin moved from the Fall River Valley to the Lookout area. Calvin's brother Henry Hall also settled in Modoc County
and, in 1875, was appointed to care for the county's indigent sick. Calvin, too, was interested in public service, becoming district clerk for
the Lookout school district in 1879. He later returned to farming,
raising vegetables and stock on his ranch in Gouger Neck. He was
relatively successful; the *Bieber Big Valley Gazette* reported that in 1899
he earned $700, then a substantial sum, and was able to pay off a
$500 mortgage on his property.[5]

The marriage between Calvin and Mary seems to have been a
shaky one, for in February, 1885, they were divorced. They remained
friends, however, and Mary continued to do housekeeping chores for
Calvin and lived just two miles from his place. Mary soon took up

with Calvin's hired man, an Indian named Wilson, and she bore him two children: Martin, born in 1887, and Agnes, born a year later. But Mary's new mate disappeared, and she raised Martin and Agnes alone.[6]

Denied a normal, stable upbringing, it is little wonder that Calvin's sons went bad. They were a wild bunch, and Frank and Jim became known as thieves. How much time Calvin devoted to his boys is not known, but during the 1890s he busied himself with Republican party politics and served as a clerk and precinct judge in three elections. A bitter political and business rivalry existed between Lookout's two storekeepers, William D. Morris and E. S. Trowbridge. Morris, who had served a term in the state legislature from 1886 to 1888, was the leader of the township's twenty-two Republican voters, while Trowbridge headed its sixty-five Democrats. Calvin Hall was a close friend of Morris's, and in the election of 1898 he worked strenuously against Bob Leventon, who was a candidate for county supervisor. Leventon lost the race, and many bad feelings were stirred up during the campaign. From then on, Hall and Leventon were bitter foes.[7]

Calvin Hall had other enemies. The worst was Isom Eades, a "squaw man" who owned a ranch six miles from Lookout. At one time Eades had wanted to marry Calvin's daughter Mary, but Calvin would not allow it. Infuriated, Eades picked a fight with the much older Hall, but a bystander separated them before Calvin could be injured. Eades, still anxious for revenge, persuaded a man named Wagner to run off with Dora Hall. Further ill will developed when Frank Hall began pursuing Eades's Indian wife, Sally, and Isom threatened to kill him unless he kept away from her.[8]

But the worst trouble of all resulted from the lawless activities of Frank Hall and his brothers. They were frequently suspected of stealing cattle and hogs and on several occasions were placed under arrest, but each time Calvin succeeded in having the charges dismissed. This seemed to encourage the Hall boys, for they became more bold. On one occasion the Lookout schoolhouse was burglarized, its windows smashed, books destroyed, and the interior ransacked. The Halls were suspected, but there were no witnesses. Enemies of the Halls began to find their horses and cattle mutilated, with severed hamstrings. Other cattle had their eyes gouged out, legs broken, or pitchfork holes punched into their bodies. On one occasion a group of Indians, unfriendly to the Halls, was at work haying on the ranch of Dillon Sherer, in Stone Coal Valley, north of Lookout. Upon returning to their camp, they found their food fouled, wagons destroyed, and their huts knocked down. The Indians trailed the vandals to the vicinity of the Hall ranch and then reported the incident to Sherer, who sent word to Frank Hall that he would be shot on sight if he ever again entered the Sherer ranch. A few days later Sherer awoke to find that his wife's pet saddle horse had been viciously mutilated, its tail and ears cut off and its flanks sliced deeply by a knife. Local ranchers were outraged, and threats of lynching were freely made. But there was no direct evidence that the Hall boys were the culprits, and no action was taken.[9]

Early in 1900 a stranger named Daniel B. Yantis showed up in the Big Valley. Forty-five years old and rumored to be a former convict, Yantis openly carried a six-gun and boasted of gunfights he had played a hand in. He rented the Lawton ranch, north of Lookout, and also purchased a woodcutting camp in nearby Round Valley. He became friendly with the Halls and developed an amorous relationship with Calvin's former wife, Mary Wilson. Frank Hall and Yantis were birds of a feather and became boon companions. They were frequently joined by nineteen-year-old Jim Hall and little Martin Wilson. Local residents dubbed this quartet the "Hall gang."[10]

Cattle thefts and burglaries in Lookout, Adin, and Bieber increased after the arrival of Yantis. Barns and houses were plundered, and cattle were killed or driven off. Harness sets, halters, clothing, and tools were stolen from outlying ranches and cow camps. Fear of retaliation kept many of the ranchers from accusing the Halls. One newspaper even advocated lynching the culprits. In June, 1900, the *Big Valley Gazette* reported that unknown persons had been killing Dillon Sherer's cattle at Mud Lake, twenty-five miles north of Lookout. "Catch them and hang them," declared the *Gazette's* editor.[11]

Apparently Calvin Hall knew of his sons' thievery. His brother Henry later said, "Calvin was kept supplied with beef for the purpose of keeping him quiet about what he knew."[12]

Things came to a head in May, 1901, when Bob Leventon discovered that a harness had been stolen from his barn and Isom Eades found that he was missing a roll of barbed wire. Early on the morning of May 25, the two appeared before Justice of the Peace Myers at his hotel and swore out search warrants for the homes of Calvin Hall, Mary Wilson, and Dan Yantis. Myers gave the warrants to Constable Carpenter to serve, and he rounded up a posse consisting of Eades, Leventon, Jervis Kresge, and Claude Brown and rode out to Mary's place, where they found only young Martin. The posse searched the house and discovered part of Leventon's harness, as well as several other stolen items. Bob Leventon looped a strap around Martin's neck and yanked him off his feet, demanding to know where the rest of his harness was.

"Don't hang me," the boy choked. "I will tell you where the stolen property is. It is under the bed at Hall's."

Carpenter confiscated the booty, arrested young Wilson, and proceeded with his posse to Calvin's ranch. Here they discovered many more articles that appeared to have been stolen, including the breast and back straps from Leventon's missing harness. When they questioned Calvin Hall about the harness straps, he replied, "I don't know how they came there."[13]

Carpenter took Hall at his word and did not arrest him. Instead the possemen rode out in search of Calvin's sons. They found Jim Hall and Dan Yantis working in a field near the Pit River. Relieving Yantis of his six-shooter, they placed the pair under arrest and returned with them to Lookout, arriving at three that afternoon. Yantis, Hall, and young Wilson were placed under guard at Myers's hotel. Then Carpenter obtained arrest warrants for Calvin, Mary, and Frank Hall and headed north again toward Gouger Neck. Three miles from town they met Frank Hall and a stockman, Walter Criss, on the road. Hall was riding a mare that he had just broken for Criss. Carpenter rode toward him and said, "Frank, you are my prisoner."

"That is all right," Hall replied coolly.

"I have a warrant for you," the constable explained.

"Read it," demanded Frank.

Carpenter did so in a nervous voice. He took a pistol from Frank, and then, without taking the precaution of handcuffing their prisoner, the posse continued on to the Hall ranch, leading Frank's horse with a twenty-foot hackamore looped around its neck. They had not gone far when Hall suddenly reached down and slipped the hackamore off his mare's nose, leaving it in a posseman's hands, and put spurs to his horse. The posse chased him to the mouth of a rough canyon that led to his father's ranch. Frank leaped from his animal and fled into the canyon. The posse abandoned its horses and followed on foot. Jervis Kresge, in the lead, threw the hackamore over Hall's neck and captured him.

They walked their prisoner to a nearby abandoned barn on the Pat Gilbert ranch, where Isom Eades fastened the rope around his neck and tossed it over a rafter. Then he, Leventon, Brown, and Kresge jerked Hall up, but his weight snapped the rope. The hackamore was repaired and Hall joisted up again, but once more the rope broke, and the gasping prisoner collapsed on the ground, half unconscious. Isom Eades pulled his six-gun and struck him over the head with the barrel.[14]

The possemen then proceeded on to the Hall ranch, arrested Calvin and Mary, and late that night returned to Lookout, where the six prisoners spent the night guarded at Myers's hotel. In the morning, May 26, they were brought before Justice Myers for arraignment. Calvin and Mary were released, but the rest were held on burglary charges. Dan Yantis's bail was set at $500 and the others at $300 each. Calvin Hall remained in town, and that afternoon he was rearrested by Constable Carpenter on a petit larceny complaint that had been sworn to by a local farmer, Robison Dunlap. A pitchfork that had been stolen from Dunlap had been found at Hall's ranch. Calvin asked that his case be delayed two days so he could obtain a lawyer, and Justice Myers released him on his own recognizance. The others, unable to raise bail money, remained under guard to await their trials, which were set for June 3.[15]

The next day Erv Carpenter swore in a friend, Jim Brown, as his deputy. Brown, forty years old, was a slightly built former butcher and was the half brother of Claude Brown. Armed with search warrants, Carpenter and Jim Brown made several more trips to Calvin Hall's and Mary Wilson's places, looking for stolen property. They also took Dan Yantis to his cabin, which he unlocked, and a number of stolen tools were found inside. In all, 104 items were identified as stolen, including dishes, spoons, and tablecloths.

The arrests of the "Hall gang" met with a great deal of public approval in Big Valley. Many hoped that they would be sent to state prison, thus leaving the valley in peace. Others, however, began to talk of a quicker and more certain way of ridding themselves of the Halls. Although various vague threats were made, the first serious proposition to lynch the men was made on Tuesday, May 28, when Deputy Constable Jim Brown approached several Lookout men and invited them to meet him at Trowbridge's store the next day to make arrangements for a hanging.[16]

Meanwhile, Isom Eades and Bob Leventon were pursuing legal methods to prosecute the thieves on felony charges. They traveled to Alturas, arriving Tuesday evening, and tried to bring the matter before the grand jury, but it had adjourned an hour earlier. They met with the district attorney, E. C. Bonner, who explained to them that no felony had been committed. The circumstances gave rise only to misdemeanor charges, which would be heard in justice court in Lookout and would result in sentences of no more than a year in the county jail, if indeed the Halls were convicted. Bonner sent a message to C. C. Auble, an attorney who lived in Adin, deputizing him to prosecute the case when it came to trial. Eades and Leventon returned home in a very unpleasant frame of mind.[17]

The next day the meeting was held in Trowbridge's store. Present were Jim Brown, Jervis Kresge, E. S. Trowbridge, John Hutton, Dick Nichols, Bob Leventon, and Justice of the Peace Myers. Brown and Myers picked out new ropes from Trowbridge's stock. Trowbridge cut them into the proper lengths, and Myers tied nooses in them. The ropes were placed in a barley sack, which Brown carried to the Leventon blacksmith shop and hid in the coal room.

That evening Jim Brown ran into Calvin Hall at the hotel. Brown had found the feet of a stolen calf's skin in Mary Wilson's stove, and he asked Calvin where the rest of the hide was.

"Right where I killed the calf!" Calvin snapped.

When Brown asked where that was, Calvin replied, "None of your damn business. Find it yourself."

"Mr. Hall, we have a right to ask you that," said Brown. "We have been instructed by the district attorney to make you produce this hide."

"Well, you are doing this business. You find it," Hall returned.

It was later reported that Brown told Calvin that if he didn't produce the hide he would be strung up until he did.[18]

While under guard at Myers's hotel, Frank and Jim Hall and Martin Wilson managed to smuggle out several letters to their parents. Frank, in a penciled note to his mother, described how he had nearly been lynched at the time of his arrest. He concealed the letter in his shoe and slipped it to his mother when she visited him at the hotel. Little Martin wrote a letter to his mother describing how he had been hung by the strap to make him talk.[19]

On Thursday afternoon, May 30, Deputy Constable Jim Brown and his brother Claude, Fred Roberts, Bob Leventon and his brother Joe, and Louis Eades (brother of Isom) rode out to Calvin Hall's ranch and placed him under arrest without any warrant of authority. Mary Wilson's young daughter Agnes was present and later said that Jim

Brown told Calvin, "You God damned son of a bitch, you have got to go to Lookout tonight. I'll fix you before I get through with you!"

Calvin refused to go, saying, "I will be at Lookout tomorrow morning at nine o'clock."

"You've got to go to Lookout right now!" Brown exclaimed, and punched the old man in the back with his rifle butt. Hall was taken to Lookout in a buggy and placed in Myers's hotel with the others.[20]

At four o'clock that afternoon another meeting was held by the Leventon brothers, E. S. Trowbridge, John Hutton, and six other men. Plans were carefully drawn up. The lynching would occur that night when the weakest guard, nineteen-year-old Sid Goyette, would be on duty with Jim Brown at the hotel. The mob would consist of two parties, one from town and the other from the country, and would disperse quietly after their work was done.

Mary Wilson and her daughter Agnes visited the prisoners in Myers's hotel. Calvin and Frank had written several more letters to Mary, but the guards had found and destroyed them. A Lookout woman, Mrs. Peter Hagerman, had got wind that something was up and passed word to Mary that it would be dangerous for her to stay in town that night. As soon as it was dark, Mary and Agnes quietly slipped out of town.[21]

Myers's hotel was a two-story structure, with a saloon and parlor downstairs and bedrooms upstairs. The prisoners were kept in the bar. The bedrooms were occupied by members of Myers's family; Erv Carpenter; Sam Parks, a sheepherder; Dennis Kane, who had defeated Bob Leventon for supervisor three years before; and a salesman. Twenty-three-year-old John Hutton tended bar and helped guard the prisoners. After supper, Hutton; Claude Morris, the twenty-three-year-old son of William D. Morris; and Myers's daughter Alice retired to the parlor to sing hymns. Old Calvin Hall, accompanied by Jim Brown, entered the room and was invited to join in the singing. He declined, saying he was unable to sing, but would stand while the hymns were rendered. Then, with the knowledge that they were about to lynch the old soldier, Hutton and Morris launched into a lusty rendition of "When Shall I See Jesus?"[22]

At midnight the two guards, Constable Carpenter and Dick Nichols, went off duty and were replaced by Jim Brown and Sid Goyette. Carpenter retired to his room upstairs, and Nichols went down the street to Trowbridge's store, as did Hutton and Morris. By one o'clock everyone in the hotel except Brown and Goyette was fast asleep. Dan Yantis, Frank and Jim Hall, and Martin Wilson bedded down on the floor of the saloon; Calvin Hall slept on a sofa in the parlor.

Meanwhile members of the lynch mob had been quietly at work. Hutton, Morris, and Nichols met Sam Parks, John Potter, and Joe Leventon behind Trowbridge's store. Earlier that day Jim Brown had talked Claude Morris into joining the mob. Brown and Trowbridge believed that if young Morris was in on the plot, his father would be less likely to press for an investigation into the lynching of his friends, the Halls. The little group then walked across a dam on the Pit River to the schoolhouse, carrying the ropes and half a dozen wagon-spoke clubs. After an hour's wait the band of twelve men from the country (outside Lookout) rode up. This group consisted of Bob Leventon; Isom Eades; Claude Brown; Fred Roberts and his twenty-three-year-old son, Harry; Louis Palmentier; Claude Marcus; Jervis Kresge; Henry Knox and his twenty-four-year-old nephew, Will McDaniels; Albert L. Colburn; and Orrin Trowbridge, a store-keeper, from Bieber, and brother of E. S. Trowbridge. Claude Brown and Fred Roberts wore pistols, and Bob Leventon carried a rifle. Each man wore a barley sack mask, and several brought ropes and sacks to use in binding and gagging the prisoners.

Jim Brown met the crowd at the schoolhouse and advised them that when he was sure everyone in the hotel was asleep, he would step onto the porch and light a cigar. He returned to the hotel and shortly after 1:30 gave the signal, and the masked band walked silently across the two bridges over the Pit River. Halfway to the hotel they stopped and held a brief counsel, choosing Claude Brown to act as the leader. Al Colburn, a husky youth who worked on Claude Brown's ranch and had had numerous run-ins with Yantis, vowed, "I'll soon get even with Dan Yantis."

Isom Eades added, "And I'll get the man who stole my barbed wire."

With Claude Brown in the lead, the mob burst into the hotel saloon. Jim Brown and Sid Goyette were covered with guns and ordered to put up their hands. The deputy constable, of course, immediately complied, as did the youthful Goyette, who was unaware of the plot and was taken completely by surprise. Martin Wilson, Dan Yantis, and the Hall brothers were seized, gagged, and their hands bound behind their backs with rope.

The commotion awoke Myers's family and his lodgers. Myers

rushed downstairs into the barroom but was turned back at gunpoint. In an effort to make it appear that he was not involved, the hotelkeeper yelled that he would kill the intruders if they did not leave. He dashed back upstairs, announcing to his wife and daughters that he wanted his gun, but the terrified women pleaded with him to stay with them.

Constable Carpenter ran downstairs but made no attempt to interfere. Calvin Hall, seventy-four years old, remained in the parlor, sound asleep. Although several of the prisoners shouted and groaned, the noise did not wake him. Frank Hall, the first man bound, was dragged out by Bob Leventon, Isom Eades, Henry Knox, and John Potter. They were followed by John Hutton and Claude Morris, who brought little Martin Wilson, then five months shy of his fourteenth birthday. The rest followed with Jim Hall and Dan Yantis. The mob started toward the bridges, but Frank Hall managed to free his hands and began to fight like a tiger. He kicked Will McDaniels a terrific blow in the stomach before one of the lynchers struck him over the head with a wagon spoke, knocking him unconscious. Frank Hall was dragged to the first bridge east of town, a low, wood structure that crossed a shallow branch. A rope was looped around his neck, the other end tied to the railing, and the unconscious prisoner shoved over the side. The fall broke his neck, killing him instantly.

The masked band continued on to the long main bridge over the river, some 140 yards from the hotel. Fred Roberts, Jervis Kresge, and Louis Palmentier hoisted Dan Yantis over the rail and dropped him down. Next these three, with Hutton and Morris, threw young Martin over, and moments later Jim Hall met the same fate. Another quick counsel was held, and one of the lynchers declared, "We'll have to hang that old Calvin Hall or he'll sock it to us if we don't."

The entire group marched back to the hotel. Five went into the parlor and woke Calvin Hall.

"Who's there? What's wanted?" Hall cried out.

"We'll show you pretty soon," was the ominous reply, and he was taken outside in his nightclothes and bound and gagged. The mob walked their captive back to the bridge, leaving Myers, Carpenter, Goyette, and Jim Brown standing idly on the hotel porch. Brown, evidently realizing that he should at least pretend to resist the mob, fired four shots into the air. Carpenter made even less of a show. He unloosed a single shot up the road and away from the crowd.

Calvin Hall was dropped over the north side of the main bridge.

The main bridge near Lookout, scene of the lynching of Calvin Hall, Jim Hall, Martin Wilson, and Dan Yantis. Courtesy Modoc County Museum.

The rope was too long and his feet struck the rocks, smashing one toe, but in moments he, too, was dead.

Then Louis Palmentier warned the band, "Now, boys, we had better keep our mouths shut."

The mob split up, its members silently returning to their homes and ranches. Strangely, the gunshots had failed to rouse any of Lookout's inhabitants, leading many to believe that few in town were unaware of the lynching plot. At daybreak, word of the hanging quickly spread, and soon every man, woman, and child in Lookout had crowded around the two bridges to view the dangling bodies. Not far from the hotel were found five wagon spokes. A rope with a hangman's noose was discovered near the bridge; it was rumored to have been prepared for Mary Wilson.[23]

Constable Carpenter made no effort to investigate the lynching. He waited until dawn to telephone the sheriff in Alturas and later claimed that the reason for his delay in reporting the quintuple murder was that he did not want to wake up the telephone operator.[24]

District Attorney E. C. Bonner, Sheriff Ben Street, and a court reporter left immediately for Lookout, arriving at six that evening. Young and inexperienced, Bonner's actions in Lookout were incompetent in the extreme. He and Adin's justice of the peace, Robert Harris, picked a local coroner's jury to investigate the affair. Bonner knew that the mob was then believed to have numbered some thirty to forty men, a figure that would have included much of the adult male population of Lookout. A blind man could have seen that if a jury of Lookout men was picked, some of them would very likely have been members of the mob themselves. But instead of delaying the inquest to obtain jurors from another locale, Bonner began the hearing with a jury of seven local men. Three of them, E. S. Trowbridge and the Leventon brothers, bore the unique duty of investigating a murder that they themselves had committed.

Jim Brown, Myers, Carpenter, Goyette, and two others testified before the coroner's jury. Brown claimed that the mob had numbered about thirty and that he and Goyette had been taken by surprise. Both Brown and Myers swore that they could not recognize any members of the mob. After taking testimony that evening and the following morning, they found, not surprisingly, that the victims had been hanged "by parties unknown to the jury." [25]

The citizens of Lookout assumed that the incident was now closed, and like scores of lynchings before it, no further attempts would be made to identify the guilty parties. Reported the *Big Valley Gazette:*

> It was thought that the matter would end with the finding of the jury, but the people of the entire state are aroused at the unprecedented lynching, and the entire press condemns the mob as wilful murderers and calls upon the State authorities to do anything in their power to bring the perpetrators to justice. [26]

The same day that the coroner's jury reached its verdict, June 1, 1901, accounts of the wholesale hanging were published on the front pages of all the leading dailies in California, and it also received prominent press coverage throughout the country. The news created a public uproar, and Governor Henry T. Gage offered a $5,000 reward for the arrest and conviction of the lynchers, stating:

> The notoriety and audacity of the crimes, if tolerated, will likely lead to a repetition of similar crimes in other localities in this State, will bring disgrace upon our law abiding people, obstruct the orderly conduct of courts of justice and will tend to render life and property insecure from the wilful and wanton acts of lawless mobs. [27]

J. W. Harrington, Modoc's single superior court judge, saw the lynching as an affront to justice and a blight upon his county. On June 3, he fired off a telegram to Attorney General Tirey L. Ford in Sacramento:

Have called Grand Jury for Friday 7th, 10 A.M. Send me an experienced State's attorney for Friday, 10 A.M. My attorney is young and inexperienced and can not conduct successfully an investigation of so horrible a crime to be submitted to the Grand Jury. Must have assistance. Answer.

Although it was improper for a judge, who is supposed to maintain a position of impartial neutrality, to initiate a criminal investigation, Ford nonetheless responded promptly that he would send a deputy. He also wired District Attorney Bonner that an attorney would be sent to assist him, and Bonner replied by telegram: "Thousand thanks for deputy. . . . Bring detective." [28]

Ford dispatched his assistant, Charles N. Post, and Deputy Attorney General George A. Sturtevant, who comprised half of his four-lawyer staff, to Alturas, where they arrived on June 7 after a long trip by rail and stagecoach. Post, an obese, timid civil servant but an able lawyer, quickly found that prosecuting the lynchers would be no simple task. Few in Lookout were willing to talk about the incident. Additional roadblocks appeared in the forms of District Attorney Bonner, Judge Harrington, and Sheriff Street. Wrote Post to Attorney General Ford:

Bonner is an incompetent; is erratic and peculiar. . . . Judge Harrington is a long ways from being a sound lawyer. The sheriff of the county is the most worthless officer that I ever saw, and gave us absolutely no assistance whatsoever. Mr. Livernash of the [San Francisco] Examiner and Mr. Bennett of the Chronicle gave us the only assistance we received in the way of getting hold of evidence and running down clews. It is absolutely necessary that a first class detective be sent to Lookout and that at once. [29]

But it was Judge Harrington who gave Post one of the first important leads: a crude, unsigned note, scratched in pencil, that had been sent to him from Lookout. It listed thirteen names as members of the mob, among them Jim Brown, Bob Leventon, Isom Eades, Jervis Kresge, E. S. Trowbridge, Claude Brown, and Fred Roberts, "pretending to be sick his consions [*sic*] is bothering him so all he needs is to be in jail and he will give every thing away. He asked some of the neighbors if god [*sic*] would for give him for a bad crime." The note, which included the names of six men who had nothing to do with the lynching, concluded, "Now you have them all go for them."[30] This was a start, but Post needed solid evidence that would stand up in court, not anonymous accusations. For twelve days he and Sturtevant grilled witness after witness in secret sessions before the grand jury in the Alturas courthouse. They had subpoenaed most of the adult men in Lookout, many of whom Post examined in Bonner's office and allowed to return home when it became evident that they could not, or would not, supply information. But fifty-one witnesses did take the stand, among them numerous members of the mob, who invariably denied any knowledge of the affair. Each day large crowds of citizens and newspaper reporters gathered outside the courthouse, anxious for news, but the grand jury's hearing was not open to the public, and little reliable information leaked out.

On June 12 a band of armed and angry Pit River Indians, thirty strong, gathered at Lookout. They had been friendly with the Halls and were particularly outraged by the murder of little Martin Wilson. With few men in town, the women and children were greatly alarmed, but the Indians' threats of vengeance were never carried out.[31]

Meanwhile, San Francisco newspapers were busy lambasting Modoc County, accusing its citizens of lawlessness and of concealing the identities of the lynchers. Perhaps the most brutal editorial appeared in the *San Francisco Chronicle* on June 13. Although acknowledging that the great majority of people in Modoc County were law abiding, in the next breath the *Chronicle* charged that

> this crime was committed in one of the most lawless and sparsely settled regions in America, whose few inhabitants have only a nominal connection with California, or any other civilized state. They were originally of bad stock, and seem reverting to savagery, but they are within the legal boundaries of this State, which must bear the odium of their bloodthirstiness.[32]

Such commentary by the leading journals of the state infuriated many in Modoc County, and local sentiment slowly began to turn in favor of any who might be implicated in the crime. Formal charges were quick to come. On June 19 the grand jury completed its investigation and returned murder indictments against Jim Brown, Isom Eades, and Bob Leventon. The most damaging evidence against them was the story that Frank Hall had been strung up at the time of his arrest and the fact the Brown and Leventon had arrested old Calvin without authority just before he was lynched. Another important witness was Albert Colburn. He denied being a member of the mob but, in an effort to cast suspicion elsewhere, testified that Jim Brown knew about the lynching plot beforehand and had boasted, "Within three days there will be no more Halls or Yantis to bother anybody." [33]

Post knew that his case was far from perfect, and he wrote to Attorney General Ford; "The evidence against the Deputy Constable, J. W. Brown, is in my judgment sufficient to convict. That against Eades and Leventon is not so strong, and, in my judgment, the best detective obtainable should be sent to Lookout immediately." [34]

Ford lost no time in retaining the services of young Eugene Thacker, son of Wells Fargo Detective John N. Thacker. Raised on his father's ranch in Humboldt County, Nevada, hardy and quick witted, Eugene was an ideal choice for the job. His courage had been tested in a number of deadly encounters with outlaws. In 1897, while riding guard on a Wells Fargo shipment in New Mexico with two other messengers, his train was halted by the Black Jack Ketchum gang. In a furious gun battle with the outlaws, young Thacker and his companions killed gang member Ed Cullin and saved the express. Seven months later, in July, 1898, he joined up with the famous lawmen Jeff Milton and George Scarborough in their hunt for the Broncho Bill Walters gang. He was present for the showdown at the Double Circle horse ranch on Arizona's Black River, when the trio shot and captured Broncho Bill and killed his partner, Bill Johnson. [35]

Eugene Thacker arrived in the Big Valley early in July, using the name of Long and posing as a laborer looking for work. He had a list of names of men who were rumored to have been in the mob, and he tried to get hired on at several of the suspects' ranches. Thacker was unable to get close to any of them but finally got a job punching cattle on a ranch, near Bieber. "They watched every stranger that came into the valley to work," he later reported, "and gave no officer a chance to get at them that way."

Thacker found a few local people who had been appalled by the lynching and were willing to assist him: Peter Hagerman, a member of the coroner's jury; Mrs. Lillian Summers, a friend of the Halls; and Bill Woodmansee, a Bieber saloonkeeper. From them he learned that John Hutton and Claude Morris had made careless remarks about the lynching to friends. "Morris and Hutton either were with the lynchers or else watched them do their work," Thacker wrote to Tirey Ford. [36]

Eugene Thacker, whose detective work resulted in the arrests of the entire lynch mob. Courtesy Wells Fargo Bank History Room.

Thacker had Woodmansee and Mrs. Summers visit William Morris at his ranch, near Lookout. Claude's father was on his deathbed, with only two weeks to live, and had expressed much bitterness about the lynching of Calvin Hall, unaware that his son had been one of the mob. Young Morris apparently felt a great deal of guilt, for when Mrs. Summers broached the lynching, telling him that he could get immunity if he would testify, in Thacker's words "he broke down and cried like a baby." Morris promised her he would meet "Mr. Long" that night in Bieber and tell him the truth about the lynching. But while on his way to Bieber, Morris ran into John Hutton on the road and told him of his mission, and Hutton convinced his friend not to talk. Morris, continuing on to Bieber, dropped into Bill Woodmansee's saloon for a drink, and Woodmansee said to him, "If you know anything, for God's sake tell it. We will see you through— see that you get protection."

Woodmansee took Morris to his house and introduced him to Thacker, who interrogated the youth for three hours, but he claimed that he knew nothing about the lynching. Said Thacker, "Hutton fixed him so we could not do a thing with him." This incident destroyed Thacker's cover, for Hutton and Morris passed the word that he was a detective. Thacker began to work openly but found that he was greatly hindered by friends of the lynchers, who put up obstacles at every turn. His letters and telegraph messages were monitored, and his movements were closely watched. The postmistress at Bieber was Jim Brown's sister-in-law, and the Wells Fargo Agent was Orrin Trowbridge. Letters sent from Bieber were found to have been opened. Nonetheless, Thacker managed to learn the names of many of the lynchers. In addition to Hutton and Morris, he reported that Henry Knox and his nephew Will McDaniels were suspects. He learned that a rancher's wife had spotted Orrin Trowbridge riding past her home on the road from Lookout to Bieber at three o'clock on the morning of the hanging. Thacker also found that Claude Marcus had told friends that he and Louis Palmentier had been invited to join the mob, and claimed that Palmentier had joined, but he had refused. "But unless we can get one of them to turn state's evidence I do not think there is much chance for conviction," wrote Thacker.[37]

In the meantime, Eades, Leventon, and Brown had been arraigned and lodged in the county jail, in Alturas, to await trial. Their attorneys, in an attempt to secure their release, filed a writ of habeas corpus with the California Supreme Court, but it was denied. They next filed a petition in the Supreme Court to prevent Judge Harrington from hearing the case on the ground that he was prejudiced against the defendants, but this, too, was rejected. Finally the case was set for their trial to begin in November.

By this time District Attorney Bonner had been ousted from the case by Post and Sturtevant. On October 20 he had written a letter to the attorney general, suggesting that the evidence was too weak to get a conviction and recommending that the indictments be dismissed. Indignant, Ford handed the letter over to the San Francisco newspapers with his own scathing reply, accusing Bonner of sympathizing with the lynchers. And on November 3, Judge Harrington sent Ford a letter accusing Bonner of aiding and giving information to the defense.[38]

The ouster of Bonner, coupled with a continuing series of negative comments about Modoc County published in the San Francisco papers, succeeded in further shifting public opinion in the county away from the prosecution and toward the defendants. Declared the editor of one Alturas newspaper shortly before the trial:

Not content with scoring some of the officers of the county, the Attorney General's office is presumably responsible for the many derogatory reports of Modoc published in the San Francisco dailies, which say in effect that Modoc is inhabited only by outlaws and ruffians, whereas the reverse is the condition. Modoc was unfortunate in having the lynching occur in her territory, but because that occurred is no reason why the whole county should be branded as wild outlaws and fools. More men were brutally beaten and killed in San Francisco during one week . . . than have ever been killed in Modoc.[39]

Jim Brown was tried first for the murder of Martin Wilson. His trial began on November 25, 1901, and was one of the most publicized and sensational in California's history. In an era when murder trials seldom took longer than a week or two, Brown's trial lasted more than three months. Almost from the start it was marked by court-room fireworks and repeated clashes between Judge Harrington and the defense attorneys.

Jim Brown was represented by G. F. Harris, a former Modoc county judge; E. V. Spencer, former speaker of the assembly from Lassen County; and John Raker, a fire-eating local lawyer who was later elected to Congress. Prosecuting the case were Post, Sturtevant, and Jim Boyd (district attorney of Lassen County), who was called in to assist during the second week of the trial. Judge Harrington and John Raker were both men of violent tempers. They had long hated each other, and there was no love lost either between Har-rington and the other two defense attorneys. Before and during the trial, Harrington accused both Raker and Harris of controlling Dis-trict Attorney Bonner and Sheriff Street.

It took more than two weeks to pick a jury. The case had received such widespread publicity that one hundred veniremen were exam-ined before twelve could be found who had not already formed an opinion about Brown's guilt or innocence. Then the prosecution opened its case, putting witnesses on the stand who testified about the arrests of the Halls, threats made of lynching them, and events at Myers's hotel on the night of the hanging. One witness, Bob Court-right, testified that he had seen Myers and some of the others tying nooses in ropes in the back room of Trowbridge's store. He was cross-examined by Raker for two days, and at one point denied that he had ever seen anyone preparing ropes in Lookout. When Raker pointed out that Courtright was testifying falsely, the infuriated wit-ness leaped from the stand and rushed headlong at the lawyer. Raker snatched up a pointing rod and struck Courtright over the head, breaking the stick in half. Sheriff Street separated the pair, and Judge Harrington ordered the witness out of the courtroom.[40]

Bitter words were exchanged frequently between Brown's lawyers and Judge Harrington, and two days later, December 20, they got into an exceptionally heated argument. Harrington reproached them for rude behavior, declaring, "There will be no such conduct while I am on the bench!"

"Well, you won't be there long," Harris snapped.

"I will be here until my term is up, Judge Harris, unless some of you assassinate me or shoot me from behind!" Harrington roared.[41]

Such clashes became commonplace. Harrington seemed to be motivated by a sincere interest in identifying the lynchers and bringing the guilty parties to justice, but his prejudice against the defense became impossible for him to conceal. Time and again he made rulings favorable to the prosecution and invariably denied motions made by Brown's attorneys. He refused to allow the defense to impeach the prosecution's witnesses and upheld objections made by Post but never by the defendant's lawyers.

John Raker, on the other hand, seemed to take a devilish delight in baiting the judge at every opportunity. He continually ridiculed and insulted Harrington and was repeatedly fined for contempt of court and on several occasions was sentenced to spend the night in jail. Spencer, to a lesser degree, took part in these frays, as did Harris, whom the judge accused of being constantly drunk in court. On December 24, Harris encountered Calvin Hall's eldest daughter, Mary, on an Alturas street. When he made an insulting remark to her, she twice knocked him down. Harris drew a knife on the woman and was promptly arrested.[42]

There was more trouble when C. N. Post made the grievous error of bringing to Alturas Dan Miller, a "state detective" and reputed gunfighter, from San Francisco. Small of stature and short of temper, Miller's ostensible purpose was to protect the prosecution's witnesses, but it was generally recognized in Modoc County that he was Post's personal bodyguard. Miller, at every chance he got, engaged in quarrels with friends of the accused lynchers and almost single-handedly sabotaged the state's case. On one occasion he met Sam Parks and Henry Knox near the courthouse and challenged them to fight. When Parks told him, "Cool off," Miller walked down the street and told a crowd of loungers, "Not a man in Modoc County will fight me."

The following evening, January 3, Miller, Post, and several witnesses ran into E. W. Brownell, a friend of Jim Brown, in the hallway of the Grand Central Hotel. Brownell made a sarcastic comment, and Miller whipped out his six-gun, yelling, "You son of a bitch! Get away from here and do it quick! You can't come making any cracks around this hotel!"

The hotel clerk rushed up and cried, "For God's sake, don't shoot him!"

Miller put up his gun, but he was later arrested, and Boyd and Sturtevant had to bail him out of jail. Unchastened, the next afternoon Miller came upon District Attorney Bonner, lawyer C. C. Auble, and several other citizens sitting on the front porch of city hall, where the grand jury was in session. Miller ordered them to move on, saying they "had no business hanging around there." An indignant Auble refused, and Miller, for once exercising self-restraint, did not press the matter. By this time Miller's bullying and imprudent actions had alienated even those who sympathized with the prosecution. So there was not a great deal of rejoicing in Modoc County when word leaked out that John Hutton and Claude Morris had confessed.[43]

Three months earlier, Eugene Thacker had procured the assistance of Reverend Jim Simmons, a local minister who was quite friendly with Isom Eades and several of the other lynchers. Simmons had attempted unsuccessfully to get Eades to confess. He had better luck with John Hutton, who had been subpoenaed as a witness and was in Alturas for the trial. Simmons met several times with Hutton in Post's office in the Grand Central Hotel, and finally, on January 1, 1902, in exchange for immunity from prosecution, Hutton broke down and made a full confession. Then Post and Sturtevant interviewed Claude Morris, who, upon learning that Hutton had confessed, admitted his guilt and agreed to turn state's evidence. Hutton was brought before the grand jury, and he told the story of the lynching, naming all those involved. The grand jury promptly returned murder indictments against Eades, Leventon, the Brown brothers, Kresge, Colburn, Parks, Palmentier, Knox, McDaniels, and Potter. Calvin's daughter Mary swore out arrest warrants for the Trowbridges, Fred and Harry Roberts, Joe Leventon, Myers, Nichols, and Marcus. All were lodged in the county jail and held without bail. At last it seemed that the lynchers would be brought to justice.[44]

On January 8, John Hutton took the stand and testified in detail about the lynching, identifying the members of the mob. Raker, unnerved and enraged by Hutton's testimony, during cross-examination

Modoc County men, 1904. Isom Eades is at far right, next to the pump.
Standing to his right is Jervis Kresge, another of the lynchers. Sheriff Ben
Street is in the back row, sixth from the left; seated at his left is defense attorney John Raker. District Attorney E. C. Bonner is seated in the front row,
at far left. Courtesy Modoc County Museum.

accused him of being a liar. At one point Raker asked Hutton, "Don't
you think a man who turned state's evidence ought to be shot?"

Such outrageous conduct in a modern court would be grounds for
discipline, but the irrepressible Raker knew that his only chance to
save Jim Brown was to discredit Hutton's testimony in as dramatic a
manner as possible. He implied that the confession had been coerced
by Dan Miller, whom he referred to contemptuously as "Danny
Miller" and "Post's bodyguard." Post objected vehemently and told
Raker that he would not dare insult Miller out of court. Raker replied sarcastically, "I never insulted Miller, because he is not a man
whom one could insult."

"I'll meet you anywhere!" shouted Miller, leaping to his feet, at the
same time reaching for his pistol in his hip pocket. Raker sprang

back, and Sheriff Street jumped between them, while women spectators fled from the packed courtroom. Never one to miss an opportunity to grandstand before the jury, Raker reached for his own pocket, as if to draw a gun, and orated dramatically, "And I command you, as sheriff of this county, to search Miller."

Judge Harrington ordered Sheriff Street to remove both Raker and Miller from the courtroom. When Street returned he told the judge that Miller had been the cause of much trouble during the trial and proposed to learn by what authority Miller carried a gun. The sheriff's words were greeted with cheers from the audience. This angered Judge Harrington, and he told Street that he would order his arrest if he continued to make such remarks. Although Miller was not punished, Raker spent the night in jail for this episode.[45]

John Hutton was subjected to rigorous cross-examination for five days, and although Raker tried his best, he was unable to shake Hutton's story. On January 15, Claude Morris took the stand and corroborated Hutton's account in all but minor details. Morris was cross-examined for four days, and although Raker tried repeatedly to impeach him, he made little headway. Like Hutton, Morris stuck to his guns.

These confessions did not sit well with the editors of Modoc county's three newspapers. They claimed that Hutton and Morris had been hypnotized and forced to make confessions. They ran editorials condemning the prosecution and referring to the state's lawyers and detectives as "head hunters" and "blood-money hunters."[46]

During the defense phase of the trial, Brown's attorneys continued to attack the confessions, hammering away at discrepancies between the testimony of Hutton and Morris and insisting that they had perjured themselves to save their necks. Friends of several of the accused lynchers swore that the suspects were in bed at the time of the hanging. In closing arguments that occasionally bordered on the incredible, Raker argued that Jim Brown, as a deputy constable, had no legal duty to resist the mob, and Spencer claimed that young Agnes Wilson, who had described Brown's threatening and striking of Calvin Hall, could not be believed because she was an Indian and thus was incapable of telling the truth. Spencer struck an extremely responsive chord when he concluded the defense arguments by saying to the jury, "Your verdict will affect not only the defendant, but the nineteen men who are implicated by Hutton and Morris. I believe your verdict will be a complete exoneration of those nineteen men. In reality you have been trying the entire community of Lookout."[47]

The closing arguments lasted nine days, and the case was finally submitted to the jury on the night of February 27, 1902. In less than half an hour they agreed upon a verdict of not guilty. When the decision was announced, loud cheers erupted from the audience. Several jurors were asked by reporters why they had voted for acquittal. One said that he had relied on alleged contradictions in the confessions of Hutton and Morris. Another had resented the "presence of armed guards and detectives in the pay of the prosecution." And a third acquitted Brown "because he did not believe in Modoc County being run by people from down below."[48]

The trial had cost Modoc County some $16,000 and left the county treasury nearly bankrupt. In addition, Attorney General Ford expended more than $5,000 in prosecuting the case. Ford was anxious to bring the other lynchers to trial, but it was impossible to find another jury in Modoc County. The eligible jury list contained but two hundred names, and there was hardly a man in the county who had not eagerly followed the progress of the trial, thus precluding him from jury service. Ford later reported to Governor Gage, "I am reliably informed that friends of the defendants have systematically attempted to disqualify jurors all over Modoc County." It was impossible to move the trials to another county, for the state constitution allowed only the defense, not the prosecution, to obtain a change of venue. Ford advised Judge Harrington of the situation, and on March 17, 1902, he ordered all the defendants released from the county jail.[49]

There were no further efforts to correct what Ford called "this gross miscarriage of justice." Despite the overwhelming evidence of Jim Brown's guilt, partisan feeling had been largely responsible for his acquittal. The clashes between Raker and Harrington, the antics of Dan Miller, the usurpation of Bonner's authority by the Attorney General, and the vicious attacks by the press on the people of Modoc County had greatly obscured the real issue of the case.

After the verdict had been rendered, John Raker gave newsmen his opinion of the case against Jim Brown. "One fact has been demonstrated—that Modoc County jurors are not to be intimidated into a verdict by imported gunfighters and detectives and without evidence." Raker called it "one of the most remarkable and disgraceful trials in the civilized world," and added, "The evidence on the part of the prosecution has been a monstrous failure all the way through."[50]

To this day, Raker's characterization of the Modoc County lynching case has been generally accepted. In popular legend and in the few written accounts of the lynching, Jim Brown and his friends are persecuted innocents. It is about time that this myth is laid soundly to rest. The conclusive evidence of their guilt, as preserved in the case files and grand jury transcripts, puts the lie to such claims. Jim Brown was not acquitted because he was innocent. In great measure it was indeed Modoc County, and not Jim Brown, that had been on trial.

Why did the Lookout lynchers take the law into their own hands? There seem to have been almost as many different motives as there were members of the mob. For some, including E. S. Trowbridge, the Leventon brothers, and Isom Eades, it was undoubtedly their hatred of the Halls that brought about their involvement. Bob Leventon and Isom Eades took part in the attempt to lynch Frank Hall in the Gilbert barn, but then changed their minds and made the long trip to Alturas in an unsuccessful attempt to convince the district attorney to prosecute the thieves on felony charges. They returned home frustrated and angry and no doubt saw lynching as the only way to rid the valley of the Halls. Some, like Al Colburn, were motivated by a desire to get revenge against the men who had stolen from them, while several of the young members of the mob, Claude Morris and John Hutton in particular, appear to have been motivated by peer pressure. For most of the lynchers, it seems to have been primarily a desire to stop the thievery; they had been pushed to the breaking point. The reason for Calvin Hall's hanging is the clearest and the most inexcusable: he died purely because the mob wanted to prevent him from pressing for their arrest and prosecution. And last, racial hatred was undoubtedly an underlying factor, despite the fact that one of the mob's leaders, Isom Eades, was married to an Indian woman. It is impossible to underestimate the depth and breadth of hatred for Indians during that era. As the editor of the *Alturas New Era* pointed out, "There is a great prejudice against Indians throughout this country."[51]

As the years passed, many legends about the lynching sprang up. The most remarkable of these was described thus: "Of all them fellers that took part in that thing, Hell overtook them, ever' one of them." There was some substance to this tale. Within a few years after the trial, James Myers and Isom Eades died, as did Jim Brown, who was killed by a train. But most unusual of all was the untimely death of young Will McDaniels. On April 10, 1903, both the *San Francisco Call* and *Chronicle* ran front-page stories that he had died of a mysterious disease of the stomach that doctors had been unable to diagnose or cure. On his deathbed at his family's home, near Lookout, McDaniels had confessed to his participation in the lynching and had revealed that in the fight with Frank Hall he had been kicked in the stomach, causing the injury he eventually died from.[52]

In many ways the Lookout lynching was identical to the 1879 hanging of Frost, McCracken, and Gibson at the Willits bridge. In that incident the lynched men had been accused of nothing more than minor crimes, but they had long terrorized the community and had destroyed the property of those who opposed them. In 1879 no attempt was made to identify or prosecute the Willits lynchers. But the passage of just twenty-two years, it seemed, all but spelled the end of lynching in California. To be sure, there were a few later lynchings, most notably at Santa Rosa, in 1920, and San Jose, in 1933, California's last. But Jim Brown's prosecution and statewide public disapproval of the Lookout mob underscored that the frontier ethic of rough justice was quickly disappearing. No longer would Californians tolerate lynch law in a modern era.

For Further Reading

AS mentioned in the Preface, books on lawlessness in frontier California are few and far between. Joseph Henry Jackson's *Bad Company* (1949) is an enormously entertaining account of early-day bandits and has long been considered a classic of its kind. Unfortunately, its chapters on Joaquín Murrieta, Tom Bell, and Rattlesnake Dick are largely unreliable. One well-researched book about a gold rush era badman is Dudley T. Ross's *Devil on Horseback* (1975), a biography of the notorious Jack Powers. Several books about Tiburcio Vásquez were published shortly after his hanging in 1875, the best being George Beers's account, which was reprinted in 1960 as *The California Outlaw*, edited by Robert Greenwood. Jim McKinney, the murderous mankiller of the San Joaquin Valley, has been the subject of two fine books: Joseph Doctor's *Shotguns on Sunday* (1958) and Guy Hughes's *Battle of the Joss House* (1968).

Three books have portrayed Evans and Sontag. Hu Maxwell's *Evans and Sontag*, an interesting contemporary account first published in 1893, was reprinted in 1981, edited by Charles W. Clough. Wallace Smith's *Prodigal Sons* (1951) tells their story from the outlaws' point of view, while C. B. Glasscock's *Bandits and the Southern Pacific* (1929) is a fairer and more balanced treatment of these controversial train robbers.

The late Frank F. Latta wrote two books on California outlaws. Although his *Joaquin Murrieta and His Horse Gangs* (1980) is not the definitive work it was meant to be, *Dalton Gang Days* (1976) is one of the best books ever written about western badmen, despite various errors about the gang's escapades in Oklahoma. Based on interviews with Littleton Dalton and Sheriff Eugene Kay, it is an exceptional firsthand account of the trials and troubles that faced horseback bandits and graphically illustrates the pain and misery the rash Dalton boys inflicted upon their family, friends, and victims.

Graphic Description of Pacific Coast Outlaws, written by Charles Howard Shinn in 1890, is a brief and somewhat inaccurate look at the career of Sheriff Harry N. Morse; it was reprinted in an improved

1958 edition, edited by J. E. Reynolds. Richard Dillon's *Wells Fargo Detective* (1969) is an excellent biography of James B. Hume and is the only full-length book about a lawman of the California frontier. A recent scholarly work on crime and crime rates in the boom camps of Bodie, California, and Aurora, Nevada, is Roger McGrath's *Gunfighters, Highwaymen, and Vigilantes* (1984).

Notes

INTRODUCTION

1. An exhaustive survey of a nineteenth-century California criminal justice system is Lawrence M. Friedman and Robert V. Percival, *The Roots of Justice: Crime and Punishment in Alameda County, California, 1870–1910* (1981).

2. For a fascinating history of California's oldest prison, see Kenneth Lamott's *Chronicles of San Quentin* (1961).

CHAPTER 1

1. Myron Angel, *History of Placer County* (1882), pp. 140, 331.

2. Ibid., pp. 139–40; *A Volume of Memoirs and Genealogy of Representative Citizens of Northern California* (1901), pp. 691–92.

3. Angel, *History of Placer County,* p. 140; *A Volume of Memoirs of Representative Citizens,* p. 693.

4. John Boggs to J. J. Valentine, Sept. 9, 1892, copy in Wells Fargo Bank History Dept., San Francisco.

5. The *Alta's* figures are quoted in Harry L. Wells, *History of Nevada County* (1880), p. 110. The comparison is based on the 1982 California homicide rate of 11.2 homicides for 100,000 population.

6. William B. Lardner, *History of Placer and Nevada Counties* (1924), pp. 252–53; *San Francisco Bulletin,* Oct. 22, 1856; San Quentin Prison Register, convicts no. 24 (Thomas J. Hodges) and no. 217 (William White); Joseph Henry Jackson's *Bad Company* (1949) has chapters on Tom Bell and Rattlesnake Dick, but both chapters contain many errors and are largely unreliable.

7. B. F. Moore, "Early Days in California," manuscript, Oct. 4, 1892, p. 9, in Wells Fargo Bank History Dept.

8. Ibid., p. 10; *Marysville Daily Herald,* Aug. 13, 1856.

9. Moore, "Early Days in California," p. 10; John Boggs to J. J. Valentine, Sept. 9, 1892.

10. Moore, "Early Days in California," pp. 10–15; *Placer Herald* (Auburn), Oct. 4, 1856; *Sacramento Union,* Oct. 2, 1856.

11. Angel, *History of Placer County,* pp. 42–43; Harry L. Wells, *History of Siskiyou County* (1881), pp. 163–65; San Quentin Prison Register, convict no. 516, Richard Barter. Several accounts have erroneously called him Richard H. Barter.

12. Moore, "Early Days in California," pp. 8–9; *Sacramento Union,* April 24, 1856.

13. Angel, *History of Placer County,* p. 331.

14. Moore, "Early Days in California," p. 18.

15. *Placer Herald,* May 1, 1858; Angel, *History of Placer County,* p. 331; Lardner, *History of Placer,* pp. 249–50.

16. *Placer Herald*, July 16, 1859; Angel, *History of Placer County*, pp. 333–34; Lardner, *History of Placer*, pp. 250–52. Jackson, in *Bad Company*, p. 116, claims that Johnston and Crutcher each fired only one shot and that a mysterious third party fired another shot that was later found in Dick's horse. "But whose bullet wounded the horse?" Jackson asks. The answer is that one of the lawmen's did; according to the editor of the *Placer Herald*, above, the "whole five" were "firing as fast as possible." Obviously, one of the posse's shots wounded the horse, and not some mysterious phantom's. Jackson also claims (p. 115) that the note found in Dick's hand never existed. This, too, is incorrect, for the note was seen and described by the *Placer Herald*'s editor, as well as by B. F. Moore; it is mentioned in every account of Rattlesnake Dick.

17. *Placer Herald*, February 20, 1858; *Sacramento Union*, Feb. 19, 20, 1858.

18. *Nevada Journal* (Nevada City), Oct. 8, 24, 1858.

19. *A History of Tuolumne County* (1882), pp. 225–27; *Placer Herald*, Dec. 4, 1858; *Tuolumne Courier* (Columbia), Dec. 4, 1858.

20. *Placer Herald*, March 26, 1859; *Nevada National*, March 26, 1859; *Nevada Democrat*, March 30, 1859.

21. *San Andreas Independent*, Jan. 15, 1859.

22. *Nevada Democrat*, June 20, 1860; *Placer Herald*, June 23, July 21, 1860.

23. Angel, *History of Placer County*, p. 140; *A Volume of Memoirs of Representative Citizens*, p. 693; *Placer Herald*, Oct. 10, 1857.

24. Angel, *History of Placer County*, p. 331.

25. Ibid., pp. 120, 123, 124, 132; *A Volume of Memoirs of Representative Citizens*, p. 693.

26. Angel, *History of Placer County*, pp. 335–36; Lardner, *History of Placer*, pp. 253–54.

27. *Placer Herald*, Aug. 27, 1881.

28. *Sacramento Record-Union*, Sept. 29, 1881.

29. Ibid. See also *San Francisco Alta*, Sept. 29, 1881, and *Placer Herald*, Oct. 1, 1881.

30. *San Francisco Alta*, Sept. 29, 1881; *Sacramento Bee*, Sept. 1, 1881; *Placer Herald*, Sept. 3, 1881.

31. *San Francisco Alta*, Sept. 2, 1881.

32. Ibid., Sept. 3, 1881; *Placer Herald*, Oct. 1, 1881.

33. Southern Pacific Company, "History of Train Robberies," manuscript, pp. 11–12; *Placer Herald*, Sept. 17, 1881; *Sacramento Union*, Sept. 12, 1881; *Sacramento Bee*, Sept. 12, 1881.

34. *Nevada City Transcript*, Sept. 13, 1881; *Sacramento Bee*, Sept. 14, 1881.

35. *Sacramento Bee*, Oct. 28, 1881; *Sacramento Record-Union*, Oct. 28, 29, 1881.

36. Southern Pacific Company, "History of Train Robberies," pp. 13–14; Lardner, *History of Placer*, pp. 255–56; Angel, *History of Placer County*, p. 337.

37. *Placer Herald*, Sept. 16, 1882.

38. Southern Pacific Company, "History of Train Robberies," p. 14; Lardner, *History of Placer*, p. 256; *Placer Herald*, Oct. 7, 1882.

39. *Placer Herald*, June 5, 1909; *A Volume of Memoirs of Representative Citizens*, pp. 693–94.

CHAPTER 2

1. *Bulletin of the Nevada County Historical Society,* Dec., 1967; "An Amateur Detective," *Harper's Weekly,* July 14, 1866, p. 444; Sven Skaar, "The Trail," *Grass Valley Union,* Dec. 31, 1959.

2. *Richmond* (Indiana) *Palladium-Item,* July 28, 1937, Aug. 25, 1959.

3. *Bulletin of the Nevada County Historical Society,* Dec., 1967; see also U.S. Census Population Schedules, 1850 Census, El Dorado County, pp. 440, 462.

4. Art Pauley, *Henry Plummer, Lawman and Outlaw* (1980), pp. 30–32, 49–50; *Nevada Journal,* May 8, 1857; *Nevada Democrat,* May 6, 1857.

5. *Nevada City Gazette,* Aug. 2, 1864.

6. Ibid., July 1, 1864.

7. *Nevada Daily Transcript,* May 21, 1891; *Grass Valley Union,* Dec. 31, 1959; *Nevada Daily Gazette,* March 16, 1864; *Daniel Snyder* v. *Stephen Venard, et al.,* case no. 945, District Court, 14th Judicial District, copy in Nevada County Historical Society Library; "Steve Venard, Who Arrested, Tried, and Executed Three Robbers," *Grizzly Bear,* Nov., 1907, p. 14.

8. William B. Secrest, "When the Ghost Met Steve Venard," *Old West,* Fall, 1968, pp. 20–21; Mrs. B. C. Truman, "Steve Venard's Chase," *Sacramento Daily Record,* March 1, 1873; *Placer Herald,* May 19, 1866.

9. Harry L. Wells, *History of Nevada County* (1880), pp. 117–18; Neill C. Wilson, *Treasure Express* (1936), p. 106.

10. *Sacramento Daily Record,* March 1, 1873; *Placer Herald,* May 19, 1866; San Quentin Prison Register, convict no. 2001, Robert Finn, California State Archives.

11. *Nevada Daily Gazette,* May 9, 1866; *Placer Herald,* May 19, 1866.

12. *Placer Herald,* May 19, 1866; San Quentin Prison Register, convict no. 2460, George W. Moore.

13. The story of this gunfight has been told and retold with varying degrees of accuracy by numerous writers. Venard's own account is taken from his testimony at the coroner's inquest as published in the *Nevada Daily Gazette,* May 17, 1866. The most accurate versions of this affair are: Secrest, "When the Ghost Met Steve Venard," pp. 22–23; *California Police Gazette,* May 19, 1866; "An Amateur Detective," *Harper's Weekly,* July 14, 1866, pp. 445–46; *Nevada Daily Transcript,* May 21, 1891; and Edwin F. Bean, *History and Directory of Nevada County* (1867), pp. 16–18.

14. "An Amateur Detective," *Harper's Weekly,* July 14, 1866; *Nevada Daily Transcript,* May 25, June 7, 1866; *Nevada Daily Gazette,* May 18, 31, 1866.

15. Paul Fatout, *Meadow Lake, Gold Town* (1969), pp. 101–102; Edmund Kinyon, *The Northern Mines* (1949), p. 94; *Grass Valley Union,* Jan. 16, 1960; *Nevada Daily Transcript,* June 3, 1866.

16. *Nevada Daily Transcript,* Aug. 7, Sept. 12, 1866.

17. Affidavits of Barclay Henley, W. B. Reynolds, and Lodi Brown; Letter, Sarah E. Watts (sister of Andrus) to Governor Newton Booth, Sept. 22, 1872; all in the pardon files of Lodi Brown and William E. Andrews [sic], Governors' Pardon Papers, California State Archives.

18. *Mendocino Democrat,* Nov. 17, 1871.

19. John Boessenecker, "Steve Venard, Wells Fargo's Ace Troubleshooter," *Golden West*, Sept., 1972, p. 13; *San Francisco Alta*, Aug. 18, 1871; *San Francisco Examiner*, Dec. 29, 1889; *Marin County Journal*, Nov. 25, 1871.

20. *Mendocino Democrat*, Nov. 17, 24, 1871; *San Francisco Examiner*, Dec. 29, 1889; *Russian River Flag* (Healdsburg), Jan. 1, 15, 1880; *Mendocino Press*, Nov. 16, 1871.

21. *San Francisco Alta*, July 12, 1872; *Mendocino Democrat*, Feb. 29, 1872; San Quentin Prison Register, convict no. 5093, John M. Brown; Pardon files of Lodi Brown and William E. Andrews.

22. *Russian River Flag*, May 16, 1872; *Mendocino Democrat*, May 16, 1872; *Marin County Journal*, March 9, 1872.

23. *San Francisco Examiner*, Dec. 29, 1889; *Russian River Flag*, Jan. 1, 1880; *San Francisco Chronicle*, Aug. 6, 1880.

24. *Sacramento Daily Record*, Jan. 29, 1876; *Amador Dispatch* (Jackson), Jan. 29, Feb. 5, 24, 1876; *Amador Ledger*, Feb. 5, 1876; *Placer Herald*, Jan. 22, Feb. 5, 1876.

25. *Nevada Daily Transcript*, March 23, 1883; *Grass Valley Union*, March 22, 23, 1883; San Quentin Prison Register, convict no. 3728, Joseph Lawrence.

26. *Grass Valley Union*, March 25, 1883.

27. Ibid., March 31, April 21, June 27, Sept. 2, 1883.

28. Ibid., March 21, 1886; *Nevada Daily Transcript*, March 21, 1886.

29. *Grass Valley Union*, Dec. 31, 1959.

30. Notice of Location of a Placer Claim, April 2, 1888, copy in Nevada County Historical Society Library; *Nevada Daily Transcript*, May 21, 1891; Register of Deaths, 1891, Nevada County Recorder.

CHAPTER 3

1. *A Volume of Memoirs of Representative Citizens* (1901), pp. 113–14; Richard Coke Wood, *Tales of Old Calaveras* (1949), p. 68.

2. Dictation of Benjamin K. Thorn, San Andreas, Calif., April 18, 1888, copy in Bancroft Library, Berkeley; *Calaveras Prospect* (San Andreas), Nov. 18, 1905.

3. Florence Finch Kelly, "Ben Thorn of Calaveras," *Los Angeles Times*, March 5, 1899.

4. *People* v. *Pedro Ybarra*, case no. 2666, California Supreme Court Records, California State Archives.

5. *A Volume of Memoirs of Representative Citizens*, pp. 114–15.

6. *San Joaquin Republican* (Stockton), July 15, 1855; *People* v. *Sam Brown and Hugh Owens*, District Court, 5th Judicial District, case file in Calaveras County Archives, San Andreas; Effie Enfield Johnston, "Wade Johnston Talks to His Daughter," *Las Calaveras* (Bulletin of the Calaveras County Historical Society), Oct., 1969, pp. 2–3.

7. *Los Angeles Times*, March 5, 1899.

8. Ibid.; *A Volume of Memoirs of Representative Citizens*, pp. 116–17.

9. *People* v. *Sam Brown and Hugh Owens*; Johnston, "Wade Johnston Talks," p. 3; San Quentin Prison Register, convict no. 762, Sam Brown; *San Francisco Chronicle*, May 1, 1892.

10. *A Volume of Memoirs of Representative Citizens*, p. 115.

11. Johnston, "Wade Johnston Talks," p. 8.

12. *A Volume of Memoirs of Representative Citizens*, p. 115; *San Andreas Independent*, April 4, Oct. 10, 1857, Feb. 20, 1858.

13. *San Francisco Alta*, Dec. 19, 1856; *A Volume of Memoirs of Representative Citizens*, pp. 117–18; *Los Angeles Times*, March 5, 1899.

14. *San Andreas Independent*, Oct. 23, 1858.

15. Johnston, "Wade Johnston Talks," p. 8.

16. *San Andreas Independent*, March 10, 17, April 21, 1860.

17. Ibid., July 25, Aug. 4, 1860.

18. Ibid., July 4, Dec. 15, 1860.

19. Ibid., Dec. 22, 1860; the *Mariposa News* item is quoted in the *San Francisco Bulletin*, Dec. 13, 1860.

20. *A Volume of Memoirs of Representative Citizens*, p. 118; *Los Angeles Times*, March 5, 1899; *San Andreas Independent*, March 23, 1861.

21. *Calaveras Chronicle* (Mokelumne Hill), Aug. 31, 1867.

22. The Calaveras County Sheriff's salary in 1871 was $3,800 a year; *Calaveras Chronicle*, March 26, 1871. The figures on graft appear in Jesse D. Mason, *History of Amador County* (1881), p. 96.

23. *Calaveras Chronicle*, Oct. 3, 1868.

24. Edna Bryan Buckbee, *The Saga of Old Tuolumne* (1935), pp. 134–35; *A Volume of Memoirs of Representative Citizens*, pp. 118–19; *Los Angeles Times*, March 5, 1899; *Calaveras Chronicle*, Nov. 7, 1868.

25. The legal history of the Coyado case is described at length in the *Calaveras Chronicle*, Feb. 4, 1871, and June 22, 1872. See also *People* v. *Coyado*, California Supreme Court Reports, vol. 40, pp. 586–93.

26. *Calaveras Chronicle*, Feb. 7, 1874.

27. *Calaveras Weekly Citizen*, Sept. 2, 1871.

28. *Stockton Independent*, Oct. 4, 1877.

29. *Calaveras Chronicle*, Feb. 13, 1875.

30. *Calaveras Weekly Citizen*, July 3, 1875; *Los Angeles Times*, March 5, 1899.

31. *Stockton Independent*, Oct. 4, 1877; *Calaveras Chronicle*, Oct. 6, 1877.

32. *Tuolumne Independent* (Sonora), Feb. 2, 1878; *Calaveras Chronicle*, Feb. 2, 1878.

33. *Calaveras Chronicle*, March 6, 1880; *Calaveras Prospect*, June 2, 1886, Nov. 18, 1905.

34. *San Francisco Examiner*, April 30, 1892, June 16, 17, 1893.

35. *San Francisco Call*, Aug. 3, 1893; *Stockton Evening Mail*, Aug. 7, 8, 9, 1893.

36. *San Francisco Chronicle*, Oct. 18, 1893. The testimony in this controversial case is detailed in the *San Francisco Chronicle*, Oct. 16, 17, 19, 20, 24, 1893; the *San Francisco Call*, March 19, 1894; the *San Francisco Examiner*, March 16, 17, 1894; and *People* v. *Evans*, Supreme Court of California, *Pacific Reporter*, vol. 41, pp. 444–45.

37. *People* v. *Evans*, p. 444.

38. Inquest into death of Abbot Thorn, May 1, 1907, copy in Calaveras County Archives; *Calaveras Prospect*, May 4, 1907.

39. *San Francisco Call*, Oct. 20, 1907; State Board of Prison Directors. Minutes, vol. 7, Aug. 17, Oct. 19, 1907, located in California State Archives.

40. *San Francisco Examiner*, Oct. 25, 1893. An excellent account of the war of

words between Ben Thorn and Jim Hume appears in Richard Dillon, *Wells Fargo Detective* (1969), pp. 269–79.

41. *San Francisco Chronicle*, Oct. 1, 2, 1897, March 10, 11, 1901; *Calaveras Prospect*, Jan. 3, 10, 1903.

42. *San Francisco Call*, Nov. 16, 1905.

CHAPTER 4

1. Lyman Palmer, *History of Mendocino County* (reprinted 1967), p. 586; *Ukiah Daily Journal*, Jan. 22, 1984.

2. Palmer, *History of Mendocino*, p. 747.

3. *San Francisco Bulletin*, March 3, 1873; *San Francisco Call*, Aug. 9, 1896.

4. *People* v. *Geiger*, California Supreme Court Reports, vol. 49, pp. 643–45; *Mendocino Democrat*, Feb. 11, 1874; Palmer, *History of Mendocino*, pp. 337–39.

5. Ninetta Eames, "Upland Pastures," *Cosmopolitan*, March, 1896, p. 528. See also *Russian River Flag*, Feb. 26, 1874; *Mendocino Democrat*, Feb. 21, 28, 1874.

6. Eames, "Upland Pastures," pp. 527–28.

7. *Mendocino Democrat*, March 21, 1874; *People* v. *Geiger*, p. 652; Palmer, *History of Mendocino*, p. 339.

8. *San Francisco Examiner*, June 8, 1892. Doc's layoff is mentioned in the *Mendocino Democrat*, March 14, 1874.

9. John Keller, *The Mendocino Outlaws* (1974), pp. xi–xii; *Bodie Standard*, Dec. 21, 26, 1877.

10. Keller, *The Mendocino Outlaws*, pp. viii–ix; *Russian River Flag*, Jan. 1, 1880.

11. Palmer, *History of Mendocino*, p. 347.

12. *San Francisco Alta*, Sept. 11, 1881.

13. Ibid.; Keller, *The Mendocino Outlaws*, pp. 3–6; Palmer, *History of Mendocino*, pp. 344–47.

14. Keller, *The Mendocino Outlaws*, pp. 6–9.

15. Palmer, *History of Mendocino*, p. 587.

16. Ibid., pp. 9–17; Palmer, *History of Mendocino*, pp. 348–49, 587–88.

17. *San Francisco Examiner*, June 8, 1892; Keller, *The Mendocino Outlaws*, pp. 19–25; Palmer, *History of Mendocino*, pp. 349–56, 588–89.

18. *San Francisco Examiner*, June 8, 1892; *Mendocino Dispatch Democrat*, July 10, 1908.

19. M. M. Marberry, *Splendid Poseur: Joaquin Miller, American Poet* (1953), pp. 217–23; *Mendocino Dispatch Democrat*, Dec. 11, 1891.

20. *Mendocino Dispatch Democrat*, Aug. 15, 1890; *San Francisco Examiner*, Aug. 12, 13, 1890.

21. David Warren Ryder, *Memories of the Mendocino Coast* (1948), pp. 38–40.

22. *Mendocino Dispatch Democrat*, Aug. 5, 1892; *San Francisco Chronicle*, Dec. 18, 1897.

23. *San Francisco Call*, Dec. 13, 1895, Jan. 1, 2, 15, 17, 22, 28, 30, 1896; *San Francisco Chronicle*, Jan. 18, 21, 1896.

24. *San Francisco Call*, Oct. 4, 1903.

25. *Mendocino Dispatch Democrat*, July 10, 1908; Palmer, *History of Mendocino*, p. 747.

CHAPTER 5

1. *Stockton Evening Mail*, July 10, 1884; George H. Tinkham, History of San Joaquin County (1923), p. 218.

2. *An Illustrated History of San Joaquin County* (1890), p. 617; J. M. Guinn, *History of the State of California and Biographical Record of San Joaquin County* (1909), pp. 213–14.

3. *San Francisco Call*, Oct. 23, 1898; Guinn, *Biographical Record*, p. 216; Hu Maxwell, *Evans and Sontag* (reprinted 1981), pp. 43–46; R. Tod Ruse, "Portrait of Thomas Cunningham," in I. N. Brotherton, ed., *Valley Trails* (1966), pp. 9–12; Theodosia Benjamin, "Sheriff Thomas Cunningham," *San Joaquin Historian*, June, 1971, pp. 1–3.

4. *Stockton Daily Record*, Nov. 28, 1900; George Beers, *The California Outlaw* (reprinted 1960), pp. 222–26.

5. *San Francisco Call*, Jan. 14, 1883.

6. These holdups are listed in Wells Fargo's *Robbers' Record*, a published report prepared by Detectives James B. Hume and John N. Thacker in 1885, copies of which are located in the Wells Fargo Bank History Dept., San Francisco, and the Bancroft Library, Berkeley.

7. *Placer Herald*, Dec. 25, 1875; *Placer Argus*, Dec. 25, 1875; *Stockton Daily Independent*, Dec. 24, 1875; *Stockton Daily Record*, Dec. 22, 24, 1875.

8. *Placer Herald*, Jan. 1, 1876; *Calaveras Chronicle*, Jan. 1, 1876; *Amador Ledger* (Jackson), March 25, 1876.

9. Hume and Thacker, *Robbers' Record*.

10. Guinn, *Biographical Record*, p. 216.

11. *San Francisco Call*, Oct. 23, 1898; *Stockton Daily Evening Herald*, Nov. 24, 1879, May 28, July 1, 1880.

12. S. D. Woods, *Lights and Shadows of Life on the Pacific Coast* (1910), p. 447.

13. *Stockton Daily Record*, Nov. 26, 1900.

14. Woods, *Lights and Shadows*, pp. 449–50; *Stockton Daily Record*, Dec. 31, 1898, Nov. 26, 1900.

15. *San Francisco Call*, Oct. 23, 1898; *Stockton Daily Record*, Nov. 26, 1900.

16. *An Illustrated History of San Joaquin County*, pp. 95–99; *Stockton Evening Mail*, July 10, 1884.

17. *An Illustrated History of San Joaquin County*, pp. 99–100; Tinkham, *History of San Joaquin County*, p. 218; Olive Davis, "Land War of Moquelemos Was Bloodless Affair," *Stockton Daily Record*, Nov. 22, 1970; *Stockton Evening Mail*, July 9, 10, 1884; *San Francisco Examiner*, July 9, 1884.

18. *Sacramento Union*, Dec. 13, 16, 1884; *San Francisco Alta*, Dec. 13, 1884; Lee Silva, "Hold-Up: They Robbed Wells Fargo—Almost," *Westerner*, Feb., 1971, pp. 10–12, 54–58.

19. Tinkham, *History of San Joaquin County*, pp. 289–90; Walker Lewis; "The Supreme Court and a Six-gun," *American Bar Association Journal*, May, 1957, pp. 415–18, 475–78.

20. George Gorham, *The Story of the Attempted Assassination of Justice Field* (1892?), pp. 105–107; *San Francisco Call*, Aug. 16, 17, 1889.

21. Guinn, *Biographical Record*, p. 215; Woods, *Lights and Shadows*, p. 442.

22. *San Francisco Chronicle,* Sept. 5, 1897; *Stockton Evening Mail,* Sept. 9, 1897.

23. *Stockton Evening Mail,* March 8, 1894, Sept. 10, 1897; *San Francisco Chronicle,* Sept. 8, 9, 12, 1897.

24. Newspaper clippings in scrapbook of C. C. Crowley, Chief Special Agent, Southern Pacific Co., pp. 88–90 (copy in Bancroft Library); *Stockton Evening Mail,* Sept. 10, 15, 1897.

25. Newspaper clipping, Sept. 16, 1897, in Crowley scrapbook, p. 89.

26. *San Francisco Chronicle,* Sept. 15, 1897; *Newman West Side Index,* Sept. 16, 1897; *Stockton Evening Mail,* Sept. 16, 1897; *San Francisco Call,* Oct. 23, 1898.

27. *San Francisco Call,* Dec. 30, 31, 1897; *Napa Journal,* Dec. 31, 1897, Jan. 7, 1898.

28. *Stockton Daily Record,* Dec. 31, 1898, Jan. 3, 1899; *Stockton Evening Mail,* Jan. 2, 3, 1899.

29. *Stockton Daily Record,* Nov. 26, 28, Dec. 6, 1900.

CHAPTER 6

1. Art Woodward, "Confederate Secret Societies in California," *Westerners Brand Book, No. 3,* Los Angeles Corral (1949), pp. 73–81; *Santa Cruz Pacific Sentinel,* Sept. 10, 1864.

2. *Santa Cruz Pacific Sentinel,* Feb. 25, March 13, 1858.

3. Asbury Harpending, *The Great Diamond Hoax* (1910), pp. 73–86; *San Francisco Bulletin,* March 16, Sept. 7, Oct. 17, 1863.

4. *San Francisco Post,* May 7, 1887; *San Francisco Alta,* July 27, 1864; *Sacramento Union,* Sept. 10, 1864.

5. *Sacramento Union,* Aug. 29, Sept. 9, 10, 1864.

6. *San Francisco Post,* May 7, 1887.

7. From the testimony of Jim Wilson at the trial of Preston Hodges, set forth in detail in the *Sacramento Union,* Sept. 10, 1864.

8. *San Francisco Post,* May 7, 1887.

9. *Sacramento Union,* Sept. 10, 1864.

10. Ibid., Sept. 9, 1864.

11. Ibid., Aug. 27, Sept. 9, 1864; *San Francisco Alta,* Aug. 27, 1864.

12. *Sacramento Union,* Sept. 9, 1864.

13. *San Francisco Alta,* July 3, 1864. See also ibid., July 2, 1864; *Sacramento Union,* July 2, 6, 7, 1864; Charles E. Upton, *Pioneers of El Dorado* (1906), pp. 130–31.

14. *San Francisco Alta,* July 27, 1864. See also ibid., July 2, Aug. 27, 1864; *San Jose Mercury,* Aug. 4, Sept. 1, 1864; Upton, *Pioneers of El Dorado,* pp. 131–38; Dillon, *Wells Fargo Detective,* pp. 89–104. This account is based primarily upon the testimony of Maria Reynolds, George Ranney, Al Glasby, and Tom Poole, which appears in detail in the *Sacramento Union,* Aug. 27 and Sept. 9, 1864.

15. *Sacramento Union,* July 6, 1864; Upton, *Pioneers of El Dorado,* pp. 135–37.

16. Sacramento Union, July 27, Sept. 9, 1864; Oct. 2, 1865.

17. Statement of John D. Van Eaton, Placerville, Sept. 26, 1865, copy in Thomas B. Poole pardon file, Governors' Pardon Papers, California State Archives.

18. *San Jose Mercury,* July 21, 1864; *Redwood City Gazette,* July 29, 1864; *San Francisco Alta,* July 17, 27, 1864; Eugene T. Sawyer, *History of Santa Clara County* (1922), pp. 133–34.

19. *San Jose Mercury,* Aug. 4, 1864; *Sacramento Union,* Aug. 5, 1864.

20. *San Jose Mercury,* Aug. 25, 1864; *Monterey Gazette,* July 22, 1864.

21. *Monterey Gazette,* July 22, 1864; *Santa Cruz Pacific Sentinel,* July 30, 1864.

22. *San Francisco Post,* April 2, 1887; *San Jose Mercury,* Aug. 11, 1864.

23. *San Francisco Post,* April 2, 1887.

24. Ibid.; *San Jose Mercury,* Aug. 11, 1864. The *Sacramento Union,* Sept. 10, 1864, reprinted a sketch of Jim Grant's career from the *Alta.* See also Sawyer, *History of Santa Clara County,* p. 133.

25. *San Jose Mercury,* Aug. 25, 1864; *Santa Cruz Pacific Sentinel,* Aug. 27, 1864.

26. *San Jose Mercury,* July 28, Sept. 8, 1864.

27. *Sacramento Union,* Aug. 26, 27, 29, 1864.

28. Ibid., Sept. 8, 9, 10, 12, 1864, Jan. 4, March 4, 1865; *San Jose Mercury,* March 23, 1865; San Quentin Prison Register, convict no. 2982, James Grant; *People* v. *Hodges,* California Supreme Court Reports, vol. 27, p. 340.

29. *San Jose Mercury,* Sept. 21, Oct. 12, 1865; *Sacramento Union,* Sept. 21, 1865; *People* v. *Poole,* California Supreme Court Reports, vol. 27, p. 572.

30. James Johnson to Governor Frederick Low, Sept. 25, 1865; Sheriff W. W. Rogers, J. B. Hume, and others, to Governor Low, Sept. 18, 1865. These and numerous other letters are located in Tom Poole's pardon file.

31. *Sacramento Union,* Oct. 2, 1865.

32. Ibid., Sept. 9, 1864.

CHAPTER 7

1. Colin Rickards, "Bill Miner, Fifty Years a Holdup Man," *Real West,* Sept. 1970, p. 23; Dawson scrapbooks, vol. 18, p. 456, in Colorado Historical Society Library.

2. Rickards, "Bill Miner," p. 22; James D. Horan and Paul Sann, *Pictorial History of the Wild West* (1954), p. 80.

3. C. A. Tweed to Governor Frederick Low, Sept. 29, 1867, and Mary J. Wellman to Governor William Irwin, Oct. 30, 1878, both in Bill Miner Pardon file, Governors' Pardon Papers; San Quentin Prison Registers, convict nos. 3248, 3313, 4902 (Bill Miner); California Volunteers, Muster Roll and Descriptive List, California State Archives.

4. *People* v. *Miner,* case file nos. 592, 594, Placer County Clerk; *Placer Herald,* Dec. 30, 1865; *Auburn Stars and Stripes,* Jan. 3, 1866.

5. *Stockton Daily Independent,* Jan. 24, 25, 1866.

6. Ibid., Feb. 23, 1866.

7. Ibid., April 4, 1866.

8. *Placer Herald,* June 9, 16, 30, 1866.

9. *Stockton Daily Independent,* Jan. 24, Feb. 7, 1871; *San Francisco Alta,* Jan. 25, 1871; *San Francisco Call,* Feb. 5, 1871; *Calaveras Chronicle,* Feb. 11, 1871.

10. *San Jose Daily Patriot,* Jan. 27, 1871.

11. *San Francisco Call,* Feb. 5, 1871; *San Jose Daily Patriot,* Feb. 1, 1871; *Redwood City Gazette,* Feb. 3, 1871.

12. *Stockton Daily Independent,* Feb. 8, 1871; *San Francisco Bulletin,* Feb. 11, 1871.

13. *Calaveras Chronicle,* March 11, 1871.

14. Ibid., Feb. 17, 1872; *San Francisco Bulletin,* Nov. 11, 1871; *People* v. *Harrington,* California Supreme Court Reports, vol. 42, p. 165.

15. San Quentin Prison Registers, convict no. 5206; San Quentin Prison, Record of Punishment, p. 32; State Board of Prison Directors, minutes, vol. 1, p. 118; all in California State Archives.

16. Hume and Thacker, *Robbers' Record; Placer Argus,* Sept. 25, 1880; *Placer Herald,* Sept. 25, 1880.

17. *Pueblo* (Colorado) *Daily Chieftain,* Sept. 30, 1880; *Denver Republican,* May 24, 1881.

18. Dawson scrapbooks, vol. 18, p. 465; Denver *Republican,* Oct. 21, 1911; Rickards, "Bill Miner," p. 22.

19. Denver *Republican,* Jan. 15, May 24, 25, 1881, April 5, 1882.

20. Dawson scrapbooks, vol. 18, p. 465; Rickards, "Bill Miner," p. 23; *San Francisco Examiner,* Dec. 21, 1881. In later years Miner claimed that after leaving Colorado he embarked on a world tour, visiting Europe, South Africa, and China, and became a slave trader in Turkey and a gunrunner in Argentina. Of course, this yarn is sheerest nonsense, for Bill could not possibly have done these things in the three months between his escape from Colorado and his November 7 holdup of the Sonora stage.

21. *Sacramento Record-Union,* Nov. 8, 1881; *San Francisco Chronicle,* Nov. 8, 1881.

22. *Sacramento Bee,* Dec. 8, 9, 1881; *San Francisco Chronicle,* Dec. 10, 1881; *Stockton Daily Independent,* Dec. 9, 10, 1881; *Sacramento Record-Union,* Dec. 8, 1881; *Calaveras Weekly Citizen,* Dec. 24, 1881; Rickards, "Bill Miner," pp. 23, 74.

23. *San Francisco Examiner,* April 19, 1884; State Board of Prison Directors, Minutes, vol. 2, pp. 68, 429, vol. 3, p. 336.

24. San Francisco Examiner, Nov. 30, 1892.

25. *San Francisco Call,* Nov. 30, 1892; *Marin County Tocsin* (San Rafael), Dec. 10, 1892; *Marin County Journal,* Dec. 15, 1892.

26. State Board of Prison Directors, Minutes, vol. 6, p. 173; San Quentin Prison Registers, convict no. 10191, William A. Miner.

27. See Rickards, "Bill Miner," and Frank W. Anderson, *Bill Miner, Stagecoach and Train Robber* (reprinted 1982) for two factual accounts of Bill's adventures in Canada and the Pacific Northwest.

CHAPTER 8

1. *San Francisco Chronicle,* Dec. 24, 1893; Charles C. Crowley scrapbook (news clippings), pp. 59–60.

2. *San Francisco Examiner,* Feb. 17, 1894; Crowley scrapbook, p. 37; Southern Pacific Company, "History of Train Robberies," pp. 64–65. In 1890 rural San Fernando Township had just 1,110 residents, and Burbank Township had only 2,996, *Census Reports, 12th Census of the United States* (1901).

3. Crowley scrapbook, pp. 37, 62; *Southern Pacific Company,* "History of Train Robberies," p. 65.

4. *San Francisco Examiner,* Feb. 17, 1894.

5. Crowley scrapbook, pp. 37–38.

6. Alva Johnson pardon file, Governors' Pardon Papers; Crowley Scrapbook, pp. 37–38; *Los Angeles Times,* March 27, 1894.

7. Court Smith, Warden of Folsom Prison, to D. O'Connell, Chief Special Agent, Southern Pacific Co., Feb. 29, 1928, located in William Thompson inmate case file, California State Archives; prison record, convict no. 618, William

Thompson, Yuma Territorial Prison State Historic Park; *San Francisco Examiner,* Dec. 14, 1894; *Los Angeles Express,* Dec. 13, 17, 1894.

8. *Los Angeles Times,* March 27, 1894; Crowley scrapbook, pp. 37–38; *Southern Pacific Company,* "History of Train Robberies," p. 66.

9. *Los Angeles Herald,* March 30, 1894; Crowley scrapbook, pp. 37–38.

10. *San Francisco Chronicle,* May 13, 1896. See also Frank F. Latta's *Dalton Gang Days* (1976) for details on Will Smith's attempts to capture the Daltons.

11. *Los Angeles Herald,* June 15, 1894; Crowley scrapbook, p. 41.

12. Crowley scrapbook, p. 31.

13. *Los Angeles Herald,* June 10, 1894.

14. The Crowley scrapbook, pp. 40–46, contains numerous articles from the Los Angeles newspapers about this trial.

15. Ibid., p. 61, Southern Pacific Company, "History of Train Robberies," p. 66; *Los Angeles Express,* Dec. 13, 1894.

16. Testimony of Will Smith, *People* v. *W. H. Thompson,* Los Angeles County Superior Court, trial transcript, May 28, 1895, in Governors' Pardon Papers; William M. Breakenridge, *Helldorado* (1928), pp. 231–33; Crowley scrapbook, pp. 60–61; *Los Angeles Times,* Nov. 3, 1894.

17. Breakenridge, *Helldorado,* p. 233; testimony of Will Smith, *People* v. *W. H. Thompson.*

18. Breakenridge, *Helldorado,* pp. 233–35; Crowley scrapbook, p. 59; Southern Pacific Company, "History of Train Robberies," p. 67.

19. *Los Angeles Express,* Dec. 14, 1894.

20. Ibid., Oct. 23, Dec. 12, 15, 1894; *Los Angeles Times,* Nov. 2, 1894; *San Francisco Examiner,* Dec. 12, 1894; Crowley scrapbook, pp. 59–61.

21. Testimony of George Smith, F. B. Kennet, A. B. Lawson, and Alva Johnson, *People* v. *W. H. Thompson;* Crowley scrapbook, pp. 61–64; Southern Pacific Company, "History of Train Robberies," p. 68.

22. *Los Angeles Express,* June 11, 1895; *San Francisco Chronicle,* Aug. 14, 1896; San Quentin Prison Registers, convict no. 16940, F. B. Kennet.

23. *San Francisco Chronicle,* April 6, 1896; *People* v. *Thompson,* California Supreme Court Reports, vol. 111, p. 242.

24. *People* v. *Thompson,* California Supreme Court Reports, vol. 115, p. 160.

25. *Los Angeles Times,* March 22, 1897.

26. Crowley scrapbook, pp. 79–81, 85–86; *People* v. *Tupper,* California Supreme Court Reports, vol. 122, p. 424.

27. *San Francisco Chronicle,* July 20, 1900.

28. Alva Johnson pardon file; *San Francisco Chronicle,* Oct. 22, 1907; William Thompson inmate case file; Southern Pacific Company, "History of Train Robberies," p. 69.

CHAPTER 9

1. The statistics on train holdups are cited in Jeff Burton, *Dynamite and Six-shooter* (1970), p. 213. For information on Evans and Sontag, see C. B. Glasscock, *Bandits and the Southern Pacific* (1929) and Wallace Smith, *Prodigal Sons* (1951). An excellent and remarkably well researched account of the Dalton boys' misadventures in California is Latta's *Dalton Gang Days.*

2. Latta, *Dalton Gang Days,* p. 139; *Tulare Register,* July 3, 1891.

3. *Tulare Register*, July 1, 2, 1891.

4. *Visalia Weekly Delta*, Sept. 3, 1891; *San Francisco Examiner*, Dec. 20, 1898; *Amsterdam* (N.Y.) *Daily Democrat*, Dec. 23, 1898.

5. *San Francisco Chronicle*, Sept. 29, 1891.

6. *Tulare Register*, Aug. 31, 1891; *Visalia Weekly Delta*, Sept. 3, 1891; *Oakland Daily Evening Tribune*, Aug. 27, 28, 1891.

7. Latta, *Dalton Gang Days*, pp. 137–39; *San Francisco Chronicle*, Dec. 30, 1893.

8. Latta, *Dalton Gang Days*, pp. 133–46; *San Francisco Chronicle*, Sept. 29, 1891; *Visalia Weekly Delta*, Oct. 1, Nov. 19, 1891; *Tulare Register*, Sept. 28, 1891.

9. *Hanford Journal*, Jan. 15, 1895.

10. Smith, *Prodigal Sons*, p. 390; *Tulare County Times* (Visalia), Feb. 20, 1896.

11. *Tulare County Times*, Aug. 29, 1895.

12. Ibid., Dec. 12, 1895, Feb. 20, 1896; *Visalia Weekly Delta*, Feb. 20, 1896; *Hanford Journal*, Feb. 18, 1896; *San Francisco Call*, Feb. 18, 1896.

13. *Tulare County Times*, Feb. 20, 1896; *San Francisco Call*, Feb. 18, 1896.

14. *San Francisco Chronicle*, March 20, 1896.

15. *San Francisco Call*, April 27, 1896.

16. *San Francisco Chronicle*, Sept. 6–9, 1896; Southern Pacific Company, "History of Train Robberies," pp. 108–109.

17. Southern Pacific Company, "History of Train Robberies," p. 110; *San Francisco Examiner*, Dec. 20, 1898.

18. *Amsterdam Daily Democrat*, Jan. 28, 1899.

19. Clarence L. Fraser, "Holdup at Cross Creek," *Los Tulares* (Bulletin of the Tulare County Historical Society), Dec. 1961; Crowley scrapbook, pp. 97–103; *Tulare County Times*, March 24, 1898; *San Francisco Examiner*, March 24, 1898.

20. *San Francisco Examiner*, March 26, 29, 30, April 1, 1898. The officers at first suspected Cliff Regan, a notorious Madera County bandit, and his partner, Walter Low. Low was arrested on May 15, 1898, by Madera County Sheriff S. W. Westfall. He was taken to Visalia and jailed but later was released when it was learned that he was not involved in the robbery.

21. *San Francisco Chronicle*, March 31, 1898.

22. *Tulare County Times*, April 7, June 2, 1898.

23. Crowley is quoted in the *San Francisco Examiner*, Dec. 20, 1898. See also Smith, *Prodigal Sons*, p. 382, and *Visalia Weekly Delta*, Dec. 22, 1898. The Cross Creek holdup is somewhat shrouded in mystery. The late Wallace Smith has a very garbled account of it in *Prodigal Sons*, pp. 381–97, in which he mixes up the Tagus Switch and the Cross Creek holdups. He calls the Johnsons, "Charles and Johnny Johnson," and claims that Jim Lee "was picked up for questioning," but in fact Lee was in Folsom Prison from Jan. 1896, to Sept. 1898, the period in which the holdups took place. Smith erroneously says that the train was robbed at Traver instead of Cross Creek, and adds this intriguing tidbit:

> Who robbed the train at Traver? One of the men who was there that night is still alive at this writing [1951]. His secret must be kept. The reader who likes to do a little amateur sleuthing is welcome to go to work on this slight clue: Six of the men who went big-game hunting more than fifty years ago and brought down a Southern Pacific express-coach were named: Anderson, Bowers, Gramley, Johnson, Larson, and Smith. This author refuses to answer any and all further questions.

Diligent inquiry has failed to unearth the answer to this riddle. It is possible that the men listed were members of the Forty Thieves and perhaps harbored the Johnson boys or assisted them in escaping. But only two men—Ben and Dudley Johnson—committed the Cross Creek holdup, a fact that, although published in the newspapers of San Francisco, Fresno, Visalia, and Hanford, seems to have eluded Mr. Smith.

24. *Volusia County Record,* Dec. 11, 1898.

25. Ibid., *Fresno Morning Republican,* Dec. 20, 1898; *Visalia Weekly Delta,* Dec. 22, 1898; *Florida Times-Union and Citizen* (Jacksonville), Dec. 12, 13, 20, 21, 22, 1898.

26. *San Francisco Examiner,* Dec. 20, 1898. Neither Ben Johnson nor Mrs. J. C. Johnston served a prison term in Florida for the murder of Deputy Kreamer, nor was Ben ever extradited back to Florida to stand trial, according to a search of prison and extradition records made by the State Archivist, Florida Department of State.

27. *Hanford Daily Journal,* Dec. 19, 1898.

CHAPTER 10

1. *Stockton Evening Mail,* April 12, 1902; *Stockton Daily Record,* April 12, 16, 19, 1902; *Amador Dispatch,* April 18, 1902; *Amador Ledger,* April 18, 1902.

2. *San Francisco Chronicle,* May 7, 1904; Crowley scrapbook, pp. 139–40.

3. *Amador Ledger,* April 25, May 9, 1902.

4. *Trinidad* (Colorado) *Chronicle-News,* Nov. 20, 21, 24, 1902; *San Francisco Chronicle,* May 7, 1904.

5. Wells Fargo & Co., wanted circular, San Francisco, Sept. 15, 1904.

6. Crowley scrapbook, pp. 139–44.

7. *Trinity Journal* (Weaverville), June 13, 1903.

8. Portland *Morning Oregonian,* July 15, 16, 18, 1903, May 7, 1904; San Francisco *Chronicle,* May 7, 1904.

9. San Francisco *Examiner,* May 10, 1904.

10. Southern Pacific Company, "History of Train Robberies," pp. 130–31; *San Francisco Examiner,* May 10, 12, 1904.

11. *San Francisco Chronicle,* April 3, 1904; *San Francisco Call,* March 21, 1904.

12. Crowley scrapbook, pp. 131–36; Southern Pacific Company, "History of Train Robberies," pp. 127–29; *San Francisco Call,* April 3, 1904.

13. *San Francisco Examiner,* May 10, 1904.

14. Ibid., May 9, 1904; *San Francisco Chronicle,* May 10, 1904; Crowley scrapbook, p. 139; Southern Pacific Company, "History of Train Robberies," pp. 129–30.

15. *San Francisco Examiner,* May 17, 1904.

16. Ibid., May 10, 11, 1904.

17. Crowley scrapbook, p. 139.

18. *San Francisco Chronicle,* April 11, 1905; Southern Pacific Company, "History of Train Robberies," p. 133.

19. *Silver City* (New Mexico) *Independent,* March 21, 1905; *San Francisco Chronicle,* April 11, 1905; *San Francisco Call,* April 11, 1905; Southern Pacific Company, "History of Train Robberies," pp. 131–33.

20. Southern Pacific Company, "History of Train Robberies," p. 133.

21. *San Francisco Chronicle,* April 11, 1905.

22. Crowley scrapbook, p. 142.

CHAPTER 11

1. Palmer, *History of Mendocino County* (1880), p. 454.

2. *Estate of Elijah Frost,* probate file no. 758, Mendocino County Clerk; U.S. Census Population Schedules, Little Lake Township, 1870, pp. 180, 200; *Ukiah Democratic Weekly Dispatch,* Dec. 5, 1879.

3. U.S. Census Population Schedules, Little Lake Township, 1870, pp. 95, 216, 217, 219. See also the addenda to the Mendocino County Historical Society's 1967 reprint of Palmer, *History of Mendocino County,* which contains a sketch of Abner Coates.

4. This affair is alluded to in the *San Francisco Bulletin,* Oct. 25, 1867, which says, "About five or six years ago one of the Coates boys and one of the Frost boys had a quarrel and a fight; from that time present there has been very bad feeling between the two families." The only account to survive appears in a manuscript written by W. C. Bunner entitled "California's Family Feud," dated at Willits, Aug. 9, 1899, pp. 2–5. It was published in the *San Francisco Call,* Aug. 6, 1899, which Jill Cossley-Batt copied almost verbatim in her book, *The Last of the California Rangers* (1928), pp. 237–40.

5. *San Francisco Bulletin,* Oct. 25, 1867; *Healdsburg Democratic Standard,* Oct. 24, 1867.

6. The best known and heretofore the most accepted account of this gunfight appears in Palmer, *History of Mendocino County,* pp. 336–37. It gives an incorrect date (Oct. 11, 1865) and has many other errors. My account is based on eyewitness testimony given at the coroner's inquest and published in the *Mendocino Herald* (Ukiah), April 24, 1868. See also *San Francisco Bulletin,* Oct. 25, 1867; *San Francisco Call,* Oct. 22, 1867; *Healdsburg Democratic Standard,* Oct. 24, 1867; Stewart Nixon, *The Redwood Empire* (1966), pp. 150–51; W. B. Held, "Vendetta of the Frosts and Coates," *San Francisco Call,* Sept. 16, 1897.

7. *Petaluma Journal and Argus,* Nov. 7, 1867.

8. *People v. Abner Coates,* case file no. 867; *People v. Isom and Martin Frost,* case file no. 361; *People v. Isom Frost,* case file no. 457; *People v. Martin Frost,* case file no. 459; all located in office of Mendocino County Clerk. Also see "Little Lake Valley," p. 2, typescript in the possession of John Keller.

9. "Little Lake Valley," p. 1.

10. Ibid., p. 3.

11. *Mendocino Democrat,* Feb. 8, July 25, 1872; *Petaluma Daily Crescent,* Feb. 7, 1872; *Russian River Flag,* Feb. 8, 15, 1872; *Mendocino County Press,* Feb. 8, 1872; *People v. John Coates,* case file no. 766, Mendocino County Clerk.

12. San Quentin Prison Registers; John Coates pardon file, Governors' Pardon Papers.

13. *James McKindley v. Elijah Frost,* case file no. 938; *People v. Taylor Frost and Robert Reynolds,* case file nos. 932, 993, 1488; *People v. Elijah Frost and Robert Reynolds,* case file no. 1171, all in Mendocino County Clerk's office.

14. *Red Bluff Sentinel,* Sept. 18, 1875; *Red Bluff People's Cause,* Sept. 18, 1875;

Weekly Butte Record (Chico), Sept. 16, 1875; *Weekly Shasta Courier* (Redding), Sept. 18, Oct. 2, 16, Dec. 18, 1875; San Quentin Prison Registers, convict no. 6809, Elijah Frost.

15. *Petaluma Weekly Argus,* Sept. 5, 1879; *Ukiah Democratic Weekly Dispatch,* Sept. 13, 1879; *Mendocino Democrat,* Sept. 6, 1879; *Ukiah City Press,* Sept. 5, 1879; *Mendocino Beacon,* Sept. 13, 20, 1879; Bunner, "California's Family Feud," pp. 13–14; *Estate of Elijah Frost,* probate file no. 328, Mendocino County Clerk.

16. *Mendocino Beacon,* Jan. 5, 1884; Bunner, "California's Family Feud," p. 16.

17. *Ukiah Democratic Weekly Dispatch,* Oct. 29, 1880.

18. *Mendocino Beacon,* March 18, 1882.

19. *Ukiah City Press,* March 17, 1882; *Mendocino Dispatch Democrat,* March 17, 1882.

20. *Ukiah City Press,* Aug. 4, 1882.

21. Ibid., Jan. 4, 1884; *Mendocino Beacon,* Jan. 5, 1884; *Mendocino Dispatch Democrat,* Jan. 4, 1884; "Little Lake Valley," p. 2; *People* v. *James Frost,* case no. 2474, Mendocino County Superior Court, typewritten notes from court record in Mendocino County Historical Society Library.

22. *Mendocino Dispatch Democrat,* July 18, 1884; *Mendocino Beacon,* July 26, 1884; statement of Jose A. Sicotte, Nov. 2, 1887, in Governors' Pardon Papers.

23. Testimony of Tom Gibson, *People* v. *Isom Frost,* case no. 2676, Mendocino County Superior Court, trial transcript in Governors' Pardon Papers.

24. *Mendocino Dispatch and Democrat,* Jan. 29, 1886.

25. *People* v. *Isom Frost,* pp. 45–101; *People* v. *David Frost,* case no. 3519, Mendocino County Superior Court, typewritten notes from court record in Mendocino County Historical Society Library; *Mendocino Dispatch Democrat,* April 18, 1885, Jan. 26, 1886; *Sacramento Union,* April 13, 1885; *Ukiah City Press,* April 17, Oct. 2, 1885, Jan. 15, 22, 1886; *Mendocino Beacon,* Oct. 17, 1885, Jan. 16, 30, 1886; *San Francisco Call,* Sept. 16, 1897.

26. *Marysville Daily Appeal,* Sept. 27, 1885; *Ukiah City Press,* Oct. 2, 1885.

27. *People* v. *David Frost,* notes, p. 3.

28. *Mendocino Dispatch Democrat,* Jan. 29, 1886; *Ukiah City Press,* Jan. 15, 22, 1886.

29. Isom Frost pardon file, Governors' Pardon Papers.

30. Death certificate of Isom Frost, Mendocino County Recorder.

CHAPTER 12

1. Statistics on lynchings in 1855 were reported in the *San Francisco Alta* in October, 1855, and republished in Wells, *History of Nevada County* (1880), p. 116; McCoy's lynching is mentioned in the *Alta,* Aug. 29, 1877; other figures are from an undated news clipping in author's collection, published about the time of the Lookout lynching.

2. *Census Reports, 12th Census of the United States* (1901), vol. 1, p. 77. The population of Lookout Township as a whole was 354 in 1900.

3. James Souther, *Legend into History: Fact and Fiction of the Lookout Lynching* (1968), pp. 30–31.

4. Calvin Hall's dictation appears in the *Fall River Tidings,* 50th Anniversary

Edition, Feb. 25, 1944; see also Souther, *Legend into History,* pp. 31–32; report of the attorney general, Modoc lynching cases, *Appendix to the Journals of the Senate and Assembly* (1903), vol. 1, p. 10.

5. *Red Bluff Sentinel,* Sept. 25, 1875; *Bieber Big Valley Gazette,* Feb. 28, 1900.

6. Souther, *Legend into History,* pp. 33, 36.

7. Ibid., p. 34; *Alturas New Era,* Aug. 9, 1901; *San Francisco Chronicle,* Jan. 4, 1902.

8. A. F. Bradshaw to Attorney General Tirey L. Ford, Oct. 9, 1901, in Modoc lynching case file, California State Archives. This file contains attorney general's correspondence, newspaper clippings, and voluminous transcripts of testimony given at the coroner's inquest and grand jury investigation.

9. Souther, *Legend into History,* pp. 37–38; William Thompson, *Reminiscences of a Pioneer* (1912), pp. 179–80; William Brown, *California Northeast: The Bloody Ground* (1951), pp. 143–44; *Alturas Plaindealer,* clipping in Modoc lynching case file, California State Archives.

10. Thompson, *Reminiscences,* pp. 180–81; Brown, *California Northeast,* p. 144.

11. *Bieber Big Valley Gazette,* June 20, 1900.

12. A. F. Bradshaw to Tirey L. Ford, Oct. 9, 1901.

13. *Alturas New Era,* Jan. 3, 1902; docket, Lookout Township Justice Court, May 25, 1901; testimony of Erv Carpenter, from grand jury hearing transcript, June 7–8, 1901, pp. 75–85. These latter two items are located in the Lookout lynching case file at the Bancroft Library, Berkeley, which contains copies of the lengthy grand jury transcripts.

14. Testimony of Walter Criss, grand jury transcript, June 7–8, 1901, p. 329. The attempted lynching of Frank Hall is described in A. F. Bradshaw to Tirey L. Ford, Oct. 9, 1901; *San Francisco Chronicle,* June 11, 1901; and *San Francisco Examiner,* June 11, 1902. Needless to say, the members of the posse denied it, and testified before the grand jury that Frank had tried to flee and they had caught him, placing a rope around his neck to keep him from escaping. But according to the *Chronicle,* "The rafter in the barn shows marks where the rope burned it."

15. Docket, Lookout Township Justice Court, May 25, 26, 1901; testimony of Erv Carpenter, grand jury transcript.

16. Testimony of Jim Brown, grand jury transcript, June 7–8, 1901; *San Francisco Chronicle,* Jan. 9, 1902.

17. Souther, *Legend into History,* pp. 43–44. *Alturas Plaindealer,* clipping in Modoc lynching file, State Archives.

18. Testimony of Jim Brown, grand jury transcript.

19. A. F. Bradshaw to Tirey L. Ford, Oct. 9, 1901.

20. Report of the Attorney General, Modoc Lynching Cases, p. 10; C. N. Post to Tirey L. Ford, June 24, 1901; *Alturas New Era,* Dec. 27, 1901.

21. A. F. Bradshaw to Tirey L. Ford, Oct. 9, 1901.

22. *San Francisco Call,* Jan. 22, 1902.

23. This account is based primarily on the confessions of Claude Morris and John Hutton, set forth at length in the *Alturas New Era,* Jan. 10, 17, 1902; *San Francisco Chronicle,* Jan. 9, 10, 12, 14, 15, 16, 1902; and *San Francisco Call,* Jan. 17, 19, 1902. See also *Sacramento Union,* June 1, 2, 1901; and testimony of James R. Myers, Erv Carpenter, and Jim Brown, grand jury transcripts.

24. Testimony of Erv Carpenter, grand jury transcript, June 7–8, 1901, p. 109. Carpenter's answers to questions posed by C. N. Post were extremely evasive. It is evident that he knew much more than he was willing to tell the grand jury.

25. Transcript of coroner's inquest, May 31, 1901, in Modoc lynching file, State Archives. See also *Bieber Big Valley Gazette,* June 5, 1901; *Sacramento Union,* June 2, 1901. According to Justice of the Peace Harris, four of the victims were buried in coffins in a single grave in the Lookout cemetery. Martin Wilson's body was carried off by local Indians, who gave him an Indian burial. *Alturas New Era,* Jan. 3, 1902.

26. *Bieber Big Valley Gazette,* June 5, 1901.

27. *Sacramento Union,* June 3, 1901.

28. This exchange of telegrams is detailed in Report of the Attorney General, p. 11.

29. C. N. Post to Tirey L. Ford, June 24, 1901.

30. This note is preserved in the Lookout lynching case file, State Archives.

31. *Alturas New Era,* June 14, 1901; C. N. Post to Tirey L. Ford, June 24, 1901.

32. *San Francisco Chronicle,* June 13, 1901.

33. Ibid., June 21, 1901; testimony of A. L. Colburn, grand jury transcript, June 17, 1901, pp. 288–97, Lookout lynching file, Bancroft Library.

34. C. N. Post to Tirey L. Ford, June 24, 1901.

35. Report of the Attorney General, pp. 11–12; John Boessenecker, "John Thacker, Train Robbers' Nemesis," *Real West,* Sept. 1976, p. 18.

36. E. J. Thacker to T. L. Ford, July 26, 1901, Lookout lynching case file, State Archives.

37. Ibid., E. J. Thacker to T. L. Ford, July 29, 1901; *Alturas New Era,* Jan. 17, 1902; *San Francisco Call,* Jan. 17, 1902.

38. Report of the Attorney General, p. 12; undated clippings from Alturas newspapers, Lookout lynching case file, State Archives.

39. Undated newspaper clipping, State Archives.

40. *San Francisco Chronicle,* Nov. 28, Dec. 7, 10, 14, 18, 19, 20, 1901; *Alturas New Era,* Dec. 27, 1901.

41. *San Francisco Chronicle,* Dec. 21, 1901.

42. Ibid, Dec. 25, 1901.

43. Ibid., Jan. 4, 5, 1902.

44. E. J. Thacker to C. N. Post, Sept. 10, 1901; Report of the Attorney General, p. 12; *Alturas New Era,* Jan. 10, 1902.

45. *San Francisco Chronicle,* Jan. 9, 1902; *Alturas New Era,* Jan. 10, 1902.

46. Report of the Attorney General, p. 13; *Alturas Plaindealer,* quoted in the *San Francisco Chronicle,* Jan. 14, 1902.

47. *Alturas New Era,* Jan. 21, Feb. 4, 21, 25, 1902.

48. *San Francisco Chronicle,* Feb. 28, 1902.

49. Report of the Attorney General, pp. 13–14; *Sacramento Union,* March 18, 1902; *Alturas New Era,* March 18, 1902.

50. *San Francisco Chronicle,* Feb. 28, 1902; *Alturas New Era,* Feb. 28, 1902.

51. *Alturas New Era,* June 28, 1901.

52. Hector Lee, *Tales of California* (1974), p. 26; Souther, *Legend into History,* pp. 19–20.

Bibliography

BOOKS

Anderson, Frank W. *Bill Miner, Stagecoach and Train Robber.* Surrey, B.C.: Frontier Books, 1982.

Angel, Myron. *History of Placer County.* Oakland, Calif.: Thompson & West, 1882.

Appendix to the Journals of the Senate and Assembly. Sacramento, Calif.: State Printing Office, 1903.

Bean, Edwin F. *History and Directory of Nevada County.* Nevada City, Calif.: Daily Gazette, 1867.

Beers, George. *The California Outlaw.* Ed. by Robert Greenwood. Los Gatos, Calif.: Talisman Press, 1960.

Breakenridge, William M. *Helldorado.* Boston: Houghton Mifflin Co., 1928.

Brotherton, I. N., ed. *Valley Trails,* Stockton, Calif.: Stockton Corral of Westerners, 1966.

Brown, William. *California Northeast: The Bloody Ground.* Oakland, Calif.: Biobooks, 1951.

Buckbee, Edna Bryan. *The Saga of Old Tuolumne.* New York: Press of the Pioneers, 1935.

Burton, Jeff. *Dynamite and Sixshooter.* Santa Fe, N.Mex.: Palomino Press, 1970.

Census Reports, 12th Census of the United States. Washington, D.C.: U.S. Census Office, 1901.

Cossley-Batt, Jill. *The Last of the California Rangers.* New York: Funk & Wagnalls Co., 1928.

Dillon, Richard. *Wells Fargo Detective.* New York: Coward-McCann, 1969.

Fatout, Paul. *Meadow Lake, Gold Town.* Bloomington: Indiana University Press, 1969.

Friedman, Lawrence M., and Robert V. Percival. *The Roots of Justice: Crime and Punishment in Alameda County, California 1870–1910.* Chapel Hill: University of North Carolina Press, 1981.

Glasscock, C. B. *Bandits and the Southern Pacific.* New York: Frederick A. Stokes Co., 1929.

Gorham, George. *The Story of the Attempted Assassination of Justice Field.* N.p., n.d.

Guinn, J. M. *History of the State of California and Biographical Record of San Joaquin County.* Los Angeles: Historic Record Co., 1909.

Harpending, Asbury. *The Great Diamond Hoax.* San Francisco: James H. Barry Co., 1910.

A History of Tuolumne County. San Francisco: B. F. Alley Co., 1882.

313

Horan, James D., and Paul Sann. *Pictorial History of the Wild West.* New York: Bonanza Books, 1954.

Hume, James B., and John N. Thacker. *Robbers' Record.* N.p., 1885.

An Illustrated History of San Joaquin County. Chicago: Lewis Publishing Co., 1890.

Jackson, Joseph Henry. *Bad Company.* New York: Harcourt, Brace & Co., 1949.

Keller, John. *The Mendocino Outlaws.* Ukiah, Calif.: Mendocino County Historical Society, 1974.

Kinyon, Edmund. *The Northern Mines.* Grass Valley, Calif.: Union Publishing Co., 1949.

Lamott, Kenneth. *Chronicles of San Quentin.* New York: David McKay Co., 1961.

Lardner, William B. *History of Placer and Nevada Counties.* Los Angeles: Historic Record Co., 1924.

Latta, Frank F. *Dalton Gang Days.* Santa Cruz, Calif.: Bear State Books, 1976.

Lee, Hector. *Tales of California.* Santa Rosa, Calif.: Letter Shop Press, 1974.

Marberry, M. M. *Splendid Poseur: Joaquin Miller, American Poet.* New York: Thomas Y. Crowell Co., 1953.

Mason, Jesse D. *History of Amador County.* Oakland, Calif.: Thompson & West, 1881.

Maxwell, Hu. *Evans and Sontag.* Ed. by Charles W. Clough. Fresno, Calif.: Panorama West Books, 1981.

Nixon, Stewart. *The Redwood Empire.* New York: E. P. Dutton & Co., 1966.

Palmer, Lyman, *History of Mendocino County.* San Francisco: Alley, Bowman & Co., 1880.

Pauley, Art. *Henry Plummer, Lawman and Outlaw.* White Sulphur Springs, Mont.: Meagher County News, 1980.

Ryder, David Warren. *Memories of the Mendocino Coast.* San Francisco: Taylor & Taylor, 1948.

Sawyer, Eugene T. *History of Santa Clara County.* Los Angeles: Historic Record Co., 1922.

Smith, Wallace. *Prodigal Sons.* Boston: Christopher Publishing House, 1951.

Souther, James. *Legend into History: Fact and Fiction of the Lookout Lynching.* New York: Vantage Press, 1968.

Thompson, William. *Reminiscences of a Pioneer.* San Francisco: 1912.

Tinkham, George H. *History of San Joaquin County.* Los Angeles: Historic Record Co., 1923.

Upton, Charles E. *Pioneers of El Dorado.* Placerville, Calif.: Published by author, 1906.

A Volume of Memoirs and Genealogy of Representative Citizens of Northern California. Chicago: Standard Genealogical Publishing Co., 1901.

Wells, Harry L. *History of Nevada County.* Oakland, Calif.: Thompson & West, 1880.

————. *History of Siskiyou County.* Oakland, Calif.: D. J. Stewart & Co., 1881.

The Westerners, Los Angeles Posse. *Westerners Brand Book, No. 3.* Los Angeles: Los Angeles Corral, 1949.

Wilson, Neill C. *Treasure Express.* New York: Macmillan Co., 1936.
Wood, Richard Coke. *Tales of Old Calaveras.* N.p., 1949.
Woods, S. D. *Lights and Shadows of Life on the Pacific Coast.* New York: Funk
    & Wagnalls Co., 1910.

PERIODICAL ARTICLES

"An Amateur Detective." *Harper's Weekly,* July 14, 1866.
Benjamin, Theodosia. "Sheriff Thomas Cunningham." *San Joaquin Histo-*
    rian, June, 1971.
Boessenecker, John. "John Thacker, Train Robbers' Nemesis." *Real West,*
    Sept., 1976.
————. "Steve Venard, Wells Fargo's Ace Troubleshooter." *Golden West,*
    Sept., 1972.
Bulletin of the Nevada County Historical Society, Dec., 1967.
Eames, Ninetta. "Upland Pastures." *Cosmopolitan,* March, 1896.
Fraser, Clarence L. "Holdup at Cross Creek." *Los Tulares.* Bulletin of the
    Tulare County Historical Society. Dec., 1961.
Johnston, Effie Enfield. "Wade Johnston Talks to His Daughter." *Las Cala-*
    veras. Bulletin of the Calaveras County Historical Society. Oct., 1969.
Lewis, Walker. "The Supreme Court and a Six-Gun." *American Bar Associa-*
    tion Journal, May, 1957.
Rickards, Colin. "Bill Miner, Fifty Years a Holdup Man." *Real West,* Sept.,
    Oct., 1970.
Secrest, William B. "When the Ghost Met Steve Venard." *Old West,* Fall, 1968.
Silva, Lee. "Hold-up: They Robbed Wells Fargo—Almost." *Westerner,* Feb.,
    1971.
"Steve Venard, Who Arrested, Tried, and Executed Three Robbers," *Grizzly*
    Bear, Nov., 1907.

UNPUBLISHED MATERIALS

Boggs, John, to J. J. Valentine, Sept. 9, 1892. Wells Fargo Bank History De-
    partment, San Francisco.
Bunner, W. C. "California's Family Feud." Manuscript. Copy in possession
    of John Keller.
Crowley, Charles C. Scrapbook. Bancroft Library, University of California,
    Berkeley.
Dawson scrapbooks, vol. 18. Colorado Historical Society, Denver.
"Little Lake Valley." Undated typescript. In possession of John Keller.
Moore, B. F. "Early Days in California." Typescript dated at Reedley, Calif.,
    Oct. 4, 1892. Wells Fargo Bank History Department, San Francisco.
Southern Pacific Company. "History of Train Robberies." Undated manu-
    script. In possession of Chief Special Agent, Southern Pacific Co., San
    Francisco.
Thorn, Benjamin K. Dictation dated April 18, 1888. Bancroft Library, Uni-
    versity of California, Berkeley.

Wells, Fargo and Co. Wanted circular for George Gates, Vernon Gates, and James Arnett, San Francisco, Sept. 15, 1904. Wells Fargo Bank History Department, San Francisco.

GOVERNMENT RECORDS

California Volunteers. Muster Roll and Descriptive List. California State Archives.

Folsom Prison. Inmate case file, no. 4077, William Thompson. California State Archives, Sacramento.

Folsom Prison Registers. California State Archives.

Governors' Pardon Papers. Pardon files of: William E. Andrews, Lodi Brown, John Coates, Isom Frost, Alva Johnson, William A. Miner, Thomas B. Poole, and Jose A. Sicotte. California State Archives.

Notice of Location of a Placer Claim, April 2, 1888. Nevada County Historical Society Library.

Register of Deaths, 1891. Nevada County Recorder.

Register of Deaths, 1928. Mendocino County Recorder.

San Quentin Prison. Record of Punishment. California State Archives.

San Quentin Prison Registers. California State Archives.

State Board of Prison Directors. Minutes, vols. 1, 2, 6, 7. California State Archives.

U.S. Census Population Schedules, 1850 Census, El Dorado County.

U.S. Census Population Schedules, 1870. Little Lake Township.

Yuma Prison Records. Yuma Territorial Prison State Historic Park, Yuma, Ariz.

COURT RECORDS

Bancroft Library, Berkeley. Lookout lynching case file.

Calaveras County Archives, San Andreas. *People* v. *Sam Brown and Hugh Owens.* District Court, 5th Judicial District.

California State Archives. Lookout lynching case file.

———. *People* v. *W. H. Thompson.* Los Angeles Superior Court. Trial transcript, May 28, 1895.

———. *People* v. *Pedro Ybarra,* case no. 2666. California Supreme Court Records.

California Supreme Court Reports. *People* v. *Coyado.* 40 Cal. 586.

———. *People* v. *Evans.* 41 Pac. 444 (unreported case).

———. *People* v. *Geiger.* 49 Cal. 643.

———. *People* v. *Harrington.* 42 Cal. 165.

———. *People* v. *Hodges.* 27 Cal. 340.

———. *People* v. *Poole.* 27 Cal. 572.

———. *People* v. *Thompson.* 111 Cal. 242.

———. *People* v. *Thompson.* 115 Cal. 160.

———. *People* v. *Tupper.* 122 Cal. 424.

Mendocino County Clerk. *Estate of Elijah Frost.* Probate file no. 328.

————. *Estate of Elijah Frost.* Probate file no. 758.

————. *James McKindley v. Elijah Frost.* Case no. 938.

————. *People v. Abner Coates.* Case no. 867.

————. *People v. John Coates.* Case no. 766.

————. *People v. Elijah Frost and Robert Reynolds.* Case no. 1171.

————. *People v. Isom Frost.* Case no. 457.

————. *People v. Isom and Martin Frost.* Case no. 361.

————. *People v. Martin Frost.* Case no. 459.

————. *People v. Taylor Frost and Robert Reynolds.* Case nos. 932, 993, 1488.

Mendocino County Historical Society, Ukiah. *People v. David Frost.* Case no. 3519. Notes from court record.

————. *People v. James Frost.* Case no. 2474. Notes from court record.

Nevada County Historical Society, Nevada City. *David Snyder v. Stephen Venard, et al.* Case no. 945.

Placer County Clerk. *People v. Miner.* Case nos. 592, 594.

NEWSPAPERS

CALIFORNIA

Alturas New Era
Alturas Plaindealer
Amador Dispatch (Jackson)
Amador Ledger (Jackson)
Auburn Stars and Stripes
Bieber Big Valley Gazette
Bodie Standard
Calaveras Chronicle (Mokelumne Hill)
Calaveras Prospect (San Andreas)
Calaveras Weekly Citizen (San Andreas)
California Police Gazette (San Francisco)
Fall River Tidings
Fresno Morning Republican
Grass Valley Union
Hanford Journal
Healdsburg Democratic Standard
Los Angeles Express
Los Angeles Herald
Los Angeles Times
Marin County Journal (San Rafael)
Marin County Tocsin (San Rafael)
Marysville Daily Appeal
Marysville Daily Herald
Mendocino Beacon
Mendocino Democrat (Ukiah)
Mendocino Dispatch Democrat (Ukiah)
Mendocino Herald (Ukiah)

Monterey Gazette
Napa Journal
Nevada Daily Gazette (Nevada City)
Nevada Daily Transcript (Nevada City)
Nevada Democrat (Nevada City)
Nevada Journal (Nevada City)
Nevada National (Nevada City)
Newman West Side Index
Oakland Daily Evening Tribune
Petaluma Daily Crescent
Petaluma Journal and Argus
Placer Argus (Auburn)
Placer Herald (Auburn)
Red Bluff People's Cause
Red Bluff Sentinel
Redwood City Gazette
Russian River Flag (Healdsburg)
Sacramento Bee
Sacramento Daily Record
Sacramento Union
San Andreas Independent
San Francisco Alta
San Francisco Bulletin
San Francisco Call
San Francisco Chronicle
San Francisco Examiner
San Francisco Post
San Joaquin Republican (Stockton)
San Jose Daily Patriot
San Jose Mercury
Santa Cruz Pacific Sentinel
Stockton Daily Evening Herald
Stockton Daily Independent
Stockton Daily Record
Stockton Evening Mail
Trinity Journal (Weaverville)
Tulare County Times (Visalia)
Tulare Register
Tuolumne Courier (Columbia)
Tuolumne Independent (Sonora)
Ukiah City Press
Ukiah Daily Journal
Visalia Weekly Delta
Weekly Butte Record (Chico)
Weekly Shasta Courier (Redding)

OTHER STATES:

Amsterdam (New York) *Daily Democrat*
Denver Republican
Florida Times-Union and Citizen (Jacksonville)
Portland Morning Oregonian
Pueblo (Colorado) *Daily Chieftain*
Richmond (Indiana) *Palladium-Item*
Silver City (New Mexico) *Independent*
Trinidad (Colorado) *Chronicle-News*

Index